Repression and Accommodation in Post-Revolutionary States

Matthew Krain

St. Martin's Press
New York

For Gary and Arlene Cooper—
parents, friends, inspirations

Library of Congress Cataloging-in-Publication Data
Krain, Matthew.
    Repression and accommodation in post-revolutionary states / Matthew Krain.
    p.   cm.
    Includes bibliographical references and index.
    ISBN 0-312-22875-9 (cloth)
    1. Latin America—Politics and government—1948   2. Iran—Politics and
government—1979   3. Revolutions.   4. Elite (Social sciences)   5. Political
persecution.   I. Title.
JL960.K7   2000
323'.044—dc21   99–045159

Design by Letra Libre, Inc.

First edition: June, 2000
10   9   8   7   6   5   4   3   2   1

Contents

Part IV
Conclusion

Figures

Tables

Acknowledgements

Scholars dispute whether Louis XIV actually uttered the famous declaration "I am the state." There can be no dispute as to whether or not I alone am this book. This project has benefited from the expertise, comments, advice, and support of many people. Without their assistance this book would not have been possible.

Chief among those to whom I am indebted is Karen Rasler, whose influence on my work goes beyond that of a former advisor. She has been perhaps *the* important force in my career thus far. Her advice is always honest and useful, and her guidance has been invaluable. Perhaps more importantly, the example she sets as a thoughtful, productive, and thoroughly professional scholar is one that I can only hope to emulate over my own career. I am equally indebted to William R. Thompson, upon whose knowledge and expertise I have drawn more often than he may care to remember.

During my time at Indiana University I sought out the expert advice of such talented scholars as Jack Bielasiak, Marjorie Hershey, Robert Huckfeldt, Michael McGinnis, Robert V. Robinson, and John Williams. Over the life of this project I also received valuable feedback from David Cingranelli, Christian Davenport, David R. Davis, Andrew Enterline, Scott Gates, Ted Robert Gurr, Roy Licklider, Michael D. McDonald, Will H. Moore, and T. David Mason. All were incredibly helpful!

Moreover, I was lucky enough to have had graduate student colleagues of unparalleled excellence. First among these is Marissa Myers—colleague, erstwhile coauthor, and valued friend. I can only describe her assistance as above and beyond the call of duty. Additionally, I must thank the members of the "Breakfast Club"—Marilyn Grobschmidt, David Kelly, Lisa Raupp Laverty, Anas Malik, Sheila Noojibail, Amanda Rose, and Sander Valyocsik—whose discussions of our works-in-progress always provided for honest, accurate, and constructive criticism. I would also be remiss if I did not tip my cap to Richard Tucker, who patiently endured numerous sessions of my clueless questions, and whose advice has saved me from more than one methodological mishap. Finally, I owe a huge debt of gratitude to Natalie Brouwer and Grace Kim, my valued colleagues and "hired guns." Most notably, Natalie's translations of speeches and interviews saved me from relying on my rusty Spanish. Both Natalie and Grace did their jobs with cool efficiency, accuracy, and aplomb. *Gracias!*

I also benefited from financial support during my graduate student year, without which I most certainly would have starved. The Department of Political Science at Indiana University was unusually generous with their time and money. My stint at *International Studies Quarterly* provided for my sustenance (both financial and academic) during the early stages of the project. A grant from the Research and University Graduate School (RUGS) at IU enabled me to focus my energies entirely on a grueling year's worth of data collection. Fenton Martin, Patrick O'Meara, and Howard Mehlinger, the Educational Testing Service (ETS), and Two Idioms provided support that enabled me to work on this project during the "off season." Finally, N. Brian Winchester and the Center for the Study of Global Change employed me during a crucial time in the life of this project. Since then I have received invaluable encouragement and support from my colleagues at The College of Wooster. The administration has been most generous, providing faculty development funds. And, of course, I must thank the editorial team at St. Martin's Press, including Karen Wolny, Ruth Mannes, Amy Reading, Gabriella Pearce, and Amy McDermott, whose patience and persistence compelled me to produce a much better final product!

Yet of all the people to whom I am indebted, perhaps none are more deserving of praise than Arlene and Gary Cooper. From childhood dinner table conversations about history and current events to encouragement, love, and support throughout too many years of school, they have had as much to do with my success as anyone. They continue to inspire me with their own struggles with life and art, words and images, and the pursuit of their dreams. No words exist with which to express how much they have meant to me. For now, I hope "thank you" will suffice.

PART I

Developing a Model
of the Post-Internal War State

CHAPTER 1

Studying the Post-Internal War State

In recent years bloody conflicts have erupted in places as different as Somalia, Bosnia-Herzegovina, Rwanda, Afghanistan, Chechnya, the former Zaire, and Kosovo. Internal wars now occur far more frequently than interstate wars.[1] Moreover, the end of the Cold War and a resurgence of ethnic and religious identifications have been cited as worrisome portents of internal conflicts to come.[2] The proliferation of such conflicts, coupled with increased international involvement in them, makes any information about the political climate in post-internal war states valuable. Yet little is known about how the post-internal war political environment evolves. Understanding these dynamics is crucial to our ability to deal with the myriad problems that these conflicts present.

In this study I examine the political development of the post-internal war state. In particular, I examine why post-revolutionary elites choose particular combinations of repression and accommodation, and demonstrate that these choices affect the domestic political environment in both the short and long run. Specifically, I show that elite perceptions of their own vulnerability, coupled with subsequent war involvement, affect the choices by elites between and among repression and accommodation. Furthermore, I examine the effect of these policy choices on the degree of opposition to the post-revolutionary regime, the subsequent development of the political system, and whether or not the elites survive in power in the long run.

The Puzzle

Internal wars pit two or more opposing sides within the same political and geographic unit in large-scale armed conflict over the future of the state structure.[3] What we know about internal wars paints a picture of extraordinary politics stemming from extraordinary domestic and international pressures. The outcome of the interaction between international pressures, elite strategic choices, and mass mobilization is a unique state forged in the fire of large-scale internal conflict.

The post-internal war state is one in which the winner has, through its internal war victory, (re)established its authority and (re)asserted its monopoly on the use of coercion. Post-internal war states are the product of rare, often bloody, state-level macrodecision, which determines the long-term path of the state's development. Victorious elites gain the ability to (re)build the state according to their wishes, buttressed by the legitimacy provided to them by their internal war victory. Yet these post-internal war states, born of similar processes, often have divergent outcomes.

Consider, for example, the parallel development of Iran and Nicaragua, whose internal wars both occurred in 1979. Similar factors conspired to create a situation in which these two U.S.-supported neo-patrimonial states crumbled under the pressure of mass-based revolution. Each ended with a decisive military victory for the opposition over the old guard.[4] Each produced stronger, more bureaucratic states, with a greater ability to mobilize the masses.[5] Yet, while Iran developed into a repressive, authoritarian state dominated by the original post-revolutionary elites, Nicaragua will soon hold its fourth consecutive nationwide, free and fair election, and the revolutionary Sandinistas are long gone from the main seat of power. Similarly, while the processes involved in both the Bolivian and Cuban revolutions look remarkably analogous, their outcomes were significantly different. "The 1959 Cuban revolution is one of the few cases universally accepted as a successful social revolution. The 1952 revolution in Bolivia, in stark contrast, has been relegated to little more than a historical footnote, a rarely invoked reference point."[6] Why do post-internal war states, seemingly so similar in origins and dynamics, exhibit such divergent outcomes?

Some work has already been done on the question of divergent post-internal war outcomes. However, much of that literature deals with the resulting *social* and *economic* policies of post-revolutionary regimes.[7] Little if any work has been done on a more *political* aspect of policymaking, the degree to which these states engage in repression and/or accommodation. Yet the use of these policies directly affects the state's ability to implement the social and economic reforms that so often define post-internal war states.[8] Therefore, this study focuses primarily on the causes and consequences of these inherently *political* choices.

In sum, this study examines how and why the historical paths of "most similar" post-internal war states diverge, and how the choice to use repression and/or accommodation affects the long and short term outcomes of internal wars. I begin below by discussing what we know so far about internal war outcomes.

The Outcomes of Internal Wars

What little we do know about internal wars answers questions about how and why they begin,[9] how they end,[10] and how they relate to other violent large-scale phenomena such as war[11] and state-sponsored mass murder.[12] We are just beginning to learn about the outcomes of internal wars, and their short- and long-term effects on domestic level processes. Below, I review in more detail the scope of our knowledge of internal war outcomes, and discuss how my study contributes to this growing body of work.

State Building and the Growth of the Post-Internal War State

Research to date has shown that internal wars produce large-scale growth in state power, as well as an increased willingness to use that power, both at home and abroad. Alexis de Tocqueville first observed that internal wars strengthen the power of the state rather than weakening it.[13] Max Weber later suggested that the processes described by de Tocqueville would lead to increased bureaucratization of the state and the establishment of a permanent, entrenched bureaucracy.[14]

Drawing upon these general observations, a number of scholars have more recently detailed the great transforming effect that revolutions have on state structures and institutions. Theda Skocpol's "revolutions from below" give rise to more centralized, bureaucratic states, as well as radical changes in the economy and social structure.[15] Ellen Kay Trimberger's "revolutions from above" yield mostly social and economic changes, with only minor political "reorganization."[16] Additionally, civil wars have been known to strengthen, rather than weaken, state power, even while fundamentally altering the very nature of state norms and institutions.[17] Regardless of the type of conflict, the nature of the state after the internal war diverges significantly from that of the pre-internal war state.[18]

Because of the unique opportunity to reshape the fundamental nature of the state, the post-internal war period is possibly the most critical juncture in the life of that state. While an internal war splits a polity into two or more competing centers of power, post-internal war periods present the opportunity to reconsolidate state power around one "center."[19] Post-internal war periods provide the winners with an advantage domestically over their rivals. Regardless of who is victorious the opportunity to reconsolidate power and reconstruct elements of the state will never be better.[20] The winning party or coalition has a preponderance of power in the short run (at least), and can use that power to impose its will, or to maneuver to better situate itself for the long haul. Yet along with this opportunity comes the pressing need for rebuilding the state and its resource base. Without vital state resources, state building cannot occur.

National political upheavals on the scale of an internal war produce situations in which the need to consolidate power and increase the resource base of the state is great.[21] Challengers to the old order attempt to change the fundamental nature of the polity by penetrating it, often made possible only by tearing down parts (or all) of the institutional structure of the polity.[22] When the old regime loses, internal wars yield new elites unprotected by the old state's power structure. Such transfers of power sweep away old structures and, in their place, create new symbols and institutions.[23] The frequent use of both coercive and cooperative measures in order to enact such transformations leads to an increasing need to extract resources to pay for them.[24]

Even when the old regime is victorious, internal wars yield an unusually high degree of state-building.[25] The unique opportunity presented to the victors to reshape the state in their image can only be taken advantage of if the tools of state-building are employed. For example, it took the extensive use of state resources for the North to reconstruct the country to its liking following the American Civil War.[26]

Necessity also plays a role in the increased levels of state building following an internal war. Successful prosecution of an internal war drains valuable state resources from the treasury. Coffers must be replenished. Damage must be repaired. Those who sided with the opposition must be either constrained, eliminated, or brought into the fold. All of these state-building activities require massive amounts of spending, which necessitates extraction of resources from a population already overtaxed by wartime extraction. Resistance, even in the wake of a loss by the opposition, may follow, requiring further state-building. Extending the United States example, the post-internal war period was characterized by reconstruction of the South, reconciliation with and accommodation of the Southern opposition, and significant opposition (and even large-scale killings) in the wake of these policies.[27] In addition, policies adopted during the war to accommodate Northern soldiers (in order to enable the conduct of the war) also led to increased mobilization of veterans to successfully demand greater benefits from the government in the post-internal war period.[28] But as Richard Bensel's work demonstrates, the American Civil War was both a product of and a solution to key problems of American political development.[29] While an increased amount of state building is a byproduct of internal war, so are internal wars byproducts of the desire for a radical rebuilding of the state.

For example, Ellen Kay Trimberger's comparative historical study of "revolutions from above" examines the ways in which military and civil bureaucrats become revolutionary, take control of institutions of the state, and then attempt to rebuild the nation's political system. Unlike most internal wars, there is little or no mass participation in these cases. Trimberger further theorizes that these revolutions can only occur in states that are economically dependent on the West. However, the outcomes of such revolutions are constrained by the same structural and historical circumstances that make them possible. Trimberger finds that the likely outcome of revolutions from above is dependent capitalistic development. She argues that only the inclusion of the working class into the revolutionary coalition would prevent such an outcome. Yet the very nature of the revolution, in which isolated bureaucratic elites sweep aside their opposition without mass mobilization, precludes this outcome.[30]

S. N. Eisenstadt, writing around the same time, also argues that the nature of the elites affects revolutionary outcomes. Eisenstadt focuses on the relationship between changes in the structure of "centers," or elites, and political violence and repression. He finds that the coerciveness of the post-revolutionary state is a function of the degree of isolation of the ruling elites from the other elites who have access to power. Eisenstadt also seizes upon the role of international pressures in adding to the ruling elite's feelings of isolation, thereby increasing the probability of the use of coercion.[31]

Theda Skocpol's work on the processes and outcomes of "revolutions from below" also includes the pressures of international competition as a major causal variable. Skocpol's structural perspective stresses "objective relationships and conflicts among variously situated groups and nations."[32] The conditions that give rise to revolutions are:

> political contradictions centered in the structure and situation of states caught in cross-pressures between, on the one hand, military competitors on the international scene and, on the other hand, the constraints of the existing domestic economy and (in some cases) resistance by internally politically powerful class forces to efforts by the state to mobilize resources to meet international competition.[33]

Once the revolution has occurred, Skocpol theorizes that reconsolidation of power by the new elites begins. She finds that the outcome is the creation by these elites of a stronger, more centralized, and bureaucratic state. In short, states make revolution and revolution makes the state.

Conflict and the Post-Internal War State

Subsequent research has examined how post-internal war state-building affects, in particular, the coercive elements of the state. In a comparative study of England, France, China, and Russia, Jonathan Adelman shows that all of these countries emerged from internal wars with larger and greatly strengthened armies.[34] Ted Robert Gurr finds that successful involvement in wars and/or internal wars leads to the post-revolutionary establishment and expansion of the secret police and other institutions of the "coercive state." This, in turn, reinforces elite political cultures that favor the use of coercion in future situations.[35] Taken together, these two studies show that internal wars, violent in nature, yield regimes prone to violent means of conflict resolution, and with the enhanced resources necessary to be able to employ coercion.

This may help explain why Zeev Maoz finds that revolutionary states are more likely to follow up an internal war with engagement in an external war.[36] Another potential reason, alluded to by Maoz and later more fully explored by Stephen Walt, is that other states, fearful that the internal war may have a destabilizing effect on the international system, may act to reverse the victory of the post–internal war regime. Additionally, Walt shows how revolutionaries may miscalculate the threat posed to them by outside forces, leading to an increased military buildup. This buildup, in turn, leads other states to perceive a threat from the revolutionary state, creating an escalating crisis situation, which often leads to war. Ironically, the war that ensues is a self-fulfilling prophecy, as perceptions and misperceptions on both sides wind up being the cause of the very conflict that both sides would prefer to avoid.[37]

Domestic challenges are also abundant in the post–internal war state. Internal wars are bloody and divisive. They involve challenges to the old order and the old institutions of the state. As discussed earlier, two or more distinct centers of power must be reintegrated into one united polity following an internal war.[38] Often this task is difficult, if not impossible. Unlike in the aftermath of international wars where winners and losers can break off relations with each other if they wish, both sides in an internal war must be able to live together in the same territory (or at the very least, contiguous territories) following the resolution of the conflict.[39] Even a decisive victory does not guarantee fewer challenges. Those who attain (or retain) power often face additional challenges, both foreign and domestic, after their initial victory.[40] The domestic upheaval produced by internal wars yields disorganization of systems, societal disorder, and eventually more violent internal conflict.[41] Thus, as Rosemary O'Kane argues, "a new revolutionary army may be needed to win foreign wars, but at home it is a new revolutionary system of internal security that is needed, under state control."[42]

A recent flurry of cross-national, longitudinal studies have established a strong connection between internal wars and the use of domestic political violence. Most document strong significant correlations between internal wars and human rights abuses.[43] And elsewhere I have demonstrated that internal war participation creates a window of opportunity in which the state may engage in the most severe form of repression, state-sponsored mass murder. This effect holds even five years after the initiation of the internal war, when many of these wars have already ended. Thus, this window of opportunity often stays open during the post–internal war period.[44] The sum of this body of research is that political violence is often the result of the opportunities and constraints provided by the unique political environment of the internal war and post–internal war state. Taken together with the works of Zeev Maoz and Stephen Walt,[45] recent research shows that internal wars beget both international *and* domestic conflict.

Framework of This Study

As Gurr pointed out two decades ago, "the systemic outcomes of revolution depend on the policies followed by revolutionary elites."[46] These "outcomes," actually functions of the modern state (state-making, war-making, quelling domestic opposition), cannot be carried out without large amounts of resources, which requires the state to further engage in state-building activities to acquire them.[47] Yet while studies of internal war outcomes assume the importance of the dynamics of state building, few develop a theory explicitly founded on this theoretic base. This study aims to do just that. Additionally, I will show that while state-building drives elite policy choices, it is these choices that help determine the political development of the post-internal war state.[48]

This study is divided into four main parts. The first section (Chapters 1 through 3) deals with developing a testable model of post-internal war political dynamics. The second section (Chapters 4 and 5) addresses the causes of repression and accommodation in post-internal war states. The third section (Chapters 6 through 8) deals with the consequences of these policy choices. In the final section, a concluding chapter reexamines these results, and looks ahead at the future of the study of internal war outcomes.

Beginning from the assumption that state building is the key to understanding the post-internal war state, I develop a historical model of post-internal war dynamics in Chapter 2. In this model I incorporate the key elements discussed above: elite perceptions, elite actions, and domestic and international conflict. Elite perceptions of their position have been shown to affect subsequent policies. Thus, I examine the effect of elite perceptions of their own vulnerability on the process of state building, and specifically on which policies (combinations of repression and accommodation) elites use to engage in this key activity. While researchers have examined how international conflict may stem from internal wars, none have examined how these wars affect the post-internal war environment. Yet external conflict has been shown to drastically affect elite policy mix choices (see Chapter 2). I therefore examine how subsequent warfare affects the state-building process via elite policy mix decisions.

In Chapter 3 I discuss the way in which cases needed to test the hypotheses derived from my model were chosen. In doing so I elaborate upon the reasoning behind the most similar systems comparative method, the criteria used to make the case choices, and the reason for this study's focus on a particular subset of post-internal war states: the post-revolutionary regime. I conclude by briefly discussing case histories for each of the four cases—Iran, Nicaragua, Cuba, and Bolivia.

In Chapter 4 I evaluate the historical process model's accuracy in depicting how events actually unfold in these cases. I discuss why the unique policy mix data set used in this study was necessary. I also explain how the data was collected. Finally, I demonstrate where and when repression and accommodation occurred in my cases of interest, and compare these observations with the expected observations posited by my model.

In Chapter 5 I employ event count models to statistically verify the relationships in my model, and to determine their levels of significance. In doing so, I control for elements that have previously been found to affect policy mix choices; namely, previous use of repression and accommodation, and domestic opposition to the state. I demonstrate that elite perceptions of their own vulnerability and war both significantly explain elite policy mix choices, even when controlling for these other powerful explanatory variables.

Once the causes of these policy mix choices have been established, I consider their consequences. In Chapter 6 I again employ event count models, this time turning the tables on one aspect of the models tested in Chapter 5. Here I examine how both war participation and the choices of repression and/or accommodation affect subsequent opposition activity. I consider both short- and long-term consequences.

Another reason why it is important to examine internal war outcomes is the growing consensus in the social scientific community regarding the strong effect of political system type on many important variables. Despite this, few studies address how regime types develop in the aftermath of internal wars. Thus in Chapter 7 I examine how post-revolutionary state building, via policy mix choices, affects the political development of the state.

Additionally, few studies have addressed the reasons why some revolutionary elites survive in the long run while others do not. Yet this, too, should impact the ability of a state to implement long-term reforms. As Migdal argues:

> No agenda is worth anything if its sponsor has not lasted through the hazards of politics. Political survival, the central issue occupying the attention of state leaders, is the prerequisite for achieving any significant long-term social change.[49]

Therefore in Chapter 8 I examine how the choices of repression and accommodation, coupled with their previous outcomes (levels of opposition activity and political system type) affect whether or not the revolutionary elites survive in power in the long run. I conclude (Chapter 9) with a look at how this study's findings should affect the way in which academics and policymakers deal with the challenges presented by post-revolutionary states specifically and post-internal war states more generally. In sum, this study will examine what affects the use of a particular policy mix by post-revolutionary war regimes, and the effect of these policy mix choices on opposition activity, the evolution of differing types of political systems, and the political survival of the elites.

CHAPTER 2

Repression and Accommodation in Post-Internal War States

I n this chapter, I develop a historical model of post-internal war dynamics. I discuss how the pressures of state building necessitate the use
of repression and accommodation by post-internal war elites. I then
discuss how war participation and elite perceptions of their own vulnerability affect the makeup of the policy mix chosen by these elites. After developing hypotheses, I construct a historical process model, and discuss the
expected outcomes for each hypothetical case type. Finally, I choose the
cases with which I will test the validity and utility of this model throughout the rest of this study. But first, I begin by discussing the setting in
which the model is constructed: the general historical framework of the
post-internal war period.

The Post-Internal War Period

The End of the Internal War

Internal wars can be short or long in duration, intense or mild, and end via
negotiated settlements or military victories. But determining the precise
moment at which a war has ended has always been a difficult problem.
Cease-fires and "peace accords" often deteriorate overnight, as happened
frequently in Bosnia during the early stages of the war. Each side dates the
end of the war according to what suits it best.

While precise dating is often difficult, some work has been done to rectify this problem. Singer and Small have collected data on internal wars, including their starting and ending dates.[1] On the theoretical front, Roy
Licklider's discussion of the termination of internal wars has been the

defining work on this subject. He asserts that the internal war ends when either "(1) the concern about living together, (2) the multiple sovereignty, or (3) the violence ends. . . ."[2]

I rely on Licklider's second indicator to determine the end of internal wars. The first indicator can be misleading, as occasionally concern about living together does not abate. If that were the main criteria for dating the end of an internal war, then the conflict in Israel between Jews and Palestinians, dated by Licklider as a one-year internal war [1948], could not yet be dated as having ended.[3] Moreover, as I will assert below, violence does not necessarily end after the termination of the internal war. The coalition-reduction and state-building phases (see next two sections) in many post-internal war cases are extremely violent. Consider for instance the excessive violence of "the Terror" immediately following the revolution in France,[4] or the genocidal rule of the Khmer Rouge in post-internal war Cambodia/Kampuchea.[5] Therefore Licklider's third indicator would also be misleading here. For my purposes, only the end of multiple sovereignty, and the reconsolidation of power into one single polity, signals the end of a given internal war.

The Coalition-Reduction Phase

Conflict often occurs even after the internal war has ended. Immediately following the end of the internal war a coalition-reduction process commences. With the old guard out of the way, the victorious coalition usually has little to hold it together. Typically the anti-regime coalition agrees over little except that the old regime must be ousted. Consequently groups splinter off and push their own policy goals once the internal war ends.[6] Bloody competition for the "soul" of the government ensues.[7]

The example found most pervasively in the literature on internal wars is that of the Terror in post-revolutionary France. Severe conflicts between the main factions of the revolutionary coalition, the Girondists and the Mountaineers, were common. Conflict within the factions, such as between the Jacobins and the Dantonists, also occurred frequently. The period of fighting within the victorious coalition led to one of the bloodiest post-revolutionary periods in modern history. Post-revolutionary Russia was also witness to conflict between factions of the revolutionary coalition. By the summer of 1918 the Bolsheviks had successfully suppressed the Mensheviks, the Anarchists, and the other opposition parties.[8] During the coalition-reduction phase, erstwhile partners revert to their previous status as contenders for power, yielding infighting, deal making, and a greater drive for power and resources.[9]

Struggles over the most fundamental issues of politics and state forms go on until relatively stable new state organizations have been consolidated.[10] At the conclusion of this process, power is consolidated in the hands of the group of elites best able to create and use these new government institutions. By this point most of the opposition at the center has either been eliminated, co-opted or appeased. Coalition-reduction is usually followed during the subsequent phase by widespread (and less critical) struggles for power in the periphery (discussed below). More importantly, once coalition-reduction has been achieved, the primary focus of the elites can shift to consolidation of power and the rebuilding of the post-internal war state.[11]

The Consolidation Phase

Once one group of elites (or coalition of groups) has eliminated or co-opted their opposition, they can proceed to implement their policies. Thus, in the phase following the reduction of the coalition the new regime consolidates its rule and begins to increase its state-building activities.[12] While post-internal war elites engage in state building during the coalition-reduction phase, permanent state construction cannot begin until after the post-internal war intra-elite conflict is resolved.[13]

The consolidation phase should typically be less violent than the coalition-reduction phase. Even when opposition remains the primary intracoalition conflicts have been settled sufficiently to produce a clear-cut winner. Despite being challenged for power, this victorious group of elites holds an edge over its opposition—it possesses a monopoly on the legitimate use of coercion. Thus a cooling-off period following the coalition-reduction phase occurs, often referred to as the "Thermidor" in the literature on revolutions.[14] During this period the new regime attempts to create a stable government and to increase the level of state building necessary for the reconstruction of the state. The internal war has either damaged or shattered the state's old symbols and institutions.[15] Repression and accommodation are the key tools that elites can employ to rebuild the post-internal war state.

How State Building Necessitates the Use of Repression and Accommodation

State building is necessary and intense in the aftermath of internal wars.[16] Internal wars either shatter, cripple, or expose the weaknesses of old institutions. New elites bring new programs to implement. Often they must alter or rebuild institutions in order to implement their agenda. In the most extreme cases attempts are made to rebuild a whole new state and society from the bottom up.[17] Repression and accommodation are key tools in rebuilding the post-internal war state because they enable elites to garner the resources necessary to engage in state building. Below I discuss what state building tasks present themselves to the new elites, and how extraction is enabled through the use of repression and accommodation.

State building is an ongoing process, which begins at the formation of the state and continues throughout its history. Tilly's model of state building encompasses four main interrelated activities:

1. War making: Eliminating or neutralizing their own rivals outside the territories in which they have clear and continuous priority as wielders of force.
2. State making: Eliminating or neutralizing their rivals inside those territories.
3. Protection: Eliminating or neutralizing the enemies of their client.
4. Extraction: Acquiring the means of carrying out the first three activities—war making, state making, and protection.[18]

These four activities overlap considerably, each reinforcing the other. However, extraction is the key to the elite's ability to engage in state building.

Extraction is necessary in order for the state to have the resources needed to finance the other three activities. Extraction may take many forms, including taxation, public borrowing, conscription, tribute, and plunder.[19] This particular state function leads to a greater need for more efficient institutions to extract or manage resources. Hence, acquisition of resources today is necessary to enable further extraction tomorrow. This leads to a deepening of the state's involvement in everyday life, again increasing the demand for state building.[20] Often a repressive arm of the state develops in order to enforce extractive claims. This repressive arm can be used for other purposes (i.e., war making, state making, protection) as well.[21] War making may also yield protection for domestic constituents, or it may enable the state to extract more from its population.[22] Because all of these activities are mutually reinforcing, state building becomes an ongoing process, driven by the ever-increasing need to acquire resources to expand the power of the state. But without the ability to extract resources to engage in state building, the state is unable to perform all the other functions required of it in any era, let alone in the high maintenance environment of a post-internal war period.

The importance of extraction to the development of the post-internal war state can be seen in post-revolutionary China, where the appropriation of land and other extractive policies of the Agrarian Reform Laws were used to win peasant allegiance and to provide the basis for subsequent state building.[23] More severe examples include the centrality of extraction to the state-building strategy of the Khmer Rouge in post-internal war Cambodia/Kampuchea. Infrastructure was leveled, banks were destroyed, currency abolished, and classes eradicated. The exclusive control of all means of production were put in the hands of the ruling elites. Despite the relative poverty of the Cambodian treasury, centralizing the totality of the state's wealth in the hands of the elites enabled them to engage in massive state-building endeavors. For example, the Khmer Rouge sponsored frequent incursions into Vietnam.[24] They also went to great lengths to eliminate all vestiges of domestic opposition and foreign influence. And they completely remade the very nature of the state. Khmer Rouge policies created a classless, agricultural, subsistence economy. They eradicated all vestiges of the old political system. The elites even went so far as to empty and level all urban areas.[25] None of these post-internal war state-building measures could have been undertaken, however, without first attending to the extraction of resources.

The Cambodian case is an atypical one in that domestic resistance was almost immediately stamped out, and little attempt was made by the elites to try to employ more accommodative strategies to ally with other elites or sectors of society. In most cases, both coalition making and resistance do play a necessary part in the process of state building. Rasler and Thompson argue that these two factors need to be incorporated into a more complete model of state building.[26]

Coalitions are formed in order to augment group resources and capabilities, which enables the state to then more efficiently carry out the four activities discussed above. Furthermore, coalition making may be employed in order to enable greater control over some group's behavior. This mitigates the immediate threat to the regime, as well as decreases the need for actions against this group in the future.[27] "Protection decisions, and, conversely, decisions to repress are thus filtered through coalitional screens."[28] In this way, coalition making may be seen as a way of implementing policies of repression or accommodation made necessary by the state-building process.

Resistance is also important in understanding the need for repression or accommodation. Without resistance, the state could extract resources from the populace without impediment, and rivals could be eliminated without opposition. But resistance does exist in most societies, especially during the course of building or rebuilding the state. Extraction yields recalcitrant populations.[29] Thus the state must temper its extractive claims, repress resistance, or engage in accommodation of resisting groups.[30] Since the former is most difficult due to the increased costs of running a modern state, repression and accommodation become the most important policy tools for state building.[31]

These policies are especially relevant to post-internal war regimes. New elites must reconsolidate power in order to both insure their protection from subsequent ouster and insure extraction for immediate state building. High levels of extraction are required in order to provide the state with sufficient resources with which to stabilize the inherently chaotic transition period between regimes. Indeed, new elites "are preoccupied first and foremost with securing their power against counterrevolutionaries and would-be separatists."[32] They do so by strengthening the state apparatus (particularly the coercive and extractive arms of the state), and by deepening the state's involvement in society.[33] This enhances extractive capability, allowing states to "deploy [resources] to maintain order at home and to compete against other states abroad."[34]

However, extractive claims will be met with opposition if the government is seen as illegitimate, or as having no claim to the resources. Winners of an internal war, unlikely to give up sovereignty claims, and desperate for consolidation of their position, will tend to react with violence or repression to resistance to extraction. In this sense, repression may be a sign of an emerging accumulation of power and an increase in state strength,[35] rather than of disorder, decay, and decreasing state power.[36] Thus, in post-internal war France, Russia, and China, it was the development of a new revolutionary system of internal security, under state control, that signaled the end of the conflicts over coalition-reduction and that became the fundamental basis of permanent state building.[37]

On the other hand, the victors may accommodate their post-war challengers in the hopes of either forming profitable alliances with or constraining the opposition. For example, with the end of the Biafran War came a reformulation of coalitions in the Nigerian political arena, which included the defeated Ibos. In the case of the American Civil War, the North went to great pains to accommodate the South in the immediate aftermath of the conflict. Andrew Johnson offered a lenient amnesty program for Southerners, and produced an ultimately unsuccessful plan, which allowed the individual Southern states to reconstruct themselves.[38] And in the aftermath of the Iranian Revolution, the tenuous alliance between the Communist Tudeh Party and the ruling Islamic clerics was a marriage of convenience for both: Tudeh felt they and the clerics had common enemies, while the revolutionary elite tolerated the Communists at first in order to focus on consolidating power and eliminating the more militant (and more threatening) Mujahedin-e Khalq. Once these goals were accomplished, the regime proceeded to dispense with the loose alliance with Tudeh and to crush them.[39]

Besides Tilly, Rasler and Thompson, other theorists focusing on the state-building process address the need for repression and accommodation. Levi's theory of the predatory state argues that the state is ruled by rational, self-interested elites who maximize power and wealth in order to supply means to their desired ends. They use repression and accommodation, described by Levi as "political resources" such as selective incentives, negative sanctions, and the ability to manipulate various other incentives, in order to extract wealth and convert it into power. Rulers are able to employ such policies in this manner because they have a monopoly on the legitimate use of coercion.[40]

Similarly, Mastanduno, Lake, and Ikenberry claim that states pursue wealth (in the form of material resources and political support) in order to provide for the state's survival and to enable the pursuit of foreign policy goals.[41] Skocpol and Trimberger reiterate this point: "States are fundamentally administrative and military organizations that extract resources from society and deploy them to maintain order at home and to compete against other states abroad."[42] State survival is maintained by using resources to co-opt or coerce challengers and to reward supporters. Furthermore, other resource-intensive state policies (be they foreign or domestic) are enabled through the use of repression and/or accommodation in accumulating these resources.

The monopoly of the legitimate use of coercion makes repression an appealing policy tool. The bloody records of post-internal war France, Russia, China, and Cambodia, to name but a few, attest to the fact that repression is an oft-used policy by victorious elites.[43] Repression enables state-building activities through enforcement. In addition, repression can be used to disrupt or uproot the opposition's organizational structure, making it exceedingly difficult for opponents to pose a significant threat.[44]

Despite the allure of repressionary measures, accommodation is also an important policy tool of state-building governments. The theories discussed so far stress the state's need to extract, but do not necessarily assume a violent extraction process. Indeed Levi, Tilly, Mastanduno, et al., and Rasler and Thompson all incorporate co-optation, deal making, and accommodation in general into their theories. The tradeoff of increased accommodation for the right of elites to increase extraction is a common and effective policy tool in the practice of state building. For example, in the case of European monarchies, accommodation fundamentally shaped long-term state development. In return for taxes, conscription, and other key resources, monarchs traded away rights to limited participation in governance. While the monarchs gained sufficient resources to fight wars, populations began to acquire what would eventually become democratic rights.[45] The relative success of Zimbabwe is a prime example of the benefits of accommodation for post-internal war states. The spirit of accommodation, which was institutionalized in the Lancaster House agreements, espoused by Mugabe's ZANU-PF government, and subsequently expanded upon, has made this one-party state one of the more stable polities in Africa.[46]

While the use of accommodation is common and often beneficial, I contend that generally state builders with limited resources should prefer repression to accommodation. Accommodation expends elites' finite political and economic capital in the short term in a way that repression does not. Once granted, rights, access, or privileges cannot easily be revoked. And while Simon and Starr show that consistent use of a strategy of accommodation brings a large improvement to the societal resource base, it does so only in the long run.[47] Repression, while it may alienate certain groups, does not forfeit sorely needed capital in the short run.[48] And states are most prone to using force when the repressive apparatus is stronger than its other capabilities.[49] Therefore post-internal war elites, already concerned with a loss of state capital following the destructive conflict, should prefer to use repression over accommodation. Yet their ability to do so may be constrained, leaving accommodation as a more costly, yet viable, alternative.[50]

Regardless, these policies are not mutually exclusive. Even the most totalitarian of states employ accommodation. Land reform in repressive countries such as Stalin's Soviet Union and Mao's China are prime examples.[51] Conversely, even the most libertarian of states must occasionally employ repression, as has been demonstrated repeatedly throughout the history of the United States. These two policy options must be considered in tandem, as potential elements of the elite decisionmakers' repertoire, or policy mix.[52] The effective use of this mix of policies of repression and accommodation to engage more efficiently in the state-building functions made highly necessary by the internal war is crucial to post-internal war development. Below I discuss what factors affect the post-internal war elites' policy mix choices.

What Affects the Policy Mix?

Elite Perception of Vulnerability

I begin my examination of the factors that affect policy mix choices by focusing on new elites' perceptions of their own vulnerability.[53] Numerous scholars have already established a strong linkage between perceptions and decisionmaking.[54] And the seminal works in this area find that perceptions of reality are more important than objective reality in explaining elites' policy choices.[55] Even if these perceptions do not mirror reality the elites still use them to evaluate their policy decisions.[56] In short, how elites perceive their milieu, or environment, directly affects their decisionmaking calculus, and thus their policy choices.

In particular, perceptions of vulnerability domestically should be important to understanding why elites choose policies of repression and/or accommodation. Elites who do not perceive themselves to be vulnerable at the outset of their rule perceive little need to relinquish assets, rights, or power to societal groups. While some opposition groups may exist, these elites expect that they can manage to survive and thrive without having to appease internal opposition. They therefore have little need to use accommodation and give up precious resource capital. This should also give them a freer hand to use repression when faced with dissension. Despite the threat of opposition to repression, secure elites are willing to utilize this policy option. Secure elites believe that they can repress without jeopardizing their positions. They feel that they do not need the support (or even the acquiescence) of the opposing groups in order to govern, build the state, and extract in order to do both. As Gamson notes, violence grows out of confidence and strength, rather than insecurity and rising pressures. Thus, secure elites should be more likely to favor repressive policies.[57]

The case of post-internal war South Vietnam illustrates this well. The South Vietnamese elites felt secure in their positions following the end of the internal conflict [1960–1965], primarily because of the support of the United States. The United States backed the new regime heavily during the internal conflict. Then, the United States increased their military presence in South Vietnam following the end of the internal war to help prop up the new government and to prosecute the Vietnam War.[58] While occasionally suspicious of the Americans, the South Vietnamese elites generally believed that the United States would not abandon them.[59] This meant that they would be provided with a nearly unending source of resources, thereby increasing their feelings of security and reducing their need to accommodate their opposition.

This relationship enabled the successive governments of Quat, Ky, and Thieu to repress more and accommodate less, and still achieve their state-building goals. The U.S. forces' backing of the South Vietnamese government and the money provided by the foreign intervener meant that the government had little need to worry about protection from internal challengers. The funds that were extracted could thus go directly towards building up the domestic repressive forces, despite the ongoing war. The costs of repression were lessened as well, as the potential failure of repression would not lead to full-scale revolution. The backing of a major international power insured the government's ability to put down even the largest of anti-government demonstrations. Indeed, the South Vietnamese elites used their repressive force liberally to put down their domestic opposition.[60]

The behavior of the North Vietnamese elites following their victory in 1975 and the reunification of Vietnam further illustrates these relationships. The victorious elites felt strengthened and more secure due mostly to the withdrawal of U.S. support for South Vietnam, the war weariness of the population of the South, and the manner in which the North took the South.[61] The post-internal war elites immediately went about consolidating their power in the country as a whole.[62] Soon after reassuring the South Vietnamese that they had nothing to fear, the severe repression began:

> the Communists proceeded to shunt four hundred thousand South Vietnamese civil servants and army officers as well as doctors, lawyers, teachers, journalists, and other intellectuals into "re-education" centers . . . those charged with infractions of the rules are beaten and shackled in the sun without water. Elsewhere, they are locked in the same "tiger cages" that the South Vietnamese government employed to incarcerate its dissidents.[63]

In addition, the new regime banned certain types of music, limited the availability of Western books, and declared all other parties except the Communist Party illegal. As the elites had expected, there was little opposition.[64] The fact that the elites did not feel vulnerable to attack or ouster by internal opponents enabled them to swiftly consolidate their power through repressive means.

Reinforcing this repressive trend illustrated above, the ability to repress freely and effectively from the outset should enable elites who do not feel vulnerable to successfully uproot much of their opposition early in their tenure. Disrupting channels of mobilization early on makes it increasingly difficult for the opposition to mobilize effectively later.[65] This is why elites in the North Vietnamese case targeted institutions and practices that could have potentially enabled mobilization. The North Vietnamese elites' successful targeting of opposition leaders, political parties, printed materials, journalists, and rights of speech and assembly made their consolidation of power more swift, broke the back of what little opposition remained, and made accommodation unnecessary.[66] When mobilization is curtailed and opposition is eliminated or neutralized there are few, if any, reasons to accommodate. If opposition cannot be sustained, then it makes little sense for elites to give away benefits or to incorporate groups. Little return can be gained from such actions.

On the other hand, if post-internal war elites begin their tenure by feeling vulnerable, they should be more likely to accommodate their opposition in hopes of retaining some power and gaining sorely needed allies. Additionally, they may be reluctant to repress, for fear of creating new enemies and further increasing their vulnerability. These patterns can be seen in the actions of the elites who emerged following the Mexican Revolution. The Mexican Revolution was preceded by the wide spread of anarchist ideals.[67] Thus when the revolutionary elites finally came to power, they had to contend with an environment in which anarchy and anti-government sentiment was not only present but encouraged. The very people who would now hold power had created a situation in which they became legitimate targets once they took power. Additionally there was little unity among the revolutionary cadre. Splits amongst the elites led to a general feeling that to maintain power and influence, they would need support of groups outside their camp, whether other elites or mass groups within the polity.[68]

To that end, the post-revolutionary Mexican elites practiced accommodation frequently. The perception of a need to win support in order to maintain power resulted in reforms such as the establishment of "municipal liberty, agrarian reform, labor legislation, nullification of foreign contracts and monopolies, tariff realignments, credits for Mexicans, and a series of promises of political readjustment."[69] The elites were also hesitant to repress, for fear of losing support from either their opposite numbers within the revolutionary elite or from constituent societal groups. These fears were not unfounded, as plots and assassinations against members of the leadership were all too frequent in the early years of the post-internal war period.[70]

The inability to use repression freely or effectively early on in the post-internal war period results in the continued existence of active opposition groups. If internal opposition remains and cannot be (or is not) dealt with effectively by repression, then these groups must be accommodated in order for elites to effectively engage in state building. These processes are depicted graphically in Figure 2.1.

In sum, elites who do not see themselves as vulnerable domestically should favor repression over accommodation, while those who see themselves as vulnerable should favor accommodation over repression. Therefore, I hypothesize:

H2.1: In the aftermath of an internal war, if the elites do not perceive themselves to be vulnerable domestically, then they will be more likely to use repression than elites who perceive themselves to be vulnerable.

H2.2: In the aftermath of an internal war, if the elites do not perceive themselves to be vulnerable domestically, then they will be less likely to use accommodation than elites who perceive themselves to be vulnerable.

War

A key breakthrough in our understanding of the origins of internal conflict was the theoretical development in the study of the role of international pressures in bringing about internal wars.[71] Changes in the international structure of political opportunities (often caused by war) have important structural effects on the national political opportunity structure.[72] Pressures to compete in the international arena lead to increased extractive claims, triggering large-scale internal conflict.[73] States fighting wars must also increase the levels of overall societal mobilization. Once mobilized, opposition groups can resist and attempt to overthrow the government. Declining threat perception or increasing unpopularity of a given war can also lead to decreased levels of societal cohesion in the postwar period, potentially leading to internal violence.[74] Additionally, war improves the likelihood of change of government via extra-constitutional means, especially in states that lose wars.[75] What is not nearly as well understood is the effect of international factors on the post-internal war period.

Whether or not a war occurs in the post-internal war period should have a great impact upon the levels of state building required, and in particular upon state's use of repressive policies. As Higgs wrote: "war, widely regarded as jeopardizing the nation's very survival, also encourages a lowering of the sturdiest barriers—constitutional limitations and adverse public opinion—that normally obstruct the growth of government."[76] Madison also believed that war threatened liberty. Writing to Jefferson in

Figure 2.1 Historical Process Model of the Causes and Consequences of Repression and Accommodation in Post–Internal War States

Case Type	Coalition-Reduction Phase (first 2–3 years)	Consolidation Phase (8–10 years)	
	Historical Process Model for Post-Internal War States	Effect of Earlier Policy Choice	War's Effect on Policy Mix
Iran (Type I)	Elites perceive themselves to be secure → Ability to use repression → No sustained opposition	Less ACC	Increase in REP
Cuba (Type II)	Elites perceive themselves to be secure → Ability to use repression → No sustained opposition	Less ACC	No war, therefore no effect
Nicaragua (Type III)	Elites perceive themselves to be vulnerable → Inability to use repression → Significant opposition remains	More ACC	Increase in REP
Bolivia (Type IV)	Elites perceive themselves to be vulnerable → Inability to use repression → Significant opposition remains	More ACC	No war, therefore no effect

Note: ACC = Accommodation; REP = Repression

1798, Madison stated, "Perhaps it is a universal truth that the loss of liberty at home is to be charged to provisions against danger, real or pretended, from abroad."[77]

The repressive mechanisms of the state are developed further as a result of war. Building on the work done by Lasswell on the "garrison state," Gurr documents the establishment and expansion of the secret police and other institutions of the coercive state as a direct result of chronic war participation.[78] This connection becomes particularly important given that states that have experienced an internal war engage in post-war conflicts with greater frequency than those that have not experienced an internal war.[79]

In addition, many studies find that war exacerbates domestic conflict directly.[80] For example, McNitt finds that the greater the external threat, the greater the number of detentions, and the greater the use of torture by the state.[81] Given this, international threats on the scale of wars should elicit the greatest use of repression. In fact, Poe and Tate find strong, persistent effects of wars on repression and human rights violations.[82] Furthermore, elsewhere I find that involvement in either internal or international wars positively affects the probability of onset and degree of severity of the most repressive policies that states can employ: state-sponsored mass murder.[83] The South Vietnamese case, discussed above, is an excellent example of this connection. This case is one in which the state was engaged in an internal war and an international war simultaneously. Barbara Harff and Ted Robert Gurr estimate that 475,000 peasants living in National Liberation Front (NLF) areas were killed by the South Vietnamese government from 1965 to 1972, in what they call a "politicide."[84] Some of these peasants were killed for harboring NLF guerrillas, some for direct opposition to the government and the war effort, and some for merely being suspected of having been infiltrated by the NLF. Regardless, all were killed in order to keep order domestically during the prosecution of the war against the North and their allies, the NLF guerrillas in the South.

States also need to compete in the global political environment. These foreign policy requirements put pressure on governments to increase the rate of state building. While post-internal war situations are particularly prone to large degrees of state building, warfare during this period should increase that amount even more. Extraction is also a necessary element in the preparation for war.[85] International conflicts require elites to secure domestic support and/or control in order to avoid a two-level conflict.[86] In addition, resources are also required to prosecute the war. Indeed, wars yield a dramatic increase in state extraction of societal resources.[87] In sum, the need for extraction increases either coercive policies or bargaining between elites and societal groups.[88] This quantum increase in extraction yields great resistance from an already overtaxed and conflict-weary populace, which in turn increases pressure on the state to respond. Therefore, I expect that engagement in war by post-internal war regimes will increase the use of repressionary policies, even in states where much of the early opposition has been suppressed. I hypothesize:

H2.3: If a state has experienced a war in the aftermath of an internal war, then the elites will be more repressive than those in a state that has not experienced such a war.

A Historical Process Model

I have constructed a historical process model based upon these hypothesized interrelationships. Table 2.1 depicts the four types of cases suggested by my hypotheses, the historical paths each are expected to take, and their eventual outcomes.

Type I cases involve elites who perceive themselves to be secure. Such perceptions allow elites to more freely use repression to remove opposition during the coalition-reduction process. Under normal circumstances we could expect little use of either accommodation or repression in the consolidation phase. Fewer opponents are left, and those who are left lack the ability to mobilize supporters. Micromobilization networks are destroyed. Those citizens who would oppose the government fear repression and therefore do not. But war intercedes, forcing elites to use repressionary measures domestically to extract more resources or to suppress internal dissent while fighting an external enemy.

Type II cases are Type I cases without the war. Thus, in Type II cases we should expect to see repression early on, but not to any great extent after

Table 2.1 Case Types

	War	*No War*
Elites perceive themselves as secure	Type I	Type II
Elites perceive themselves as vulnerable	Type III	Type IV

the coalition-reduction process has finished, as it is not required. Accommodation will also be unnecessary in the consolidation phase because a majority of the opposition will have been rooted out by early repression.

Type III cases feature elites who sense their vulnerability at the outset of their regime. They are unable to use repression effectively, either because they are forced to share power (and thus control over the repressive apparatus) or because they fear that repressing their opponents would mean alienating necessary domestic allies. This inability to use repression early in the coalition-reduction process means that opposition remains (and sometimes thrives) into the consolidation phase. The elites must therefore accommodate them or risk non-cooperation, a breakdown in domestic alliances, or even rebellion. War intercedes in Type III cases, however, having a curious double-edged effect. In addition to employing accommodation often in this period, the elites must repress often in order to maintain order at home during the national emergency. Thus Type III cases should employ both types of policies frequently during the consolidation phase.

Finally, Type IV situations, like Type III, contain elites who perceive themselves to be vulnerable. They must accommodate during the state-building phase due to an inability to repress during the coalition-reduction process. Without the pressures of war, repression does not occur on any grand scale even after the coalition-reduction process ends.

Of course, these case types are ideal types. I do not expect that the cases I analyze will perfectly fit these patterns. Unforeseen critical events such as major crises short of war, deaths of key leaders, peace treaty negotiations, and the like may cause temporary deviations from the historical patterns described in the model above. However, these "blips" should be explainable within the context of the model, and I expect that, in general, the hypothesized patterns will hold.

In sum, I expect that elite perceptions of their own vulnerability and war participation are the prime causal factors in explaining which elites choose repression and which choose accommodation in the period following the end of the internal war. In Chapters 4 and 5 I test these propositions and evaluate the historical process model presented above. In order to empirically test the model I need to choose cases to examine that correspond with the four types of cases that my model predicts. In the next chapter I engage in careful case selection.

CHAPTER 3

You Say You Want a Revolution: Selecting Test Cases

The historical process model developed in the previous chapter yielded a number of testable hypotheses, based on four hypothetical case types. In this chapter, I discuss the selection process for the cases that will be used to test these hypotheses. The cases examined throughout the rest of this book are (with the dates of their respective internal wars in brackets): Bolivia [1952], Cuba [1958–59], Iran [1978–79], and Nicaragua [1978–79]. Below I begin by discussing how and why these cases were chosen from among the pool of potential cases, and then provide a brief sketch of these revolutionary conflicts.

Case Selection

I employ a small-n structured-focused "most similar case" comparative design to test the hypothetical implications of my model.[1] This method is particularly useful in situations like these where cases that appear to have multiple commonalties experience different outcomes. The researcher's objective is to identify the dissimilar variable(s) between and among the cases examined (the independent variable[s]) and determine whether they causally explain the differing outcomes (the dependent variable).[2]

In order to do so, the researcher must first insure that the cases are indeed "most similar" in terms of other key factors that could possibly affect the outcomes. Hence, one controls for variables that might otherwise provide alternative causal explanations for variance in the outcome.[3] This allows the researcher to create a set of *ceteris paribus* assumptions[4]—for instance: *assuming that the cases examined are similar on (control) variables X1,*

X2, and X3, how does (independent) variable X4 affect (dependent) variable Y1?[5]
In short, cases are selected based on similarity on key control variables as
well as variation on the independent variable(s) of theoretical interest. One
can then examine whether differences in the independent variable(s) have
the expected effects on the dependent variable in a more methodologically
rigorous manner.

The four cases employed throughout the rest of this study (Bolivia
[1952], Cuba [1958–59], Iran [1978–79], and Nicaragua [1978–79]) were
chosen from the pool of internal wars that forms a subset of the larger
Correlates of War (COW) data project.[6] I then attempted to assure that the
cases chosen for examination were most similar. Below I enumerate the
control variables used to help select the cases to be examined.

Temporal Boundaries

First I selected cases based on their temporal location. I selected only cases
whose internal wars began after 1945 and ended before 1983. The latter
boundary insured that there were at least 13 observable years after the internal war. This allows for observations of up to three years for the coalition-reduction phase and up to ten years for the consolidation phase. The
lower boundary keeps the cases bounded within the Cold War era. While
much variance was present in the international system during these years,
the amount is much less than the variance between the environment of
that era and that of the previous era(s). By bounding the cases within the
Cold War years I effectively controlled for the general alignment of the international system.

Internal War Type: Revolutions vs. Civil Wars

Next I selected cases based on internal war type. Internal wars pit two or
more opposing sides within the same political and geographic unit in
large-scale armed conflict over the future of the state structure. Revolutions and civil wars are subsets of this larger concept of internal wars.[7] In
a revolution, each side (government and opposition) fights to control or
alter the existing state structure. As discussed earlier (Chapter 1), mass-
based revolutions from below attempt to create more centralized, bureaucratic states, as well as to instigate radical changes in the economy and
social structure.[8] Elite-driven revolutions from above attempt mostly social
and economic changes, and only minor political reorganization.[9] Civil
wars can be understood loosely as armed conflicts in which one side

wishes to rule the state from a unified center, while another side seeks to split the state, and rule the remainder from a second center of power.[10] In all of these cases multiple sovereignty exists throughout the duration of the internal war.

For this study I selected only those cases of mass-based revolution, or revolution from below, in order to insure that the cases examined are most similar in nature. I acknowledge that the model presented in this study should also be tested using cases of civil wars and/or revolutions from above in order to ascertain the generalizability of the theory to all internal wars. However, given time, space, and resource limitations, I leave such an endeavor for future studies (see Chapter 9).

Success vs. Failure

From the remaining Cold War era revolutions from below I chose only cases where the outcome was the successful overthrow of the old regime. If the old government is victorious, then much of the old system will remain intact. However, if the opposition wins, then much of the old system will be either torn down or revamped to the specifications of the new regime. Because I am most interested in examining situations that call for the most drastic state-building measures, I prefer to focus on successful transfers of power. J. David Singer and Melvin Small's Correlates of War data set codes the "winner" of the internal war as either "government" or "opposition." I rely on their coding of an "opposition" win to determine revolutionary success.[11]

Internal War Duration

I then controlled for internal war duration. A number of studies find that conflict duration affects post-conflict policies, following both interstate and internal wars.[12] Longer conflicts are bloodier, more draining on state resources, and engender more subsequent repression than shorter conflicts. Thus, so as to eliminate conflict duration as a potential factor in determining subsequent levels of repression, I chose only cases that experienced relatively short (less than two year) revolutions.

Internal War Termination Type

Additionally, how internal wars are terminated influences subsequent internal war outcomes.[13] Negotiated settlements force differing groups to live together, and enable them to defend themselves from each other as well. Military victories by definition enable the winner to set the terms of the post-conflict period. This may include the decision to punish the losing side. Indeed, military victories to internal wars are more likely to be followed by severe repression than negotiated settlements.[14] Thus, if I wish to eliminate it as a potential influencing factor in determining post-revolutionary policy mix choices I must control for termination type.

It was fortuitous then that all of the cases that remained after controlling for conflict type, duration, and success were terminated in the same fashion—through military victory. War weariness helps account for termination type: "the longer a civil war has lasted, the more likely the participants are to seek a negotiated settlement as the conflict drags on."[15] Therefore one would expect that internal wars that end in a military victory would be, on average, shorter than those ended via negotiated settlements. Additionally, it is rare that opposition groups successfully supplant their government opponents via negotiated settlement. More often, revolutionary groups succeed by ousting the old regime militarily.

Economic Status

All remaining cases are also "most similar" on another key indicator that may otherwise affect the choice of policies by the elites—economic status. A number of studies have established that economic status plays a role in conditioning the use of repression.[16] For example, Michael Freeman argues that "[t]he weakness of many states in the world economic system and the economic expectations of their peoples may lead to rebellions and ruthless repressions . . . ."[17] Therefore, economic status is controlled for by insuring that all cases chosen have a GNP per capita below $1,000 (in 1972 dollars) in the first year of the post-revolutionary period.

Ethnic Heterogeneity

Societal homogeneity should also affect the degree to which regimes engage in state building. State building inherently involves "attempts at eliminating subnational differences that might serve as counterloyalties to the state."[18] Such divisions, especially if drawn along communal lines, impede the state's ability to mobilize resources effectively.[19] Heterogeneous societies present a large number of groups with their own agendas, ideas, and demands on the state. Thus heterogeneity requires policies or solutions to be more diverse as well, making them harder to pay for, implement, and enforce. Beyond the obvious ideological imperatives, these increased costs may help explain the apparent incentive for heterogeneous post-revolutionary states to homogenize the society at large.[20]

Ethnicity, in particular, appears to many theorists to be an extremely powerful identifier and barrier between groups. Indeed, while other differences are often important, most communal conflict centers around the primary cleavage of ethnicity. Ethnicity tends to sweep away other cross-cutting cleavages, and is a powerful driving force in domestic conflict.[21]

Therefore, I attempt to control for the potential impact of ethnic heterogeneity on policy mix choices of post-revolutionary regimes. The cases chosen should therefore have similar levels of ethnic fractionalization. Elsewhere I have constructed a continuous ethnic fractionalization index:

> Operationalizing the variable requires first calculating the proportion of the population of each ethnic group to the total population of the country and then squaring it. Next, I summed the squared proportions for all groups—and subtracted that number from one to come up with the fractionalization measure. A low score, such as Japan's 0.01 (the minimum) indicates asymmetry between groups—a huge majority (99%) of one group and a very small minority (1%) of another. A high score, such as Nigeria's 0.87, indicates many groups with small or relatively equal percentages of the population. In Nigeria, Igbo, Yoruba, Hausa, and Fulani all comprise substantial proportions of the population.[22]

All cases to be examined in this study should be relatively heterogeneous, and roughly within the same range of ethnic fractionalization—preferably in a medium to high range—with a score over 0.33 and under 0.67.[23]

The result of this selection process is that the four remaining cases—Bolivia [1952], Cuba [1958–59], Iran [1978–79], and Nicaragua [1978–79]—are most similar in internal war type, termination type, success, and duration, are bounded within the same era in international politics, are generally considered to be less-developed states, and have similar levels of ethnic heterogeneity. They also vary as needed on my two key independent variables—war participation and elite perceptions of vulnerability.[24] Table 3.1 shows how the four cases vary on the explanatory variables. Iran [1978–79] is a Type I case—elites who perceive themselves to be secure, and the presence of a post-revolutionary conflict (the Iran-Iraq War). Cuba [1958–59] is a Type II case—secure elites

Table 3.1 Cases To Be Examined (by Key Independent Variables)

	War	No War
Secure	Iran (Type I)	Cuba (Type II)
Vulnerable	Nicaragua (Type III)	Bolivia (Type IV)

but no post-revolutionary conflict. Nicaragua [1978–79] is a Type III case—elites who perceive themselves to be vulnerable coupled with the presence of a post-revolutionary conflict (the Contra War). Finally, Bolivia [1952] is a Type IV case—vulnerable elites and no post-revolutionary conflict.

Excellent detailed studies abound about each of these revolutions.[25] I do not propose to delve deeply into their respective histories, as the primary interest of this study is the post-revolutionary period. However, in order to provide some necessary background information for the remainder of this study, I present a thumbnail sketch of these four revolutions in the next section.

Four Revolutions

Bolivia

After a 1943 coup in Bolivia, the military-backed National Revolutionary Movement (MNR) instituted a middle-class, nationalist, semi-fascist regime.[26] The regime was overthrown in 1946, and the MNR realized it needed a new, strengthened social base.[27] In order to appeal to the working classes, the MNR began to reposition itself as a left-leaning populist party in favor of, among other things, universal suffrage, tin nationalization, and land reform.[28] But the alliances with labor and peasants were fragile, and "fraught with mutual distrust and uncertainty."[29] Nevertheless, the MNR successfully contested elections in 1951. However, the election results were overturned, the MNR was outlawed, and the government was turned over to the military.

The MNR and their allies attempted to retake the reigns of power in April of 1952. What began as a coup attempt grew into a mass-based revolution, as the loose alliance of opposition groups, including the powerful labor unions and peasant organizations, became better armed and more radicalized.[30] The revolution itself was rather brief and relatively bloodless.

Within less than a week the MNR-led coalition had ousted the military and taken control of the state.

Cuba

In 1952 a military coup brought Fulgencio Batista back to power in Cuba. The dictator's corrupt and predatory rule galvanized opposition to the regime.[31] It was clear by late 1956 that a large segment of the population desired radical change. Student groups and labor unions began holding anti-government strikes, demonstrations, and sit-ins. Returning from exile, Fidel Castro led a group of revolutionaries against Batista's army. After devastating losses during their landing in Cuba, Castro and his army set up camp in the Sierra Maestra mountains. During this period the revolutionaries won the peasants over to their cause, creating a broad anti-regime coalition necessary for a successful mass-based revolution.[32]

1957 and early 1958 saw bloody but sporadic and mostly unsuccessful urban guerrilla assaults against the government. The fighting increased to full-scale internal war by mid-1958. As popular support grew for the rebels, anti-government successes increased dramatically. By January 1, 1959 the revolutionary army had taken the capital, Havana, and Batista had fled the country.[33] The revolutionaries immediately stepped into the power vacuum and began shaping post-revolutionary Cuba.[34]

Iran

In 1953, with help from his sponsor, the United States, Mohammed Reza Pahlavi—the Shah of Iran—overthrew the government of reformist prime minister Mohammed Mossadeq.[35] The Shah proceeded to marginalize religious leaders and Westernize Iranian political, economic, and social life. He also cultivated and employed brutal coercive mechanisms of the state, including a powerful army and much-feared secret police (SAVAK).[36] The reforms drew Iran closer to the West. However, domestically the reforms mainly benefited the rich.[37] The Shah rejected claims by most societal groups, including peasants, unions, bazaaris (merchants), intellectuals, professionals, and religious leaders. Opposition was harshly suppressed.

The oil shock of 1978 devastated the Iranian economy, prompting national strikes and massive street protests. This time the Shah's inconsistent use of repression, coupled with the clever use by religious leaders of the 40-day mourning period to consistently spur on mass mobilization, escalated rather than reduced dissent.[38] Despite serious differences, even among religious leaders, the opposition united toward the common goal of ousting the Shah's government. The most powerful factions of the opposition were those following exiled religious leader Ayatollah Ruhollah Khomeini, who favored replacing the monarchy with an Islamic theocracy. His more militant followers led massive street protests in major cities throughout the country. Deciding he could no longer control events in Iran, the Shah left the country on January 16, 1979.[39] The remnants of government soon fell to the revolutionaries.[40] A vast and unstable revolutionary coalition, ranging from Communists to merchants to religious zealots, took power. On February 1, 1979 Khomeini returned from exile to direct the post-revolutionary reconstruction of Iran.

Nicaragua

During the early to mid-1970s various factions within Nicaraguan society began to converge toward a unified goal—opposition to Anastasio Somoza Debayle's corrupt, brutal, neopatrimonial dictatorship. Residents of the capital, Managua, had never recovered from a massive earthquake in 1972, nor had they forgiven Somoza for misappropriating funds designated as disaster relief and profiting off of the disaster at their expense.[41] The rural poor were devastated by Somoza's harsh economic reforms, instituted at the behest of the International Monetary Fund. The middle class was angered over massive government corruption, and by their exclusion from their traditionally modest role in Nicaraguan politics. Numerous pressure groups formed among agricultural, industrial, commercial, and financial interests, and were reinforced by clergy espousing Liberation Theology and encouraging mass revolutionary behavior.[42] The movement was spearheaded by the Sandinista Front for National Liberation (FSLN), a left-wing organization made up of three "cells" ranging from far-left Communists to moderate socialists.[43] The revolutionary coalition was thus an odd, diverse, and unstable combination of Socialists/Communists and clergy, peasants, and bourgeoisie. Yet it was effective in the one goal shared by all groups involved—Somoza's ouster.

Popular demonstrations and the formation of neighborhood defense committees in the cities, coupled with effective guerrilla tactics in the countryside, yielded a weakening of the government.[44] In addition, the United States, Somoza's former patron, withdrew support for the regime as a result of President Carter's new human rights-based foreign policy.[45] After weeks of intense fighting in May and June of 1979, and pressure from the United States government, Somoza fled Nicaragua. Somoza's elite force, the National Guard, soon disintegrated, and in July 1979 the Sandinista-led coalition took control of Nicaragua.

In this chapter I have chosen cases to be used throughout the rest of this study. Because of the desirability of a most-similar-systems design, all cases chosen were those that had experienced a revolution. Therefore, for the duration of the study I will refer primarily to a subset of post-internal war states, post-revolutionary states.

In the next chapter I proceed to test the validity and utility of the model I outlined earlier using these post-revolutionary states as my test cases. First I discuss why a unique data set was necessary for this study, and how this data was collected. Then I evaluate the historical process model's accuracy in depicting how events actually unfold in post-revolutionary Iran, Nicaragua, Cuba, and Bolivia using that data. I demonstrate where and when repression and accommodation occurred in these cases, and compare my results with the expected observations posited by the historical process model.

PART II

The Causes of Repression and
Accomodation in Post-Revolutionary States

CHAPTER 4

Charting Policy Mix Choices:
Event Data and the
Historical Process Model

A revolution is not cut off square. It has always some necessary undulations before re-turning to the condition of peace, like a mountain on descending towards the plain.

- Victor Hugo (*Les Miserables*, X. ii.)

In Chapter 2 I developed a historical process model of factors affecting policy mix choices in post-internal war states. In this chapter I evaluate the model's accuracy in depicting how events actually unfold in the four post-revolutionary states discussed in Chapter 3. I demonstrate when and where repression and accommodation occurred in these cases, and compare those observations with the expected observations posited by the model. A close fit between expectations and observations gives me more confidence that the model accurately depicts the dynamics of policy mix choices in post-revolutionary states.

Policy Mix Data: Repression and Accommodation

Repression and accommodation are central to the questions examined in this project. In Part II of the project (Causes) these policy mix choices are the dependent variables to be explained. In Part III (Consequences) they are the primary explanatory variables.[1] Thus proper evaluation of the theoretical model developed earlier requires accurate data on the use of these policies. Yet data on repression and accommodation is either poor or nonexistent. Below I discuss the type of data required for this study, evaluate the available pool of data sets, and explain the method I employ to collect the repression and accommodation data used in this project. I begin by discussing the nature of the measures typically used in the collection of internal conflict data.

Choosing between Event Data and Standards-Based Measures

The collection of data on internal conflict and state policies is a complex process. Data collection rules must be systematically constructed and followed, variables must be carefully operationalized, and materials must be gathered and evaluated. However, the first decision the researcher must make is in regard to the nature of the measure of the dependent variable. In the study of government policy choices affecting rights, liberties, and political freedoms there have typically been two types of measures used: standards-based measures and event data.

Many recent data-intensive projects on the study of human rights and violations to personal integrity have employed a standards-based approach to the dependent variable in question.[2] This approach involves placing countries on an ordinal scale, based on the researchers' reading and evaluation of human rights information sources. Typically a single source is evaluated over time, such as *Amnesty International Reports*[3] or *State Department Reports*,[4] although it is becoming standard practice to check one source against another.[5] Multiple measures may be employed in combination in order to locate a given country on this ordinal scale. For example, Mitchell and McCormick use different variables to measure two conceptually distinct dimensions of human rights.[6] Cingranelli and Richards employ a Mokken scale approach to construct a single score per country-year representing that country's levels of both political rights and civil liberties.[7]

These approaches mirror those employed by Freedom House to construct similar country-year scores for political rights and civil liberties.[8]

The standards-based approach, as used to date, has a key flaw that makes it a sub-optimal measurement strategy for policy mix choices. Aggregation of these coded instances into a two, three, four, or five-point scale, as is common practice, leads to the loss of much, if not most, of the information on these instances. Specifics are sacrificed in return for an aggregate "score" determining a country's level on that particular indicator for that particular year. For example, Mitchell and McCormick look at indicators of "torture/killings" and "imprisonment" to evaluate human rights violations.[9] Cingranelli and Richards create a two-variable measure of political rights ("freedom from government censorship," "freedom to participate politically") and a three-variable measure of civil liberties ("freedom to form or join unions," "freedom of religion," "freedom of movement").[10] Neither of these attempts to systematize data on repression of human rights can get at qualitative differences between these indicators, or between these indicators and others not examined (but which occur with alarming frequency) such as mass rape, forced labor, seizure of assets, declaration of martial law, and many others. The indicators used in standards-based approaches are useful but limited in scope. The wealth of information potentially available is lost in the aggregation of these variables into country-year rankings.

The use of event data helps to circumvent these problems. Each instance of repression or accommodation is considered a separate data point. This produces a continuous (rather than ordinal) scale of repression and/or accommodation, allowing for greater variation. Information is not lost due to needless aggregation, although aggregation is still possible (and potentially useful). Moreover, the greater use of information creates an incentive for the researcher to differentiate beforehand between the multitude of different types of each policy. Thus stricter guidelines can be created in advance, which more rigidly guide the researcher during the collection of the data. The resulting data set is richer in content, containing not only information on how many events, but also a wide variation in the type of events coded and the qualitative differences between them. The researcher can then employ counts of events, weighted events, or a standards-based scale with equivalent ease in examining the data.

This project's particular needs are better served by event data. Event count data provides greater variation on the dependent variables without sacrificing accuracy. Variation in degree of severity of each type of policy is captured more easily by event data. These advantages provide the researcher with opportunities to employ multiple methods in analyzing the data. Event count models can be used to test the effects of particular variables on the likelihood of an event occurring or not occurring. Categorical data analysis methods such as (multinomial) logit or probit models can be easily employed if aggregation is deemed necessary. Finally, more differentiated data provides a more reliable test of the historical process model discussed in the previous chapter. In short, event data provides numerous and varied opportunities to analyze a richer source of data. Therefore I choose to employ event data in this project.

Some event data sets of internal conflict already exist. However, I find that original data collection is required. In the next section I discuss the data sets available, the reasons why they are inadequate for this project, and the development of the Post-Internal War Accommodation and Repression (PIWAR) data set.

Existing Internal Conflict Event Data Sets

International relations scholars have been blessed with useful event data about conflict and cooperation among states in the international system. The Conflict and Peace Data Bank (COPDAB)[11] and World Event / Interaction Survey (WEIS)[12] presented researchers with daily dyadic, cross-national, longitudinal conflict and cooperation event data.[13] Unfortunately, similarly useful data have not been available for the study of internal conflict. While COPDAB does present data on conflict and cooperation within nation states, it is aggregated at the national level. There is no way to distinguish between and among actors within the state. Thus, despite some internal conflict data, COPDAB data cannot be used here. Even if this were not the case, temporal limitations of the COPDAB series (1948–1978) make it unusable for this project.

The World Handbook of Political and Social Indicators provides "Daily Political Events Data" on a range of conflict events.[14] However, no scaling system for the events is developed, and only a small number of types of events are coded. The World Handbook also does not account for the cooperative end of the spectrum of events. Without this data, evaluations of policies of accommodation are impossible.[15] And as with the COPDAB series, temporal limitations preclude the use of the The World Handbook data for this project.[16]

The Violent Intranational Conflict Data Project (VICDP)[17] followed the conflict-cooperation scale model of COPDAB, but did not aggregate data at the national level, thereby rendering it more useful in the study of government-opposition interactions. The weighted 15-point scale model used by COPDAB was retained, increasing the potential variation of interaction types beyond those possible using standards-based measures. Additionally, Moore demonstrates that VICDP conflict-cooperation data can be converted into data on repression, accommodation, and both violent and nonviolent opposition data with relative ease.[18] However, the countries covered by VICDP do not include any of the countries of interest in this project.[19]

The Intranational Political Interactions (IPI) data set is a larger scale version of VICDP, and subsumes the latter.[20] IPI conflict and cooperation data are also scaled according to intensity. Each event is also grouped with other like events and given a particular code, enabling more detailed evaluations of particular policies. IPI also includes a large number of actor/target codes to allow users flexibility in choosing appropriate levels of aggregation. However, despite the fact that the range of cases covered by IPI is much more extensive than the VICDP range, it still falls short of covering my cases of interest.[21] Additionally, as of this writing the full IPI data set is not yet generally available. Thus, I cannot utilize the IPI data for this project.

Other, machine-coded data sets with information on internal conflict are currently available or are in development, including the Global Event Data System (GEDS),[22] the Kansas Event Data System (KEDS), and the Program for the Analysis of Nonviolent Direct Action (PANDA).[23] But these either cover short periods of time or deal with a narrow range of cases.[24] Unfortunately, none of these machine-coded data sets as yet provide event data for the cases and time frames that would make this project possible.

International relations and comparative politics scholars have begun to realize the utility of collecting systematic events data for the study of internal conflict situations. Some of the data-collection projects described above are moving in the direction of a comprehensive internal conflict event data set. However, none of the currently available data sets can be employed in the context of this project. Therefore, I am compelled to create a new data set that will allow me to test the model described earlier on my cases of interest. For this, I have created the Post-Internal War Accommodation and Repression (PIWAR) data set. The development of this data set, including the compilation of a list of policy mix choices and their weights, the coding procedure used, descriptions of the specific data collected, and the reliability of the data is discussed below.

Developing a Weighted Scale List of Policies of Repression and Accommodation

I began by compiling a list of types of repressive and accommodative policies. These particular policies were drawn from key works in the literature, both theoretical and case-oriented. Lists of particular policies of repression and accommodation and the sources in which they are discussed appear in Tables 4.1 and 4.2.

Once these lists were compiled, the policies needed to be assigned a value or score. Each repressive or accommodative policy can be counted as either one unit with equal value to all other units or as one unit with some greater or lesser value than other units. If Country A represses five times in a given year, restricting freedom of speech each time, while Country B represses five times that year, but each time it engages in genocidal massacres of a domestic group, then it does not seem right to say that Country A is as repressive as Country B. Not all types of repression and/or accommodation are of similar severity, and this needs to be taken into account.

Unfortunately no adequate scale currently exists to allow measurement of these policies in such a manner. VICDP, IPI, and COPDAB have all created weighted scales of conflict and cooperation. But none of these projects can distinguish adequately between and among specific policies of repression and accommodation. As such, these scales are too dissimilar to employ here. I therefore endeavored to create a unique scale of repression and accommodation based upon the judgment of experts.[25]

In order to derive values or scores for each particular policy I polled 30 experts in the field. A copy of the survey and cover letter sent to each respondent appears in Appendix A. A list of the experts contacted appears in Table A.1 in the Appendix. Of the expert judges contacted I received 15 valid responses, a 50 percent response rate.[26] Each respondent was asked to rank the specific types of repression and accommodation on a scale of one to five. For repression, a score of one indicated the least repressive, and five the most repressive policy. For accommodation, one was the least accommodative policy, and five the most. Tables 4.3 and 4.4 list the scores assigned by each individual expert to policies of repression and accommodation respectively.[27]

The experts' scores were then averaged, and the averages rounded to the nearest whole number, to get the assigned score for each indicator. These scores are integers ranging from one to five. This scale is a slight improvement over simply counting the number of repressive or accommodative events. However, finer distinctions can still be made between and among the different types of policies. In order to capture differences that might have been lost due to rounding error I created a second, weighted score. The weighted score equals the experts' raw averaged score squared. Weighted scores range from 1 to 25. The original scores for repression and accommodation are highly correlated (0.95 and 0.91 respectively) with the weighted scores. Thus weighting the scores allows for greater differentiation among policy types without significantly diverging from the original scale. Tables 4.5 and 4.6 show the rounded scores (SCORE) and weighted scores (SCORE^2) for each specific policy. Once the list of possible policies and their relative weights were established, I was able to begin collecting data on repression and accommodation. In the next section I discuss the coding procedure employed.

Coding Procedure

I used in-depth archival research to provide the data for the dependent variables: repressive or accommodative policies. I coded repression and accommodation for up to 13 years following the end of each case's internal war.[28] An instance of repression or accommodation was counted for the purposes of this data set only if found and confirmed in at least two archival sources. The multi-step procedure for coding instances of repression or accommodation was as follows:

STEP 1. Initially, I employed an international news source. I used *Keesing's Contemporary Archives* as the primary data source in place of the more traditionally-favored *New York Times Index* because of the latter's history of underreporting certain types of events in the developing world and other potential problems.[29] Many other event data projects, including VICDP, COPDAB, and the International Military Interventions data set (IMI),[30] have used *Keesing's* as a primary source in systematically collecting their data.[31] Although not a primary source, I did use the *New York Times Index* in STEP 4 (below) to corroborate unconfirmed instances of repression or accommodation.

STEP 2. Next, I employed regional news sources. No one regional news source was available that covered all four cases over time. Therefore I employed different sources in order to grant the most coverage of potential events. I used *Foreign Broadcast Information Service* (FBIS) reports whenever possible because FBIS is compiled from a variety of regional sources both inside and outside the country of interest. It therefore has a wider range of coverage and is generally more reliable.[32] However, FBIS reports were only available for two of my cases of interest—Iran and Nicaragua.

Events in Bolivia were covered well by *Hispanic American Report* (HAR). HAR consists of in-depth monthly summaries of events in Latin America by a team of academic experts at Stanford University. As with FBIS, HAR draws upon information from multiple regional sources. HAR coverage runs from 1952 to 1964, conveniently the time span in which Bolivia is examined in this study.

44

Table 4.1 Sources—Policies of Repression

Policy	Source
Armed attack	Moore & Lindström (1996), Leeds, et al. (1995), Harff (1986)
Arresting opposition leaders	Moore (1996), Leeds, et al. (1995), Tilly (1978), Gamson (1975)
Compellance: punishing nonperformance	Kiernan (1993), Stohl & Lopez (1984; 1986)
Concentration camps	Rummel (1994), Kuper (1981), Horowitz (1980), Fein (1979)
Disappearances	Mason & Krane (1989), Stohl & Lopez (1984; 1986)
Disruption of group organization	Rummel (1994), Tilly (1978), Gamson (1975)
Establishment of a secret police/special forces	Mason & Krane (1989), Gurr (1988), Lasswell (1962)
Exemplary punishment/deterrent	Tarrow (1994), Carey (1990), Stohl & Lopez (1984; 1986)
Exiles/expulsions	AI (1994)
Expulsion or purge from party or ruling elite	Leeds, et al. (1995), Tilly (1978)
Forced conscription	Porter (1994), Tilly (1978)
Forced labor	Rummel (1994), Gurr (1993), Kiernan (1991; 1993)
Forced resettlement	Rummel (1994), Gurr & Harff (1994), Kiernan (1993)
Forced subjugation/integration of communities	Gurr (1992; 1993), Kiernan (1993), Kuper (1977; 1981)
Illegal detentions	Tarrow (1994), Rummel (1994), Gurr & Harff (1994)
Making groups more visable, easily spotted	Kiernan (1991; 1993), Kuper (1981), Fein (1979), Tilly (1978)
"Manufactured" famine or drought	AI (1994), Rummel (1994), Kiernan (1993) Malhuret (1985)
Martial law declared	Moore & Lindström (1996), Stohl & Lopez (1984; 1986)
Mass killings	Krain (1997), Rummel (1994; 1995), Harff & Gurr (1988)
Mass rape	Tetrault (1995), Rummel (1994; 1995), Brownmiller (1975)

(continues)

Table 4.1 *(continued)*

Policy	Source
Ousting group from government	Leeds, et al. (1995), Gurr (1993), Skocpol (1979), Tilly (1978)
Outlawing organizations, groups, industries	AI (1994), Tarrow (1994), Gurr (1993), Tilly (1978)
Political executions	Rummel (1994), Gurr & Harff (1994), Mason & Krane (1989)
Prohibitive fines, taxes, fees, regulations	Moore (1996), Kuper (1981)
Public threat of violence	Moore & Lindström (1996), Stohl & Lopez (1984; 1986)
Religious suppression/persecution	AI (1994), Rummel (1994), Gurr (1993), Harff & Gurr (1988)
Restricting access to resourcses, necessities, jobs	Moore (1996), Rummel (1994), Gurr (1993), Kiernan (1993)
Restricting assembly	Tarrow (1994), Gurr (1993), Kiernan (1991; 1993), Tilly (1978)
Restricting communication of information, speech	Moore & Lindström (1996), Rummel (1994), Tilly (1978)
Restricting emigration, mobility	AI (1994), Rummel (1994), Gurr (1993), Kiernan (1993)
Seizing assests	Rummel (1994), Gurr (1993), Horowitz (1980), Tilly (1978)
Show of force	Moore & Lindström (1996), AI (1994), Harff (1986)
Show trials/political trials	Moore (1996)
"Special" extra-legal courts set up	AI (1994)
Suspending or censoring news media/speech	Moore & Lindström (1996), Stohl & Lopez (1984; 1986)
Suspension of part of constitution or the regular workings of government	Moore & Lindström (1996), Stohl & Lopez (1984; 1986)
Trials in absentia	AI (1994), Kiernan (1993)
Use of torture	Mason & Krane (1989), Stohl & Lopez (1984; 1986)
Violent putdown of demonstration/insurrection	Moore & Lindström (1996), Tilly (1978), Gamson (1975)
Widespread use of spies and informants	Gurr (1988), Stohl & Lopez (1984; 1986), Tilly (1978)

Note: AI (1994) = Amnesty International (1994)

Table 4.2 Sources—Policies of Accommodation

Policy	Source
Abandoning project hurtful to group	Moore (1996), Leeds, et al. (1995)
Allowing emigration	AI (1994)
Allowing return from exile	Gurr & Harff (1994), O'Donnell & Schmitter (1986)
Broad statement of guarantee of rights	Moore & Lindström (1996), Leeds, et al. (1995)
Compromise reached	Moore & Lindström (1996), O'Donnell & Schmitter (1986)
Direct aid (money, forces) to challanger	Gurr & Harr (1994), Gurr (1993), Tilly (1978)
Encouraging/allowing separatism	Moore & Lindström (1996), Gurr (1993)
Freeing prisoners	Moore (19996), Leeds, et al. (1995), AI (1994)
General amnesty	Moore & Lindström (1996), O'Donnell & Schmitter (1986)
Giving positive publicity to group	Pion-Berlin (1984), Tilly (1978)
Incorporation into government	O'Donnell & Schmitter (1986), Gamson (1975)
Increasing access to information	Gurr & Harff (1994), Gurr (1993)
Increasing access to markets	Eckstein (1982; 1985)
Increasing opportunies for participation	Tarrow (1994), Eckstein (1982; 1985), Kelly & Klein (1981)
Increasing security of target group	Leeds, et al. (1995)
Introducing enabling mechanism/ necessary entitlement	AI (1994)
Large-scale redistribution of assets/ resources	Eckstein (1982; 1985), Kelly & Klein (1977; 1981)
Legalizing group membership	Tarrow (1994), Gurr (1993), Tilly (1978), Gamson (1975)
Low-level concession	O'Donnell & Schmitter (1986)
Negotiations begin	Moore & Lindström (1996), O'Donnell & Schmitter (1986)
Outlawing repressive apparatus, institution, practice	Moore (1996), Leeds, et al. (1995)
Prosecution of enemies target group	AI (1994)
Providing selective incentives	Lichbach (1994; 1995), Gamson (1975), Olson (1965)

(continues)

Table 4.2 *(continued)*

Policy	Source
Reduction in fines, taxes, fees	Kiser & Barzel (1991), Tilly (1975), Hintze (1975)
Removing restrictive law/regulation	Leeds, et al. (1995), Eckstein (1985), Kelly & Klein (1981)
Small scale-diversion of resources in group	Gurr & Harff (1994), Pion-Berlin (1984)
Stays of executions	AI (1994)

Note: AI (1994) = Amnesty International (1994)

Unfortunately HAR covers only half of the years of interest for Cuba (1959–64). However *The Times of the Americas* (TOTA) began publication in 1964, and continues up to and beyond 1971, the final year required for complete coverage of Cuba in this study.[33] In order to check for continuity in reporting, I coded TOTA and HAR for the only year in which they overlap, 1964. HAR reported all events published in TOTA for that year, plus a few more. While not perfect correlation, it is close enough to enable its use here as one of many sources for identifying events. The use of multiple data sources should provide any information not covered by TOTA from 1965 through 1971.

One potential problem with this source is that TOTA was published by anti-Castro dissidents. This calls into question the degree to which this source might be biased in favor of reporting more repression and less accommodation than actually occurred. At the opposite spectral extreme is *Granma,*[34] the Communist Party newspaper in Cuba, which should be biased in favor of reporting more accommodation and less repression than actually occurred. I coded both sources for two years (1970, 1971) as a quick test of TOTA's reliability. Interestingly, all events reported by *Granma* during these years were reported in TOTA. In addition, while TOTA did report more repression than Granma as expected, it also reported more accommodation than the Communist Party paper. TOTA appears to be a generally valid source,[35] and is therefore used for Cuba for the years 1965–71.[36]

STEP 3. Next, I used historical accounts. These accounts may be more sensitive to the subtleties of forced day-to-day inhumane living conditions, other quiet repressive tactics, and non-newsworthy or unspectacular forms of accommodation that are typically missed by media sources.[37] Historical

Table 4.3 Experts' Weighted Sources—Policies of Repression

Policy						Expert #									
	1	2	3	4	5	6	7	8	9	10	11	12	13	14	15
Armed attack	4	5	4	5	2	4	5	3	3	–	1	2	3	4	3
Arresting opposition leaders	3	3	4	2	2	3	3	2	3	3	3	1	2	3	3
Compellance: punishing nonperformance	3	2	2	–	2	1	4	1	3	–	1	1	2	1	–
Concentration camps	3	3	4	3	4	4	5	4	3	3	3	5	4	4	4
Disappearances	5	1	5	5	4	5	5	4	4	5	5	4	4	5	5
Disruption of group organization	1	3	3	1	1	2	2	2	2	3.5	3	2	2	2	2
Establishment of a secret police/special forces	3	4	3	1	2	1	3	2	3	2	3	3	–	1	3
Exemplary punishment/deterrent	3	2	3	4	3	3	3	3	4	–	1	2	3	2	–
Exiles/expulsions	2	1	4	3	4	3	5	2	2	3	2	2	–	3	3
Forced conscription	2	3	4	2	1	3	3	3	2	3	2	4	–	3	3
Forced labor	3	3	4	2	4	3	4	3	5	3	3	4	4	3	3
Forced resettlement	3	3	4	3	4	4	5	4	3	3	3	5	4	4	4
Forced subjugation/integration of communities	3	3	3	4	2	3	3	4	3	–	3	5	2	4	4
Illegal detentions	3	2	3	2	3	3	3	3	4	2.5	3	3	3	3	3
Making groups more visable, easily spotted	3	2	2	2	1	1	1	3	3	2.5	–	1	2	2	–

(continues)

Table 4.3 *(continued)*

Policy	Expert #														
	1	2	3	4	5	6	7	8	9	10	11	12	13	14	15
"Manufactured" famine or drought	3	4	3	5	5	5	5	4	5	4	5	5	4	4	4
Martial law declared	3	4	3	2	3	3	3	4	3	2.5	3	4	3	3	3
Mass killings	5	5	5	5	5	5	5	5	5	5	5	5	5	5	5
Mass rape	4	5	5	4	5	4	5	5	5	4	4	5	5	5	4
Ousting group from government	1	4	3	1	1	1	2	2	2	2	2	3	1	1	2
Outlawing organizations, groups, industries	3	4	3	2	2	1	3	2	3	2	3	3	2	2	3
Political executions	4	3	4	4	4	5	5	4	4	5	5	2	4	4	5
Prohibitive fines, taxes, fees, regulations	3	2	2	1	1	1	1	3	3	2	–	3	3	2	1
Public threat of violence	3	3	1	4	1	3	1	1	3	2	1	1	–	2	3
Religious suppression/ persecution	2	2	2	2	4	2	4	3	1	3	3	5	3	3	–
Restricting access to resources, necessities, jobs	1	3	1	3	2	1	2	3	3	2.5	1	4	2	1	1
Restricting assembly	2	3	2	2	1	2	2	1	2	3	3	2	2	2	2
Restricting communication of information, speech	1	1	3	1	1	1	2	2	2	–	3	1	1	1	1

(continues)

Table 4.3 *(continued)*

Policy	Expert #														
	1	2	3	4	5	6	7	8	9	10	11	12	13	14	15
Restricting emigration, mobility	2	2	3	2	1	2	2	3	2	–	3	3	3	2	1
Seizing assets	2	3	2	3	2	2	3	2	3	3	1	2	3	1	2
Show of force	2	3	2	1	1	2	1	2	3	–	2	1	1	2	–
Suspending or censoring news media/speech	2	4	3	1	2	2	3	2	3	2	3	2	2	2	3
Use of torture	5	2	5	3	5	4	5	4	4	4	4	3	3	3	4
Violent putdown of demonstration/insurrection	3	1	3	1	3	3	4	4	3	–	4	1	3	2	3
Widespread use of spies and informants	3	3	3	1	3	1	3	2	3	2	1	4	3	2	3

Table 4.4 Experts' Weighted Sources—Policies of Accommodation

Policy	Expert #														
	1	2	3	4	5	6	7	8	9	10	11	12	13	14	15
Allowing return from exile	3	2	3	3	2	3	3	3	2	3	2	3	3	2	4
Compromise reached	4	5	4	3	4	3	3	4	3	3	2	5	2	3	5
Direct aid (money, forces) to challanger	4	2	4	4	2	3	4	3	3	4	3	3	2	4	3
Encouraging/allowing separatism	5	3	3	5	5	5	5	3	1	5	4	5	5	5	5
Freeing prisoners	4	2	5	2	1	4	3	3	4	3	3	2	4	2	3
General amnesty	4	4	2	5	3	4	4	3	3	3	2	4	5	3	5
Giving positive publicity to group	3	3	3	3	2	2	2	1	2	4	–	1	1	1	1
Incorporation into government	5	4	5	4	5	5	4	5	5	5	4	5	2	5	3
Increasing access to information	1	2	4	2	1	1	1	1	3	2	3	1	1	1	2
Increasing opportunies for participation	3	3	4	4	4	2	1	3	2	4	4	3	2	2	–
Large-scale redistribution of assets/resources	3	4	4	5	3	5	4	5	5	5	1	5	5	5	3
Legalizing group membership	3	4	4	4	2	2	5	3	3	4	3	4	2	3	4
Low-level concession	1	1	1	1	1	2	2	1	2	1	1	1	1	1	1
Negotiations begin	3	3	4	2	3	2	2	2	2	1	1	3	1	3	4
Providing selective incentives	1	2	5	5	2	–	3	3	2	4	–	3	2	1	1

(continues)

Table 4.4 *(continued)*

Policy	Expert #														
	1	*2*	*3*	*4*	*5*	*6*	*7*	*8*	*9*	*10*	*11*	*12*	*13*	*14*	*15*
Reduction in fines, taxes, fees	2	3	4	1	1	1	2	1	3	2	1	2	2	1	1
Removing restrictive law/regulation	3	3	3	1	2	2	2	3	3	4	3	2	2	2	—
Small scale–diversion of resources in group	1	2	2	3	1	3	2	3	2	4	1	1	1	2	2
Stays of executions	3	1	5	1	1	2	2	3	4	3	1	1	3	2	3

Table 4.5 Weighted Scores for Policies of Repression

Policy	Score	Score^2
Mass killings	5	25
Mass rape	5	21
Disappearances	4	19
"Manufactured" famine or drought	4	19
Concentration camps	4	18
Political excutions	4	17
Use of torture	4	15
Forced resettlement	4	14
Armed attack	3	12
Forces labor	3	12
Forced subjugation/integration of communities	3	11
Martial law declared	3	10
Explary punishment/deterrent	3	8
Illegal detentions	3	8
Religious suppression/persecution	3	8
Show rials/political trials	3	8
Trials in absentia	3	8
Violent putdown of demonstration/insurrection	3	8
Arresting opposition leaders	3	7
Exiles/expulsions	3	7
Forced conscription	3	7
Outlawing organizations, groups, industries	3	6
Establishment of a secret police/special forces	2	6
"Special" extra-legal courts set up	2	6
Suspending or censoring news media/speech	2	6
Widespread use of spies and informants	2	6
Restricting access to resources, necessites, jobs	2	5
Restricting assembly	2	5
Restricitng emigration, mobility	2	5
Seizing assets	2	5
Compellance: punishing nonperformance	2	4
Disruption of group organization	2	4
Making groups more visable, easily spotted	2	4
Prohibitive fines, taxes, fees, regulations	2	4
Public threat of violence	2	4
Suspension of parts of constituion or the regular workings of government	2	4
Expulsion/purge from party or ruling elite	2	3
Ousting group from government	2	3
Show of force	2	3
Restricting communication or information, speech	2	2

Table 4.6 Weighted Scores for Policies of Accommodation

Policy	Score	Score^2
Incorporation into government	4	19
Encouraging/allowing separatism	4	18
Large-scale redistribution of assets/resources	4	17
General amnesty	4	13
Compromised reached	4	12
Direct aid (money, forces) to challenger	3	10
Legalizing group membership	3	10
Freeing prisoners	3	9
Increasing opportunites for participation	3	9
Increasing access to markets	3	9
Allowing return from exile	3	7
Providing selective incentives	3	7
Allowing emigration	3	6
Introducing enabling mechanism/necessary entitlement	3	6
Outlawing repressive apparatus, institution, practice	3	6
Removing restrictive law/regulation	3	6
Negotiations begun	2	6
Stays of execution	2	5
Broad statement of guarantee of rights	2	4
Giving positive publicity to group	2	4
Small-scale diversion of resources to group	2	4
Abandonng project hurtful to group	2	3
Increasing access to information	2	3
Reduction in fines, taxes, fees	2	3
Increasing security of target group	1	1
Low-level concession	1	1
Prosecution of enemies of target group	1	1

sources are therefore valuable tools in this kind of data collection effort, and are employed here. I engaged in an on-line library catalog search to create the list from which I selected 15 historical sources. I chose broad surveys of the post-internal war period whenever possible. Table 4.7 lists the historical materials used in this step.

While general books about the state, region, or time period were preferred, occasionally I substituted academic articles when the information provided in these articles was particularly useful and not covered in book form. In other instances I included more specific books if coverage of a particular group or time frame was generally ignored by the other historical accounts. For example, the literature on Iran largely ignores policies of the government toward the Baha'is. To remedy this deficiency I added a good source on the state's actions with regard to this group,[38] allowing for more accurate coding of government policies. Another example is the addition of Anoushiravan Ehteshami's work on the Iranian Second Republic to insure adequate coverage of this period (1989–91+).[39]

STEP 4. Finally, I used the *New York Times Index* only to verify whether instances found in one of the above three steps, but not confirmed subsequently, were in fact eligible for inclusion in this data set.[40] No new cases were added at this stage. However, any event confirmed in this step was included as a useable data point.

Data Collected for the PIWAR Data Set

Each event received its own coding sheet. Each coding sheet allowed for information on each of the following: case and event identification, date of event, type of policy, (weighted) scores for each policy, a brief description of the event (optional), targets of the policy, actions that triggered the use of this policy, reactions to the policy, and data sources used. Appendix B contains a copy of the coding sheet used in data collection for the PIWAR project.

Once an event was found, I assigned it a unique reference number made up of the Singer and Small COW war number, followed by "R" for repression or "A" for accommodation, followed by a policy event number.[41] So, for example, the fifteenth accommodation event coded for Iran would have the following reference number: 904-A-15; the one hundred and twenty-second repression event for Cuba would be numbered 829-R-122. Events were numbered in order of discovery rather than by temporal sequence.

To the best of my ability I ascertained the date on which the policy was first implemented. A new event was coded if the event overlapped into the next year. Otherwise it was coded as one event, regardless of duration (up to one year). Many times specific dates were unavailable. In such situations, year and month were usually found.

Once the type of policy was determined I ascertained which specific type of repression or accommodation was being used. Each specific policy was given a unique number, found in the PIWAR project's codebook,

Table 4.7 Historical Case Materials Used in Step 3 of the Coding Process

Bolvia	*Cuba*
Alexander (1958)	del Aguila (1984)
Andrade (1976)	Betto (1987)
Calderon (1972)	Brenner, LeoGrande, Rich, and Siegel (1989)
Corbett (1972)	Chilcote and Edelstein (1974)
Dunkerly (1984)	DiFronzo (1991)
Eckstein (1985)	Gonzalez (1974)
Kelly and Klein (1981)	Halebsky and Kirk (1985)
Klein (1992)	Luce (1968)
Ladman (1983)	Matthews (1975)
Malloy (1971a)	Nelson (1972)
Malloy (1970)	Randell (1981)
Malloy and Thorn (1971)	Sobel (1964)
Mitchell (1977)	Suarez (1967)
Ostria Gutierrez (1958)	Szulc (1986)
Queiser Morales (1992)	Urrutia (1964)
Iran	*Nicaragua*
Arjomand (1988)	Americas Watch Committee (1988)
Bakhash (1984)	Belli (1985)
Baktiari (1996)	Benjamin (1989)
Benard and Khalilzad (1984)	Close (1988)
DiFronzo (1991)	DiFronzo (1991)
Ehteshami (1995)	Dunkerley (1988)
Hiro(1985)	Grynspan (1991)
Keddie and Hooglund (1986)	Harris and Vilas (1985)
Menashri (1990)	Miranda and Ratliff (1993)
Moshiri (1991)	Nietschmann (1989)
Parsa (1989)	Ruchwarger (1987)
Ramazani (1990)	Selbin (1993)
United States Congress (1988)	Stahler-Sholk (1995)
Wright (1989)	Valenta and Duran (1987)
	Walker (1991)

presented in Appendix C. I then assigned the event a score and a weighted score based upon the scales listed in Tables 4.5 and 4.6.

I also recorded which groups or individuals were targeted by these government policies. Each type of target was assigned a unique number, which can also be found in the PIWAR project's codebook (Appendix C). I listed up to five targets in order of importance.

If the primary targeted group was targeted in the course of combat during war (i.e.- Contras in Nicaragua during the Contra War; Mujahedin-e-Khalq who fled Iran to fight with Iraq during the Iran-Iraq War) then the event was excluded from the data set. First, the targeted groups in these instances are groups that operate outside of the domestic arena. Second, these events will be captured once war is incorporated into the model. Thus, counting them at this stage is problematic on two fronts: it would not be a true accounting of "domestic" policy mix choices, and it would double-count events in this variable and the war variable.

When a group was targeted for multiple reasons they were coded twice, once for each way in which they were identified by the state. For example, when the Khmer Rouge slaughtered residents of the Eastern Zone of Cambodia in the 1970s many of the victims were targeted both because they lived in that region and because they were ethnic Chams.[42] If I were to code the killing of such people I would list them twice. First, I would record them as having been residents of a specific geographic region [32]—the primary reason for being targeted. I would also list them again as a second type of target—members of a specific ethnic group [72]. If others were also killed in that incident, they would be listed subsequently. To continue the example, if Buddhist Monks were also killed during this event, they would be listed as tertiary targets, and coded as clergy [75].[43]

I also recorded the type of event or action that triggered the use of the policy being examined, as well as the reaction by the target to that policy. Take for example an instance where a sit-in occurs, and the state responds by beating the protesters, killing one and injuring many others. The protesting group reacts by taking to the streets to avenge that death and winds up rioting. The trigger would be coded as non-violent resistance [TRIGGER=3], the government policy as violent put-down of a demonstration [POLICY TYPE=1; SPECIFIC POLICY=222], and the group's reaction would be coded as violent resistance [REACTION=4]. The most common triggers and reactions range from cooperation/acquiescence to non-cooperation to non-violent or violent resistance. A list of the range of possible triggers and/or reactions appears in the codebook (Appendix C).

Finally, I recorded up to five sources used to code each event, although only two were necessary to validate each event as a legitimate data point in the PIWAR data set. A list of the sources used appears at the end of Appendix C.

Coding Reliability

To test the reliability of the data, a second, independent researcher coded a sample of the overall materials. Both the primary investigator and the second coder used the same instrument and sample data. The second coder was instructed regarding the use of the instrument, but no aid or suggestions regarding specific instances to be examined were given. Intercoder reliability for the PIWAR data was 0.85. When these results were disaggregated, intercoder reliability was found to be 0.86 for the repression data and 0.83 for the accommodation data. Two coders working independently with the same instrument and sample data yielded similar results. I therefore feel more confident in the reliability of the PIWAR data and the instrument used to collect it.

Another key test involved the degree of fit of the data to the expectations laid out by Lichbach and others. Following from the work of these writers, I argued earlier that policy mix choices are not mutually exclusive—that elites can employ both repression and accommodation. Table 4.8 demonstrates that this is in fact correct. Note that in some years the monthly correlations of repression and accommodation were at or around 0.5.

Results

Using the Data to test the Dynamics of the Historical Process Model

Now that the data set has been constructed and evaluated, I can assess the model's accuracy in depicting how events actually unfolded in my four cases of interest. Below I demonstrate when and where repression and accommodation occurred in these cases, and compare those observations with the expected observations posited by the model. If a close fit between expectations and observations can be established, then I will have more confidence that the model accurately depicts the dynamics of policy mix choices in post-revolutionary states.

Figure 4.1 restates the expected relationships shown originally in Figure 2.1, with case names included, and with their corresponding case types in parentheses. To reiterate, given the model developed in the pre-

Table 4.8 Repression and Accommodation: Total Number of Events and Correlation Between Uses of Repression and Accomodation

	Iran				Cuba		
Year	Rep	Acc	Corr	Year	Rep	Acc	Corr
t	69	37	0.2538	t	45	17	0.4861
t + 1	53	15	-0.4733	t + 1	42	6	0.3017
t + 2	51	6	0.1887	t + 2	22	8	0.1757
t + 3	53	8	-0.3910	t + 3	20	15	0.0675
t + 4	31	9	0.5773	t + 4	11	6	-0.3025
t + 5	17	4	0.0842	t + 5	8	5	0.2946
t + 6	17	5	0.5477	t + 6	5	3	-0.2585
t + 7	9	2	-0.2335	t + 7	18	5	0.3770
t + 8	16	5	-0.3629	t + 8	9	3	0.7970
t + 9	30	12	0.0408	t + 9	19	4	0.3525
t + 10	17	14	0.3101	t + 10	5	3	-0.1879
t + 11	26	10	0.6059	t + 11	4	2	-0.2582
t + 12	13	8	-0.1642	t + 12	8	5	-0.0756

	Nicaragua				Bolivia		
Year	Rep	Acc	Corr	Year	Rep	Acc	Corr
t	37	37	0.3022	t	23	20	0.3552
t + 1	24	25	-0.0333	t + 1	18	19	0.2665
t + 2	29	16	-0.1925	t + 2	6	10	-0.2748
t + 3	25	9	-0.1590	t + 3	3	8	-0.3828
t + 4	17	16	-0.1252	t + 4	8	8	0.2124
t + 5	12	22	0.2808	t + 5	5	8	0.1572
t + 6	30	13	0.1126	t + 6	5	9	-0.0511
t + 7	18	12	0.2444	t + 7	8	11	0.3927
t + 8	10	25	0.1846	t + 8	9	13	0.2550
t + 9	15	22	0.2463	t + 9	10	10	0.5076
t + 10	5	27	-0.0847	t + 10	4	1	0.3233
t + 11	8	25	0.3869	t + 11	6	5	0.5030
t + 12	7	18	0.1736	t + 12	9	6	0.0113

vious chapter, I expect that the Type I case, Iran, will experience high levels of repression throughout, and generally low levels of accommodation. The Type II case, Cuba, should experience high levels of repression early on during the coalition-reduction process, but little repression in

Figure 4.1 Historical Process Model of the Causes and Consequences of Repression and Accommodation in Post-Revolutionary States

Case Type	Coalition-Reduction Phase (first 2–3 years)	Consolidation Phase (8–10 years)	
	Historical Process Model for Post-Internal War States	Effect of Earlier Policy Choice	War's Effect on Policy Mix
Iran (Type I)	Elites perceive themselves to be secure → Ability to use repression → No sustained opposition	Less ACC	Increase in REP
Cuba (Type II)	Elites perceive themselves to be secure → Ability to use repression → No sustained opposition	Less ACC	No war, therefore no effect
Nicaragua (Type III)	Elites perceive themselves to be vulnerable → Inability to use repression → Significant opposition remains	More ACC	Increase in REP
Bolivia (Type IV)	Elites perceive themselves to be vulnerable → Inability to use repression → Significant opposition remains	More ACC	No war, therefore no effect

Note: ACC = Accommodation; REP = Repression

the consolidation phase. Accommodation levels should be low throughout for Cuba. The Type III case, Nicaragua, should experience generally high levels of accommodation throughout, and high levels of repression only during the war years. Finally, the Type IV case, Bolivia, should experience very low levels of repression and high levels of accommodation throughout the entire period of observation.

The Use of Repression

Time series plots of repressionary events (Figure 4.2) and weighted events (Figure 4.3) confirm that, as expected, Iran is the most repressionary of the four cases during the coalition-reduction process. Iran also maintains a higher level of repression than the other states throughout the series, with the exception of two years (t+6, t+7). Cuba, as expected, is highly repressionary during the coalition-reduction process, and significantly less so in its aftermath. Nicaragua is less repressive in the first few years than the previous two cases, and more repressive during the consolidation phase than Cuba (and even more than Iran during year t+6). Finally, Bolivia remains consistently the least repressive of the four cases throughout the period of examination.[44]

Type I—Iran. As Figure 4.4 indicates, the first few years in Iran, the coalition-reduction phase, saw severe factional infighting, including polarizing conflicts over the governments of Bazargan and Bani Sadr.[45] The terror spread by the Revolutionary Committees, as controlled by the dominant Islamic clerics, was effective in putting down much of the leaderless opposition against the emerging theocracy.[46] Yet by the third year of the new regime the leadership questions had been resolved.[47] The coalition-reduction process had yielded a loose alliance between fundamentalist clerics and their pragmatic counterparts under the leadership of the *faqih,* the Ayatollah Khomeini.[48]

Intense fighting also arose out of related conflicts between left-wing forces, particularly the Mujahedin-e Khalq, and the ruling clerics during this period. Once the Mujahedin was all but destroyed,[49] the regime turned to eliminating other opposition groups such as the Communist Tudeh Party and the Fedayeen.[50] Almost all potential resistance was effectively crushed by the end of 1982 (t+4). Thus, with the issues of coalition-reduction settled, repression began to drop off considerably. Yet compared with the other cases, relatively high levels of repression continued to be employed by the elites throughout the period under observation. This is primarily as a result of the war in the Persian Gulf.

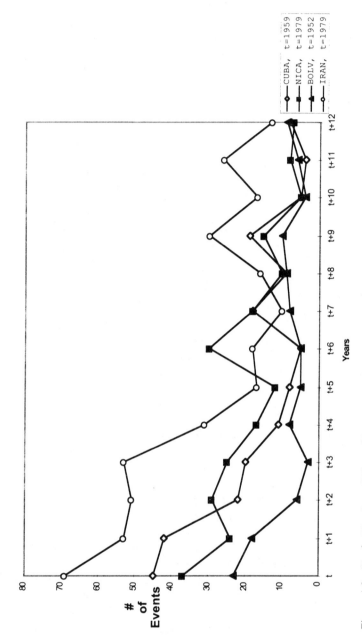

Figure 4.2   Yearly Number of Uses of Repression

63

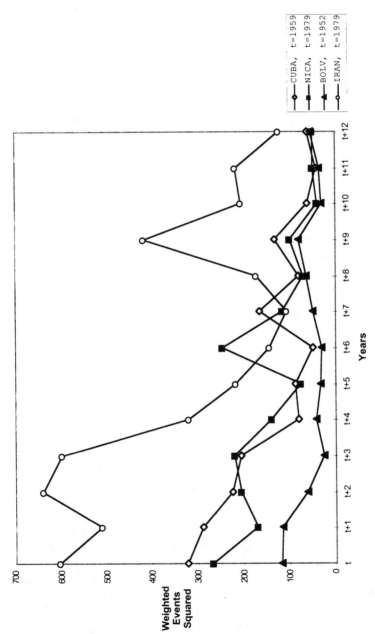

Figure 4.3   Yearly Uses of Repression, Weighted Events Squared

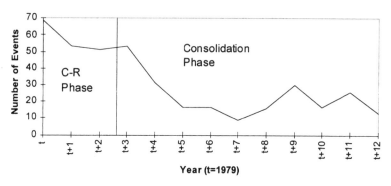

Figure 4.4   Yearly Uses of Repression—Iran

The Iran-Iraq War appears to have had a significant impact upon Iranian repressionary policies. The level of repression remains high, falling off only a year after the war ended (t+11). In fact, many of the targets of repression during this period were directly related to the war. For example, coercive measures short of all-out war were employed against the Kurds, Baluchis, and other minorities who took advantage of the war effort (and of support from the enemy) to press their claims.[51] Other repressionary measures were often justified as a function of the war or the necessities of the war effort. The war even provided additional opportunities to engage in repression. For example, the regime relied on a small army of secret agents in the armed forces to gather information on the domestic opposition during the war.[52]

Type II—Cuba.   Cuba, as expected, is highly repressive during the coalition-reduction process, and significantly less so in its aftermath. As Figure 4.5 indicates, the coalition-reduction process was swift, as enemies of the revolution were brought before a firing squad, often to the cheers of *Paredon!* (*"to the wall"*) by large crowds of Castro supporters.[53] Eventually, the moderate first president of the new regime, Manuel Urrutia, was forced to resign, and Fidel Castro took up the position of premier.[54] In reality, through an effective reduction of the revolutionary coalition, Castro had become Cuba's *jefe maximo*. Coalition-reduction effectively ended in midyear 1959, with the arrest of the only potentially dangerous rival to the new government, Major Huber Matos.[55] Subsequent repression focused on quick appropriation of the means of production.[56]

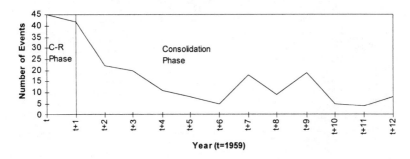

Figure 4.5   Yearly Uses of Repression—Cuba

Remarkably, as Figure 4.5 demonstrates, Cuba's level of repression was actually on the decline during 1961 and 1962, crisis years in which Cuba faced two historic external threats - the Bay of Pigs invasion and the Cuban Missile Crisis. Successful reduction of the revolutionary coalition, and the subsequent absence of an effective opposition domestically, helped Castro's regime avoid excessive repression during these crises. The lack of the need to mobilize resources for a full-scale war, or to quell disorder at home during the prosecution of a war, had made large-scale repression, on the order of that which was experienced in Nicaragua and Iran during that point in their histories, unnecessary.

Type III—Nicaragua.   Figure 4.6 shows that Nicaragua used significantly less repression during the coalition-reduction process (t, t+1) than at least two of the other cases (Iran and Cuba), as predicted. Interestingly, the difference between Cuba's pattern and Nicaragua's pattern diminishes when one weights the repressionary events. As Figure 4.3 demonstrates, Nicaragua actually represses *less* than Cuba in year t+2 when repression is weighted.[57] The new regime went to great lengths to avoid repression, which it feared would fracture the already shaky coalition with the middle class.

As the fighting that would eventually become the Contra War began, repression increased (t+2, t+3). From this period on, and throughout the years of the war, Nicaragua repressed more than Cuba and Bolivia, and even more than Iran on two occasions (t+6, t+7). The targets were frequently those engaged in actively sympathizing with the Contra rebels.[58] Additionally, the Miskito and other indigenous peoples became victims of

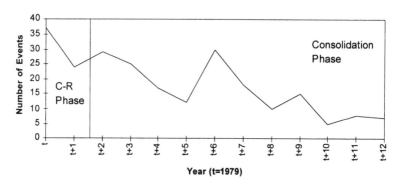

Figure 4.6   Yearly Uses of Repression—Nicaragua

the war, as the government used repressive policies such as forced reset-tlements to remove them from the war zone.[59] This only angered these communities, and often pushed them toward siding with the Contras, making them targets yet again.[60] By the mid 1980s the regime was overextended, engaging in both repression and accommodation, in pros-ecuting a war and consolidating a revolution.[61] The combination became too much to bear. Thus the high level of repression dropped again begin-ning in year t+8 (1987), with the unveiling of the Arias Peace Plan. In the waning days of the war and beyond, Nicaragua scaled back its repression-ary policies significantly.

Type IV—Bolivia. Bolivia is the least repressionary of these cases, as hy-pothesized. At no time in the first 11 years did any other country repress less than Bolivia. When the events are weighted, that increases to 12 years. It was only in the last year or so of the revolutionary government's rule that repression rose above the levels of Cuba and Nicaragua, and even then the increase is slight.[62]

The Bolivian revolutionary party, *Movimiento Nacionalista Revolucionario* (MNR), fearful of offending the powerful labor unions, avoided repressing their sometime ally.[63] The MNR also did their best to avoid offending the peasants, even when the peasants went beyond the revolutionary bound-aries set forth by the MNR. For example, the peasants actually made the MNR's plan for small-scale agricultural reform a moot point in 1953 by taking the land for themselves, effectively creating their own large-scale "reform."[64] Not only were the peasants not punished by the regime, but

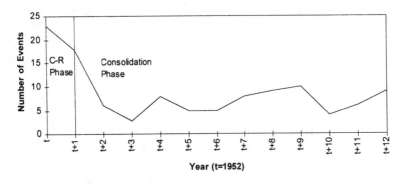

Figure 4.7   Yearly Uses of Repression—Bolivia

the MNR actually legitimized the seizures by appropriating the issue and calling for more sweeping reforms.[65]

The Use of Accommodation

As seen in time series plots of the number of uses of accommodation (Figure 4.8) and weighted accommodation (Figure 4.9), while all four regimes accommodate heavily in the first year (t), this attempt at unity soon falls away as the coalition-reduction process takes over. The figures confirm that, as expected, post-internal war Iran and Cuba are the least accommodating regimes.

More interestingly, Bolivia and Nicaragua, as expected, are heavily accommodating. Each find that there is significant opposition left following the coalition-reduction phase, and that they must increase accommodation in order to maintain their positions. The Sandinista government continued to accommodate more than any of the other regimes, even during Contra War.

Type I—Iran.   As predicted, Iran's levels of accommodation were rather low. Iran's elites had little need for accommodation in the wake of their effective use of repression in rooting out the opposition during the coalition-reduction process.[66] What little opposition remained typically came from within the government, and was often encouraged by Khomeini himself.[67] The war years also presented little reason for the regime to accommodate. Some opposition groups such as the Mujahedin-e Khalq fled

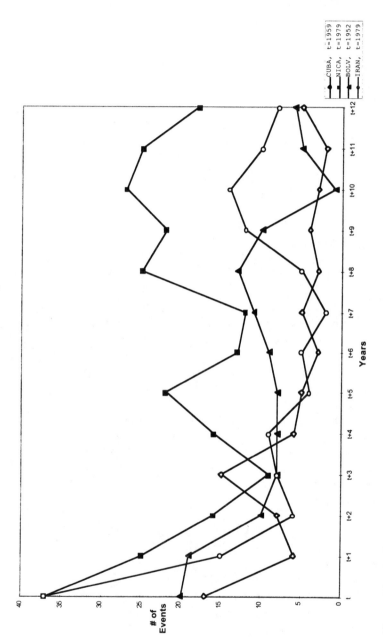

Figure 4.8   Yearly Number of Uses of Accommodation

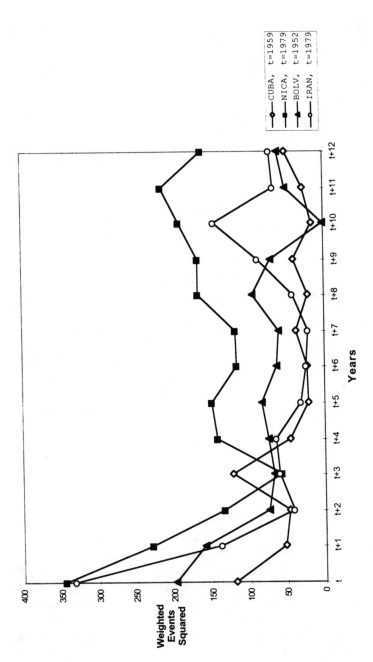

Figure 4.9   Yearly Uses of Accommodation, Weighted Events Squared

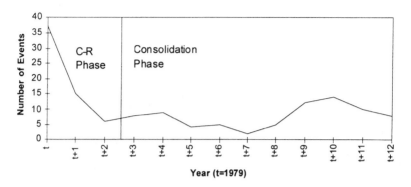

Figure 4.10   Yearly Uses of Accommodation—Iran

Iran to fight on the side of Iraq.[68] Others rallied behind the regime against the external foe across the border (Iraq) and/or across the globe (the United States).

As Figure 4.10 shows, accommodation levels only began to rise somewhat in response to the failing health of the Ayatollah Khomeini (t+9). Iran's elites continually fought amongst themselves, even while Khomeini was alive. In fact, Khomeini often pitted moderates against extremists to maintain a balance amongst the elites.[69] With the deterioration of Khomeini's health and his subsequent death in 1989, the other elites knew that factions in government might increase the levels of contention.[70] To counter this the elites employed accommodation. In fact, half of the accommodative policies employed in 1989 targeted factions in government and/or legitimate political parties in the Majlis.

Type II—Cuba.   As Figure 4.11 demonstrates, with the exception of the initial year of the revolution, 1959 (t), and 1962 (t+3), Cuba's levels of accommodation (and weighted accommodation) were low, and fairly uniform. This is consistent with the expectations derived from my model. Cuba had little reason to accommodate following the successful use of repression to root out opposition during the coalition-reduction phase. Much of the opposition fled the country for Miami.[71] With little opposition left, and with most of the major political, economic, and social transformations coming in the first year, further accommodation was deemed unnecessary.[72]

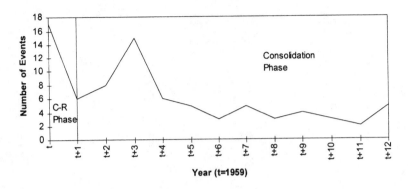

Figure 4.11   Yearly Uses of Accommodation—Cuba

The 1962 spike is troubling, however. Considering Cuba's lack of use of repression during the 1961 and 1962 crises discussed above, it is possible that the Cuban elites decided to use accommodation as a method of coping with crises short of war. They could do so by accommodating targets affiliated with the United States in order to insure calm throughout a contentious period, and to signal their preference for a peaceful settlement. A closer examination of the data reveals that, in fact, almost half of the policies of accommodation employed by the Cuban government in 1962 affected a target affiliated with the United States.

Type III—Nicaragua.   Nicaragua, as expected, was highly accommodating. Significant opposition remained in the consolidation phase because of the regime's attempts to accommodate the middle class during the coalition-reduction process.[73] With such a strong opposition left in the consolidation phase, the Sandinistas had to increase accommodation again in order to maintain their positions.[74]

As shown in Figure 4.12, even in the face of the most terrible fighting of the Contra War (t+4 through t+7), the Sandinista government continued to accommodate more than any of the other regimes. They tried to keep the loyalty of much of the middle class, and went to great lengths to rectify the problems they had created for themselves by mishandling the Miskito situation in the early days of the new regime. Finally, the regime decided that the best way to keep opposition groups from defecting to the Contras was a dual strategy. They repressed direct collaborators and kept order domestically, and

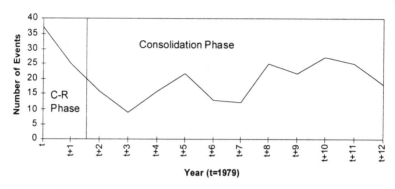

Figure 4.12 Yearly Uses of Accommodation—Nicaragua

did their best to accommodate the population at large by continuing to implement revolutionary programs even in the face of a dwindling treasury drained by the war.[75] Despite decreasing resources, accommodation increased in a gradual incremental fashion from 1982 (t+4) through 1990 (t+11).[76] And when the Arias Peace Plan was unveiled in 1987 (t+8), accommodation in Nicaragua increased yet again. The Sandinistas did their best to show the world that they were serious about peace with the Contras.[77]

Type IV—Bolivia.   Bolivia's level of accommodation was generally high from 1952 to 1964. The coalition-reduction phase saw little actual reduction in the revolutionary coalition. In fact, labor (COB) actually gained in power relative to the rest of the alliance partners.[78] The MNR then spent the rest of the initial Victor Paz Estenssoro administration (1952 to 1956) and the Hernan Siles Suazo administration (1956 to 1960) keeping the left-wing COB (labor), the peasants, and the MNR's right wing (middle class) happy.[79] This strategy of widespread accommodation was born of perceived necessity. Both administrations saw labor, peasants, and the right wing of the party as crucial to the stability of the MNR's rule.[80]

Bolivia's accommodation levels were also generally higher than Iran and Cuba's, save for the last few years, under the second administration of Victor Paz Estenssoro (1960 to 1964, or t+9 through t+12). In this period the ruling revolutionary party (MNR) began to extract itself more completely from the control of the labor unions and the left wing of the party.[81] The last two years saw a brief upswing in accommodation, as Paz's government

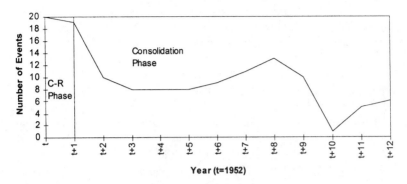

Figure 4.13   Yearly Uses of Accommodation—Bolivia

first tried to assuage labor, and then entered into an alliance with the military, leading eventually to the 1964 coup, which ended the life of the revolutionary regime.[82]

Conclusion

The relationships suggested by the historical process model developed in Chapter 2 are borne out by the data presented here. The Type I case, Iran, experienced high levels of repression throughout, and generally low levels of accommodation, save for a period punctuated by the unusual circumstance of the death of the Ayatollah Khomeini. The Type II case, Cuba, experienced high levels of repression early on during the coalition-reduction process, but leveled off afterwards. As expected, accommodation levels were generally low. The Type III case, Nicaragua, experienced generally high levels of accommodation throughout, and high levels of repression only during the war years. The signing of the Arias Peace Plan signaled the coming of the end of both the Contra War and the repression that accompanied it. Finally, the Type IV case, Bolivia, experienced very low levels of repression throughout, and medium to high levels of accommodation up until the change in policy and alliance partners by the second Paz Estenssoro government in the early to mid-1960s.

The one constant seems to be a frequent use of accommodation, across all four regimes, in the first year following the end of the revolution. This occurs irrespective of elite perceptions. The most likely explanation is that elites engage in a process of trial and error in their first year in office, employing both repression and accommodation. This would also explain why in the less repressive regimes some of the highest levels of repression are found in the first year.

The evidence presented here points to the conclusion that elite perceptions of their own vulnerability have both short-term and long-term consequences. In the short term, elites who perceive themselves to be secure in their power position domestically feel freer to use repression early, thereby reducing the need to accommodate later. Vulnerable elites fear repression will make them more vulnerable, and prefer instead to accommodate early. This leads to more demands and more accommodation in later years as well. Additionally, war leads to significantly increased levels of repression, as the need to extract without giving up valuable state resources increases, and the need to keep order domestically also increases.

In this chapter I developed a unique data set, and used it to test the ability of the historical process model to predict when each post-revolutionary state would employ repression and/or accommodation. But it is possible that the relationships discussed above are spurious. Maybe what was observed to be the effect of elite perceptions of their own vulnerability or war is actually a function of opposition activity, or a previous history of either repression, or accommodation, or both. These relationships need to be tested in a more systematic fashion. In the next chapter, I employ a negative binomial event count model to more rigorously test the comparative effects of these variables on the policy mix choices of post-revolutionary elites.

CHAPTER 5

The Use of Repression and Accommodation in Post-Revolutionary States

Revolutions have never lightened the burden of tyranny; they have only shifted it to another shoulder.

—G. B. Shaw[1]

All government, indeed every human benefit and enjoyment, every virtue, and every prudent act, is founded on compromise and barter.

—Edmund Burke[2]

The analysis in the previous chapter evaluated the historical process model's accuracy in depicting how events actually unfolded in post-revolutionary Bolivia, Cuba, Iran, and Nicaragua. In this chapter I employ event count models to statistically verify these relationships, and to determine the degree of their significance. In doing so, I control for elements that others have shown affect the use of the implements of state building—namely, previous use of these implements, and domestic opposition to the state. The results demonstrate that elite perceptions of their own vulnerability directly affect elite policy mix choices, even when controlling for these other powerful explanatory variables. I then show that war participation and previous uses of repression indirectly affect policy mix choices, via their effects on elite perceptions. I begin by discussing alternative explanations for the findings of the previous chapter.

Alternative Explanations

Despite what appears, in the previous chapter, to be a good fit between model expectations and empirical observations, it is possible that these results are spurious. The observed effects of both war and how elites perceive the vulnerability of their power position may actually be a function of opposition activity. Alternatively, they may be a function of a country's previous history of repression or accommodation or both. These relationships need to be tested in a more systematic fashion. In this section I discuss these two rival explanations, and derive testable, alternative hypotheses to be included in tests of my model.

Opposition Activity

Any examination of factors affecting elite policy mix choices needs to consider the population at large, at whom these policies are directed. The choice to employ repression and/or accommodation may be in response to, or may be triggered by, increases in opposition activity. Yet scant attention has been given to the impact of opposition activity on the regime's use of repressive measures.[3] Much of the work on the connection between policy mix decisions and opposition activity has focused on repression's effect on dissent.[4] However, the assumption that both violent and nonviolent activities of opposition groups lead regimes to undertake repressive measures is less prevalent in the literature.[5] The dearth of knowledge is even more glaring regarding the effects of opposition activity on policies of accommodation. Yet scholars acknowledge that political dissent should impact elite policy mix choices.[6] Some empirical support exists for this claim.[7] Yet simply counting the frequency of opposition activity has yielded insignificant results.[8]

Some authors have established that there are significant differences between the effects of violent and nonviolent opposition on state response. For example, in her examination of the emergence of terrorism in West Germany, Sabine Karstedt-Henke finds that different types of opposition activity trigger corresponding policy mix responses.[9] She finds that regimes typically repress more radical elements of the opposition in order to send signals that violence will not be tolerated. This also sends signals to the citizens at large that these opposition tactics are dangerous, and therefore must be repressed. As Davenport observes:

When dissidents are portrayed as being dangerous and threatening to other citizens' lives, the regime is in a better position to attempt behavioral regulation. The citizenry would be more likely to see the government's behavior as legitimate, and they may even call for it themselves. This would tend to increase the likelihood of its application because less resistance to the particular government policy would be apparent.[10]

Thus, regimes repress violence because they can, and because it further enhances their legitimacy in the eyes of the public. This is consistent with most studies of the effects of opposition on policy mix choices, which find that violent opposition provokes state repression.[11] In order to control for this relationship, I hypothesize:

H5.1: In the aftermath of an internal war, if levels of violent opposition activity increase, then the use of repression should also increase.

And because regimes can use repression in such situations, they can avoid the costly tradeoffs made necessary by policies of accommodation. Therefore I Hypothesize:

H5.2: In the aftermath of an internal war, if levels of violent opposition activity increase, then the use of accommodation should decrease.

Karstedt-Henke further argues that regimes will facilitate more moderate groups who employ either less violent or nonviolent strategies. This sends a signal to these groups that less violent strategies are preferable to the alternative, and tells the citizenry that the government is being reasonable in dealing with more "legitimate" opposition tactics.[12] Therefore I hypothesize:

H4.3: In the aftermath of an internal war, if levels of nonviolent opposition activity increase, then the use of accommodation should also increase.

Additionally, if the regime were to repress such nonviolent tactics, then the citizenry might respond by viewing the government as less legitimate, and might actually join the protesters.[13] This, too, acts as a constraint on the use of repression in response to nonviolent opposition. I hypothesize:

H5.4: In the aftermath of an internal war, if levels of nonviolent opposition activity increase, then the use of repression should decrease.

Previous Policy Mix Choices

Previous policy mix choices should also affect future choices.[14] For example, Karen Rasler finds that, in a post-war environment, previously nonaccommodating administrations are likely to rely on repressive measures, and previously accommodating regimes are less likely to employ repression.[15] Rasler's study differs from this one, however, in that she examined previous history of accommodation during major crisis periods such as wars or depressions. Nevertheless, these results raise the possibility that previous accommodation and the use of repression may be inversely related in a post-internal war environment. Therefore I hypothesize:

H5.5: In the aftermath of an internal war, if the elites have a history of accommodation, then the use of repression should decrease. Conversely, if elites were previously nonaccommodating, then the use of repression should increase.

Karstedt-Henke's study, discussed above, involves a multiple phase theoretical model. She tests her model and finds that after an initial phase in which the elites employ repression, a second phase emerges in which elites combine continued repression of some groups with efforts to appease other groups by using concessions.[16] Repression at time t may give way to increased levels of accommodation at time t+1. Therefore I hypothesize:

H5.6: In the aftermath of an internal war, if the elites have a history of repression, then the use of accommodation should increase subsequently. Conversely, if elites were not previously repressive, then the use of accommodation should decrease.

Repression also begets repression. Some researchers have focused on the high degree of "bureaucratic inertia" involved in the application of repression.[17] The use of repression is grounded in the historical experience of the state. Once repressive behavior is employed, regimes become habituated into using it. "Successful use of coercion enhances the leaders' assessment of its future utility."[18] Additionally, the mechanisms of coercion are particularly abundant in states that have previously employed coercion. The development of the coercive "garrison" state is often a consequence of repeated use of repressive measures.[19] In short, repression is made more likely by the previous use of repression. Therefore I hypothesize:

H5.7: In the aftermath of an internal war, if the elites have a history of repression, then the subsequent use of repression should increase.

Finally, given Karstedt-Henke's argument, accommodation should also breed accommodation. Remember that she argues that regimes will respond to nonviolent tactics with accommodative measures. If opposition groups see that their nonviolent tactics have been successful in generating government acquiescence (or at the very least, recognition of the validity of their claims), then they should choose to continue employing the successful strategy. In turn, this second wave of nonviolent opposition should again be countered with government policies of accommodation. Thus a logical extension of Karstedt-Henke's argument is that previous levels of accommodation should positively affect subsequent levels of accommodation. I hypothesize:

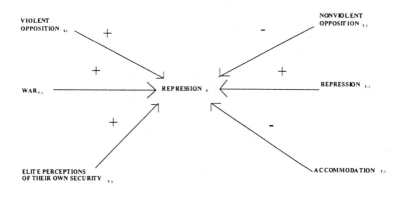

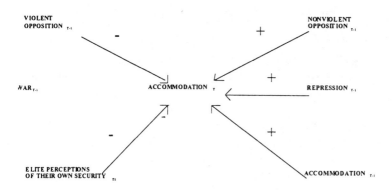

Figure 5.1   Hypothesized Relationships

H5.8: In the aftermath of an internal war, if the elites have a history of accommodation, then the subsequent use of accommodation should increase.

Figure 5.1 depicts the relationships discussed in this study to date. As discussed in the previous chapter, when elites do not perceive themselves to be vulnerable they are able to increase the use of repressive policies and decrease the use of accommodation. Perceptions of vulnerability should increase the use of accommodation and decrease repression (Hypotheses H2.1 and H2.2). Additionally, war should increase the use of repressive policies (Hypothesis H2.3). I also include relationships that I have controlled for in this chapter, in Hypotheses 5.1 through 5.8. Increased levels of violent opposition activity should increase the use of repression and decrease levels of accommodation. Increased levels of nonviolent opposition activity should increase the use of accommodation and decrease levels of repression. Accommodation should decrease subsequent levels of repression, and repression should increase subsequent levels of accommodation. Finally, the hypotheses predict autocorrelation in the dependent variable: repression begets repression, while accommodation yields future accommodation.

Now that I have accounted for other potential causes of repression and accommodation in post-internal war states, I can move on to systematically testing my hypotheses. In order to do so I need to operationalize my variables. In the previous chapter I discussed my dependent variables, repression and accommodation, in detail. In the next section I discuss how I operationalize my independent variables.

Operationalization of the Independent Variables

Independent Variables

Elite Perceptions of Security / Vulnerability. Elite perceptions of their own security or vulnerability are coded as a continuous variable ranging from zero to one. A high score denotes elites who perceive themselves to be relatively secure, while lower scores denote elites who perceive themselves to be vulnerable. Perceptions of vulnerability are determined by content analysis of speeches and interviews by the elites in question. The unit of analysis was the individual document as a whole.

I established a coding procedure and an instrument to be used on all documents collected. I began by compiling a list of words and phrases denoting either vulnerability or security, shown here in Table 5.1. Next, the document in question was searched (see below) for these words or phrases. If they referred to the (in)security of the speaker, his/her colleagues in the governmental elite, or the revolution in general, vis-à-vis domestic actors, they were coded. If they did not refer to the speaker, the other governmental elites, or the revolution in general, and/or if they were not in reference to domestic actors, the items were left uncoded. Once these were coded I tallied all the coded words or phrases that denoted vulnerability and security within the document. If the former outnumbered the latter the document was coded as a whole as projecting elite perception of vulnerability. If the latter outnumbered the former it was coded as projecting perception of security. If the numbers were identical, the document was

**Table 5.1 Elite Perceptions of Their Own (In)Vulnerability—Word/
Phrase List**

Vulnerability Words	Security Words
Challenged	Arrogant
Defeat	Assurance
Defensive	Confident
Discord	Fearless
Divided	Indestructible
Doubt	Indispensible
Exposed	Invincible
Fear	Invulnerable
Impotent	Popular
Insecure	Power/Powerful
Instability	Protected
Intimidated	Safe
Limitations	Secure
Precarious	Shielded
Sabotage	Solidarity
Scared	Stable
Subvert/Subversion	Strong/Strength
Suspicious	United
Threat/Threaten	
Uncertain	
Unpopular	
Unprotected	
Vulnerable	
Weak/Weakness	
Wounds	

Vulnerability Phrases	Security Phrases
are subject to pressures	can OR will not be defeated
attempt to destroy us	does not bother us
in a state of chaos	it is impossible to defeat us
our needs are so great	no one would dare attack us
their support is crucial	support of the people
this situation is dangerous	they are united behind us
we are having major difficulties	vote of confidence
we are struggling to _____	we are afraid of nothing
we must be on the alert	we don't need (GROUP X)
we must be very cautious/careful	we won't be brought to our knees

Note: All words or phrases used in the negative sense or denoting the inverse of a sense of
SECURITY are considered words or phrases denoting VULNERABILITY. All words or
phrases used in the negative sense or denoting the inverse of a sense of VULNERABILITY
are considered words or phrases denoting SECURITY.

coded as projecting neither perceptions of vulnerability nor of security. Once each document was coded, I took the ratio of the number of documents coded as "secure" to the total number of documents for a given time period. That ratio was then taken as the value used to code perceptions of security. The lower the score, the more vulnerable the elites feel.[20] Appendix D contains a copy of both the codebook and the coding sheets used in the collection of data on elite perceptions.

A list of source materials employed can also be found in Appendix D. A majority of the textual materials for Iran and Nicaragua were located through searches of *FBIS* reports. A majority of the Cuban materials were acquired from an on-line archive of Fidel Castro's speeches, located at *gopher://lanic.utexas.edu/11/la/Cuba/Castro*. It was difficult to find one comprehensive source for the Bolivian materials, so I employed diverse U.S. weekly news magazines and regional periodicals. Collections of speeches and interviews for all four cases were also used, but I relied upon these most heavily for Bolivia. All of the materials were already translated into English with the exception of about half of the collections of Bolivian speeches. Those were translated and coded by both the author as well as a bilingual second coder. Both coders used the same instrument and sample data. The second coder was instructed regarding the use of the instrument, but no aid or suggestions regarding specific instances to be examined were given. Intercoder reliability for the translated materials was 0.81. The second coder also coded a sample of the overall materials for all four countries. Intercoder reliability for this larger sample was 0.84. Two coders working independently with the same instrument and sample data yielded similar results.

As Table 5.2 demonstrates, the overall results were surprisingly consistent. Elites in Bolivia and Nicaragua were coded as perceiving themselves to be vulnerable over the entire 13-year period examined. Conversely, elites in Cuba and Iran were coded as perceiving themselves to be relatively secure vis-à-vis their internal opposition over the entire 13-year period examined. The ratios fluctuated to some degree, but the overall tenor of those documents was constant within each case. A more detailed breakdown of these statistics can be found in Appendix D.

War.   Presence or absence of war during the post-internal war period is denoted by a dichotomous variable, with "1" for any country participating in at least one war within the time frame examined, and "0" for any country that does not participate in a war in that period. Wars are operationalized as both international wars and internal wars occurring between 1816

Table 5.2 Elite Perceptions of Security—Total Documents Coded and Score Received (by Year)

Year	Iran (t = 1979)		Cuba (t = 1959)		Nicaragua (t = 1979)		Bolivia (t = 1952)	
	Total	Score	Total	Score	Total	Score	Total	Score
t	21/24	0.88	37/44	0.84	8/21	0.38	5/16	0.31
t + 1	27/30	0.90	38/47	0.81	7/17	0.41	2/10	0.20
t + 2	11/12	0.92	23/29	0.79	5/14	0.36	1/14	0.07
t + 3	9/10	0.90	27/36	0.75	7/20	0.35	1/16	0.06
t + 4	12/14	0.86	21/26	0.81	5/16	0.31	1/19	0.05
t + 5	8/11	0.82	8/10	0.80	3/12	0.25	1/15	0.07
t + 6	16/20	0.80	4/17	0.82	5/14	0.36	1/17	0.06
t + 7	10/13	0.77	12/15	0.80	6/18	0.33	1/12	0.08
t + 8	10/12	0.83	9/12	0.75	5/21	0.24	2/18	0.11
t + 9	21/25	0.84	12/14	0.86	4/15	0.27	1/10	0.10
t + 10	20/25	0.80	12/15	0.80	2/13	0.15	2/13	0.15
t + 11	11/13	0.85	12/16	0.75	3/18	0.17	1/10	0.10
t + 12	11/14	0.79	34/42	0.81	6/21	0.29	2/18	0.11

Notes: All ratios above represent number of documents denoting security to number of total documents

Score = Perception of security (high = high degree of security; low = low degree of security)

These totals are disaggregated into the component parts (speeches and interviews) in Appendix D

Sources used are also listed in Appendix D

and 1994, as determined by the Correlates of War (COW) data set. International wars include wars of any type (interstate wars, extra-systemic wars, and colonial wars) in which at least 1,000 battle deaths resulted during the course of the war.[21] Internal wars are revolutions or civil wars in which "(a) military action was involved, (b) the national government at the time was actively involved, (c) effective resistance (as measured by the ratio of fatalities of the weaker to the stronger forces) occurred on both sides and (d) at least 1,000 battle deaths resulted during the civil war."[22]

The only wars that occurred in the time periods and cases examined in this study were the Iran-Iraq War [September 1980 to August 1988] and the Contra War [March 1982 to April 1990]. Some may argue that these two conflicts were fundamentally different kinds of wars, and as such are not comparable. The former is considered an interstate war, while the latter is often considered an internal war.[23] However, each war was perceived at the time by the elites engaged in it as an international war. As such, these wars' effects on policy mix choices should be similar. The fact that the Iran-Iraq War was perceived by both sides as an international war is not in dispute. Below I discuss how the Contra War was viewed by the elites.

The Contra War, although fought on Nicaraguan soil, was viewed by all sides as a war between the United States and the Sandinista government of Nicaragua. Evidence suggests that the U.S. administration viewed the conflict as one between the United States and the Sandinista government, with the Contra soldiers as proxy combatants for the U.S. forces.[24] And despite the fact that the EPS (the Nicaraguan Sandinista army) was engaged in fighting directly with the Contas, the Sandinista leaders understood that they were, in reality, engaged in a war with the United States.[25] Roger Miranda, a top aide to EPS chief Humberto Ortega from 1982 to 1987, and William Ratliff, a specialist in Latin American politics, describe the perceptions of the Sandinista elites as follows:

> The Sandinista government always claimed that the Contra War was a U.S. terrorist mercenary operation seeking to restore the Somoza dictatorship—with or without Somoza himself—and U.S. domination of Nicaragua. In Bayardo Arce's colorful terms, the Contras were merely the "clowns" in an American circus.[26]

Regardless of whether the war was overt or covert, both the U.S. government and the Sandinistas perceived the other to be the enemy with whom they were at war. As such, the Contra War and the Iran-Iraq War are more similar than might originally have been thought. Regardless, both wars represent external threats to the new regimes, and therefore hold similar roles. These wars are therefore used as cases of war during the post-internal war period.

Opposition.   Opposition is coded as the total number of opposition activities per month. Opposition is defined as any anti-government protest, strike, plot, assassination attempt, or armed attack attributed to or claimed by any group in news accounts. Two main sources were used to locate opposition activity. The regional news sources employed earlier to code repression and accommodation were used again here. Also, I employed the *New York Times Index* in order to pick up cases where the regional news was censored but the event was nonetheless picked up by the international press.[27] Information collected includes date of the event, type of opposition activity, target, and source used to code the data. Appendix E contains a copy of both the codebook and the coding sheets used in the collection of data on opposition activity.

To test the reliability of the opposition data, the independent researcher employed to code a sample of the PIWAR data (see previous chapter) also coded a sample of the opposition data. Both the primary investigator and the second coder used the same instrument and sample data. The second coder was instructed regarding the use of the instrument, but no aid or suggestions regarding specific instances to be examined were given. Intercoder reliability for the opposition data was 0.81. Each coder, working independently with the same instrument and sample data, yielded similar results. I therefore feel more confident in the reliability of both the instrument used to collect the opposition data and the data itself.

Previous Policy Mix Decisions.   I code previous policy mix decisions by lagging the results of the dependent variables—repression and accommodation. While not all previous policy mix decisions are incorporated into the hypothetical model discussed above, all are considered here. Those not included above (previous repression in the repression model and previous accommodation in the accommodation model) are included here in order to control for autocorrelation in the data.

Methodology

I employ event count models in this study because my dependent variables are counts of discrete events. Event count models are modifications of the basic regression model, using maximum likelihood estimators, and accounting for both distribution and a continuous underlying process.[28]

Repressive events are not necessarily independent of each other, and thus have a distribution unlike that of an OLS regression's dependent variable. The same can be said of accommodation. Yet, the most common strategy used by researchers in such situations is to employ OLS regression despite the nature of the dependent variable. This strategy can lead to methodological problems. Estimators can be inefficient, biased, and/or inconsistent. OLS does not account for the unique properties inherent in counts of events. For example, one cannot observe a *negative* number of events. Yet OLS regression models assume that negative integers are part of the normal distribution of events. The answers that one gets using OLS are therefore not just inefficient, but are also substantively meaningless.[29] Standard modifications to an OLS model's dependent variable, such as taking the log or adding a small constant, have been shown to bias the estimates as well. In general, event count models more accurately account for the way in which events are distributed.[30] Thus, when estimating models of frequency counts of events I employ the more appropriate event count models.

The choice of which event count model to use is dependent upon the type of dispersion of the correlated dependent variable. Event count models are based on the assumption that events have a particular distribution. These models have exponential functional forms, with the variance of the dependent variable equal to the expected value of the dependent variable times the degree to which the events are independent, such that $V(Y_i) = \lambda_i \sigma^2$, assuming that $\lambda_i > 0$ and $\sigma^2 > 0$, with σ^2 being an extra parameter measuring the degree of independence of the events.[31] Independence among events makes $\sigma^2 = 1$, making the variance equal to the mean. The simplest event count model, the Poisson regression model, meets this stringent requirement. In the study of regime policies and internal conflict, however, events are often not independent. Correlated events create situations of either overdispersion ($\sigma^2 > 1$) or underdispersion ($\sigma^2 < 1$), which can be accounted for by more complex count models such as the negative binomial model.[32] Negative binomial models include a random component reflecting the uncertainty about the true rates at which the events occur for individual cases.[33] This allows for a more variable dispersion by relaxing the rigid independence of events assumption.

Table 5.3 shows the results of goodness-of-fit chi-square tests, which help to determine what type of event count model is most appropriate for this study. The null hypothesis is that the data are Poisson distributed.

Table 5.3 Test of Poisson Distribution of the Dependent Variable

Repression Models		Accomodation Models	
Case	Goodness of Fit χ^2	Case	Goodness of Fit χ^2
Type I—Iran	35.74★★★	Type I—Iran	29.49★★★
Type II—Cuba	46.13★★★	Type II—Cuba	16.88★★★
Type III—Nicaragua	11.81★	Type III—Nicaragua	18.52★★★
Type IV—Bolivia	16.50★★★	Type IV—Bolivia	25.35★★★

Note: ★★★ = p < .01; ★ = p < .10

Table 5.4 Likelihood Ratio (LR) Test of Negative Binomial Models vs. Poisson Models

		Repression Models		
Case Type	Case Name	Coefficient [ln (alpha)]	LR Test vs. Poisson (χ^2)	Log Likelihood
Type I	Iran	–0.779★★★	55.135★★★	–298.830
Type II	Cuba	–0.525	22.705★★★	–205.963
Type III	Nicaragua	–0.108	54.807★★★	–239.767
Type IV	Bolivia	–1.026	3.448★	–162.903

		Accommodation Models		
Case Type	Case Name	Coefficient [ln (alpha)]	LR Test vs. Poisson (χ^2)	Log Likelihood
Type I	Iran	–0.348	17.769★★★	–170.968
Type II	Cuba	–0.940	1.744	–122.626
Type III	Nicaragua	–1.080★★★	23.422★★★	–252.913
Type IV	Bolivia	–1.659★	1.825	–169.976

Note: ★★★ = p < .01; ★ = p < .10

The overwhelming significance of the goodness-of-fit chi square indicates that the Poisson regression model is inappropriate. To check this result I ran Likelihood Ratio (LR) tests of negative binomial models for the overall models against Poisson models of the same data. The results, presented in Table 5.4, demonstrate that indeed the Poisson model is inappropriate in most cases. The large chi-square values and high levels of significance confirm that the assumption of a strict Poisson distribution of both the repression and the accommodation data is inappropriate. Subsequent tests show that, despite the presence of a Poisson distribution in some cases (specifically, for the accommodation models for Cuba and Bolivia), results do not change significantly if a negative binomial model is used. Therefore, for the sake of consistency in data presentation, I employ negative binomial models for all cases.

As Tables 5.3 and 5.4 also show, I employ separate models for each case as well as for each policy type. I cannot pool the cases in my analysis, as I wish to be able to test the effect of the independent variables on the different types of policy mix choices within each case. I also wish to account for differences between cases. Running a separate negative binomial model for each case allows me to test the dynamics of my hypothesized model in each case, and to compare these dynamics across cases.[34]

I also wish to test a time-dependent relationship. My historical process model hypothesizes that elite perceptions (and their resulting policy mix choices) during the coalition-reduction phase affect policy mix choices in the subsequent consolidation phase. Therefore I create a coalition-reduction phase dummy variable as a time element. I then create an interaction variable between this time element and the perceptions variable. This allows me to account for the effect of perceptions during the coalition-reduction phase on policy mix choices throughout the life of the post–internal war state.

Finally, I should note that in all of the models employed in this study the independent variables are lagged one month. Lagging the independent variables eliminates possible simultaneity bias between independent and dependent variables measured contemporaneously.[35] This allows one to make causality arguments that would have been impossible if both independent and dependent variables were examined at time (t).[36] While lagging the variables a week or a series of days might have been preferable, limitations of the data prevent employment of such a strategy. Below I present and interpret the results of these models.

Findings

Tables 5.5 and 5.6 present the results of negative binomial event count models testing which factors affect the use of repression and accommodation. Table 5.5 depicts a strong significant impact of elite perceptions of security on the use of both repression and accommodation in the four post-revolutionary states. More importantly, the interaction between perceptions and the time element is highly significant. As expected, the per-

Table 5.5 Negative Binomial Model of Factors Affecting the Use of Repression (by Month)

Independent Variables	Iran	Cuba	Nicaragua	Bolivia
Elite perceptions of security in C-R phase	0.826***	0.725***	3.685**	4.797***
	(2.656)	(2.272)	(2.101)	(3.647)
Elite perceptions of security (t – 1)	0.793*	0.673	0.673*	1.312*
	(1.892)	(1.196)	(1.915)	(1.827)
Coalition-reduction phase dummy variable	0.689*	0.554	0.689	0.697*
	(1.741)	(1.811)	(1.221)	(1.733)
War (t – 1)	0.159	—	-0.155	—
	(0.828)		(-0.526)	
Violent opposition (t – 1)	0.022	0.196***	-0.091	0.067
	(0.502)	(3.329)	(-0.851)	(0.581)
Nonviolent opposition (t – 1)	0.114	0.260	0.066	0.108
	(0.221)	(1.431)	(0.609)	(1.079)
Repression (t – 1)	0.96***	0.112***	0.027	-0.015
	(3.387)	(1.842)	(0.473)	(-0.138)
Accommodation (t – 1)	0.040	0.075	-0.054	0.058
	(0.677)	(0.603)	(-1.082)	(0.608)
Constant	0.234	-0.621***	0.387	-0.787***
	(1.228)	(-3.810)	(1.305)	(-4.175)
Ln (alpha)	-0.779***	-0.525	-0.108	-1.026
	(-3.210)	(-1.543)	(-0.432)	(-1.499)
N	155	155	149	151
Chi-square	35.74***	46.13***	11.81*	16.50***
Log-likelihood	-298.830	-205.963	-239.767	-162.903
LR test vs. Poisson	55.135***	22.705	54.807***	3.448

Notes: (t – scores in parentheses) *** = $p < 0.01$, ** = $p < 0.05$, * = $p < 0.10$ (two-tailed tests)

ceptions of relative security in the coalition-reduction phase led to an increased use of repression in that period in all four cases. War, however, does not appear to significantly affect repression. Instead, it appears to decrease the levels of accommodation used by Iranian elites. The only other significant relationship found is a positive effect of previous levels of repression on subsequent uses of repression.

Table 5.5 shows the significant impact of elite perceptions of security during the coalition-reduction phase on the use of repression in post-internal war Cuba. Once again, this led to an increased use of repression in that period. Perceptions are also hypothesized to lead to a decrease in the levels of accommodation employed in the subsequent (consolidation) phase. However, no significant effect is found. The only other significant relationships appear to be a strongly significant positive effect of opposition activity on repression and a slightly less significant positive effect of previous levels of repression on subsequent uses of repression. War is not a factor, as none occurs in the period under examination. Finally, repression breeds more repression in Iran and Cuba, which may help to explain why these two states are the most repressive of the four. Nicaragua and Bolivia do not see such an escalatory effect.

Table 5.6 depicts a strong significant impact of elite perceptions of security, and particularly perceptions of security during the coalition-reduction phase, on the use of both repression and accommodation. As expected, the perceptions of relative security also lead to a decrease in the levels of accommodation employed in the consolidation phase. Interestingly, war does not significantly affect accommodation in post-revolutionary Nicaragua, but does in Iran.

Discussion

Choices of repression and/or accommodation can be traced back to particular factors that affect their use. What is most apparent from the findings presented in Tables 5.5 and 5.6 is that both elite perceptions of their own security and the phase in which the post-internal war state finds itself are key in understanding elite policy mix choices. As my model predicted, elite perceptions of their own security were shown to have a strong, significant impact on policy mix choices. Vulnerable elites cannot repress early on in the post-internal war period, and are forced to increase levels of accommodation subsequently. Secure elites can and do repress, making accommodation less necessary and less likely later on. Therefore, if we wish to reduce the potential for repression in post-internal war

Table 5.6 Negative Binomial Model of Factors Affecting the Use of Accommodation (by Month)

Independent Variables	Iran	Cuba	Nicaragua	Bolivia
Elite perceptions of security in C-R phase	-1.114***	0.105	-2.445***	-4.352***
	(-2.469)	(0.201)	(-2.945)	(-3.366)
Elite perceptions of security (t – 1)	-0.685*	0.217	-0.912**	2.167**
	(-1.942)	(0.167)	(-2.121)	(2.685)
Coalition-reduction phase dummy variable	0.551	0.429	0.588*	0.733*
	(1.243)	(0.598)	(1.717)	(1.739)
War (t – 1)	-0.707***	—	0.193	—
	(-2.465)		(0.884)	
Violent opposition (t – 1)	0.018	0.106	0.054	0.017
	(0.277)	(1.388)	(0.895)	(0.160)
Nonviolent opposition (t – 1)	-0.312	0.269	0.010	-0.058
	(-1.536)	(1.196)	(0.132)	(-0.562)
Repression (t – 1)	0.006	0.133	-0.025	0.130
	(0.131)	(1.601)	(-0.571)	(1.530)
Accommodation (t – 1)	0.050	0.014	0.069*	0.005
	(0.602)	(0.087)	(1.741)	(0.059)
Constant	0.682**	-1.463***	0.835***	0.339
	(1.923)	(-3.269)	(3.169)	(1.149)
Ln (alpha)	-0.348	-0.940	-1.080	-1.659*
	(-0.866)	(-1.019)	(-3.352)	(-1.842)
N	155	155	149	151
Chi-square	2.949***	16.88***	18.52***	25.35***
Log-likelihood	-170.968	-122.626	-252.913	-169.976
LR test vs. Poisson	17.769***	1.744	23.422	1.825

Notes: (t – scores in parentheses) *** = p < 0.01, ** = p < 0.05, * = p < 0.10 (two-tailed tests)

states, we may wish to consider ways in which post-internal war elite perceptions are shaped. If we know what factors affect perceptions, then we may be able to affect them in such a way as to reduce the likelihood of repression's use.

War did not significantly increase the use of repression, contrary to my model's prediction. In fact, in Iran war negatively affected levels of accommodation rather than positively affecting repression. The lack of a concrete, significant finding might make sense in light of comparisons at different times within cases. In Nicaragua, for example, the PIWAR data shows that much of the domestic repression that the state employed during the Contra War was directed at either Contra sympathizers or those who stood in the way of the battleground (i.e., the Miskito). In other words, most of the repression employed was in some way war-related. However, the levels of repression during this period were not nearly as severe as during the coalition-reduction period preceding it. Similarly in Iran, wartime uses of repression domestically were frequent, and were often directed at Iraqi allies or sympathizers. However, wartime repression pales in comparison to the use of repression in the coalition-reduction phase in Iran.

Yet comparative analysis shows some relationship between war and repression. As I demonstrated in the previous chapter, both war-torn Iran and Nicaragua experienced considerably higher levels of repression than war-free Cuba and Bolivia during the same time period. However, when examining this factor in light of other controlling factors within one country over time, war appears to have little or no effect.

It is possible that war does have an effect, but that it is indirect, via war's effect on elite perceptions of security or vulnerability, and therefore not captured by my analysis. Considering the debate in the literature as to whether war increases or decreases domestic cohesion, no theoretical assumption is obvious regarding the direction or degree of this potential effect.[37] Adding to the confusion is the lack of work done on the effect of war on elite perceptions of their own vulnerability. Therefore, a brief brush-clearing exercise, and as a way to tease out potential indirect effects of war on policy mix choices, may be justified. Additionally, it is also possible that the effects of the other variables, which were not found to be significant, actually affect policy mix choices via effects on elite perceptions. To reiterate, while this study does not purport to be an explanation of elite perceptions of their own security or vulnerability, a quick check of the effects of the variables already employed in earlier analyses on elite perceptions is justified here.

Indirect Effects Via Elite Perceptions
of Their Own Security or Vulnerability

Using OLS regression, I examine the effects of war, violent and nonviolent opposition, previous repression and accommodation, and phase of the post-revolutionary period on elite perceptions of their own security or vulnerability. The results are presented in Table 5.7. As these results demonstrate, war does appear to have a significant, positive effect on elite perceptions of their own security. There are a number of possible explanations for this counterintuitive finding. The two most credible explanations center around opposition reaction to the war and the ability of the elites to further consolidate their power.

First, it is possible that war has a "rally-round-the-flag" effect. A number of researchers have demonstrated that war creates an environment in which domestic opposition drops its objections to the regime, instead rallying around it and against the foreign opponent.[38] If in fact dissent decreases in the face of conflict then elites may perceive the domestic threat to have lessened, thereby increasing their perceptions of security in their power position. However, there is also research that suggests that not only is there no such "rally-round-the-flag" effect, but that in fact war *increases* levels of domestic dissent.[39] This is an empirical question, one that will be addressed further in the next chapter.

Another explanation for this puzzling effect is that war provides opportunities for revolutionary leaders to more effectively consolidate their power. The revolution and immediate post-revolutionary period sees the development of organizational networks by the elites. If effective, these networks provide the basis for the establishment of a "revolutionary identity" and common goals among regime supporters. However, not all post-revolutionary regimes can justify taking complete control of these networks. War provides the leaders with the justification for the establishment of a centralized controlling authority over them.[40] If able to take control of these key networks, elites may feel more secure in their power position domestically.

Regardless of the reasons why, war seems to have a positive effect on elite perceptions of their own security domestically. The war-driven increase in perceptions of security would then translate into an increased willingness to use repression, given earlier findings. Thus, indirectly, war does affect the choice by post-revolutionary elites to use repression. However, because of the minimal degree of impact of war on perceptions, one should be careful not to overestimate war's impact on policy mix choices. Its effect is significant and indirect, but not terribly strong.

Table 5.7 Factors Affecting Elite Perceptions of Their Own (In)Vulnerability

Independent Variables	Iran	Cuba	Nicaragua	Bolivia
Elite perceptions of security (t − 1)	0.141***	0.220***	0.181***	0.242***
	(6.104)	(6.369)	(8.189)	(6.815)
War (t − 1)	0.101*	—	0.010*	—
	(1.942)		(1.976)	
Violent opposition (t − 1)	0.007	0.000	0.002	−0.000
	(1.314)	(0.323)	(1.191)	(−0.307)
Nonviolent opposition (t − 1)	−0.000	−0.000	−0.003	0.001
	(−0.269)	(−0.080)	(−1.388)	(0.659)
Repression (t − 1)	0.001	−0.001	0.001	0.003**
	(1.336)	(−0.990)	(1.021)	(2.139)
Accommodation (t − 1)	−0.001**	0.003***	0.000	−0.000
	(−2.100)	(2.673)	(0.411)	(−0.359)
Coalition–reduction phase dummy variable	0.005*	−0.001	0.012	0.018**
	(1.787)	(−0.135)	(1.378)	(2.592)
Constant	0.047***	0.063**	−0.008	0.011***
	(2.498)	(2.293)	(−1.017)	(3.179)
N	155	155	149	151
R^2	0.96	0.85	0.96	0.95

Notes: (t − scores in parentheses) *** = $p < 0.01$, ** = $p < 0.05$, * = $p < 0.10$

Causes and Consequences: Looking Back and Forward

This study has, to this point, provided a guide to the factors that affect the use of repression and/or accommodation in post-revolutionary states. The way in which elites perceive the security of their positions in power plays a significant role in determining elite policy mix choices. These choices are made necessary by the extreme levels of state building required by the political environment of the post-revolutionary state. Additionally, the political environment, as affected by war participation and previous levels of repression, also affects state-building needs, elite perceptions, and subsequent policy mix choices.

While this knowledge adds to our understanding of the post-revolutionary environment, it does not go far enough. If we are to deal successfully with the myriad internal conflicts breaking out across the globe, then the consequences of these policy mix choices must be examined as well. Short-run effects, such as the direct effect of policy mix choices on degrees and type of opposition activity, need to be examined if we are to determine whether, and how, post-revolutionary elites are able to keep order domestically.

Additionally, we need to know how these policy choices, and subsequent opposition responses, affect the development of the political system writ large. Do bargains made to accommodate challengers set the stage for democracy, as they did in early modern Europe? Or do they help absolutist regimes keep opposition in check, facilitating a further centralization of power? Does the use of repression inhibit democracy and pluralism? Or is the use of repression a tool to enable the construction of a more pluralistic system?

Finally, we need to understand how short-term choices of repression and/or accommodation, coupled with the long-term development of the political system, affect the political survival of the post-revolutionary elites. Does repression make too many enemies, leading to the fall of the elites from power? Or does it make continuation in power possible? Does accommodation buy more time for the elites? Or does accommodation come at the price of their power positions? These factors may affect who leads these states beyond the first decade of post-internal war politics and, therefore, how they are led.

The ability to answer these questions will provide a more complete picture of the politics of the post-revolutionary state. Therefore, the next section of this study is devoted to examining the long- and short-term consequences of the use of repression and accommodation by post-revolutionary elites. I begin, in the next chapter, by examining the more immediate effects of policy mix choices on levels of opposition activity.

PART III

The Consequences of Repression and Accommodation in Post-Revolutionary States

CHAPTER 6

Responding to Revolution: Opposition in Post-Revolutionary States

The first half of this study has examined what factors affect elite policy mix choices during the crucial post-revolutionary period. This focus on elite behavior presents an incomplete picture of the dynamics of that period. Mass behavior must also be considered. Therefore, in this chapter I examine the factors that affect opposition activity in the post-revolutionary state. I begin by examining how closely the observed levels of opposition activity conform to expected levels.

Opposition Activity in the Post-Internal War State

Domestic opposition is abundant in the post-revolutionary state. Those who have gained power often face additional challenges, both foreign and domestic, after their initial victory.[1] As discussed earlier, there are serious complications implicit in reconsolidating power in the aftermath of a revolution. Two or more distinct centers of power must be reintegrated into one united polity.[2] All sides must be able to live together in the same territory.[3] Elites must consolidate their power.[4] Finally, the new regime must bring its desired policies to fruition.[5] To accomplish these goals the victorious elites must engage in state building. But the extraction necessary for state building yields recalcitrant populations.[6]

Levels of opposition activity should be high in any post-internal war period. As Doug McAdam notes: "Generalized political instability destroys any semblance of a political status quo, thus encouraging collective action by *all* groups sufficiently organized to contest the structuring of a new political order."[7] Indeed, this problem of *over-mobilization* is common in post-internal war environments. Too many groups remain active in the aftermath of the fall of the old regime. This stems from the fact that it takes a larger mobilized mass to seize power than to maintain it.[8] Empirical examples abound, including the high levels of opposition activity following such diverse internal conflicts as the American Civil War,[9] the Russian Revolution,[10] and revolutionary wars of the late twentieth century in Ethiopia and Afghanistan.[11]

Levels of violent opposition activity should be particularly high in the immediate aftermath of revolution. With the old guard out of the way, the victorious coalition usually has little to hold it together. Groups splinter off and push their own policy goals. Erstwhile partners revert to their previous status as contenders for power,[12] and bloody competition for the "soul" of the government ensues.[13] Thus we should expect to see high amounts of violent opposition activity during the coalition-reduction phase.

The consolidation phase should be less violent than the coalition-reduction period. Once the regime has established some degree of order, opposition activity should decrease to normal levels. By this point most of the opposition at the center has either been eliminated, co-opted, or appeased. Even when opposition remains, the primary intracoalition conflicts have been settled sufficiently to produce a clear-cut winner. A cooling-off period, sometimes referred to as the "Thermidor," follows the coalition-reduction phase.[14]

This is not to say that opposition activity will fall off altogether. Indeed, coalition-reduction amongst the primary contenders for power is usually followed during the subsequent phase by widespread (and less violent) struggles for power with peripheral actors. This should be particularly true in the two cases, Bolivia and Nicaragua, where the state was unable to use repression early on in the coalition-reduction phase. In Iran and Cuba the

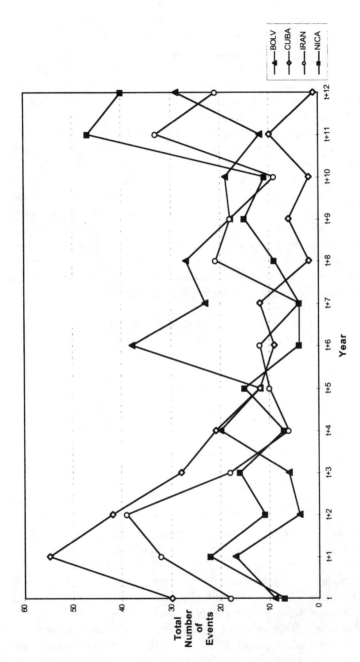

Figure 6.1   Total Opposition Activity

use of repression wiped out much of the opposition in the first few years of the new regime. Thus it would be surprising to see significant opposition activity in the consolidation phases in Cuba and Iran. But in Nicaragua and Bolivia the inability of the new regime to use repression early left much of the opposition intact. In fact, it may even have emboldened groups to oppose them, albeit via nonviolent means. By refraining from the use of repression, elites signal to opposition groups that less violent strategies are preferable to the alternative.[15] Therefore we should see some increases in nonviolent opposition activity in these two states after the first few years.

In short, given my model, in each case I expect to see high levels of opposition activity in the coalition-reduction phase, followed by lower levels in subsequent years. After disaggregating the effects, I expect to find high levels of violent opposition activity during the coalition-reduction phase, followed by a dramatic reduction in violent opposition activity during the consolidation phase. Finally, nonviolent opposition activity should increase during the consolidation phase in the two states (Bolivia and Nicaragua) whose elites were unable to employ repression during the coalition-reduction phase.

Using the opposition data discussed in the previous chapter (see also Appendix E), I plotted opposition activity in the post-internal war period across my four cases. Figure 6.1 shows the overall levels of opposition activity. Figures 6.2 through 6.5 disaggregate opposition activity into violent and nonviolent opposition respectively, by country. An examination of the data collected for this project reveals that levels of opposition activity vary within and among post-revolutionary states. However the expected patterns hold, for the most part.

Figure 6.1 demonstrates that opposition activity was highest during the coalition-reduction phases in Iran and Cuba. In Nicaragua only the last two years, associated with the post-Sandinista regime, find more opposition than the initial coalition-reduction years. Bolivia is the only case that runs directly contrary to explanation. Opposition activity is at its highest during the middle and later years of the post-revolutionary regime. Disaggregating the opposition data into its component parts may help explain this anomaly.

Figures 6.2 and 6.3 show that violent opposition activity was extremely high during the coalition-reduction phases in both Cuba and Iran. Violent opposition was not as prevalent in Nicaragua and Bolivia during this period, but were still higher than in a majority of the subsequent years (see Figures 6.4 and 6.5). Figures 6.2 and 6.3 also show a considerable drop-off

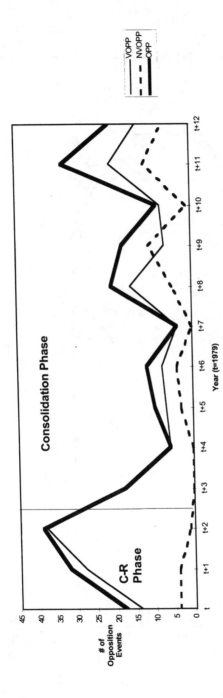

Figure 6.2   Opposition Activity—Iran

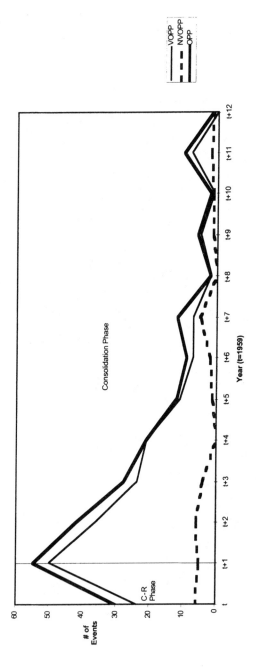

Figure 6.3   Opposition Activity—Cuba

in levels of violent opposition activity in Cuba and Iran during the consolidation phase. Additionally, Iran and Cuba exhibited little nonviolent opposition activity throughout the post-internal war period, with the exception of two of the four later Iranian years—1988 and 1990. These may be attributed to the uncertainty surrounding the declining health of the Ayatollah Khomeini and the succession following his death.[16]

Conversely, both Nicaragua and Bolivia (Figures 6.4 and 6.5) see only a slight drop-off of opposition activity following the end of the coalition-reduction phase. Nicaragua experiences little if any opposition following the coalition-reduction phase. Of course, this is partly due to the fact that all the opposition by those joining the Contras is considered warfare and therefore not counted here. A major aberration appears in the last two years of the Nicaraguan series. The high levels of violent opposition in that period (1990–91) are primarily associated with the extremely contentious elections, the transition process following the Sandinista loss, and the unrest of the first year of Violetta Chamorro's UNO regime.[17]

Figure 6.5 demonstrates that, as expected, Bolivian nonviolent opposition activity increased dramatically from the coalition-reduction phase to the consolidation phase. It is that nonviolent protest that appears to be driving the overall Bolivian opposition activity trends.

In sum, the model appears to fit the data. Yet despite this relatively good fit between observation and expectation, some minor aberrations exist. Additionally, as with the observations in Chapter 3, there is no way to know whether this apparent fit is actually a spurious one. Statistical tests will determine more conclusively whether the data fits the model. Therefore, below I examine statistically why levels of opposition activity vary within and among post-internal war states. I begin by examining the factors that may affect opposition activity, including repression, accommodation, war, and previous opposition activity.[18]

Factors Affecting Levels of Opposition Activity

How Repression Affects Opposition Activity

The relationship between repression and opposition activity is perhaps the most studied relationship in the field of political violence. Unfortunately, numerous studies, ranging from cross-national, longitudinal statistical analyses to formal models to single case and comparative case analyses, have found a plethora of potential relationships between these variables.

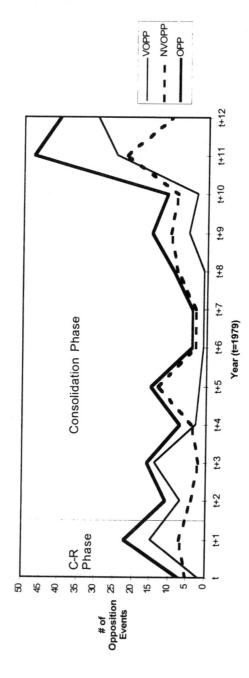

Figure 6.4   Opposition Activity—Nicaragua

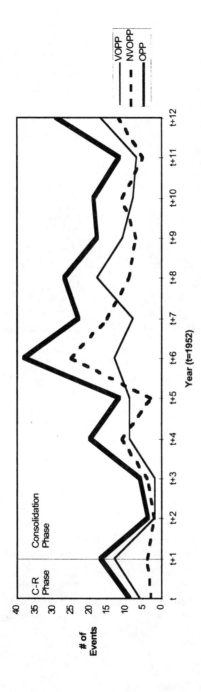

Figure 6.5   Opposition Activity—Bolivia

Deterrent Model: Repression Decreases Opposition Activity. Some research has uncovered a linear negative relationship between repression and opposition activity. Proponents of Resource Mobilization and Political Process Model explanations of collective action argue that the use of repression by the regime limits the ability of opposition groups to mobilize resources and supporters. This, in turn, limits the ability of the opposition to act effectively.[19] Some proponents of Rational Choice explanations argue that repression has a negative impact on mobilization levels because it increases the costs of collective action for each individual participant.[20] Regardless of whether they focus on the group or the individual, these studies argue that repression works, in that it leads to a decline in collective action. As William Gamson notes: "When authorities used extralegal and violent means to control the challenger, it didn't backfire on them."[21]

H6.1: In post-internal war states, if the regime increases the use of repression, then opposition activity will decrease.

Conversely, the inability or unwillingness to use repression may lead to increases in dissent. Opposition groups may see a regime that refrains from the use of repression as signaling official tolerance of dissent. Thus a nonrepressive regime appears to give the opposition a license to engage in protest activities.[22]

However, some researchers have found this negative relationship between repression and opposition activity to have only borderline significance.[23] Additionally, the relationship appears to be strongest after the opposition has moved from nonviolent to violent tactics.[24]

Escalation Model: Repression Increases Opposition Activity. Others argue that regime repression leads to an increase in opposition activity.[25] These escalation models hypothesize that regimes that use repression lose popular legitimacy at the cost of increased levels of authority. An increase in the level of coercion employed by the state is capable of provoking outrage rather than restraint.[26] Repression therefore becomes the catalyst for mobilizing previously neutral actors against the regime. Additionally, repression hardens the resolve of the previously mobilized members of the opposition. Thus opposition membership increases and becomes more radicalized and more committed. In support of these hypotheses, Hibbs found that increases in repression led to increases in levels of both nonviolent and violent protest.[27] Gurr and Duvall also found that "coercive elite policies breed civil conflict more often than civil peace."[28]

More recently, in his study of political violence in the West Bank, Khawaja found that repression consistently increased the rate of popular resistance. He argues that repression helps foster an environment conducive to further collective action by overcoming social cleavages, strengthening collective identity, and rearranging factional groupings into a unitary whole. Therefore, in an environment conducive to resistance, continued repression will not suppress collective action and political violence.[29] This is consistent with Koopmans' work, which argues that the use of coercion actually drives home the anti-regime message by underlining the defensive and repressive nature of the regime.[30] In sum, the escalation hypothesis can be expressed as follows:

H6.2: In post-internal war states, if the regime increases the use of repression, then opposition activity will increase.

Repression Has Differential Effects on Different Types of Opposition Activity. However, there is also evidence that repression has different effects on different types of opposition activity. Olivier's study of collective action in South Africa found that state-sponsored repression increased the overall rate of opposition. However, Olivier found that levels of repression had different effects on either type of opposition. High levels of repression increased the probability of more violent events, but decreased the rate of nonviolent opposition.[31] And as noted earlier, Davis and Ward found that the relationship between repression and opposition activity appears to be strongest after the opposition has moved from nonviolent to violent tactics.[32] These hypotheses can be expressed as follows:

H6.3: In post-internal war states, if the regime increases the use of repression, then violent opposition activity will increase.

H6.4: In post-internal war states, if the regime increases the use of repression, then nonviolent opposition activity will decrease.

Curvilinear Models. Others have hypothesized a U-shaped, curvilinear relationship between repression and opposition activity. These theorists proposed that increasing levels of repression should make carrying out opposition difficult, thereby yielding an initial drop in opposition activity until some critical threshold is reached. As repression increases beyond that threshold, support for the opposition among the general populace rises due to moral outrage against the regime. Previously unmobilized members of the population join the opposition, making anti-regime activity possible again. Thus, up until that threshold is reached, repression decreases opposition activity. Beyond that critical threshold, repression increases the levels of opposition activity.

Yet another strain of the literature argues that collective action levels should be low when repression is either high or low, but high when repression is at moderate levels. This *inverted* U-shaped curve thesis argues that low levels of repression avoid creating much anti-regime sentiment, thereby keeping levels of opposition low. When the regime increases its use of repression it imposes a new set of grievances upon the populace, thereby inciting opposition activity. However, if high levels of repression are employed by the regime, opposition activity decreases, as fear overcomes anger. In such cases the use of severe repression has a deterrent effect on opposition activity. A wide range of empirical studies confirm the existence of an "inverted-U" relationship between repression and opposition activity.[33]

A recent variation on this theme was proposed by Ronald Francisco. He finds that, for the most part, the inverted-U curve hypothesis appears valid. However, the highest levels of repression accelerate protest. Based on these results, Francisco suggests that "the inverted-U curve might yield another rise in protest at the high end of coercion."[34] The resulting nonlinear function would be something like a rounded N-curve.

Generally, all of these above models have different expectations for dissent depending on levels of repression. These concerns can be expressed as follows:

H6.5: In post-internal war states, the relationship between regime repression and opposition activity will be curvilinear.

Repression's Short- and Long-Term Effects on Opposition Activity.   The above discussion illustrates the key problem in the study of repression–dissent dynamics. Different researchers have found different effects of repression on opposition activity. The result is that repression appears to have both positive and negative effects on dissent.[35] But precisely how repression can simultaneously escalate and deter protest was unclear for many years.[36]

Two key and interrelated problems with this research are the lack of consideration of direct versus indirect effects, and the lack of temporal controls.[37] Studies that account for the potential for both short- and long-run effects of elite policy mix choices should be better able to capture repression-dissent dynamics. Two recent studies may have finally clarified Lichbach's "deterrence/escalation puzzle."[38] Opp and Ruehl and Rasler present a slightly more complicated, but more accurate depiction of the relationship between repression and opposition, incorporating these concerns.[39]

In their study of opponents of nuclear power in West Germany, Opp and Ruehl theorize that repression is a cost, and therefore will have a direct negative effect on opposition activity.[40] However, they also argue that this effect can be nullified, or even reversed, when repression launches micromobilization processes. In some cases this may raise the incentives for protest, yielding an indirect positive effect of repression on dissent. Their results confirm their hypothesis.

Karen Rasler took the revelation of the existence of both direct and indirect effects of repression and made the argument more dynamic:

> If Opp and Ruehl (1990) are correct in their analysis of the indirect effects of repression on protest, overall levels of repression should have a short-term negative effect on dissent because of the time lapse required for micromobilization processes to occur, but a long term escalatory effect.[41]

Indeed, Rasler found that in the short run, dissidents during the Iranian Revolution decreased their anti-regime activity. In the long run, however, repression increased opposition. Thus each repressive act has both a negative "instantaneous effect" and a positive "lagged effect" on opposition activity. This more dynamic hypothesis can be expressed as follows:

H6.6: In post-internal war states, if the regime increases the use of repression, then opposition activity will decrease initially, but increase subsequently.

How Accommodation Affects Opposition Activity

There is little agreement as to the connection between repression and opposition. Similarly, there is little agreement as to the relationship between concessions and dissent.[42] This presents an *accommodation-dissent puzzle* akin to the repression-dissent problem examined by Mark Lichbach.[43] Below I discuss the research to date on the effects of accommodation on opposition activity.

Accommodation Increases Opposition Activity. Accommodation may signal to the opposition that their previous collective efforts were successful. Therefore when a regime employs accommodation it enhances the perceived influence of the accommodated opposition, increasing the probability that others will join them in mass action.[44] These "victories" over the government assure both current and prospective opposition members that further opposition activity will pay off.[45] Additionally, accommodation may signal a regime's vulnerability, which increases the expected value of further action for many potential opponents of the regime at the same time.[46] Thus accommodation, usually employed in order to appease and diffuse opposition, may have the unintended consequence of stimulating even more domestic disorder.[47] Empirical examinations of this relationship have lent support to this hypothesis. For example, Rasler finds that government concessions increased both violent and nonviolent protests during the Iranian Revolution.[48] In sum:

H6.7: In post-internal war states, if the regime increases the use of accommodation, then levels of opposition will increase.

Accommodation Decreases Opposition Activity.　Conversely, accommodation may signal willingness on the part of the regime to negotiate the claims of the opposition. Such a willingness to move the field of contention from the streets to the bargaining table may preempt and/or substantially reduce domestic conflict.[49]

Accommodation may also be employed as a way of smothering opposition groups rather than appeasing them. Historian Paul W. Schroeder argues that alliances between nation-states are often made with the intention of "restraining or controlling the actions of the partners in the alliance themselves."[50] The same logic can be applied to the domestic alliance made between the accommodators and the accommodated. Ruling elites can and often do accommodate in order to co-opt potential adversaries. And, as Gamson shows, co-optation can lead to reduced opposition activity.[51] With many of their demands satisfied, and with more immediate access to the state granted, opposition groups will have a harder time convincing potential members of the urgency of action. Additionally, co-optation provides the state with a way to keep an eye on the opposition groups. Advance warning of opposition plans can then allow the state to act to preempt the opposition, thereby short-circuiting opposition activity before it begins.[52] Such a hypothesis can be expressed as follows:

H6.8: In post-internal war states, if the regime increases the use of accommodation, then levels of opposition will decrease.

How Previous Levels of Opposition Affect Subsequent Opposition Activity

One area where there is some agreement is in the study of opposition's self-stimulating effects. Researchers have also found that previous levels of opposition activity can be crucial in determining subsequent opposition. Granovetter develops a threshold model of collective behavior in which a given rational individual's decision to participate in collective action depends to a large degree on how many others have already decided to participate.[53] Because different individuals require different levels of safety before participating, and because different individuals derive different benefits from such actions, these cost-benefit calculations vary from person to person. If opposition activity has already been occurring, a chain reaction might then occur in which a smaller number of key participants at the outset trigger participation by others over time. This same logic can be applied to groups in opposition as well.

Kuran develops a similar "bandwagon model" to explain how seemingly invulnerable regimes may crumble at the slightest shock. Kuran shows that a privately hated regime may enjoy seemingly widespread public support because of people's reluctance to take the lead in publicizing their opposition. Kuran finds that a significant shock, in this case the presentation of some even small opposition, can put a bandwagon process in motion, which leads to greater and greater opposition.[54]

Davis and Ward provide additional empirical support for this argument. In their study of political violence in Chile from 1966 to 1986, Davis and Ward find that rebellion was self-stimulating. Their study shows that previous opposition activity and deaths from political violence, rather than government sanctions, determined subsequent levels of opposition.[55] Therefore I hypothesize:

H6.9: In post-internal war states, if there is a history of opposition, then subsequent opposition will increase.

How War Affects Opposition Activity

Davis and Ward also find that international sources of conflict affect opposition levels indirectly, through their effects on deaths from political violence. In addition, they find that high levels of opposition activity help explain involvement in international conflict.[56] International conflict and opposition activity are part of a continuous feedback loop, with increases in one increasing the levels of the other. In short, the domestic-international conflict nexus may be one of the keys to understanding the dynamics of domestic political violence.

The most severe form of international conflict is war. It stands to reason that war involvement should have a pronounced impact on opposition activity. A number of studies have examined this question, either theoretically or empirically. While there are some convincing arguments for a negative effect of war on domestic opposition, the dominant view in the literature is that war increases opposition activity.

War Increases Opposition Activity. War may lead directly to increases in opposition activity by stimulating the mobilization of domestic opposition groups.[57] States fighting wars must increase the levels of overall societal mobilization.[58] Once mobilized, opposition groups can resist and attempt to overthrow the government.

Wars also influence the mobilization of new domestic groups indirectly. Wars require the state to extract additional resources from their populations.[59] In the previous chapter I showed that war indirectly affects those policy choices—repression and accommodation—that enable extraction for state building. War was found to increase elite perceptions of security, thereby indirectly increasing the ability or willingness to use repression. In turn, this extraction can be too much for the population to bear, and lead to widespread opposition.[60] Therefore, war should have yet another indirect effect, this time increasing opposition activity.

Additionally, war increases the degree of mobilization of opposition groups by enhancing their economic and social positions. Wartime economic mobilization, coupled with war-induced pressure on opposition groups to normalize relations with the state, may lead to the co-optation of these groups.[61] Their status is improved, but this yields further demands for power and resources. Once again, this effect should be particularly strong in the wake of an internal war. Post-internal war social mobility, coupled with wartime social mobility, leads to increased demands on the part of the opposition.

Finally, war also creates a window of political opportunity for opposition groups.[62] As Boudreau notes, "[s]tructural shifts . . . influence the probable ramifications of collective action, and therefore change how participants behave." Works ranging from Skocpol's study of revolutions to Kriesi's study of New Social Movements find that changes in the international political opportunity structure, often caused by war, have important structural effects on the national political opportunity structure.[63] These openings in the domestic political opportunity structure may lead to challenges to the regime because they signal the vulnerability of the state.[64] Opposition groups know that the government is distracted by the war effort, and in need of domestic allies and/or internal cohesion in order to successfully prosecute a war. Additionally, changes in the domestic political opportunity structure may provide opposition groups with expanded political access and/or greater incentives to act collectively.[65] Therefore, opposition groups see international and internal wars as propitious moments to press their claims.[66] Indeed, empirical studies such as Gurr and Duvall's and Ward and Widmaier's find that international dispute involvement leads to increases in opposition activity (and levels of domestic conflict in general).[67] In short, war creates a new political space in which movements may act, thereby increasing opposition activity.[68] The sum total of all of this work is the following hypothesis:

H6.10: In the presence of a war, levels of opposition in the post-internal war period will increase.

War Decreases Opposition Activity. Despite the overwhelming support for the hypothesis of a positive effect of war on opposition activity, a case can be made for a negative effect. For example, decreases in opposition activity following war initiation are consistent with the ingroup/outgroup hypothesis, as advanced by Coser and Simmel.[69] The essence of this hypothesis is that groups react to external pressure by increasing internal coherence. This "rally-round-the-flag" effect has been used to account for the rise in popularity of leaders during war.[70] Additionally, some scholars have hypothesized that leaders will purposely engage in war in order to increase unity domestically.[71]

However, evidence supporting this hypothesis is mixed. Recent analyses of the literature have determined that this effect is less likely than had been previously thought.[72] As Levy notes: "there is a considerable discrepancy between the theoretical and historical literature, on the one hand, and the quantitative empirical literature on the other."[73] And Stein points out that declining threat perception or increasing unpopularity of a given war can also lead to *decreased* levels of societal cohesion in the postwar period, potentially leading to *greater* opposition activity.[74]

Perhaps a more convincing argument comes from a reexamination of Gamson's concept of co-optation, this time from the side of the co-opted.[75] Gamson finds that war-induced pressure on opposition groups to normalize relations with the state leads to the co-optation of these groups. And recall that co-optation may actually lead to *reduced* opposition activity. In addition to the benefits of co-optation discussed earlier (in the discussion of how accommodation might decrease opposition activity), co-optation gives the opposition group in question a stake in the success of the regime. A weakened regime means access to fewer resources, or an alliance with a lesser partner. In some cases, co-opted opposition groups may decide to throw in with the regime, even if they do not care for their politics, so that both may profit.[76] Therefore, while it is likely that war leads to an increase in opposition activity, the potential of a negative effect cannot be ignored. This potential effect is hypothesized as follows:

H6.11: If a war occurs during the post-internal war period, then levels of opposition will decrease.

Testing the Determinants of Opposition Activity

The sum of the above survey of the factors that impact opposition activity is that researchers are fairly certain that repression, accommodation, war, and previous opposition activity affect subsequent dissent. What is unclear is the nature and direction of these effects. Conflicting theories and evidence cloud the picture. I propose to test the determinants of opposition activity, incorporating these key variables, as well as indicators that will test the soundness of my own model.

The crux of my explanation relies on the ability of the new regime to employ repression during the coalition-reduction phase. The ability and willingness to wield this potent policy tool should remove or suppress most of the relevant opposition early during the regime's tenure. Thus, as a result of the use of repression during the coalition-reduction phase, we should expect to see less overall opposition in the subsequent (consolidation) phase. Conversely, the inability to use repression early means that opposition groups remain. Additionally, dissenters may be emboldened by either the regime's reluctance to use repression, or by their reliance on accommodation. Thus, as a result of low levels of repression during the coalition-reduction phase, we should expect to see opposition levels increase in subsequent years. In short, I hypothesize:

H6.12: If post-internal war regimes employ high levels of repression during the coalition- reduction phase, then opposition activity will decrease. Conversely, low levels of repression during the coalition-reduction phase will result in an increase in opposition activity.

Operationalization of Variables

In order to test my main hypothesis, as well as the various hypotheses discussed above, I employ variables that I previously used to examine the determinants of policy mix choices in these cases. Therefore, I refer the reader to the operationalization of these variables (opposition activity, war participation, repression, accommodation, the coalition-reduction phase dummy variable), which are discussed in Chapter 5. Additionally, lags are handled in a similar fashion as in the previous chapter.

I also create an interaction term between the coalition-reduction phase dummy variable and the measure of repression. This variable accounts for the key mechanism driving my theoretical model—the use of repression in the coalition-reduction phase.

Methodology

The methodology used in Chapter 5 is also employed in this analysis. The dependent variable, opposition activity, is measured as counts of events. To determine what type of event count model is most appropriate, I ran goodness-of-fit chi–square tests, shown in Table 6.1. The overwhelming significance of the goodness-of-fit chi-square indicates that the Poisson regression model is inappropriate.

To check this result I ran Likelihood Ratio (LR) tests of negative binomial models against Poisson models of the same data. The results, presented in Table 6.2, demonstrate that the Poisson model is, in fact, inappropriate in these cases. The large chi-square values and high levels of significance confirm that the assumption of a strict Poisson distribution of both the repression and the accommodation data is inappropriate. Therefore I employ negative binomial models in my analysis of all four of my cases.

Findings

Table 6.3 presents the results of negative binomial event count models testing which factors affect opposition activity in post-revolutionary Bolivia, Cuba, Iran, and Nicaragua. The most striking result is that no one factor is significant across all four cases. War is significant in both cases in which it is present. However, the effect is contrary to the expectations of the majority of the literature. A post-internal war state involved in a subsequent

Table 6.1 Test of Poisson Distribution of the Dependent Variable

	Total Opposition Activity	
Case	Goodness of Fit χ^2
Type I—Iran	259.286★★★
Type II—Cuba	216.623★★★
Type III—Nicaragua	243.487★★★
Type IV—Bolivia	292.766★★★

Note: ★★★ = p < .01

**Table 6.2 Likelihood Ratio (LR) Test of Negative Binomial Models vs.
Poisson Models**

		Total Oppositional Activity		
Case Type	*Case Name*	*Coefficient [ln (alpha)]*	*LR Test vs. Poisson (χ^2)*	*Log Likelihood*
Type I	Iran	−0.807★★★	25.617★★★	−241.932
Type II	Cuba	−0.511★★★	8.215★★★	−224.184
Type III	Nicaragua	−0.705★★	25.847★★★	−223.257
Type IV	Bolivia	−0.400★★★	40.342★★★	−251.606

Note: ★★★ = p < .01; ★★ = p < .05

war experiences a significant decrease in levels of domestic opposition, all else held constant at the mean. Perhaps this lends some credence to both the utility of co-optation and the "rally-round-the-flag" effect.

More important for this study, however, is that repression during the coalition-reduction phase significantly decreases levels of opposition activity in three of the four cases. The effective use of repression in Cuba and Iran enables the elites to oust most of the opposition early. This results in low levels of opposition subsequently, as predicted. And in Bolivia the same negative relationship between repression and opposition holds. The state's choice to use low levels of repression early leads to increases in opposition activity. Only in Nicaragua does my hypothesized model break down. The relationship is in the wrong direction, but the variable is not significant.

However, repression in and of itself (lagged either one or two months) does seem to reduce opposition activity in Nicaragua. In fact, while not reported here because of space considerations, a negative binomial model examining the effect of repression, lagged from one to six months on opposition activity, reveals that the effects of repression on opposition activity in Nicaragua are consistently negative. Thus, while the timing of repression is important in understanding levels of dissent in the three other post-revolutionary cases, repression in general, irrespective of when it was used, reduced domestic dissent in Nicaragua.

Repression in general is also strongly significant (p < .01) in cases where it is used early by elites (Iran and Cuba). This makes sense given findings in Chapter 5. In both Iran and Cuba, previous repression leads to subsequent repression. Thus, once repression is employed initially, it has an escalatory effect on both subsequent repression and opposition activity.

Table 6.3 Negative Binomial Model of Factors Affecting Total Oppostion Activity (using total number of repression and accommodation events)

Independent Variables	Bolivia	Cuba	Iran	Nicaragua
Opposition (t − 1)	0.039	0.220***	0.120***	0.134***
	(0.680)	(5.387)	(3.165)	(2.646)
Repression (t − 1)	0.001	0.258***	0.125***	−0.127*
	(0.005)	(4.464)	(3.075)	(−1.745)
Repression (t − 2)	−0.092	−0.066	0.017	−0.122**
	(−0.851)	(−1.288)	(0.507)	(−2.139)
Accommodation (t − 1)	0.107	−0.065	−0.199**	0.001
	(0.988)	(−0.620)	(−1.952)	(0.023)
Accommodation (t − 2)	−0.057	0.073	−0.255**	0.085*
	(−0.547)	(0.745)	(−2.066)	(1.741)
War (t − 1)	—	—	−0.585***	−0.526**
			(−2.803)	(−2.209)
Coalition-reduction phase	0.487	1.187***	1.531***	−0.841
	(1.222)	(3.920)	(3.338)	(−0.441)
Interaction: Repression in the coalition-reduction phase	−0.432*	−0.292***	−0.352***	0.176
	(−1.634)	(−3.270)	(−3.571)	(1.579)
Constant	0.402***	−0.511***	0.429**	0.530**
	(2.480)	(−3.595)	(2.009)	(2.022)
Ln (alpha)	−0.400	−1.535***	−0.807***	−0.705**
	(−1.520)	(−3.102)	(−2.503)	(−2.228)
N	150	154	154	149
Chi-square	6.04	80.25***	48.32***	25.35***
Log-likelihood	−251.606	−224.184	−241.932	−223.257
LR test vs. Poisson	40.343***	8.215***	25.617***	25.847***

Notes: (t − statistics in parentheses) ★ = p < 0.10 (two-tailed tests), ★★ = p < 0.05 (two-tailed tests), ★★★ = p < 0.01 (two-tailed tests)

Yet the other policy mix option, accommodation, is not much help in understanding opposition activity across these cases. It is significant and negative in Iran (p < .05), but nowhere else. And accommodation lagged an additional month is significant and negative in Iran (p< .05), but significant and positive in Nicaragua (p < .10). One reason for this discrepancy might be that Iran employed accommodation very rarely, so when it did use this policy tool, mass level groups decided to encourage concessions by not engaging in opposition activity. In Nicaragua, however, the use of accommodation was frequent. This signals the perceived vulnerability of the elites to opposition groups.[77] Such groups would then be eager to try dissent again in order to gain even more concessions. This explanation does not satisfy, however, because it cannot be applied to the other two cases in the study. Accommodation has no significant effect on opposition activity in either Bolivia or Cuba.

Finally, as expected, previous levels of opposition activity positively affect future levels of dissent in three of the four cases analyzed here. These effects are highly significant (p < .01). Only in Bolivia is there a lack of autocorrelation in dissent.

In sum, my model appears to explain opposition activity across these four post-internal war cases. However, it is also possible that in aggregating opposition activity into one overall category I have missed some more nuanced effects. Below, I rerun the above statistical models using first violent and then nonviolent opposition as the dependent variable.

Disaggregating Opposition Activity

Methodology

To determine what type of event count model is most appropriate for these models, I ran goodness-of-fit chi-square tests, presented here in Table 6.4. The overwhelming significance of the goodness-of-fit chi-square for violent opposition activity indicates that the Poisson regression model is inappropriate for these models.

To check this result I ran Likelihood Ratio (LR) tests of negative binomial models against Poisson models of the same data. The results, presented in Table 6.5, demonstrate that the Poisson model is, in fact, inappropriate in three out of my four cases. The large chi-square values and high levels of significance confirm that the assumption of a strict Poisson distribution of both the repression and the accommodation data is inappropriate. However, mixed results from these two tests regarding the Bolivian case lead me to suspect that a Poisson model might be more appropriate. I therefore employ negative binomial models in my analysis of violent opposition activity for all four of my cases, and include an additional table comparing results for Bolivia using both negative binomial and Poisson models.

The overwhelming significance of the goodness-of-fit chi-square for nonviolent opposition activity indicates that the Poisson regression model is inappropriate in the Nicaraguan and Bolivian models. However, the lack of such evidence for Iran and Cuba suggests that a Poisson model might best account for the dispersion of the dependent variable in these cases.

As a second check I again ran Likelihood Ratio (LR) tests of negative binomial models against Poisson models of the same data. The results (Table 6.5) confirm the appropriateness of Poisson models in the Cuban case, but question the appropriateness of Poisson for analyzing the Iranian nonviolent opposition data. The large chi-square values and high levels of significance confirm that the assumption of a strict Poisson distribution of both the repression and the accommodation data is inappropriate in three of the four cases. Therefore, for the sake of consistency in data presentation, nonviolent opposition is analyzed using negative binomial models for all four of my cases. However, I include an additional table comparing results for both Cuba and Iran using negative binomial and Poisson models. This rather conservative measure protects against the possibility that I have misidentified the appropriate model in the Iranian case.

Findings

Violent Opposition. Table 6.6 presents the results of negative binomial event count models testing which factors affect violent opposition activity in Bolivia, Cuba, Iran, and Nicaragua. Again, no factor significantly impacts opposition levels in all four cases. The only factor that affects more than two cases is previous levels of violent opposition. In Cuba, Nicaragua, and Iran, violent opposition begets more violent opposition. However, only in Cuba do increases in nonviolent opposition also lead to increases in violent opposition.

Unlike in the aggregate analysis, war does not retain consistently significant effects on violent opposition. Participation in the Contra War significantly decreased Nicaraguan levels of violent domestic opposition (p < .01).[78] However, the Iran-Iraq War had no such effect on violent opposition in Iran. While negative, the relationship is not significant. Results for war's effect on violent opposition are therefore mixed.

Table 6.4 Test of Poisson Distribution of the Dependent Variable

	Violent Opposition Activity	
Case	*Goodness of Fit χ^2*	
Type I—Iran	254.843★★★	
Type II—Cuba	222.795★★★	
Type III—Nicaragua	181.891★★★	
Type IV—Bolivia	180.592★★★	

	Nonviolent Opposition Activity	
Case	*Goodness of Fit χ^2*	
Type I—Iran	143.745	
Type II—Cuba	96.986	
Type III—Nicaragua	181.484★★★	
Type IV—Bolivia	215.938★★★	

Note: ★★★ = $p < .01$

Table 6.6 also shows that neither repression nor accommodation have notable effects on violent opposition activity, even given lags of an additional month for both. Among policy mix choices, only accommodation in Cuba affects violent opposition. That effect is positive, but barely significant ($p < .10$). Table 6.6a, a comparison between negative binomial and Poisson models of the Bolivian case, reveals that the only major difference between the two models is that moving from the former to the latter makes accommodation barely significant in Bolivia as well. In short, policy mix choices on their own have little, if any, effect on opposition activity.

Neither do they have much effect when in combination with the phase dummy variable. While the previous tests showed that my model did a good job of explaining three out of the four cases, Table 6.6 demonstrates that it performs poorly when analyzing only violent opposition. The interaction term is only significant ($p < .01$) in Bolivia. My model says little about what affects violent opposition in the other three states. And the coalition-reduction dummy variable on its own also lacks broad explanatory power. It is significant in two of the four cases, but it is an odd combination of cases (Bolivia and Iran), which suggests little as to why these in particular can be explained by the temporal control variable.

Table 6.5 **Likelihood Ratio (LR) Test of Negative Binomial Models vs. Poisson Models**

Case Type	Case Name	Coefficient [ln (alpha)]	LR Test vs. Poisson (χ^2)	Log Likelihood
Violent Opposition Activity				
Type I	Iran	−0.490	25.909★★★	−220.675
Type II	Cuba	−0.694★★★	14.240★★★	−201.660
Type III	Nicaragua	−0.628	10.037★★★	−157.197
Type IV	Bolivia	−1.513★	2.280	−177.689
Nonviolent Opposition Activity				
Type I	Iran	0.589	12.744★★★	−101.139
Type II	Cuba	−15.937	0.001	−75.534
Type III	Nicaragua	−0.943	4.448★★	−162.365
Type IV	Bolivia	−0.389	16.826★★★	−173.458

Note: ★★★ = p < .01; ★★ = p < .05

In short, there appears to be little to explain violent opposition activity within and across these four cases other than previous violent opposition. And even that variable is only significant in three of the four cases.

Nonviolent Opposition. An analysis of the factors that affect nonviolent opposition activity produces even more confusing results. Figure 6.7 shows that, once again, the strongest factor affecting the dependent variable appears to be autocorrelation. Here, however, previous nonviolent opposition significantly increases future nonviolent opposition in only two of the four cases—Bolivia and Iran.

No other factor significantly affects Bolivian nonviolent opposition levels. And not a single factor considered significantly impacts Nicaraguan levels of nonviolent opposition. Previous levels of violent opposition, accommodation, lagged accommodation, lagged repression, the dummy variable for the coalition-reduction phase, and the interaction term (representing the engine of the historical model) all fail to significantly explain

Table 6.6 Negative Binomial Model of Factors Affecting Violent Opposition Activity (using total number of repression and accommodation events)

Independent Variables	Bolivia	Cuba	Iran	Nicaragua
Violent Opposition (t – 1)	0.006	0.312★★★	0.131★★	0.283★★★
	(0.050)	(5.502)	(2.188)	(3.158)
Nonviolent Opposition (t – 1)	0.048	0.632★★★	0.120	0.044
	(0.537)	(2.933)	(0.987)	(0.374)
Repression (t – 1)	0.110	–0.175	0.065	–0.077
	(0.763)	(–1.539)	(1.575)	(–0.861)
Repression (t – 2)	–0.129	–0.009	0.020	–0.124
	(–1.151)	(–0.138)	(0.534)	(–1.584)
Accommodation (t – 1)	0.172	0.196★	–0.145	0.043
	(1.530)	(1.644)	(–1.383)	(0.618)
Accommodation (t – 2)	–0.138	0.060	–0.149	0.061
	(–1.172)	(0.532)	(–1.356)	(0.928)
War (t – 1)		—	–0.188	–0.926★★★
			(–0.770)	(–3.155)
Coalition-reduction phase	1.204★★★	0.412	1.094★★	–0.043
	(2.855)	(1.000)	(2.030)	(–0.086)
Interaction: Repression in the coalition-reduction phase	–0.820★★★	0.202	–0.156	0.043
	(–2.510)	(1.362)	(–1.437)	(–0.258)
Constant	–0.303★	–0.694★★★	–0.055	0.010
	(–1.700)	(–4.094)	(–0.214)	(0.030)
Ln (alpha)	–1.513★	–0.863★★	–0.490	–0.628
	(–1.903)	(–2.075)	(–1.522)	(–1.326)
N	150	154	154	148
Chi-square	13.38	67.28★★★	29.27★★★	36.51★★★
Log-likelihood	–177.689	–201.660	–220.675	–157.197
LR test vs. Poisson	2.280	14.240★★★	25.909★★★	10.037★★★

Notes: (t – statistics in parentheses) ★ = p < 0.10 (two-tailed tests), ★★ = p < 0.05 (two-tailed tests), ★★★ = p < 0.01 (two-tailed tests)

Table 6.6a Negative Binomial Model vs. Poisson Model of Factors Affecting Violent Opposition Activity in Bolivia (using total number of repression and accommodation events)

Independent Variables	Cuba	
	Negative Binomial	Poisson
Violent Opposition (t − 1)	0.006	0.006
	(0.050)	(0.059)
Nonviolent Opposition (t − 1)	0.048	0.053
	(0.537)	(0.665)
Repression (t − 1)	0.110	0.127
	(0.763)	(0.948)
Repression (t − 2)	−0.129	−0.129
	(−1.151)	(−1.257)
Accommodation (t − 1)	0.172	0.170★
	(1.530)	(1.665)
Accommodation (t − 2)	−0.138	−0.138
	(−1.172)	(−1.282)
War (t − 1)	—	—
Coalition-reduction phase	1.204★★★	1.205★★★
	(2.855)	(2.855)
Interaction: Repression in the coalition-reduction phase	−0.820★★★	−0.811★★★
	(−2.510)	(−2.748)
Constant	−0.303	−0.317★
	(−1.700)	(−1.913)
N	150	150
Chi-square	13.38	16.82★★★
Log-likelihood	−177.689	−178.829
LR test vs. Poisson	2.280	—
Goodness-of-fit (chi-square)	—	180.592★★★

Notes: (t − statistics in parentheses) ★ = p < 0.10 (two-tailed tests), ★★ = p < 0.05 (two-tailed tests), ★★★ = p < 0.01 (two-tailed tests)

nonviolent opposition activity in *any* of the four post-internal war states examined in this study.

Short-term effects of repression may play a role, albeit a minimally significant one (p < .10). Both Cuba and Iran exhibit some effect of repression on nonviolent opposition. However, in Cuba repression increases violent dissent, while in Iran repression decreases it.

Table 6.7 Negative Binomial Model of Factors Affecting Nonviolent Oppostion Activity (using total number of repression and accommodation events)

Independent Variables	Bolivia	Cuba	Iran	Nicaragua
Violent Opposition (t − 1)	-0.192	0.060	0.058	0.129
	(-1.251)	(0.641)	(0.469)	(1.388)
Nonviolent Opposition (t − 1)	0.205★★	0.460	0.831★★★	0.073
	(2.231)	(1.453)	(3.741)	(0.743)
Repression (t − 1)	0.116	0.190★	-0.260★	-0.138
	(0.614)	(1.910)	(-1.657)	(-1.520)
Repression (t − 2)	-0.011	0.043	0.042	-0.036
	(-0.076)	(0.441)	(0.434)	(-0.516)
Accommodation (t − 1)	0.023	-0.143	0.080	0.038
	(0.159)	(-0.503)	(0.517)	(0.655)
Accommodation (t − 2)	0.047	0.140	-0.124	0.078
	(0.364)	(0.621)	(-0.794)	(1.469)
War (t − 1)	—	—	-0.622	0.380
			(-1.459)	(1.085)
Coalition-reduction phase	-0.635	0.626	-1.133	-0.005
	(-0.886)	(0.561)	(-0.951)	(-0.008)
Interaction: Repression in the coalition-reduction phase	-0.116	-0.361	0.346	0.172
	(-0.332)	(-0.610)	(1.423)	(1.161)
Constant	-0.389★	-2.244★★★	-0.981★★	-0.872★★★
	(-1.843)	(-7.301)	(-2.219)	(-2.287)
Ln (alpha)	-0.127	-15.937	0.589	-0.943
	(-0.336)	(-0.016)	(1.260)	(-1.500)
N	150	154	154	148
Chi-square	8.90	12.21★★★	21.52★★★	12.29
Log-likelihood	-173.458	-75.534	-101.139	-162.365
LR test vs. Poisson	16.830★★★	0.001	12.744★★★	4.448★★

Notes: (t − statistics in parentheses) ★ = $p < 0.10$ (two-tailed tests), ★★ = $p < 0.05$ (two-tailed tests), ★★★ = $p < 0.01$ (two-tailed tests)

Finally, while negative binomial models of my cases do not uncover an effect of war on nonviolent opposition activity, a check of Poisson models for Iran reveals a slightly significant (p < .10) negative effect of war on violent dissent (see Table 6.7a). Where war involvement in Nicaragua led to decreases in violent opposition activity domestically, the Iran-Iraq War led to decreases in internal nonviolent dissent.

Discussion

Perhaps the most consistent finding is that opposition activity is self-stimulating. Previous violent opposition and total opposition levels affect subsequent levels in all cases but Bolivia. Non-violent dissent leads to more of the same in Bolivia and Iran. In short, in each of the four cases at least some type of opposition activity is self-stimulating.

Yet even given these effects, the historical process model developed in this study accounts rather well for overall levels of opposition activity in three of the four post-internal war states. That may not be a perfect track record, but the historical process model still explains dissent better in these four cases than do the other explanations that I have examined. The key findings concern the importance of the timing of repression and of the effects of war participation on opposition activity. Below, I discuss the implications of my findings for the different types of cases analyzed in this study.

Timing: States Which Employ Repression during the Coalition-Reduction Phase. Time plays a key role in determining overall levels of dissent in post-revolutionary states, particularly in cases where the elites felt secure enough to employ repression (Case Types I and II). As predicted, opposition in these states was higher during the coalition-reduction phase than subsequently. And the ability to use repression during this period goes even further toward reducing the threat posed by opposition groups.

In Cuba and Iran, the ability to use repression during the coalition-reduction phase helped to reduce the amount of dissent faced by the regime. The elites ousted dissenters early, leaving little in the way of an effective opposition. Yet, despite the negative interactive effect of repression and time, repression by itself had a positive short-run effect on levels of opposition. While repression increases opposition (in the short run), repression during the crucial coalition-reduction phase acts to reduce the overall level of opposition faced by the regime over time. Support exists for the hypothesis that repression has dual and dynamic effects. However, the effect

Table 6.7a Negative Binomial Model vs. Poisson Model of Factors Affecting Nonviolent Oppostion Activity in Cuba and Iran (using total number of repression and accommodation events)

Independent Variables	Cuba		Iran	
	Negative Binomial	Poisson	Negative Binomial	Poisson
Violent Opposition (t – 1)	0.060	0.069	0.058	-0.021
	(0.641)	(0.724)	(0.469)	(-0.257)
Nonviolent Opposition (t – 1)	0.460	0.507	0.831★★★	0.707★★★
	(1.453)	(1.457)	(3.741)	(6.269)
Repression (t – 1)	0.190★	0.163	-0.260★	-0.174★
	(1.910)	(1.095)	(-1.657)	(-1.696)
Repression (t – 2)	0.043	0.046	0.042	0.021
	(0.441)	(0.416)	(0.434)	(0.278)
Accommodation (t – 1)	-0.143	-0.187	0.080	0.018
	(-0.503)	(-0.697)	(0.517)	(0.132)
Accommodation (t – 2)	0.140	0.110	-0.124	0.012
	(0.621)	(0.541)	(-0.794)	(0.127)
War (t – 1)	—	—	-0.622	-0.576★
			(-1.459)	(-1.875)
Coalition-reduction phase	0.626	-0.100	-1.133	-0.718
	(0.561)	(-0.125)	(-0.951)	(-0.795)
Interaction: Repression in the coalition-reduction phase	-0.361	0.131	0.346	0.187
	(-0.610)	(0.147)	(1.423)	(1.130)
Constant	-2.244★★★	-2.204★★★	-0.981★★	-0.955★★★
	(-7.301)	(-7.121)	(-2.219)	(-3.029)

continues

Table 6.7a *(continued)*

Independent Variables	Cuba		Iran	
	Negative Binomial	Poisson	Negative Binomial	Poisson
Ln (alpha)	−15.937	—	0.589	—
	(−0.016)		(1.260)	
N	154	154	154	154
Chi-square	12.21★★★	12.25	21.52★★★	40.263★★★
Log-likelihood	−75.534	−75.720	−101.139	−107.511
LR test vs. Poisson	0.001	—	12.744★★★	—
Goodness-of-fit (chi-square)	—	96.986	—	143.745

Notes: *(t − statistics in parentheses)* ★ = *p* < 0.10 *(two-tailed tests)*, ★★ = *p* < 0.05 *(two-tailed tests)*, ★★★ = *p* < 0.01 *(two-tailed tests)*

found here is contrary to that which has been uncovered elsewhere. Previous research has examined non–revolutionary and revolutionary situations.[79] Perhaps post–revolutionary states present different dynamics altogether, and therefore different opportunities for and costs and benefits of opposition. The centrality of the timing element points to this as a possible explanation.

In sum, repression during this period has long-reaching implications for potential opposition. Yet, repression during the consolidation phase has only short-term effects. This may help to explain why levels of opposition rose in Iran yet fell in Cuba during the latter part of the post-internal war period. In Iran, repression continued throughout the entire period. In Cuba, however, repression dissipated after the end of the coalition-reduction phase and did not rise significantly thereafter. Thus, the use of repression early on leads to an overall decline in opposition levels. However, when these regimes employ repression subsequently, they spur on micromobilization processes, reviving opposition activity.

Timing: States Which Do Not Employ Repression during the Coalition-Reduction Phase. This exercise has unfortunately yielded little information about opposition activity in states that do not repress during the outset of the post-internal war period (Case Types III and IV). Remember that elites who see themselves as vulnerable cannot repress early on, and eventually fall back on accommodation. Thus, the timing of repression should be as important here as in cases with secure elites. Yet, timing was found to be a key variable in only one of these two states. The inability of the Bolivian elites to repress during the coalition-reduction period left them facing an emboldened opposition, as the historical process model predicts. This may explain why all types of opposition activity increased substantially following this crucial phase. While the same time-dependent relationship does not hold in Nicaragua, repression itself does have an immediate and longer term negative relationship to overall levels of dissent. However, when dissent is disaggregated into its constituent parts, the effect disappears.

War and Policy Mix Choices: Direct and Indirect Effects. Given the lack of reliability of the time element in explaining opposition in Nicaragua, what accounts for the exceedingly low levels of violent domestic opposition during the middle of this state's post-revolutionary period (see Figure 6.2)? The other policy mix option, accommodation, appears to have no significant effect on opposition levels in either Bolivia or Nicaragua. However, war involvement goes a long way toward explaining this unexpected dip in dissent. The Contra War significantly decreases overall levels of Nicaraguan non-Contra related opposition.

However, when dissent is disaggregated, it is revealed that this relationship is due to the negative effect of war on violent opposition. Nonviolent opposition continued on unaffected in wartime Nicaragua. Perhaps this is because the states of emergency frequently declared by the Sandinista government were aimed at reducing the loudest and most destructive forms of opposition.[80] The Sandinistas required the existence of some kind of opposition in order to legitimate their claims of reform and accommodation to domestic and international audiences. In addition, one of the main stated goals of the revolution was the empowerment of the population at large.[81] By allowing less violent opposition to go relatively unchallenged, these claims could be legitimately espoused while the regime was simultaneously suppressing violent opposition (see Chapter 4).

An alternative explanation is that opposition groups, realizing that an already vulnerable regime is fighting a costly war, lower their demands, and change their tactics to suit these new demands. Riots and violent strikes are not often used to acquire low-level concessions. And strategies such as nonviolent strikes and demonstrations are more apt to be considered by the regime. While it is difficult to infer causality, there is evidence that opposition groups did lower their demands once the Contra War broke out in order to support the Sandinista government.[82] Once the war was concluded, opposition activity, and demands, rose sharply.[83] This explanation is consistent with the "rally-round-the-flag" hypothesis espoused by theorists who argue that war decreases opposition activity.

Perhaps this also helps to explain the counter-intuitive finding from the previous chapter that war increased the perceptions of security of the Sandinistas. While the war itself was devastating and led to a division of Nicaraguans into pro- and anti-Contras, many who opposed the Sandinista regime reined in their more severe anti-regime activity in favor of more passive resistance. Thus, vulnerability and war (Type III) have the effect of encouraging the opposition to rally around the regime, and subsequently leading the elites to perceive their power positions to be more secure. This, in turn, leads to increases in the use of accommodation, which, as seen in Table 6.3, has a negative long-term effect on opposition activity. In addition, because accommodation is self-stimulating, opposition activity declines even further. In sum, war appears to have both direct and indirect negative effects on opposition activity in states with vulnerable elites. These more complex relationships are depicted in Figure 6.6.

The relationship between war and opposition in Iran, however, is even more complicated. The first clue comes in comparing the effects of accommodation in generally nonaccommodating regimes (Types I and II). Iran's rare uses of accommodation prompted decreases in dissent. However, no such effect is evident in Cuba. Perhaps this is due to the impact of the Iran-Iraq War. Recall that in the previous chapter I found that the Iran-Iraq War led to a significant decrease in levels of accommodation employed by the Iranian regime. And war is found in the current analysis to decrease levels of dissent directly. Given these findings, I conclude that war has a negative direct effect and a positive indirect effect on opposition activity in Type I cases. I elaborate below.

War has three effects in Type I cases. Figure 6.7 illustrates these complex relationships. War's primary effect is an immediate decrease in opposition activity. Mass actors rally around the government in opposition to the foreign aggressor. However, war has two positive indirect effects which, in the long run, counter the immediate negative effect of war on opposition.

War increases dissent via perceptions of security, and the use of repression. Table 5.7 (Chapter 5) shows that war increased perceptions of security among Iranian elites. And Table 5.5 in the previous chapter shows that these reinforced perceptions of security lead to increases in the use of repression. In addition, more repression feeds on itself directly and indirectly. Repression is self-stimulating, creating a repression–repression positive feedback loop. It also increases perceptions of security, creating a repression-perceptions positive feedback loop. These increases in repression lead to more opposition activity, yielding war's very complex and indirect secondary effect.

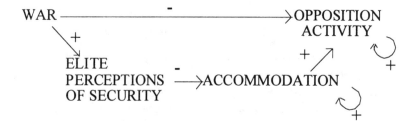

Figure 6.6   Observed Relationship between War and Opposition Activity in Type III Case (Nicaragua)

War's tertiary effect is a decrease in accommodation, and therefore an increase in opposition. War in nonaccommodating regimes makes the use of accommodation even rarer. But less accommodation leads to more opposition in Iran. What had been pro-regime support becomes anti-regime activity. Thus war's effect of decreasing the use of accommodation indirectly leads to an increase in opposition activity.

Perhaps this helps to clarify the accommodation-dissent puzzle. Researchers disagree as to the effect of concessions on opposition activity. In fact, there is no uniform effect across cases. Rather, in post-revolutionary states with secure elites, war creates a negative relationship between concessions and dissent where it might not have existed otherwise. War also has differential effects on opposition when elites have different perceptions of the security of their power positions. Vulnerable elites who must endure war enjoy a decrease in opposition activity (particularly violent opposition). Secure elites find that opposition decreases in the short run, but increases in the long run.

Conclusion

This chapter is a tentative first step in clarifying the accommodation-dissent puzzle. Accommodation has different effects on different types of regimes. When war strikes states with secure elites (Type I), accommodation has a dual effect: it decreases opposition activity in the short run, but increases levels of dissent in the long run. But vulnerability at the outset of war (Type III) has the effect of reducing opposition activity overall. Finally,

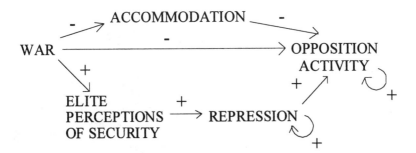

Figure 6.6   Observed Relationship between War and Opposition Activity in Type I Case (Iran)

concessions have no effect on opposition in states that are able to avoid war (Types II and IV).

Additionally, the other relationships suggested by my historical process model hold, for the most part, when examining the determinants of opposition activity in post-revolutionary states. Repression is important, but the timing of repression is critical. The effects of repression employed at the outset impact opposition levels throughout the post-revolutionary period. Given that perceptions of security or vulnerability influence the use of repression during the coalition-reduction phase, one can also say that elite perceptions have long-lasting indirect effects on opposition. In short, it appears that, while not a perfect explanation of levels of dissent, a historical model incorporating perceptions, war, and their interdependent outcomes (policy mix choices and opposition activity) goes a long way toward explaining the dynamics of repression, accommodation, and opposition in post-revolutionary states.

This chapter has examined an immediate concern of post-revolutionary regimes, namely, the maintenance of domestic order. It has also incorporated the actions of mass actors into what is primarily an elite-driven model. However, the analysis of the political dynamics of the post-revolutionary state remains incomplete. In particular, the incorporation into the model of unconventional behavior of mass actors begs the following question: To what degree can mass actors participate conventionally in the political life in these states? In the next chapter, I examine how elite policy mix choices, opposition, and war participation impact the development of different regime types and their corresponding political institutions within the post-revolutionary state.

CHAPTER 7

Sharing the Cake:
Political System Development
in Post-Revolutionary States

All men would be tyrants if they could.

—Daniel Defoe [1]

*The saddest life is that of a political aspirant under democracy. His failure is igno-
minious and his success is disgraceful.*

—H. L. Menken [2]

R evolutions generally produce stable forms of governance.[3] However, it is rare when these post-revolutionary political systems
evolve into what we know as stable democratic regimes.[4]

The reason for this failure is that the process of revolutionary power struggles leads to the concentration of power in the hands of revolutionaries, and
the persecution and purging of their opponents. This process is highly in-
imical to the toleration and compromise between contending parties that is
essential to stable democracy.[5]

Indeed, when democracies have resulted from revolutions in this century, they
have typically followed a pattern of expansion of suffrage and single-party

dominance with regulated political competition.[6] The PRI's Mexico and ZANU-PF's Zimbabwe are prime examples.[7] Occasionally, semi-democracies emerge, in which serious political competition occurs despite the dominance of one party. Bolivia's political system, dominated by the MNR but contested vigorously by the Socialist Falange Party, illustrates these post-internal war semi-democracies.[8] In some rare cases, this phase is followed by multi-party contestation and the consolidation of democracy. The recent turnovers in government within the framework of a democratic system in Hungary, Poland, and Bulgaria, in the early 1990s, and in Nicaragua in both 1990 and 1996 underscores the possibility of this outcome.[9]

More often, however, post-revolutionary states yield institutionalized autocracies.[10] These non-democratic post-revolutionary regimes are a distinct form of authoritarianism. In most authoritarian states political parties are either absent or play limited roles. Leaders in these states seek either public apathy or active demobilization of the masses. But overmobilization of mass actors in the early stages of the post-revolutionary period requires institutionalized arrangements for controlling and channeling mass participation. Therefore, political parties play key roles in post-revolutionary states. The dual structures and resources of party and state put these elites in a unique position regarding their ability to wield the instruments of coercion and control.[11] In this century there are numerous examples of single-party-dominated authoritarian states that grew out of revolution. Consider the role of the Communist Party in Soviet Union, China, Cuba, Vietnam, Cambodia, and Ethiopia, as well as the development of party-driven theocratic regimes in Iran and Afghanistan.

Both types of post-revolutionary outcomes, whether democratic or authoritarian, rely on political parties.[12] Both are the consequences of similar processes of conflict. So how is it that some post-revolutionary states develop democratic tendencies, while others do not? The internal wars examined in this study provide unique laboratories in which to examine the dynamics of political system development. In this chapter, I examine how the historical processes examined thus far—involving leaders' policy mix choices, opposition activity, and involvement in international conflict—contribute to the political development of post-internal war states.

Political System Development: The Chicken or the Egg?

What is the relationship between elite-mass interactions and political system development? Recent findings by Benson and Kugler show that government effectiveness in the extraction of resources from society, combined with the consolidation of democratic institutions, reduces levels of domestic political violence.[13] The crux of their argument is that politically efficient governments are much more likely to avert internal challenges than inefficient extractors. Serious challenges can only be waged by a well-organized opposition that approaches power parity with the regime. They argue that efficient extraction removes the threat of parity by dramatically increasing the regime's resources, allowing for the consolidation of democracy. Additionally, the consolidation of democracy allows for more efficient extraction by reducing extra-institutional domestic challenges. In other words, the effects of extraction and regime type reinforce each other.

Two puzzles remain: First, which came first, extraction or democracy? In post-internal war periods, where a new regime and new institutions have yet to be created, extraction of resources *must* come first. Second, we know that all successful regimes extract with some degree of efficiency. This begs the question: do the *methods* that regimes use to extract resources affect political system development? I argue that they do. Additionally, I argue that the timing of the use of these methods is crucial.

Elites who employ repression early in the post-revolutionary period are able to oust most of their domestic opposition, leaving little need to accommodate. Without an effective opposition to mollify there is little need to trade away democratic rights and privileges, and little time spent developing norms of give-and-take necessary for democracy to develop. Conversely, elites who cannot use repression early on leave an effective opposition in place. These elites must then accommodate their opponents, often by trading rights and privileges for compliance. Additionally, interactions between regime and opposition during this accommodative period help develop the cooperative norms necessary for democracy to develop.

In short, the timing of elite policy mix choice is crucial to the development of the political system in post-revolutionary states. Yet examination of this relationship has been overshadowed recently by the study of the inverse of this relationship—the effect of regime type on policy mix choices. Below, I elaborate on the connection between regime type and elite policy mix choices, beginning with the latter, more studied relationship.

Regime Type's Effects on Elite and Mass Strategies

A growing literature has developed analyzing the effects of regime type on the use of repression. The general consensus among scholars is that regime type is strongly associated with levels of state repression.[14] Violence is more likely to be used in non-democracies to quell domestic dissent than in democracies. Leaders in democratic states refrain from repression because of the potential for adverse popular reaction through institutionalized means of participation.[15] Such political participation minimizes the power of elites and maximizes the power of non-elites. Particular institutions are cited for their ability to reduce state repression, including parliamentary executives,[16] consociationalism,[17] elections,[18] and universal adult suffrage.[19]

This is not to say that democratic states do not employ repression. Longitudinal case analyses[20] and cross-national longitudinal studies[21] have demonstrated that democratic states can and do employ repression. However, democratic states employ repression at a significantly reduced rate than their non-democratic counterparts.[22]

Regime type also impacts levels of opposition activity. Policy-making structures may determine both opportunities for mobilization and movement success.[23] Electoral politics in particular suppresses the possibilities for protest.[24] Additionally, violent opposition activity is discredited in democratic systems because of the available channels through which groups may address grievances.[25] Democracy is even cited as an inhibitor of revolutions and civil wars.[26]

Yet the period of *transition* to democracy is rife with conflict. Domestic repressive behavior increases substantially, if but for the short term, as states move toward democracy.[27] New democracies are subject to significant levels of domestic conflict.[28] These states have been found to have a propensity to respond to opposition with repression. For example, the most serious types of internal conflict, including ethnopolitical conflict and state-sponsored mass murder, have been found to be unintended consequences of efforts to democratize.[29] Compounding this problem is the propensity of transitional democracies to redress these conflicts through the use of repression.[30]

One reason for transitional states' reliance on repressive tactics is that transition periods are characterized by increases in demands of all types of opposition groups.[31] The opening up of the political opportunity structure allows previously dormant claims to be resurrected. The added problem of overmobilization during and after a revolution means more groups who took part in the overthrow of the *ancién regime* have active claims on the state.[32] In short, transition periods are often as conflict-ridden as are periods of autocratic rule.[33]

It is evident that the effects of regime type are well-studied. Yet few have examined how the use of elite policy mix choices and their effects on opposition activity impact the development of the political system. I address this problem below.

The Effect of Policy Mix Choices on Political System Development

The majority of the research on the connection between regime type and policy mix choices focuses on how democracy reduces repression and encourages accommodation. Yet few of these studies consider the possibility that researchers have misidentified the direction of causality. Is it possible that policy mix choices in post-revolutionary states affect political development and regime type?[34] In the study of democratization, what have been emphasized as independent variables might be more fruitfully conceived of as dependent variables.[35]

It also makes sense to focus primarily on elite actions when exploring the proximate causes of democratization. Transitions to democracy are processes involving strategic interactions between elite and mass actors. Yet while democracy is almost always the fruit of popular struggle, the political choices necessary to construct a workable democratic regime are the work of political elites.[36] Thus elite policy mix choices and their subsequent effects on opposition activity[37] should heavily impact a post-internal war state's political system development.

Accommodation. Elites who perceive themselves to be vulnerable will act to insure their security. However, their inability and/or reluctance to repress leads to a reliance on accommodation. In these cases the emergence of democracy is due (at least in part) to the absence of any one group capable of suppressing its competitors and dominating the system.[38] Under such conditions, the competitors must agree to cooperate. It is this reliance on accommodation that should make it more likely that the resulting political system will become more democratic.

In the short term, the purpose of these concessions is to broaden support for the existing regime and convince the population of the regime's benevolent intentions.[39] If concessions are accompanied by a hardline crackdown, this sends a mixed message that is likely to generate popular distrust and generate more severe opposition rather than broaden support for the regime.[40] Therefore, once accommodation is established as the policy of choice in dealing with the opposition, it is difficult to employ repression. The elites must therefore continue to employ accommodation when faced with demands.

In the long run, the elites know that they are not only satisfying immediate interests, but are also establishing the norms, rules, and procedures that will determine who will be winners and losers in the future.[41]

Accommodating elites allow others to gain from, and participate in, the political process in return for allowing the state to extract valuable resources from society.[42] Once benefits are gained, groups are loathe to give them up, and may even ratchet up their claims on the state.[43] At the moment that leaders allow the opposition participation rights, a Rubicon is crossed, which eventually leads to more protest and greater reforms.[44] In this way, liberalization through accommodation is inherently unstable.[45]

Additionally, the pace of liberalization has increased throughout this century. Once some initial accommodation has occurred, it is much more difficult to deny citizens rights and access than it was for earlier liberalizing countries.[46] Thus accommodating elites know from observing liberalization in other countries they will have to continue to give in to demands as the masses move to institutionalize their gains.[47] This leads to the toleration of, growth of, and often institutionalization of opposition to the government.[48] As these cooperative interactions between elites and masses increase, the elites become habituated to the use of accommodation to resolve disputes. As Gurr notes, "frequent success in the use of reforms, concessions, and displacement to manage internal challenges leads to the development of the institutions and norms of democratic rule."[49]

In short, accommodating elites leave the opposition intact, creating further need to make concessions, and leading to the habituation of cooperative behavior and democratic practices.[50] Therefore, I expect that elites who cannot repress, and must therefore accommodate persistent domestic opposition, will develop a democratic or semi-democratic political system. I hypothesize:

H7.1. In the aftermath of an internal war, if the elites employ high levels of accommodation, then that state's resulting political system will be more democratic than a state's whose elites employ less accommodation.

The literature on transitions to democracy appears to support this hypothesis. Transitions to democracy are necessarily characterized by accommodation. The aim of the transition process is to find both social consensus about the goals of society and the means to achieve them.[51] The drive to achieve some broad consensus is made necessary be the elite perceptions of their weakened power position relative to societal challengers. A transition pact (implicit or explicit) benefits all parties to some degree and insures both the "rules of the game" and the possibility that any group may take power eventually.[52] This precludes the need for some elite or mass actors to attempt to overthrow the regime. This threat is especially real in the first few years of the new state, and perceived to be more threatening by elites who see themselves in a vulnerable position. A transition pact makes the threat of extra-constitutional overthrow less likely.[53]

Thus vulnerable elites turn to the democratic processes as a way to increase their security domestically. Democratic elections give them added legitimacy if or when they win. Democratic processes also provide a security net so that if the elites are ousted, they can be assured that they will be safe, and may even be able to return to power eventually.[54] This possibility of return to power decreases the uncertainty of political interactions.[55] For example, as Higley, Kullberg, and Pakulski point out, the return to power of former Communist elites in post-1989 Eastern Europe is a sign not of rollback of democracy, but of a high degree of security for all parties involved.[56] In short, the primary task of transitions to democracy is developing tolerance and a sense of mutual security among those participating in the political system.[57] As such, elites who use accommodation in an attempt to stay in power and continue to engage in state building will be more likely to move toward adopting democratic institutions and practices.

However, the ability of the elites to retain control of the state does not depend solely on the use of accommodation. They might also rely directly on other resources to circumvent or eliminate mass participation in the political process.[58] The frequent and timely use of one such resource, repression, leads to the development of a centralized, non-democratic state.

Repression. Repressive regimes do not have to allow conventional political participation by mass actors. If elites who see themselves as secure do not feel the need to ease up and accommodate, and are willing to use force beyond the initial stages of the post-internal war era, then one should expect that attempts on the part of societal groups to move toward pluralism would be either pre-empted or crushed. Because repressive elites are able to crush the opposition early on they can set up the "rules of the game" in their own favor. Del Aguila sums this argument up best as follows:

> In systems in which no viable opposition exists, or in which the prospects that anti–status quo forces would organize and forge compelling coalitions are nonexistent, defining the rules of the game freezes the political process and suspends the potentially democratic option. In such cases, the process of institution building does not lead to genuine liberalization, or to the expansion of effective participation; instead, and quite purposely, it leads to the politics of controlled participation and one-party hegemony.[59]

In other words, success in the use of repression early in the post–internal war period leads not only to the suppression of democratization, but also to the development of autocratic norms and institutions.[60] And Karen Remmer's study of authoritarian regimes in Latin America finds that the use of repression, and the negative influence that this policy choice had on opposition activity, negatively influenced political change in these countries.[61] In sum, I expect that post–internal war states with elites who employ repression early on will eventually develop autocratic regimes. Therefore I hypothesize:

H7.2. If, in the aftermath of an internal war, the elites are able to employ repression during the coalition-reduction phase, then that state's resulting political system will be less democratic than a state's whose elites are unable to employ repression early on.

War's Effect on Political System Development

War can usher in liberalization, but it can also strengthen anti-democratic tendencies. In some cases, mass mobilization for war empowered some groups and led to significant moves toward greater democratization. Examples include the impact of World Wars I and II on the expansion of suffrage in Canada, Great Britain, and the United States, the acceleration of further democratization in Sweden and the Netherlands, and the reestablishment of democracy in Germany, Austria, and Italy.[62] However, war may not have uniform effects across countries. For example, war had a greater impact on democracy in Europe than in other regions.[63] Indeed, these positive effects of war on democratization are typically found in states that have already consolidated democracy, or have a recent history of democracy.

More often than not, and particularly in post-revolutionary states, war participation yields less democratic regimes. Eisenstadt's survey of the outcomes of revolutions finds that hostile international pressures commonly lead to the retardation of the development of pluralism in post-revolutionary states.[64] Kiser and Barzel's examination of the origins of democracy in Europe finds that external shocks on the scale of wars slow the development of the rule of law.[65] And Thompson suggests that the absence of a peaceful environment has frequently thwarted movements toward democratization.[66] These arguments are consistent with the "garrison state" hypothesis: repeated experience with war produces repressive, less democratic, praetorian states.[67] Indeed, involvement in war has been found to lead to the development of militaristic, autocratic regimes in places as different as nineteenth-century Latin America and interwar Germany, Spain, and Italy.[68] In short, war should inhibit the development of democratic or protodemocratic institutions and practices. Therefore I hypothesize:

H7.3. In the aftermath of an internal war, if a state becomes involved in a subsequent war, then its political system will become less democratic than that of a state that has not experienced an internal war.

Figure 7.1 summarizes my expectations regarding the historical sequence of factors hypothesized to affect the development of post-internal war political systems.

Operationalizing Regime Type

Given the numerous ways in which democracy is defined,[69] I prefer to rely on what Karl calls a "middle-range specification,"[70] or what Dahl calls the "procedural minimum."[71] As such, democracy encompasses several dimensions: contestation, participation, and accountability.[72] A necessary condition for democracy which touches on all three of these elements, is the presence of constitutional political opposition.[73] As Lawson (1993:194) notes, "where there is no possibility of alternation in power between governing elements and oppositional elements through a peaceful process of fair and free elections, there is no constitutional opposition, and therefore no genuine democracy."[74] Thus democratic regimes, for this analysis, will be those that allow contestation of elections and policy decisions, conventional and unconventional participation, and accountability of the elites.

Of course, no regime in this study will rate as a "true" democracy. The very nature of these governments as post-revolutionary regimes makes them inherently transitional. They are in the process of building a new state through extraction and reallocation of resources and through interaction with the masses. The "second transition," during which these regime types are consolidated, takes longer than can be observed in this study.[75] Therefore one cannot expect any of the regimes under examination here to measure up to democracy as we know it, even at this level of a "procedural minimum." What can be observed is whether these regimes attempt to fulfill the procedural minimum, whether they are moving in the direction of a democratic state. I call states that fulfill these requirements "protodemocracies." These are states that, on a continuum from autocracy to democracy, fall somewhere in the middle. As such, they can be defined by their degree of democraticness.

Figure 7.1 Historical Process Model of the Causes and Consequences of Repression and Accommodation in Post-Revolutionary States

Case Type	Coalition-Reduction Phase (first 2–3 years) Historical Process Model for Post-Internal War States	Consolidation Phase (8–10 years) Effect of Earlier Policy Choice	War's Effect on Policy Mix	Long-Run Outcomes Level of Democracy
Iran (Type I)	Elites perceive themselves to be secure → Ability to use repression → No sustained opposition	Less ACC	Increase in REP	Low
Cuba (Type II)	Elites perceive themselves to be secure → Ability to use repression → No sustained opposition	Less ACC	No war, therefore no effect	Low
Nicaragua (Type III)	Elites perceive themselves to be vulnerable → Inability to use repression → Significant opposition remains	More ACC	Increase in REP	High
Bolivia (Type IV)	Elites perceive themselves to be vulnerable → Inability to use repression → Significant opposition remains	More ACC	No war, therefore no effect	High

Note: ACC = Accommodation; REP = Repression

Historical Process Tracing of
Political System Development

Below I examine the historical record of each of the four cases in this study to determine the degree to which the procedural minimum for democracy are met or attempted. In the process, I elaborate upon the way in which the elite perceptions, policy mix choice and timing, opposition activity levels, and war participation (when applicable) affected political system development.

Type I—Iran. The *ulama* (clerical leaders) and their diverse revolutionary coalition partners took power in Iran in early 1979. Perceiving themselves to be secure, the clerics, led by Ayatollah Khomeini, went about systematically removing their opponents.[76] The coalition-reduction process ended in early 1982 with the neutralization of the Mujahedin–e Khalq, the clerics' most violent and dangerous opponent.[77] In between, the quick and effective use of repression enabled the regime to oust nearly all other dissenters, including those from amongst the clerical ranks.[78] What opposition remained acquiesced with little struggle.[79]

The Islamic Revolutionary Party (IRP) further consolidated its hold on power by remaking the state's institutions in an Islamic image.[80] From the very beginning, the revolutionary regime in Iran was an authoritarian state first and a presidential-parliamentary hybrid system second.[81] The drafting of the constitution in 1979 led to the establishment of an Islamic basis for the post-revolutionary state.[82] Khomeini, as *faqih* (ruler/jurist), acquired far-ranging veto powers over the *majlis* (parliament), effectively negating any democratic benefits that such a legislative body might provide.[83] Successive governments were led by elected officials who opposed the *faqih* and the *ulama*. Both Medhi Bazargan, the revolutionary state's first prime minister, and Abul Hasan Bani Sadr, it's first president, soon found themselves in direct conflict with Khomeini and the more radical clerics.[84] Each was eventually ousted from power.[85]

The Iranian regime had developed into an illiberal theocracy that recognized few civil and political rights.[86] The press and the legal system were brought under the jurisdiction of the *ulama*.[87] The Revolutionary Guards were given a mandate of military support and intelligence gathering.[88] Even the army came under the watchful eye of the clerics.[89]

Elections were held, but only involved candidates approved by the *ulama* and the IRP.[90] The electoral process in Iran severely limited citizen participation.[91] When participation was allowed, it was often rigged in favor of the *ulama*. For example, Skocpol points out that in practice the system required a largely illiterate population to gain the clerics' help in voting.[92] By the late 1980s the public political sphere was restricted to radical and moderate factions within the closed circle of clerical leadership.[93] Vigorous contestation occurred, but only by elements within that limited political sphere.[94]

Particularly during its initial stages, the war with Iraq served to solidify the *ulama's* political system.[95] It provided a convenient excuse to oust Bani Sadr, to isolate the *majlis* from foreign policy, and to reassert clerical rule.[96] It allowed the regime to blame any domestic problems on the aggression by the Iraqis and their international supporters, and helped the government suppress the opposition and rally the masses around the flag.[97] Finally, the war created the cover under which the regime could deal harshly with the rebellious minority communities within the country.[98] However, the foundations for the autocratic regime that developed had been laid a year prior. Thus, while the war did not directly cause the development of an illiberal regime, it made it easier to justify measures necessary for the consolidation and institutionalization of the revolution.

In post-revolutionary Iran, power was centralized at the top, and rule was autocratic in nature. The Islamic regime had been successfully institutionalized, primarily because of the ability of the clerics to oust their opposition within the first few years of their rule. With little domestic opposition left, the elites did not need to give up political rights to participation and contestation, and had little incentive to allow for accountability of the elites to the masses. Even a major war with Iran's neighbor to the west did not shake the hold of the *ulama* on the political system. If anything, it helped them to solidify their power and further entrench the institutions of an autocratic state.[99]

Type II—Cuba. At the onset of the post-revolutionary period in Cuba, the new elites, led by Fidel Castro, found themselves in a very favorable position. The lack of an organized alternative to the revolutionaries, coupled with the outpouring of support by the masses, boosted the perceptions of security of Castro and his inner circle.[100] Therefore, upon assuming power, the elites went about quickly eliminating all potential rivals.[101] Counterrevolutionaries were either executed or fled into exile in the United States. Large numbers of former Batista military and police officers were arrested, tried, and executed.[102] Yet this severe repression actually increased the regime's popularity. While the firing squads offended some North Americans, it won the approval of many Cubans whose families had suffered under the Batista regime.[103] Aided by his immense personal popularity, Castro even ousted rivals within the elite, including his hand-picked president Manuel Urrutia.[104] The coalition-reduction process culminated with the trial of Major Huber Matos, the only other extremely popular figure (and therefore potential threat) in Cuba, in October of 1959.[105]

Once the opposition was removed, the elites were able to relax their repressive grip somewhat and concentrate instead on consolidating the revolution. However, this did not entail the institutionalization of the revolution.[106] It certainly did not result in the development of democracy in Cuba—when institutions were implemented, they had little power, and tended to increase rather than decrease Castro's influence.[107] The first major institutionalization of the revolution took place in 1976, more than 15 years after the end of the revolutionary conflict.[108] Yet even these attempts at incorporating the masses into the political decisionmaking process failed to meet the procedural minimum of democracy discussed above.[109]

Writing a generally favorable report in the middle of 1960, Herbert Matthews outlined the successes of the first year of the Cuban Revolution. Despite a glowing account of Cuban revolutionary progress, Matthews depicts post-revolutionary Cuba as the antithesis of a democracy:

> What we have not seen in Cuba is progress toward democracy on the political side. Quite the contrary is true. The regime is a dictatorship, without freedom, under the control of one man. Law is an arbitrary concept.[110]

From its very inception, it was clear that post-internal war Cuba would not move toward democracy. Not much has changed in Cuba almost 40 years later. Cuba's laws and institutions are not designed to protect basic civil and political rights. The political system does not allow its citizens an effective voice in policy determination.[111] Despite the introduction of "direct democracy," policy is routinely dictated from the top echelons.[112] The state does not tolerate dissent or any other kind of freedom of expression and/or association, nor has it since the inception of the post-revolutionary regime.[113]

At first the justifications for the lack of democratic freedoms and institutions ranged from the argument that it was not possible to make a revolution and hold elections at the same time to the notion that strong leadership was necessary to direct a drastic revolution like the one in Cuba.[114] Leaders emphasized that an institutional framework would limit the flexibility necessary to successfully alter society. Later, the Western conception of democracy was rejected outright, in favor of "direct democracy" and democratic centralism.[115] In this way, the development of the Cuban political system bears an odd resemblence to the path chosen years later in Iran.

As in Iran, regardless of the stated reasons, it was not in the interests of the Cuban elite to move toward democracy. With little to no opposition left on the island, the Cuban elites did not need to give up political rights to participation and contestation, and had little incentive to allow for accountability of the elites to the masses. What opposition did exist came from within the United States, and even that was manipulated to increase societal cohesion and further mobilize regime support.[116] When accommodation was occasionally employed, it was in the absence of the kind of large-scale repression used by Iran during its consolidation phase. The accommodative policies used by the Cuban elites, typically distributive policies, expanded the regime's support and placed its opponents on the defensive.[117]

In short, the regime was able to oust its opponents early in the postrevolutionary period through the effective use of repression, and then keep the rest of the populace satisfied with the occasional use of accommodation during the consolidation phase. No opposition existed that could present a viable alternative.[118] Therefore, Cuban elites had little reason to give up power and authority to the people. Instead, a centralized, personalistic, autocratic regime developed.[119]

Type III—Nicaragua. In July of 1979 a broad-based coalition led by the Sandinistas seized power in Nicaragua.[120] Realizing their potential vulnerability as first among many powerful but disorganized interests within the coalition, the Sandinistas shied away from repressing key groups, particularly the more conservative middle class. Instead, they chose to employ more inclusive policies of accommodation to maintain their hold on power.[121] In doing so, the Sandinistas attempted to maintain rather than reduce the revolutionary coalition. Consequently, they were faced with strong domestic opposition groups with escalating demands.[122] While occasionally employing repressive measures, the regime was forced to continue the costly policy of accommodation throughout their tenure.

The ruling directorate of the Sandinista National Liberation Front (FSLN) had begun its rule with the idea of holding off democratic institutionalization until its power was firmly consolidated.[123] Indeed, they did not seriously consider holding elections in the early 1980s.[124] Even then there was serious concern that elections would send the revolution down a path toward "a sort of directionless populism (à la Mexico in the 1920s and 1930s and Bolivia in the 1950s)."[125] However, the dual pressures of strong domestic opposition groups and powerful "external" enemies (including the Contras and their patrons, the United States government) forced the Sandinistas to liberalize further.[126] Massive literacy and voter registration drives were undertaken.[127] The Sandinistas instigated the development of numerous grassroots level mass organizations in an effort to create a democratic civil society.[128] A new constitution was issued, allowing for more regional autonomy on the Atlantic Coast.[129] Opposition parties were given more freedom to campaign and criticize freely.[130] First the Council of State, and then later the National Assembly became more representative of the population, and a place where opposition politics, rather than factional politics, could be practiced.[131] And, over the objections of a significant portion of the ruling FSLN directorate's objections, the first nationwide election was called for June of 1984.[132]

Despite U.S. propaganda to the contrary, popular participation was high and professional observers judged the 1984 elections as conforming to democratic standards.[133] As expected, the Sandinistas won by a large majority.[134] Despite the boycotting of the elections by the main opposition party, non-Sandinista parties won approximately 33 percent of the votes.[135]

However, the political landscape of the mid-1980's featured significant autocratic elements despite these liberalizing efforts. The United States-sponsored Contra War contributed to some of the most egregious violations of the principles of democracy during the rule of the Sandinistas. Relations between the FSLN and their opposition became increasingly hostile.[136] The regime frequently declared states of emergency that officially banned certain types of assembly, including labor strikes.[137] Press censorship restricted freedom of speech.[138] And the mishandling of the situation in the Atlantic Coast resulted in bloody conflict between the regime and Nicaragua's indigenous peoples.[139]

Democracy developed in Nicaragua despite the external and internal pressures of the war. While the FSLN's tolerance of the opposition declined as the war intensified, their use of repression to deal with the opposition did not significantly increase (see Table 5.6 in Chapter 5). The signing of the 1987 Esquipulas Accords as part of the process ending the Contra War provided external validation—Nicaragua's neighbors were willing to recognize the institutionalization of the revolution.[140] The Sandinistas even amended the electoral laws to benefit the opposition.[141] And while the war had eroded some of the democratic progress that had been achieved, democracy in principle and in practice was reaffirmed in 1990 with the end of the war, the election of the UNO coalition, and the honoring of the election results by the FSLN.[142] The UNO further legitimized the political system during its tenure in office by leaving intact most of the political changes resulting from the revolution.[143]

While not a fully consolidated democracy by 1991 (the last year examined in this study), post-revolutionary Nicaragua exhibited the procedural minimum necessary to be considered, at the very least, a broadly legitimate pluralist protodemocracy.[144] It should be noted that Nicaragua from 1984 to 1990 was far more democratic than any other Central American country with the exception of Costa Rica.[145] Nevertheless, questions remained regarding the commitments of both the Sandinistas and the former Contras to democratic consolidation.[146]

The development of a loose political alliance between the UNO and the Sandinistas,[147] the split within the FSLN,[148] and the 1996 election of Arnoldo Aleman and his Liberal Constitutionalist Party (PLC) put these fears to rest for the most part.[149] The 1996 election was the third free and fair nationwide election in only 17 years since the revolution.[150] Given the criteria set forth by scholars of democratic transitions, with two successful turnovers in power and the development of a new, more democratic, political culture, Nicaragua has become a successful case of democratic consolidation.[151]

In sum, in order to insure their security, the Sandinistas accommodated their opposition rather than repress and oust them. As accommodation spiraled out of their control, the opposition grew stronger. The combination of internal and external pressures finally resulted in an institutionalized opposition, greater political freedoms, regular free and fair elections, and eventually a consolidated democracy.

Type IV—Bolivia. The revolution ended quickly, and the National Revolutionary Movement (MNR), which had led the opposition, assumed control.[152] The MNR saw itself as immensely popular but fundamentally insecure. The elites' first moves were cautious, emphasizing their legitimacy based in the past rather than in revolutionary plans to fundamentally change the Bolivian state.[153] The MNR elites had hoped to hold power alone, but knew they needed a firmer basis of legitimacy and needed to rein in the well-armed and more radical workers and peasants. Unable to repress for fear that their allies would turn on them, the MNR elite began to accommodate their opposition.

Labor unions gained the most in terms of power and access, winning both shop-floor power and *co-gobierno* (co-rule), or corporate status in government.[154] *Co-gobierno* meant that the newly created COB, a worker's party and union, had veto power over policy decisions, possessed cabinet seats, the vice presidency and many ministries, and shared in the management of the newly nationalized tin industry, under the auspices of a national mining company, COMIBOL.[155] In granting the COB power and access to resources, and by recognizing the COB as the voice of the left, the MNR in effect granted the union both semi-sovereign status over the workers of Bolivia and institutionalized opposition to the regime.[156] *Co-gobierno* also prevented the MNR from being able to structure the nature of political, social, and economic interactions unilaterally.[157]

The MNR knew that how they dealt with labor would be critical to their political success.[158] The strength and power of the COB made the MNR uneasy, and led to further accommodation in hopes of assuaging the powerful union.[159] It also led to the simultaneous accommodation of a rival, more conservative, mass group—the peasants.[160] The leaders of the MNR thought they could contain liberalization by playing one group off of the other.[161]

Some democratization began immediately following the 1952 revolution. On June 21, 1952 the MNR decreed universal suffrage, including a large illiterate portion of the peasant population.[162] The measure expanded suffrage from 200,000 to almost one million.[163] Peasant political participation of all kinds saw an enormous increase.[164] Peasants also gained a cabinet post, as well as a new local bureaucratic structure linking them for the first time to the government. But often the peasants were not satisfied with their gains, and went beyond the lines drawn by the elite. For example, the peasants seized land in a near-spontaneous uprising against former landlords, very much against the wishes of the elites.[165] The MNR's right-wing faction demanded the suppression by force of the land seizures.[166] Unwilling to anger the well-armed and numerous peasant masses, the MNR declared sweeping land reform, despite the fact that it merely ratified a *fait accompli*.[167]

Another element of elite insecurity, the fear of the army that had propped up the old regime, was confirmed within the first year of the post-revolutionary period, after a failed coup attempt.[168] The attempt, a response by the far-right faction of the MNR to the party's handling of the peasant land seizures and the demands of the workers, made the ruling elites even more insecure than before, and wary of the army in particular. In response, the elites disbanded the armed forces, purged the far right from the party leadership, and increased their accommodation of workers and peasants even further.[169] The government could not protect itself, and decided that relying instead on popular militias in return for access to power and resources was a way to enhance their security.[170] In this way, heightened elite perceptions of insecurity led to a strengthened left.[171]

The unions and peasants, powerless before the revolution, now had political clout. And each group (and many others) had competing claims on the government. They were soon joined by right-wing factions of the MNR, which split from the main revolutionary party.[172] Parties like the Bolivian Falangist Party (FSB), a Catholic party with fascist leanings, opposed the MNR via conventional and unconventional participation.[173]

The proliferation of these parties and factions made it impossible for the MNR to rule without consulting other sectors of society. Regular elections were held in four year increments for national elections and two-year increments on the local level. Two peaceable transfers of the presidency from one person to another (albeit within the same party) occurred in the MNR's 12 1/2-year rule.[174] Competition in these elections was, for the most part, free and fair.[175] Institutions were established that could better channel political participation in the rural areas.[176] Most press and speech freedoms were respected.[177] In short, the political landscape in post-revolutionary Bolivia was pluralistic, competitive, and in many ways very democratic.

Indeed, Rueschemeyer, Stephens, and Stephens consider the post-revolutionary period in Bolivia (1952–64) to be one of unqualified democratic rule.[178] And as Alexander points out, the 12 1/2-years of the post-revolutionary regime was the longest period of stable civilian government in Bolivia since the early 1900's. Nevertheless, it should be noted that the MNR never intended to establish a pluralist competitive system. In fact, it preferred the model, as illustrated by the PRI in Mexico, of single-party control operating behind a facade of democratic institutions.[179] But their perceptions of their own position vis-à-vis other groups immediately following the end of the internal war led the elites to accommodate heavily in the first few years. As Malloy notes:

> From 1952 to 1959 the MNR core elite was seldom in control of the events taking place around it. Having lost the ability to use force, the party's center had to rely on demand satisfaction in its desperate struggle to hold the various sectors of the society at least nominally in its orbit.[180]

Thus the elites, in order to insure their security, traded away political rights and access to power and resources on which they would have otherwise preferred to hold a monopoly. The end result was an institutionalized opposition, greater political freedoms, regular free and fair elections, decentralized power, and a fairly healthy protodemocracy.[181]

Conclusion

As expected, states that could not repress early in the post-revolutionary period found themselves having to deal with a significant opposition. In response, elites continued to accommodate, trading valuable rights and privileges in hopes of gaining security. Both Nicaragua and Bolivia began to develop a democratic system in this fashion despite significant opposition within each ruling party to democratization.[182] Each engaged in free and fair elections between multiple parties and had a tolerated opposition. Nicaragua went further, experiencing two peaceful turnovers in government by 1996, thereby becoming a consolidated democracy.

On the other hand, Iran and Cuba developed into autocratic states. The ability of the elites to use repression during the coalition-reduction process enabled them to oust their opposition early in the post-revolutionary period. Without significant opposition pressuring them to liberalize the political system, secure elites have little incentive to give away rights and privileges.

War had an effect on the development of the political system, but not uniform effect across both cases. In Iran, war helped the regime consolidate its power. Even long-term increases in opposition resulting from war's effects on policy mix choices were ineffective once the elites had been able to institutionalize and consolidate the revolution. Alternatively, war made the Nicaraguan elites push their liberalization plans up while simultaneously leading to rollback of some existing freedoms. In this way, war led eventually to the consolidation of an autocratic regime in Iran and a democratic turnover in government in Nicaragua.

War's mixed results show that while examinations of structure are important in the study of revolutionary outcomes, often an understanding of agency and process is vital. Elite policy mix *choices* at a particular moment in time help to determine the historical development of the political system. Thus, the possibility is always present for transition to democracy, even in nations that may not appear to be most hospitable to democracy (i.e., Nicaragua, Bolivia). However, certain elites close off these opportunities by repressing early in their tenure and ousting the opposition necessary for the development of a democracy. And without the pressures of a strong opposition, post-revolutionary elites are loathe to give up rights and resources.

These findings suggest that regime type is both the result of policy mix choices as well as a determinant of future elite choices. The post-revolutionary period is a critical juncture in the life of a state, precisely because the policies chosen during this phase will affect the type of political system set up. Future policies therefore depend on key choices made early in the life of the new state. As such, further study is warranted to better understand other factors that affect the development of the state.

One of these factors is whether the original revolutionary elites survive in the long term, beyond the post-revolutionary period under examination here. If they do not survive in power it is unlikely that their policies be carried out by their successors.[183] In short, the survival of the elites is yet another crucial outcome of elite policy mix choices. Therefore, I examine the determinants of elite survivability in the next chapter.

CHAPTER 8

Only the Good Die Young: Political Survival of Revolutionary Elites

"If a due participation of office is a matter of right, how are vacancies to be obtained? Those by death are few; by resignation, none."

—The Declaration of Independence (Thomas Jefferson, 1776)

"your kingdom is temporary and will be washed away"

(Daniel, 5:25)[1]

Political survival is the primary concern of politicians.[2] While political, economic, and social policy goals may be important to those in power, these ends cannot be achieved without the elites' ability to retain that power.[3] As Joel Migdal argues:

> No agenda is worth anything if its sponsor has not lasted through the hazards of politics. Political survival, the central issue occupying the attention of state leaders, is the prerequisite for achieving any significant long-term social change.[4]

In addition, survivability concerns affect which policies elites choose to employ. In a series of studies of elite succession in the Soviet Union, Eastern

Europe, India, and numerous advanced industrial democracies, Valerie Bunce's work shows that new leaders mean new policies, regardless of political system type.[5] If elites wish to see their preferred policies carried out they need to insure either their own personal survival or, at the very least, the survival of those with similar goals. This is particularly important in the aftermath of a revolution. Victorious elites have the opportunity to shape both the present and future political, economic, and social environment of the post-revolutionary state. But actions to insure continuation of their policies into the future are conditional upon political survival of those in favor of that agenda.

Survivability concerns are particularly felt in states where the old guard has been ousted. In such states, that ouster sets a precedent that elites can be removed from office, especially through violent means.[6] Elite survival in and of itself is often considered remarkable in post-revolutionary states, where institutions, norms, and power bases are either being fundamentally reshaped or created anew.[7] This is consistent with Henry Bienen and Nicholas Van de Walle's finding that unconstitutional entry into power substantially raises a leader's risk of being ousted early on in his/her tenure.[8] As some scholars have argued, contrary to the typical social scientific focus on change, "in an era of upheaval, it is continuity and stability that need explanation."[9]

Indeed, many sets of post-revolutionary elites lose their grip on the main seat of power within the first decade or so following the internal war. Some elites are thrown out by extra-constitutional means, as in the coups in Bolivia in 1964 and Grenada in 1983.[10] Others pave the way for their own removal from power, seen most clearly in the electoral defeats in the early 1990s of the Sandinistas in Nicaragua and Solidarity in Poland.[11] Conversely, many post-revolutionary states are dominated by the original victorious elites long after the internal war has concluded. Consider, for example, the long tenures of the revolutionary elites in the Soviet Union, China, Cuba, and Iran. Obviously some post-internal war elites survive well beyond the consolidation phase while others do not. What accounts for this set of divergent outcomes?

Below I demonstrate that elite political survival is a function of a historical sequence of events triggered by elite policy mix choices made early on in the life of the post-revolutionary regime. These choices, in turn, affect levels of opposition activity experienced in these states (Chapter 6), and the degree of democracy allowed to develop (Chapter 7). The sum of these factors determines the likelihood of the elites surviving (politically) beyond the consolidation phase of the post-revolutionary period.

Why Policy Mix Choices, Opposition Activity, and Regime Type Affect Elite Survivability

Leaders are strategic actors who generally seek to implement policies they expect will enhance their political survival, or alternatively will provide the most influence over their successors.[12] Additionally:

> leaders recognize the existence of opposition and the designs of others on the office they hold. They consequently select policies to minimize the opportunities available to those seeking to remove them from power.[13]

Indeed, studies have shown that political survival is dependent to a large degree on the strategic use of policy mix choices by elites.[14] Earlier (Chapter 6) I demonstrated that these choices affect levels of opposition faced subsequently by these leaders. And Andrew Enterline and Kristian Gleditsch note: "the position of executives can be considered reasonably secure as long as potential contenders lack the necessary support or control over the means to mount successful challenges to their position."[15] Political strategies employed by the elites to depoliticize society help to keep these same elites in power.[16]

Additionally, some political systems create more opportunities to oust political leaders than others. Elections, public opinion, and alternative institutions in pluralistic, democratic societies provide such opportunities.[17] Indeed, democracy by its very nature is government *pro tempore*.[18] Authoritarian political systems present few, if any, institutional opportunities to oust elites.[19] In sum, political system type tells us the degree to which the institutional windows of political opportunity are open to such changes. Thus, regime type should help explain elite survivability.

This logic is consistent with Henry Bienen and Nicholas Van de Walle's finding that, over time, risks of ouster decline at a greater rate for authoritarian leaders than for democratic leaders.[20] They suggest two possible explanations: first, authoritarian elites are able to overcome illegitimacy over time; second, authoritarian elites are able to wield their coercive power to effectively put down any opposition. Bienen and Van de Walle's first reason is not generally applicable to post-internal war cases. By virtue of their success in overthrowing the old regime and securing a leadership position at the beginning of the post-internal war period, these elites have some measure of legitimacy at the onset of their rule.[21] Therefore, when considering post-internal war cases, Bienen and Van de Walle's second explanation rings truer. Elites who can successfully wield repression and oust their opposition early on in the process will have a significantly lower risk of being ousted from power themselves. This is not surprising, given that political system type is a result of the elite policy mix choices made early in the life of the post-internal war state (see Chapter 7). Below I discuss, in greater detail, how the longevity of particular rulers is a direct result of both the use of repression and the type of political system set up.

How Policy Mix Choices, Opposition Activity, and Regime Type Affect Elite Survivability

Repression can prove to be the most effective of strategies employed by a regime to insure its survival.[22] Elites who continue to repress into the consolidation phase are able to hold back what little opposition might remain, and thus survive longer in power.[23] Historical evidence shows that elites can survive even when they impose heinous amounts of suffering on their peoples.[24] Examples of elites who repressed heavily in both phases and survived for great lengths of time afterwards include the Communist Party leaders in post-revolutionary Russia and China.

Those elites who employ repression in the coalition-reduction phase but do not need to repress in the consolidation phase create a situation in which the gradual easing of restrictions over time actually legitimizes their rule. Following Machiavelli, elites who repress early (and quickly) and then relax their grip throughout the state-building process should tend to be seen as more legitimate, and thus will not be quickly opposed:

> Whence it is to be noted that in taking a state, the occupier ought to reason out all those offenses that are necessary for him to do; and do them all at one stroke in order not to have to renew them daily. He is thus able, by not innovating them, to assure men and gain them to himself by benefiting them. Whoever does otherwise, either from timidity or bad counsel, is always necessitated to hold knife in hand; nor can he ever rely on his subjects, since they are unable, because of fresh and continuous injuries, to assure themselves of him. For all the injuries ought to be done all together, for being tasted less, they offend less. The benefits ought to be done little by little, so that they may be tasted better.[25]

Elites who use repression early on should be most likely to survive for a substantial period of time beyond the state-building phase.[26]

In addition, the successful use of repression early on leaves little opposition left to accommodate subsequently. In such situations, patterns of concessions and the give-and-take interactions necessary for pluralism to develop do not occur. Thus elites who are able to oust their opponents early on are then able to set up the "rules of the game" without having to consult the opposition.[27] In such cases, elite survival comes at the cost of potential civil and political rights for portions of society.[28]

However, those who cannot repress during the coalition-reduction phase must construct rules of the game that accommodate their opposition, thereby creating a system in which the elites can "lose." A more democratic system emerges due to the development over time of cooperation between elites and the masses (or groups), and the idea that out-groups can "win" (become "in-groups") in the current political environment.[29] But this very process leads to situations that make it more likely that the elites will not be able to survive in power for very long.[30]

Elections or other types of power transfers are likely to occur in environments in which repression early on was rare, leading to a healthy opposition, and the development of some of the key elements of democracy. A recent example is the reliance of the elites on accommodation in the immediate aftermath of the 1989 Polish Revolution. The system set up was a democratic one, in which the victorious elite, Solidarity, could (and indeed did) lose power.[31]

The inability to repress and thus rid themselves of their opposition early on forces elites to accommodate. By being inclusionary, elites are forced to allow participation at the national and local levels, weakening their grip on power. A recent example is South Africa, where despite the huge success of the African National Congress in 1994, some local regions were dominated by other parties with hostile and competing agendas. Furthermore, loss of autonomy leaves them open to the possibility of loss of power due to shifting alliances. For example, in post-revolutionary Bolivia the necessity of "co-government" and alliance-shifting between the elites and worker and peasant militias led to the 1964 coup.[32]

It appears that the ability to use repression in the coalition-reduction phase, the effects of this policy choice on opposition activity, and the subsequent development of the type of political system, affect elite political survival. Therefore I hypothesize:

H 8.1: If, in the aftermath of an internal war, the victorious elites are able to use repression during the coalition-reduction phase, then they will survive longer than elites who use less repression in the coalition-reduction phase.

The hypothesized effects can be seen in Figure 8.1. In Type I and Type II cases elites can and do repress early in the life of the post-internal war state. This enables them to oust their opposition early on, making accommodation less likely. Because elites have little need to accommodate, they

Figure 8.1 Historical Process Model of the Causes and Consequences of Repression and Accommodation in Post-Revolutionary States

	Coalition-Reduction Phase (first 2–3 years)		Consolidation Phase (8–10 years)		Long-Run Outcomes	
Case Type	Historical Process Model for Post-Internal War States		Effect of Earlier Policy Choice	War's Effect on Policy Mix	Level of Democracy	Probability of Elite Survival
Iran (Type I)	Elites perceive themselves to be secure	→ Ability to use repression → No sustained opposition	Less ACC	Increase in REP	Low	High
Cuba (Type II)	Elites perceive themselves to be secure	→ Ability to use repression → No sustained opposition	Less ACC	No war, therefore no effect	Low	High
Nicaragua (Type III)	Elites perceive themselves to be vulnerable	→ Inability to use repression → Significant opposition remains	More ACC	Increase in REP	High	Low
Bolivia (Type IV)	Elites perceive themselves to be vulnerable	→ Inability to use repression → Significant opposition remains	More ACC	No war, therefore no effect	High	Low

Note: ACC = Accommodation; REP = Repression

do not develop patterns of concessions and the give-and-take interactions necessary for pluralism to develop. They therefore do not need to subject themselves periodically to elections that threaten their political survival. In addition, because elites have successfully routed the opposition they will survive well beyond the first years of the post–internal war state-building process. With no institutional mechanism of elite accountability and no opposition strong enough to oust them, elites can remain in power indefinitely.

Alternatively, Type III and Type IV cases feature elites who feel they cannot or do not repress during the coalition-reduction phase. As a result, opposition remains, and the elites choose to accommodate it. Continual accommodation leads to the acquisition by the masses of greater political rights. A pluralistic system emerges due to the development over time of cooperation between elites and the masses (or groups), and the idea that outgroups can "win" (become ingroups) in the current political environment. But this very process leads to situations that make it more likely that the elites will not be able to survive in power for very long.

Does War Directly Affect Elite Political Survivability?

In previous chapters I have shown that war affects perceptions, policy mix choices, and opposition activity. As such, war should have an indirect effect on elite survivability via these variables. However, the question remains as to whether war *directly* impacts the survival of the elites.

Elite survival may depend to a large degree on the interaction of intense international pressures with domestic concerns. As Bruce Bueno de Mesquita and Randolph Siverson write: "The desire to remain in power . . . provides the linchpin between the threats and uncertainties of the international system and the inevitable imperatives of fending off the domestic opposition."[33] Specifically, recent studies have shown that war involvement directly impacts survivability.

Bueno de Mesquita, Siverson, and Gary Woller find that war participation nearly doubles the chances of violent overthrow of a regime by its domestic opponents.[34] In addition, they find that this propensity is aggravated further by instability in the prewar regime as a result of violent regime changes. Therefore one might expect that survivability should be very difficult in states that have experienced violent regime change (i.e., revolution, civil war, coup) followed soon after by a war. If so, one might hypothesize:

H 8.2: In the aftermath of an internal war, if a state is involved in another war, then its elites will not survive as long as elites in a state that has not experienced such a war.

However, this assumes the presence of an effective opposition. An underlying process may be at work, which acts to remove that opposition. In other words, in regimes that participate in another war following the internal war, if the opposition can be uprooted early on, then the elites may still be able to hold onto power. Because elites who perceive themselves to be secure can and do use repression early on to oust their opposition, I expect that these elites will survive in the long run, regardless of whether or not they have experienced another war.

Remember that earlier (Chapter 6) I found that the Contra War decreased levels of opposition both directly and indirectly in Nicaragua. This does not mean, however, that opposition disappeared altogether. Indeed, the graphical depictions of opposition activity (Figures 6.1 through 6.3) show that opposition activity rose significantly following the end of the conflict. Thus, despite the short-run effects of war on opposition, the timing of the use of repression may best explain long-term opposition, and therefore elite survivability. An examination of the Iranian case yields a similar conclusion. The Iran-Iraq War directly decreased opposition activity in the short run, but led to an increase in opposition in the long run. However, due to the initial use of repression by the regime, the overall levels of opposition were small. Therefore, the timing of repression should have a greater effect on elite survival than should war involvement.

Additionally, regime type plays a role in conditioning any effect that war might have on elite political survival. Andrew Enterline and Kristian Gleditsch examine the effect of domestic and interstate conditions on leadership tenure in Latin America from 1946 to 1992.[35] They find that the use of force abroad by institutionally constrained regimes has a negative effect on elite political survival. In other words, even given war involvement, political system type appears to have an effect on elite survivability. And since political system type, like levels of opposition, is a function of elite policy mix choices, I expect that any effect of war on survivability will be at the very least conditioned by (if not totally overshadowed by) the effect of these choices. Therefore I assume that Hypothesis 8.2 is a null hypothesis, and hypothesize alternatively:[36]

H 8.3: In the aftermath of an internal war, if a state whose elites were able to use repression during the coalition-reduction phase experiences another war, then its elites will survive longer than elites who used less repression in the coalition- reduction phase and subsequently experienced another war.

In sum, I expect that the timing of elite policy choices, and the effects these choices have on opposition activity and regime type, is the key to explaining why certain elites survive in the long run while others do not. Below I test these hypotheses by examining the survival of the elites, and the historical reasons for the length of their tenure. In order to do so effectively, I must first define the dependent variable: elite survivability.

Operationalization: Elite Survivability

I code elite survivability as a dichotomous variable, with "1" for elites who survive in the long run and "0" for elites who do not survive beyond the consolidation phase. Survivability is evaluated based on the length of continuous tenure by the elites who were victorious in the revolution and the coalition-reduction process. These are coded by using historical accounts to determine length of tenure. Survivability is not determined by the tenure or lifespan of a particular leader (i.e., Ayatollah Khomeini, Fidel Castro, Daniel Ortega, or Victor Paz Estenssoro). Rather, I consider elite survival as the hold on power by a particular *group* of elites that came to power immediately following the revolution. For example, the revolutionary elites retained power in the Soviet Union until 1989, despite the fact that Lenin died in 1924. Alternatively, while the Communist Party elites in Poland engaged in the political system after 1991, they did not retain a hold on the center of political power after the first election. The fact that they regained that power position in the second post-transition election shows not survival but resiliency.

A Preliminary Test

As a preliminary test of the hypotheses, I mapped out the variable patterns for each case using truth tables.[37] Table 8.1 indicates that war is neither necessary nor sufficient for elite ouster. Elites survive long-term in both the presence (Iran) and absence (Cuba) of war. Elites are also ousted in both the presence (Nicaragua) and absence (Bolivia) of war. In short, while war may or may not have an impact, it definitely does not alone determine survivability, nor does it have *the same* impact on the long-term survival of elites in all post-revolutionary states.

However, as expected, the pattern exhibited by Types I (Iran) and II (Cuba) states—elite perceptions of security, their use of repression during the coalition-reduction phase, the subsequent reduction in opposition activity

Table 8.1 Truth Table of Factors Affecting Elite Survivability in Post–Internal War States

	Independent Variables						Dependent Variable
Cases	Elite Perceptions of Security	Repression in Coalition-Reduction Phase	Subsequent Levels of Accommodation	Opposition Activity Levels	Political System (Regime) Type	War Participation (Post-Revolution)	Elite Survival Beyond Post–Internal War Period
Iran	1	1	0	0	0	1	1
Cuba	1	1	0	0	0	0	1
Nicaragua	0	0	1	1	1	1	0
Bolivia	0	0	1	1	1	0	0

Notes:

Key Independent Variables

Elite Perceptions of Security: 1 = Secure; 0 = Vulnerable

Repression During the Coalition-Reduction Phase: 1 = High; 0 = Low

Subsequent Levels of Accommodation: 1 = High; 0 = Low

Opposition Activity Levels: 1 = High; 0 = Low

Political System (Regime) Type: 1 = Proto-Democratic; 0 = Non-Democratic

War Participation (Post-Revolution): 1 = War; 0 = No War

Dependent Variable

Elite Survival Beyond the Post–Internal War Period: 1 = Yes; 0 = No

and therefore in need to employ accommodation, and the development of an authoritarian political system—is associated with elites who survive beyond the post-internal war period. Additionally, the opposite pattern, associated with Types III (Nicaragua) and IV (Bolivia) states—elite perceptions of vulnerability, the inability or reluctance to use repression during the coalition-reduction phase, the presence of opposition activity and the use of accommodation to deal with it, and the development of a protodemocratic political system—is associated with elites who do not survive beyond the post-revolutionary period. Truth tables confirm that these relationships may exist. A more detailed analysis of the historical interactions of these variables reveals why.

Mapping the Historical Processes

Below I examine the historical record of each of the four cases to determine the degree to which the elites in each state survive beyond the post-revolutionary period. In the process, I elaborate upon the way in which the elite perceptions, policy mix choice and timing, opposition activity levels, regime type development, and war participation (when applicable) affected elite survivability.

Type I—Iran. The ability of the Iranian revolutionary elites to employ repression early in the post-revolutionary era was crucial in insuring their survival.[38] Once the opposition was ousted there were few if any domestic groups with the power or resources to challenge the regime.[39] Additionally, participation in the Iran-Iraq War allowed the regime to further deal with potential opposition in two ways: first, it created a short-term rally-round-the-flag effect that mobilized supporters against an external threat and its internal allies;[40] second, it enabled the regime to institutionalize the use of force domestically in dealing with the remaining dissenters. Even after the devastating war was over there were few groups willing or able to challenge the regime. In short, "opposition forces are fragmented, disorganized, leaderless, and ineffectual, while the leadership of the Iranian regime has up to now been highly committed and repressive."[41]

The political system set up in post-revolutionary Iran also played a major role in insuring the survival of the elites. The autocratic style of rule closed off most institutional avenues for ouster of the elites. Even when elections were held, either for the *majlis* or for nationwide office, the candidate choices were typically limited to members of factions of the ruling elite, rather than true opposition parties.[42] Final authority rested in the hands of the clerics, and this ensured the defeat of all alternatives to the revolution.[43] Yet, while the new Iranian regime was autocratic, it was more widely legitimate than the Shah's regime.[44] Popular legitimacy without accountability may have also contributed to the survival of the Iranian elites in power.[45] This was also the case in the Cuban post-revolutionary state (see below).

Finally, Khomeini's insistence on the centralization of power at the top coupled with collective clerical leadership insured that the elites would survive and thrive despite the removal of key individuals.[46] Therefore the elites continued to hold power despite a massive and generally successful assassination campaign waged against them by the Mujahedin–e Khalq in 1981.[47] Additionally, succession, which had been a worrisome issue for the regime from the early to mid-1980s, was dealt with smoothly and successfully following the death of Khomeini in 1989.[48] Old elites such as Ali Khameini and Hashemi Rafsanjani continued to wield power, although from different positions, following the death of the revolutionary leader.[49]

Factional politics continues to this day in Iran.[50] However, the Islamic clerics as a group remain in power nearly 20 years after the revolution ended.[51] The recent election of Mohammed Khatami may signal popular preferences for moderation in policy, but does not foreshadow a coming ouster of the clerics from power. The nature of the Iranian regime and the severe weakness of the opposition forces make that outcome unlikely in the near future.[52]

Type II—Cuba.   Fidel Castro and his inner circle have been remarkably resilient. They still dominate Cuban politics almost 40 years after their revolutionary victory.[53] They have even outlasted the leaders of the opposition-in-exile.[54] What explains the remarkable survival of the Cuban revolutionary elites, despite decades of international pressures, economic crises, and the collapse of Communism in Eastern Europe?[55] Well-timed elite policy mix choices and their effects on both opposition activity and the development of the political system enabled Castro and his surrounding clique to survive well beyond the post-internal war period. As in Iran, popular legitimacy, combined with a lack of accountability, helps explain the survival of the Cuban elite to this day.

The Cuban revolutionary elites saw themselves as secure at the outset of their regime. This enabled them to repress early. Their effective reduction of the revolutionary coalition left Cuba bereft of an organized opposition domestically.[56] Despite an opposition-in-exile, they have not been successful in generating sufficient domestic dissatisfaction with the regime.[57] Furthermore, the regime's shrewd use of a few accommodative policies to expand their domestic support has placed its opponents even further on the defensive.[58] Given these conditions, extralegal ouster from power was unlikely.

Additionally, no institutional mechanisms existed in the Cuban political system to hold elites accountable and enable the masses to oust them through legal means.[59] The successful use of repression and accommodation resulted in little in the way of domestic opposition. Therefore there was little reason to engage in democratic reforms. Instead Cuba developed an authoritarian state. The abandonment of democratic institutions in favor of centralized, personalistic autocracy does not allow for institutionalized windows of political opportunity. In short, while the shrewd use of policy mix choices decreased the *willingness* of the masses to oust their leaders, the type of political system that developed in Cuba decreased the *opportunities* that any potential opposition might have had to attempt to oust the elite. The result is a cadre of revolutionary elites who survived well beyond the post-revolutionary period.

Type III—Nicaragua. In a sense, the Nicaraguan post-revolutionary elites were responsible for their own ouster in the 1990 elections. The Sandinistas lost power because they created a type of political system where they could lose power.[60] By relying too heavily early in their tenure on accommodation rather than repression the FSLN allowed domestic opposition groups to survive and thrive.[61] This led to the need for further accommodation. Once the Contra War was underway the elites feared driving alienated groups into the Contra camp. But accommodation eventually led to increases in domestic opposition activity and demands (Table 6.3 in Chapter 6), further escalating liberalization.[62]

The most accommodating steps involved increasing the pace and scope of democratization, which led to the development of a system with institutional opportunities to oust the elite.[63] Elections were then undertaken by the Sandinistas as a tactic for maintaining both internal and international support, and for institutionalizing the revolution.[64] But given the opportunity, Nicaraguan voters cast their ballots for an end to the devastating political and economic crises associated with the Contra War.[65]

The economic, social, and human costs of the Contra War had eroded support for the government.[66] The political concessions made in the Esquipulas pact to end the war proved to be difficult for the FSLN to bear as well. The pact was an informal recognition that the Contras were a legitimate part of the opposition, and led to both U.S. and Contra influence in the 1990 election.[67] To facilitate a quicker end to the war the FSLN moved the elections forward from November to February 1990. At least one member of the elite now feels that this action cost the FSLN the election.[68] Finally, many Nicaraguans voted for the UNO coalition because they thought it was the only way to guarantee an end to U.S. military and economic aggression.[69] Thus the Contra War acted first to roll back democracy during the conflict, and second to spur on turnover in government after the war. Elite turnover led to greater democratization, but lesser involvement by those who began the process. The calculation that it was better to affect change as an opposition party than to be completely removed from the arena insured the ability of the Sandinistas to contest future elections, and to one day regain power via legitimate venues.[70]

The FSLN allowed a viable alternative to develop by accommodating the opposition at a critical juncture. This led to further elite insecurity, as healthy opposition groups with the potential to aid the Contras became a greater threat. Insecurity led to even more accommodation, and a quicker pace of liberalization than had been planned by the elites.[71] By creating a political system in which they could lose power, the Sandinistas provided an institutional window of political opportunity. An opposition that was allowed to survive and thrive defeated a revolutionary party weakened economically and politically by war and over-accommodation. While not expected by either experts or participants, hindsight makes it clear that the defeat of the Sandinistas in the 1990 election was inevitable.[72] What is remarkable is that the FSLN abided by the popular decision and became the opposition party in a revolutionary state of their own making.[73]

Type IV—Bolivia. When the National Revolutionary Movement (MNR) took power they faced a situation in which numerous powerful actors were demanding more resources and greater access. The MNR was unable to employ repression effectively to remove this potential opposition. Instead, they relied upon accommodation to deal with mounting pressures and demands, particularly from peasants and workers.[74] But this accommodation led to some groups gaining too much power, particularly in their ability to veto or frustrate MNR policy. The MNR had created a pluralistic, protodemocratic system, but had also sewn the seeds for their eventual ouster from power.

After the coalition-reduction process had concluded, group demands began to conflict. While the workers pushed for greater change, the peasants were a more conservative force.[75] Paz Estensorro and the other MNR elites understood this, and began to play one side off the other.[76]

The strategy worked in the short run—the cleavage between peasants and the working class widened, and each competed with the other, rather than with the MNR.[77] However, in the long run swings in loyalty and changing domestic alliances contributed to the fall of the revolutionary government.[78]

Another key factor in the change of fortunes for the MNR was the resurrection of the armed forces. As the MNR continued to pit the workers against the peasants, their alliances with these societal groups withered. The left became increasingly marginalized.[79] The peasants began to regard local strongmen, rather than the central government, as the most legitimate authority in Bolivia.[80] Popular support eroded, partly because of these machinations,[81] and partly because of a strict stabilization plan employed by the regime.[82] No group remained but the military to sustain the MNR in power.[83]

The military had been officially dissolved within the first year of MNR rule.[84] However, elites continued to feel insecure about having to rely on worker and peasant militias for defense.[85] They lacked the desire to repress, but felt it necessary to at least have the wherewithal to do so. The elites soon attempted to recreate the armed forces in the image of a revolutionary army, one which would be subordinate to the revolutionary party, as in Mexico.[86] But the reestablishment of the armed forces proved to be one of the MNR's fatal mistakes.[87] As factional conflict tore the party apart, and demands of the workers and peasants increased, the MNR was overwhelmed, and their ability to hold the country together waned. The army saw little choice but to step in and restore order, particularly in peasant strongman-controlled areas like the Cochabamba Valley.[88]

The MNR had grown reliant on the military, but the military had grown tired of the MNR's mismanagement and political machinations.[89] The final straw came when Paz Estensorro manipulated the MNR party convention to renominate himself as a candidate for the presidency, as well as to alienate both left- and right-wing factions of the party.[90] Even the inclusion on the 1964 MNR ticket of vice presidential candidate General Barrientos did not forestall a military coup—engineered by Barrientos and General Ovando—soon after the elections.[91]

In sum, the weakness of an MNR government that could not consolidate its power effectively was its eventual downfall. The MNR felt vulnerable to ouster by strong worker and peasant groups, and accommodated them excessively. In doing so, they democratized the political system, weakening their own position. This fed their insecurity, leading to the politics of factional manipulation and the reinstatement of the armed forces.

Increasing infighting and pressures from multiple societal groups made the fall of the MNR inevitable.

Conclusion

As expected, political elites in Bolivia and Nicaragua did not survive beyond the post-revolutionary period. These elites felt vulnerable, avoided repression early, and over-accommodated throughout their tenure. This created an entrenched opposition that had to be dealt with throughout the post-revolutionary period. The elites liberalized their political systems in an attempt to deal with their opposition. By generating institutional opportunities for ouster and/or willingness on the part of the opposition to remove the elites, these post-revolutionary leaders effectively dug their own political graves.

Conversely, revolutionary elites survive, even to this day, in both Cuba and Iran. These leaders saw themselves as secure, and were therefore more willing to employ repression to reduce the post-revolutionary coalition. With few, if any, opposition groups left to challenge the regime during the consolidation phase, there was little need to trade away rights and privileges. As such, the early ouster of their opposition created a clear path down which these elites could travel throughout the post-revolutionary period and beyond.

War, however, does not have uniform effects on survival. In Iran, war helped the regime consolidate its power early. Even long-term increases in opposition resulting from war's effects on policy mix choices (see Figure 6.5 in Chapter 6) were ineffective once the elites had been able to institutionalize and consolidate the revolution, and remain in power longer. Alternatively, war made the Nicaraguan elites push their liberalization plans up while simultaneously leading to a degree of rollback in existing freedoms. War also negated many of the gains of the revolution, making it difficult for the Sandinistas to point to successes when campaigning. The result was an antagonized opposition in a stronger position than they had been before, making it nearly impossible for the Sandinistas to successfully survive the crucible of a post-conflict election. In sum, war had a large effect on elite survival in both cases, but did not have the *same* effect. Perhaps the nature of the regime is the intervening variable here. We know that democratic elites do not fare well in elections following losses in wars, while non-democratic elites do not have to subject themselves to such electoral contests.[92] Future research may consider examining the interrelationship between these variables more closely.

In many ways the findings in this chapter are not all that surprising. It is clear that leaders in non-electoral regimes have lower risks of ouster than those in electoral ones.[93] But how these regimes came to be is often overlooked as the reason behind this relationship. Cuban and Iranian elites survived because they wiped out their opposition early, and were therefore able to institute an autocratic regime. Nicaraguan and Bolivian elites failed to survive, as much because of their policy mix choices as because of the institutional windows of opportunity that they created.

The implications of these findings go beyond the immediate post-revolutionary period. For instance, Guy Whitten and Henry Bienen recently found that surviving in power longer lowers the chance of violence from below, but has no effect on violence from above. Thus "the longer a leader has been in power, the lower the probability that there will be any large scale political violence that the leader does not control."[94] Additionally, Bienen and Van de Walle find that length of time in office leads to further survival of leaders.[95]

The longer the elites are able to hold power, the less opposition they face, and therefore the longer they continue to survive in power subsequently. As such, both governance and survivability should be easier for a Fidel Castro or an Ali Khameini now because these elites have been in power for many years. Additionally, the decrease in opposition also suggests that these elites will have little internal incentive to liberalize the political systems that keep them in power. This is consistent with Bienen and Van de Walle's finding that the chance of constitutional ouster of elites decreases as time progresses. In short, "[p]ower begets power; it is hard to remove entrenched leaders, and they rarely remove themselves."[96]

The first years after the revolution appear to be crucial to elite survivability. Elites who survive beyond the post-revolutionary period do so by repressing their opposition early. An insignificant opposition decreases chances of extra-constitutional removal from power. Additionally, these same elites develop authoritarian political systems, which add to their chance of continued survival. An authoritarian system eliminates institutional avenues for ouster. As such, it appears likely that, barring death or external intervention, the Cuban and Iranian elites will continue to inhabit their respective centers of power for years to come.[97]

PART IV

Conclusion

CHAPTER 9

What Is To Be Done?: Concluding Thoughts on Political Dynamics in Post-Internal War States

When this project began back in 1995, the Dayton Accords had not yet been signed. The genocide and civil war in Rwanda was but a year in the past, as was the revolutionary uprising in Chiapas, Mexico. The revolution in what was then called Zaire was two years away, although rumblings could be heard from the small but externally supported opposition.[1] Chechnya had just become a part of the global consciousness, and the Taliban had yet to solidify their hold on power in Kabul in the ongoing conflict within Afghanistan.[2] At that time, it seemed more important to both scholars and policymakers to understand how these conflicts originated and might be resolved, rather than what their aftermath might yield. Indeed, the literature of the day turned increasingly to the study of the origins of ethnic conflict,[3] nationalism,[4] genocide,[5] and internal wars,[6] and how these conflicts might be resolved.[7]

Yet with hindsight one can see why ignoring the dynamics of the post-internal war period was not a wise strategy.[8]

Peacekeeping in internal conflicts became more frequent following the end of the Cold War.[9] With this new global initiative came the need to deal with the problems of the post-internal war environment. Yet scholars and policymakers knew little about the outcomes of internal wars, and were thus ill-equipped to deal with what followed. Despite policymakers' deep interest in both peacekeeping and post-internal war state building,[10] the disastrous involvement in Somalia showed that the international participants did not understand the implications of the job.[11] A year later, the U.S. administration promised a quick pullout from Bosnia, despite the obvious need to remain longer. The demands and perils of state building, as much as those of peacekeeping, keep them there as of this writing.[12]

Perhaps more pertinent to the cases examined in this study is the situation in the post-revolutionary Democratic Republic of Congo, formerly Zaire.[13] Recent evidence of mass killings of Hutu refugees from the Rwandan conflict by the new government of Laurent Kabila testifies to the persistence of political violence in this post-internal war state.[14] The new regime has repressed at a level that reminds some of the neo-patrimonial Mobutu regime it replaced.[15] Opposition is not tolerated, and promised democratic reforms have been delayed repeatedly, probably shelved for good.[16] A secure Kabila has even openly mocked one of its original supporters, the United States, during Secretary of State Madeline Albright's attempt to smooth over relations with the new regime.[17] The Democratic Republic of Congo appears headed down the path traveled by Iran and Cuba, not to mention the Soviet Union, China, Cambodia, and numerous other repressive post-revolutionary regimes in the past century. Unfortunately, as this study indicates, much of the future path of a state such as the former Zaire can be gleaned from an understanding of the political dynamics of the coalition-reduction phase.

Implications of This Study's Findings

The Coalition-Reduction Phase as a Critical Period

This study suggests that the first years after a revolution are crucial to the future of the post-revolutionary state. Table 9.1 and Figure 9.1 depict these historical processes and their outcomes. Secure elites survive beyond the post-revolutionary period because they repress their opposition during the coalition-reduction phase. They are able to cripple or oust dissenters, which decreases chances of extra-constitutional removal from power. Additionally, these same elites develop authoritarian political systems, which add to their chance of continued survival by decreasing institutional avenues for ouster.

These results echo earlier work, which suggests that internal wars and their consequences are significant factors in accounting for subsequent repression and human rights violations up to and including state-sponsored mass murder.[18] These results may also explain why some have attributed this tendency towards severe repression to regime type.[19] Indeed, political systems develop because of the use of particular policy mix choices. However, ultimately, in post-revolutionary states decisions to repress and political system type derive from the same factors—elite perceptions of their own vulnerability and subsequent war participation. As such, not all internal wars lead to the development of repressive states. Indeed, some post-revolutionary elites, unable or unwilling to employ repression, develop a decidedly more accommodating repertoire of policy mix choices.

Elites that feel vulnerable following the end of the revolution cannot employ repression as freely. Because they accommodate dissenters during the coalition-reduction period, these elites subsequently find themselves having to deal with a significant opposition. The elites over-accommodate in hopes that they can curb or satisfy opposition demands. But this creates an entrenched opposition that has to be dealt with throughout the post-revolutionary period. Liberalization of the political systems occurs as a result of cooperative interactions in response to opposition demands. But political elites in these states do not survive beyond the post-revolutionary period. By generating institutional opportunities for ouster that democracy provides, and by strengthening the ability of the opposition to remove the elites, these post-revolutionary leaders effectively dig their own political graves.

Nevertheless, the suggestion that a post-revolutionary state might find relative peace and democratic political stability is an intriguing one. Yet the era of internal wars has also been the tail end of the third wave of democratic transitions.[20] Observers note that the same factors that sow the seeds for political violence—a permissive world community, increased mass mobilization, elite fragmentation—also create fertile ground for democratic transitions.[21] And other scholars note that transitions can be violent periods in the life of a state.[22]

Previous studies, even those addressing dynamic historical processes, have focused on the importance of the transition *moment* (pacts, revolutions, etc.) as the key to understanding the nature of regime transitions.[23]

Table 9.1 Historical Process Tracing of the Politcal Dynamics of Post–Internal War States

	Path A		Path B	
Common starting point:	Internal war (successful revolution)		Internal war (successful revolution)	
Main independent variables:				
Elite perceptions:	Secure		Vulnerable	
War perceptions:	War	No War	War	No War
Political outcomes:				
Use of repression in the coalition-reduction phase:	High		Low	
Consequences for thr opposition:	Opposition ousted		Significant opposition remains	
Use of accommodation in the consolidation phase:	Low		High	
Type of political system set up:	Autocracy		(Semi)democracy	
Survivability of elites:	Elites survive beyond the consolidation phase		Elites do not survive beyond the consolidation phase	
Cases:	Iran (Type I)	Cuba (Type II)	Nicaragua (Type III)	Bolivia (Type IV)

Note: The format and style of this table is loosely based on the Theda Skocpel's depiction of "Categories and Explanatory Variable Clusters in Barrington Moore's Social Origins of Dictatorship and Democracy" (Skocpel, 1973:Table 1.1)

Other studies have jumped ahead, focusing on the determinants of regime consolidation.[24] This study suggests a missed step—the importance of policy choices in the early years of the post-revolutionary state. In such states, elite-mass interactions in the first few years help to determine the type of political system that develops. Given the importance of this critical period, we need to better understand transitional states and the *dynamics* of international and internal politics in them. Some studies have addressed the dynamics of politics in transitional states,[25] although most focus on the behavior of these states in the international arena.[26] Future studies, particularly those in the area of democratic transitions, should

175

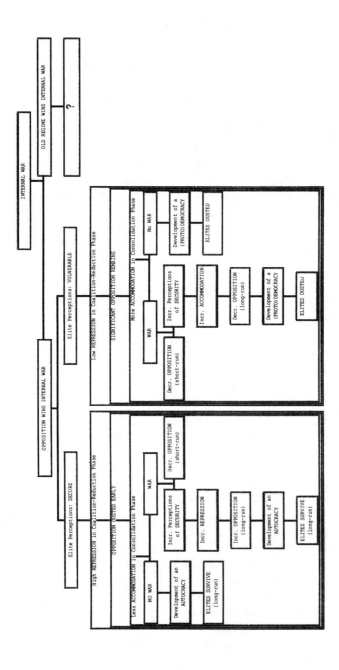

Figure 9.1   Mapping a Historical Process Model of the Political Outcomes of Internal Wars

abandon the static notion of a threshold or moment and consider adopting a more dynamic analysis of elite-mass interaction to better understand political system development.

Finally, this study's findings suggest why states that end their revolutions by military victory are not all as likely to engage in large-scale political violence and mass killings subsequently. Military victory is defined by the ability to threaten the opposition with impunity, and that it is therefore possible for these regimes to engage in such activity. However, while military victories are more likely to be followed by mass killings than are negotiated settlements, they only result in the severest forms of repression 14 percent of the time.[27] This study sheds some light on this problem. Military victory provides an opportunity to employ severe repression, but elite perceptions of security provide the willingness to do so. Elites who do not feel secure in their power position following a military victory avoid repression when possible, engaging in more conciliatory behavior with the opposition.

The Consequences of War in Post-Revolutionary States

This study also demonstrates that subsequent war involvement affects the post-revolutionary state. However, its effects are situational, and therefore complex. Initially, opposition groups react to the onset of war by supporting the regime. War's short-term rally-round-the-flag effect increases the elites' perceptions of security. And more secure elites are less skittish about repressing opposition. Additionally, the war further decreases the resources available to devote to concessions at home. Thus, war indirectly leads to either an increase in repression or a decrease in accommodation or both.

Opposition groups then react to changes in elite policy mix choices due to the war. If regimes decrease their use of accommodation, dissenters place these changes in the context of previous regime actions. When war makes concessions impossible in states that have previously relied on accommodation, opposition groups understand that the regime would accommodate if it could, and are therefore willing to forgo some demands in the short-run. But regimes that did not employ much accommodation before the war, and must lower that level even further during the war, draw the ire of dissenters, who are left with little. The only thing keeping these groups from trying to oust the elites is the fact that the regime weakened these groups earlier through the use of repressive policies. Finally, if repression increases as a result of war, opposition groups take to the streets in anger, replacing wartime nationalist slogans with dissenters' demands. In short, war has different short- and long-term effects on dissent, depending upon political context and elite reactions.

War does not have uniform effects on political system development or elite survival either. In states that have already begun the process of coalition-reduction through the use of repression, war helps the regime consolidate its power. Even long-term increases in opposition resulting from war's effects on policy mix choices are ineffective once the elites had been able to institutionalize and consolidate the revolution. This, in turn, helps these elites to remain in power longer.

In states that have had to rely on accommodation, however, war drives vulnerable elites to liberalize faster than they might otherwise prefer in hopes of avoiding a two-front conflict—at home and abroad. But a weakened regime, whose resources are being simultaneously pumped into both a war effort and domestic accommodation, cannot deliver on its promises, and will therefore not last long. The probability of ouster increases for one of three reasons: first, the state is weaker and the opposition is stronger, making extra-constitutional ouster a more likely possibility;[28] second, dissenters have the opportunity to successfully contest elections against a politically weakened opponent; third, if the war effort is not successful, the likelihood of elite ouster increases.[29] In short, in states that are unable to repress early, war hastens the development of a more democratic political system, but leads to a greater chance of ouster of the elites.

These findings have implications for our understanding of the development of garrison states. Ted Robert Gurr suggests that garrison states develop as a consequence of repeated experience with both international and internal conflict. Additionally, Gurr hypothesizes that post-revolutionary states that face internal resistance in the immediate aftermath of the revolution tend to become police states.[30] But not all states that experience both an internal war and a subsequent war within a few years of each other develop into garrison states. For example, it is true that Iran became a coercive regime, remaining heavily repressive beyond the Iran-Iraq War.[31] However, Nicaragua relied primarily on accommodation, rather than repression, in dealing with their non–Contra-related opposition. They therefore developed into a democratic polity rather than a garrison state, despite the Contra War. Additionally, while the use of repression did increase during the war, it dropped off precipitously after the Arias Peace Plan was signed. In short, while coercive states may be the product of the early use of repressive tactics, not all post-internal war states employ these tactics as consistently as suggested. And while garrison states may be the product of repeated experience with war, as the

Nicaraguan case suggests, not all states that experience multiple conflicts within a short time frame develop into garrison states.

Policy Implications

In post-revolutionary states, how elites perceive their power position relative to domestic opposition is crucial to their decisions between and among policy mix choices. Timing is crucial, as actions in the first few years (the coalition-reduction phase) determine to a large degree subsequent policy mix choices, the strength of the opposition, the development of the political system, and the survival of the elites in the long run. War has important effects, but they are less predictable, as they are conditioned by elite and mass interactions.

Given these findings, if international actors wish to get involved in post-revolutionary situations, they would be best advised to do so immediately after the conflict has ended. Waiting too long runs the risk of allowing a chain of events to begin, which could potentially be difficult to reverse later on. Unfortunately, peacekeeping/state-building operations take some time to come together.[32] Therefore, one implication of these findings is that a more rapid response is necessary if these missions are to be successful.

The type of involvement is also important. Actors in the international system may already understand that early involvement is the key to successfully swaying the course of events in post-revolutionary states. This would account for the fact that post-revolutionary states are very likely to be involved in warfare soon after the internal war has concluded.[33] It may also account for the fact that post-revolutionary states are more often than not the targets, rather than the initiators, of these conflicts.[34] But starting an overt war with a revolutionary state may have unintended consequences. In the short run the opposition in these states is likely to rally around the new regime when the state is attacked. This helps the new regime consolidate its power, and makes the revolutionary state a more unified enemy. In some cases, dissenters continue to refrain from opposition activity, even in the face of the regime's reduced ability and/or willingness to accommodate. Another option, covert action, while sometimes successful, may drag out into a long, bloody, costly war, essentially becoming an overt conflict. On the other hand, wars against post-revolutionary states can push regimes to liberalize, and may play a role in their eventual ouster from power.

A less risky but often ineffective strategy is to condemn and punish repressive behavior, with the hope of influencing policy and political system development. Unfortunately, such aggressive sanctions may even lead to greater repressive behavior. Elites who lose the ability to extract from international actors will increase their extraction domestically in order to make up the difference. And sanctions without teeth merely boost the elites' perceptions that they have nothing to fear from external actors. Finally, antagonistic behavior in general can lead to a situation where such action actually helps elites consolidate their rule by providing a convenient external enemy.

Unfortunately, these types of responses to post-revolutionary states have become standard operating procedures in the international arena. International actors react with shock and indignation at the necessary early attempts to consolidate power and reduce the victorious coalition. Most states are initially hostile to revolutionary regimes, and tend to dictate terms by which these new states must abide, while insinuating threats if they do not. It is no wonder that post-revolutionary states have such a conflict-ridden history.

Short of direct military intervention, then, what is to be done? The results of this study point to a possible alternative solution to dealing with post-revolutionary states. Punishing repression, even if successful, is a short-term solution. Regimes that employed repression in the past are more likely to continue to do so into the future. Early action on the part of international actors to reward accommodation, rather than punish repression, may lead to longer-term beneficial effects.

In the absence of international action, elites in post-revolutionary states see repression as the cheaper policy in terms of a cost-benefit analysis. International efforts can make accommodation a better, cheaper, domestic policy option for resource extraction by providing incentives to the elites if they employ concessions. While the elites would have to give away resources that would be hard to recoup, including perhaps rights and privileges, they would gain the ability to extract resources externally. Given the usual way in which international actors react to these regimes, this option is usually closed to post-revolutionary states.[35] In short, there is a distinct possibility that rewarding accommodation could lead to the development of patterns of interaction associated with less repressive, more liberal regimes.

Let us assume that a post-revolutionary state accepts this bargain, and increases its use of accommodation in return for resources from abroad. If action is taken in the first year or two of the life of the new regime, perhaps the opposition may survive the coalition-reduction phase. This makes them a force to be reckoned with. Assuming the elites wish to continue receiving said resources, they will become more likely to continue to accommodate, and perhaps eventually liberalize the political system. But the combination of a strong opposition and a democratic system may result in the ouster of these same elites. If elites realize this, they might not consider adopting democratic reforms.

However, I point to both Nicaragua and Poland to suggest that this does not have to be the case. In both places, the elites who led the revolution lost an election and were ousted from power. But as of this writing, both of these sets of actors have become vital parts of a vibrant political system. They have learned through experience that, at any given moment, out-groups can become in-groups, and can do so legitimately. It is this realization that makes the accommodating option worth taking, even at the risk of ouster.

More importantly perhaps, other states have learned this lesson by example. Before the mid-1980s, the democratic option in post-revolutionary states did not seem viable. There were no concrete examples to speak of in which elites had led a revolution and then submitted themselves to popular accountability in free and fair elections. By 1996 consolidated democracies following revolutionary change had become a reality.

Given a change in the international environment, and a change in what we now know (and can demonstrate) is possible, perhaps the international community now has a tool that it could not have used before. In the current international environment, rewarding accommodation early in the life of post-revolutionary states may be the safest and most efficient way to reduce human rights abuses, encourage cooperation, and sow the seeds of democracy.

Implications for the Way We Do Research

This study also suggests numerous ways in which social scientists can better study political dynamics of post-revolutionary states. First, most studies of elite-mass interactions focus either exclusively on repression or on a dichotomous trade-off between repression and accommodation. However, as this study demonstrates, these policies are not mutually exclusive. Elites in repressive states do employ accommodation when necessary. Elites in more accommodating states employ repression. And these policy choices have particular effects at different times. Students of elite-mass interactions need to heed Mark Lichbach's suggestion to view these policies as elements of a repertoire or policy mix from which leaders can choose at the appropriate time.[36]

The importance of timing highlights the necessity of historical analysis when examining political interactions. Yet all too often static theories or methods are employed to examine inherently dynamic phenomena such as repression and political system development.[37] While structural elements do impact political interactions, this study demonstrates the necessity of incorporating process into the equation.

Additionally, this study demonstrates the importance of examining phenomena using multiple levels of analysis. In this case, factors in all three levels of analysis—international, national, and individual levels—played important roles in explaining the causes and consequences of policy mix choices in post-revolutionary states. Elite perceptions (individual) and war (international) were found to affect domestic policy mix choices, which in turn have effects on national level politics for years to come. An analysis of these phenomena that had restricted itself to only one (or even two) levels of analysis would have missed key elements of the puzzle.

Finally, theories of political violence, revolutions, social movement dynamics, war, state building, and political system development are all compatible. This study is but one of many that suggests that these phenomenon are inextricably interrelated. As such, an understanding of each theoretical literature enriches the analysis as a whole. Scholars have recently begun to search for common ground within the more general context of conflict analysis and political violence.[38] This project implies the importance of such efforts.

Where to Next?

While this study is an important first step, scholars are just beginning to scratch the surface in the study of political dynamics of the post-internal war state. With the knowledge such work can acquire we can pursue answers that will aid us in dealing with states undergoing this difficult period. Below I discuss four ways in which this project can be expanded and improved upon to aid scholars in this endeavor.

Generalizability

The first place to improve upon the work presented here is to expand its generalizabiltiy. In considering which cases with which to test my model, I chose only cases of successful revolutions in order to keep them most similar. While this was an effective research strategy, it limited the ability to generalize beyond post-revolutionary states in which the opposition was victorious. However, the state must be rebuilt even following a victory by the old regime.[39] Therefore cases of unsuccessful revolution should also exhibit most of the dynamics that this study has uncovered.

Additionally, the demands for state building are just as great in post-civil war cases, as the American Civil War suggests.[40] Elites in these states must grapple with choices between and among repression and accommodation to the same degree. And civil wars also experience subsequent conflicts, as the history of Lebanon suggests.[41] Finally, Roy Licklider suggests that the type of internal war does not affect post-internal war outcomes as much as expected.[42] Thus, in theory, the model examined in this study should be generalizable to other post-internal war cases. However, this is an empirical question that needs to be addressed.

Finally, while state-building needs are not as great following revolutions from above than following those from below, perhaps some of the same dynamics are present, but to a lesser degree. Future work might also attempt to extend a modified version of my historical process model to cases of smaller-scale internal political conflict.

Examining Actors and Interactions More Closely

A second way to move beyond this study is to deepen the analysis by examining the actors involved and the interactions between them in more detail. Parsimony has some serious drawbacks. The model developed and tested in this project is, by necessity, simple. In reality, neither elites nor the opposition in post-internal war states are monolithic. Each jockey for position. Alliances can be made across elite-mass lines, or between factions. This also has ramifications for our understanding of elite policy mix choices. A particular policy can be designed to repress one group while simultaneously accommodating another. Hence, inter-group conflicts amongst elites and the opposition, as well as alliances between polity members and challengers, need to be taken into account. Future analyses of the post-internal war state should consider changing the focus from a dyadic (elite-mass interactions) to a multi-actor analysis incorporating factions within the elites and multiple elements within the opposition.[43]

A deeper analysis, one that can differentiate between and among actors more easily, would have additional benefits. Most notably, it would enable a more detailed analysis of who the targets of the elite policy mix choices are and why they, specifically, are targeted. One would expect that different phases of the post-internal war state might lead to different targets being chosen, as targets present different challenges at different times. Repression, for example, is selective by type of actor faced.[44] And different types of repression affect dissent differently.[45] Perhaps communal targets are more likely to be dealt with after the coalition-reduction phase. Certainly this was the case with the Kurds in Iran and the Miskito in Nicaragua.[46] Perhaps economic targets are dealt with first, in order to reduce the need to acquire resources subsequently. This would explain the rash of confiscations within the first few years in all four cases examined here. Finally, regimes may use different tactics on different types of groups. Might this explain the severity of ethnopolitical conflict? Might this also explain the difference between treatment of urban and rural sectors, or labor and capital, or clergy and layperson, in post–internal war states? Future work should examine the targets of elite policy mix choices in more detail to better understand how and why specific policies are adopted.

Future work also needs to incorporate more dynamics into the study of the post–internal war state. Theoretical models that can account for the interaction between dissent and policy mix choices are particularly lacking in the study of elite-mass tactical choices.[47] While the model presented in this project accounts for overall trends across the first 13 years following an internal war, the particular dynamics of protest cycles within this period are still not well accounted for. Some recent work has focused on historical sequencing in protest cycles to better get at the particular patterns of interaction between elite and mass policies.[48] Future work should consider the use of these strategies in studying the elite-mass dynamics of the post–internal war state.

How Political Choices Affect Economic and Social Policies

A third place to improve upon this study is to address the impact of political choices on economic and social outcomes. I began my discussion of the study of the post–internal war state by pointing out that much work has been done on the economic and social outcomes of internal wars, but that an understanding of political dynamics was limited. This study has provided a base from which to begin linking these two interdependent sets of dynamics. Future studies should examine how elite policy mix choices and their effects on dissent, political system development, and elite survivability affect the economic and social outcomes of internal wars.

How the Domestic Affects the International

Finally, in the same vein, this study can be expanded upon by addressing the impact of political choices in post–internal war states on subsequent behavior in the international arena. This project focused primarily on the effect of international factors on domestic processes. However, the relationship is not unidirectional. The key elements examined in this study—perceptions, war participation, policy mix choices, dissent, regime type, and survivability—affect the foreign policy and war propensity of post-internal war states.[49] Future work should examine the impact of post-internal war domestic political dynamics on behavior in the international arena.

Conclusion

Many scholars argue that revolutions will continue to be a part of the global political landscape in the twenty-first century.[50] Others warn that internal wars writ large will continue to be the dominant threat in the international system.[51] The desire of members of the international community to involve themselves in these conflicts, and to engage in both peacekeeping and state building, does not appear to be waning.[52] Given these predictions, a better understanding of political dynamics in post-internal war states can only insure a more effective foreign policy in the uncertain post–Cold War era.

APPENDIX A.

Survey of Experts on Repression and Accommodation

Professor XXXXXXXX
Department of XXXXXXXX
XXXXXXXX College/University
XXXXXX, XX XXXXX

December 14, 1995

Dear Professor XXXXXXXXX:

In the coming months I shall be working on a project entitled: "Repression and Accommodation in Post-Revolutionary States." In the course of this work I will need to code different types of governmental policies of repression and accommodation for four different post-internal war states. There appears to be no easy way to rank order the scores which I wish to create for these variables. Yet such a ranking or "weighting" is necessary to distinguish different types of policies and their relative severity.

In order to do so in a non-arbitrary manner, I am polling a number of experts in the field to get their thoughts on rank ordering these policies. I was hoping that you, as a major figure in this field, might assist me.

Enclosed you will find two survey sheets, one for repression, and one for accommodation. Please rank each policy on a severity scale of 1–5. For repression, a score of 1 indicates the least repressive and 5 the most repressive policy. For accommodation, 1 is the least accommodative policy, and 5 the most. Also, if I have omitted key types of either policy, feel free to list them in the spaces provided below, and indicate where you would place them on this scale.

Your research has already been extremely influential in my work to date. I hope that you can assist me yet again (this time in a more direct way) in this new project. Thank you very much for your time and assistance in this matter.

Sincerely,
Matthew Krain

POLICY (REPRESSION) . . .

_____mass killings
_____mass rape
_____forced conscription
_____disruption of group organization
_____restricting communication or information
_____restritcing emigration, mobility
_____politcial executions
_____disappearances
_____forced subjugation / integration of communities
_____violent putdown of demonstration
_____martial law declared
_____exemplary punishment as a deterrent
_____ousting group from government (i.e.- Cabinet)
_____armed attack
_____establishment of a secret police
_____arresting opposition leaders
_____religious suppression / persecution
_____exiles
_____forced resettlement
_____use of concentration camps
_____"manufactured" famine or drought
_____use of torture
_____forced labor
_____compellance: punishing nonperformance
_____seizing assets
_____outlawing organizations or groups
_____suspending or censoring news media
_____widespread use of spies and informants
_____restricting access to resources, necessities
_____restricting assembly and association
_____illegal detentions and excessive arrests
_____prohibitive fines, taxes, fees
_____making groups more visible, easily spotted
_____public threat of violence
_____show of force

OTHERS not listed here: [list below, with scores you would assign]

____ _____

____ _____

____ _____

____ _____

POLICY (ACCOMMODATION) . . .

____legalizing group membership

____encouraging / allowing separatism

____granting additional civil rights/civil liberties

____freeing prisoners

____stays of executions

____increasing access to information

____providing selective incentives to join group

____giving positive publicity to group

____reduction in fines, taxes, fees

____allowing return from exile or safe havens for exiles

____general amnesty

____negotiations begun

____compromise reached

____increasing opportunities for participation

____removing restrictive law / regulation

____direct aid (money, forces) to challenger

____incorporation into government (cabinet post, corporate partnership, etc.)

____large scale redistribution of assets / resources

____legalizing citizenship for group members

____officially recognizing group

____low level concession

____small scale diversion of resources to group

____enlarged priveleges for group

____consultation of group on a regular basis

OTHERS not listed here: [list below, with scores you would assign]

____ _____

____ _____

____ _____

____ _____

TABLE A.1

Experts Polled to Create Weighting Scales for Repression / Accommodation

Alyson Brysk	Guillermo O'Donnell
David Cingranelli	Mancur Olson
David Davis	David Pion-Berlin
William Gamson	Frances Fox Piven
Scott Sigmund Gartner	Steven Poe
Ted Robert Gurr	G. Bingham Powell
Edgar Kiser	Rudolph J. Rummel
Mark I. Lichbach	Philippe Schmitter
Roy Licklider	Matthew Soberg Shugart
Arend Lijphart	Michael Stohl
George Lopez	Sidney Tarrow
T. David Mason	C. Neal Tate
Andrew McNitt	Charles Tilly
Joel Migdal	Arturo Valenzuela
Will Moore	Aristide Zolberg

APPENDIX B.

Post-Internal War Accommodation And Repression [PIWAR] Data Project

Matthew Krain, Principal Investigator

Coding Sheet

(___) Entered   Ref. No. _____-_____-_____
                                 (Warnum)-(R/A) -(Event#)

DATE   *CASE*

_____ Year   Year: _____   Warnum: _____ Event: _____
_____ Month   Month: ___   Ccode: _____
_____ Day   Day: _____   Cname: _____

POLICY

_____ Policy Type   Policy Type: _____
_____ Policy Score   Policy Score: _____
_____ Specific Policy   Specific Policy: _____
_____ See Decription   Description: _____
                         _____

TARGETS

_____ Target #1   Target #1: _____

_____ Target #2   Target #2: _____

_____ Target #3   Target #3: _____

_____ Target #4   Target #4: _____

TRIGGERS / REACTIONS

_____ Trigger?   Trigger: _____

                                  _____

_____ Reaction?   Reaction: _____

                                  _____

DATA SOURCES

_____ Source #1   Source #1: _____

_____ Source #2   Source #2: _____

_____ Source #3   Source #3: _____

_____ Source #4   Source #4: _____

_____ Source #5   Source #5: _____

APPENDIX C.

Repression and Accommodation in Post-Revolutionary States (Codebook)

Principal Investigator: Matthew Krain

I. Case Identity Information

1. REF. NO   .= Unique reference number for each event:
                   (WARNUM)-(R/A)-(EVENT#)

2. WARNUM   = Internal war number
                   as coded by Singer and Small (1994)

   811 = Bolivia (1952)
   829 = Cuba (1958–1959)
   904 = Iran (1978–1979)
   907 = Nicaragua (1978–1979)

3. EVENT#   = Number for event found per case and policy;
                   sequential by discovery, not temporal order

4. CCODE   = Country code of country "hosting" internal
                   war, as coded by Singer and Small (1994)

   40 = Cuba
   93 = Nicaragua
   145 = Bolivia
   630 = Iran

5. CNAME   = Name of country "hosting" internal war

II. Date

1. YEAR   = Year event began
2. MONTH   = Month event began
3. DAY   = Day event began

III. Policy

1. POLICY TYPE

   1= Repression
   2= Accommodation
   9= Unsure / Don't Know

2. POLICY SCORE   = See Below

3. SPECIFIC POLICY NUMBER   = See Below

4. SEE DESCRIPTION?   = Is it necessary to refer to the coding sheet for a more detailed description of the event?
   0 = NO
   1 = YES

4A. DESCRIPTION   = Additional description, if needed (six lines, maximum)

IF POLICY TYPE = 1 (REPRESSION) . . .

#	Specific Policy	Score	Score^2
111	restricting access to resources, necessities, jobs	2	5
112	restricting assembly	2	5
113	illegal detentions	3	8
114	prohibitive fines, taxes, fees, regulations	2	4
115	making groups more visible, easily spotted	2	4
116	public threat of violence	2	4
117	show of force	2	3
118	forced conscription	3	7
119	disruption of group organiztion	2	4
120	restricting communication on information, speech	2	2
121	restricting emigration, mobility	2	5
129	expulsion/purge from party or ruling elite	2	3

#	Specific Policy	Score	Score²
130	show trials/political trials	3	8
131	suspension of parts of constitution or the regular workings of government	2	4
221	"special" extra-legal courts set up	2	6
222	violent putdown of demonstration/ insurrection	3	8
223	martial law declared	3	10
224	exemplary punishment/deterrent	3	8
225	compellance: punishing nonperformance	2	4
226	seizing assets	2	5
227	outlawing organizations, groups, industries	3	6
228	suspending or censoring news media/ speech	2	6
229	widespread use of spies and informants	2	6
331	establishment of a secret police/ special forces	2	6
332	arresting opposition leaders	3	7
333	religious suppression/persecution	3	8
334	exiles/expulsions	3	7
335	trials in absentia	3	8
336	forces subjugation/integration of communities	3	11
440	mass rape	5	21
441	political executions	4	17
442	disappearances	4	19
443	forced resettlement	4	14
444	concentration camps	4	18
445	"manufactured" famine or drought	4	19
446	use of torture	4	15
447	forced labor	3	12
448	ousting group from government	2	3
449	armed attack	3	12
551	mass killing	2	25

IF POLICY TYPE = 2 (ACCOMMODATION) . . .

#	Specific Policy	Score	Score²
111	increasing access to information	2	3
112	providing selective incentives	3	7
113	giving positive publicity	2	4
114	reduction in fines, taxes, fees	2	3

115	introducing enabling mechanism/ entitlement	3	6
221	negotiations begun	2	6
222	compromise reached	4	12
223	increasing opportunites for participation	3	9
224	removing restrictive law/regulation	3	6
225	low-level concession	1	1
226	small-scale diversion of resources to group	2	4
227	abandoning project hurtful to group	2	3
228	allowing emigration	3	6
230	outlawing repressive apparatus instituion, practice	3	6
231	prosecution of enemies of target group	1	1
232	broad statement of guarantee of rights	2	4
233	increasing security of target group	1	1
234	increasing access to markets	3	9
332	freeing prisoners	3	9
333	stays of executions	2	5
334	allowing return from exile	3	7
335	general amnesty	4	13
441	legalizing group membership	3	10
442	encouraging/allowing separatism	4	18
551	direct aid (money, forces) to challenger	3	10
552	incorporation into government	4	19
553	large-scale redistribution of assets/ resources	4	17

IV. Targets

Targets are the groups that policies are aimed at influencing. Up to five targets can be coded for each policy. The top five will be coded in order of importance. Some targets will fall under more than one category. These will be coded based on which "category" is being targeted, or which appears to be the primary identification of the target by the state (coder's discretion).

TARGET#		TARGET DESCRIPTION
General Targets	0	= no (apparent) target
	1	= population at large
	2	= citizens living abroad
	3	= other country's nationals
	4	= prominent individual / celebrity
	5	= all potential targets

	6	= men
	7	= women
	8	= prisoners (general)
	90	= other
	91	= veterans
	92	= disabled
	99	= n.a. / don't know
Political Targets	9	= army officer
	10	= army - main
	11	= army - splinter / rogue group
	12	= member of government (current)
	13	= royalty
	14	= government or party faction
	15	= government agency
	16	= non-government agency within state bureaucracy
	19	= political party
	20	= counterrevolutionary political party
	21	= political interest group
	22	= former political leaders (ousted enemies)
	23	= (general) political opponents
	24	= secret police / spy network
	25	= media / journalists
	26	= intellectuals / artists / teachers
	27	= professionals
	28	= students
	29	= war criminals
	80	= counterrevolutionaries - foreign
	81	= counterrevolutionaries - domestic
	82	= sympathizers with counterrevolutionaries
	85	= social movement organization
	86	= civic group
	87	= voluntary organization
	88	= fraternal organization
Geographical Targets	30	= residents of urban area
	31	= residents of rural area
	32	= specific geographic region
Extra-border Targets	40	= other country
	41	= intervener: friendly
	42	= intervener: neutral
	43	= intervener: hostile
	44	= non-intervening country

	45	= multinational force
	46	= breakaway republic or region
	47	= principality or colony
	48	= international community (in general)
	49	= international non-governmental organization
Economic	50	= labor union
Targets	51	= other union
	55	= particular industry / private enterprise
Class	61	= peasant group
Targets	62	= urban lower class group
	63	= middleman group
	64	= merchant group
	65	= lower middle class group
	66	= middle class group
	67	= upper middle class group
	68	= upper class group
Communal	71	= linguistic group
Group	72	= ethnic group
Targets	73	= racial group
	74	= religious group
	75	= clergy
	76	= other communal group

V. Triggers of Policy / Reactions to Policy

Targets' actions as a trigger for new policy, and / or reaction by target to new policy. Two-line description if necessary.

1. TRIGGER? = action by target that triggered a government response?

    0 = no previous action - this is first interaction between actors
    1 = acquiescence / cooperation
    2 = non-cooperation
    3 = non-violent resistance, statements, etc.
    4 = violent resistance
    5 = response to intervention by outside party
    6 = response to previous intervention
    7 = current policy not in response to action from target group
    8 = demand / accusation
    9 = n.a. / don't know
    10 = exogenous event
    11 = other

2. REACTION? = reaction by target to new government policy?

0 = no reaction
1 = acquiescence / cooperation
2 = non-cooperation
3 = non-violent resistance, statements, etc.
4 = violent resistance
5 = response to intervention by outside party
6 = response to previous intervention
7 = reaction appears present, but is in response to something else
8 = demand / accusation
9 = n.a. / don't know
10 = exogenous event
11 = other

VI. Data Sources

At least two sources must be cited for any event to count in this data set. Sources are cited by type and page number on left-hand side of coding sheet, by (author, year: page number) on right-hand side.

#	SOURCE TYPE
0	= No Source Available
1	= Keesing's Contemporary Archives
2	= United States Government Documents
3	= Other Newspaper / Periodical
4	= New York Times (NYT)
5	= Foreign Broadcast Information Service (FBIS)
6	= Hispanic American Report (HAR)
7	= The Times of the Americas (TOTA)
8	= The Times of Havana (TOH)
9	= Other Regional News Source
10	= Historical Account- Primary Source
20	= Historical Account- Secondary Source
30	= Historical Account- Tertiary Source
40	= Facts On File (Regular)
45	= Facts On File Publication
70	= Human Rights Watch Publication
71	= Freedom House Publication
72	= Amnesty International Publication
99	= N.A. / Don't Know

Coding Procedure Is as Follows for All Instances of Repression or Accommodation:

Initially, Keesing's *Contemporary Archives* (1) is used as an international source. Next, regional news sources are used (5–8). Then historical accounts (10, 20, 30, 40, 45, 70, 71, 72) are employed (gathered via on-line searches). Finally, The *New York Times* (4) is used *only* to check unsubstantiated cases (cases with only one citation). *No new cases may be added at this point.*

APPENDIX D.

Coding Elite Perceptions of Their Own Security / Vulnerability (CODEBOOK)

1. *Source ID #:* write the WARNUM number . . .

   Bolivia = 811
   Cuba = 829
   Iran = 904
   Nicaragua = 907

   . . . followed by the last two digits of the year . . .
   . . . followed by a three digit case number . . .

   EXAMPLES: A speech given by Fidel Castro in 1966, which has been coded first would be numbered "82966001"; that is: "829" for CUBA, "66" for 1966, and "001" because it is the first case to be coded. If the next Cuban item coded is an interview given by Raul Castro in 1959 then that case would be coded "82959002."

2. *Source Type*   Source of document.

   New York Times (or NYT Index)   = 4
   Foreign Broadcast Information Service (FBIS)   = 5
   Collection of Speeches/ Historical Source Book   = 10

3. *Day/Month/Year:* Use two digits for each entry.

   EXAMPLES:
       December 19, 1970 = 12/19/70
       February 1, 1967 = 01/02/67

4. *Page(s):* Enter page number(s) from source if available.

5. *Source Name:* Any/all info. needed to be able to identify it in case one needs to track down source later.

6–17. *Content Information:* Enter all key words/phrases that appear in the text of the document that appears to refer to the elites, to "the revolution," or to the "state." Do not use words that refer directly to other groups.

> EXAMPLE: " . . . *The Falange is a WEAK group* . . ."
> - DO NOT use a quote like this one!

All words or phrases appear on the Word/Phrase List on the next page. Note the number of times this word or phrase appears in such a way within the document in parentheses (___) at the far right of the coding sheet.

18. *Overall Perceptions:* If number of vulnerable statements outnumber secure statements, check box [1]. If secure outnumber vulnerable, check box [2]. If the sums are equal, check box [3].Write the number in the checked box on the line _____ .

19–23. *Trigger(s):* List groups or types of people to which the speaker refers who might be catalysts for this perception.

> EXAMPLE: *"The Contras have weakened our position . . ."*
> . . .in this case, the Contras would be a trigger. If it is unclear or there is no discernible trigger, leave blank.

Elite Perceptions of Their Own Security / Vulnerability (CODEBOOK)

Word/Phrase List

WORDS

VULNERABILITY	*SECURITY*
CHALLENGED	ARROGANT
DEFEAT	ASSURANCE
DEFENSIVE	CONFIDENT
DISCORD	FEARLESS
DISPENSIBLE	INDESTRUCTIBLE
DIVIDED	INDISPENSIBLE
DOUBT	INVINCIBLE
EXPOSED	INVULNERABLE
FEAR	POPULAR

IMPOTENT	POWER/POWERFUL
INSECURE	PROTECTED
INSTABILITY	SAFE
INTIMIDATED	SECURE
LIMITATIONS	SHIELDED
PRECARIOUS	SOLIDARITY
SABOTAGE	STABLE
SCARED	STRONG/STRENGTH
SUBVERT/SUBVERSION	UNITED
SUSPICIOUS	
THREAT/THREATEN	
UNCERTAIN	
UNPOPULAR	
UNPROTECTED	
VULNERABLE	
WEAK/WEAKNESS	
WOUNDS	

SAMPLE PHRASES

VULNERABILITY
are subject to pressures
attempt to destroy us
in a state of chaos
our needs are so great
their support is crucial
this situation is dangerous
we are having major difficulties
we are struggling to _____
we must be on the alert
we must be very cautious/careful
NOTE: All words or phrases used
in the negative sense or denoting
the inverse of a sense of SECURITY
are considered words or phrases
denoting VULNERABILITY

SECURITY
can/will not be defeated
does not bother us
it is impossible to defeat us
no one would dare attack us
support of the people
they are united behind us
vote of confidence
we are afraid of nothing
we don't need *(GROUP X)*
we won't be brought to our knees
NOTE: All words or phrases used
in the negative sense or denoting
the inverse of a sense of
VULNERABILITY are considered
words or phrases denoting
SECURITY

ELITE PERCEPTIONS OF THEIR OWN SECURITY/VULNERABILITY

"Repression and Accommodation in Post-Revolutionary States"

Coding Sheet

SOURCE INFORMATION

1. Source ID #: _____ (WARNUM-YR-NUMBER)
2. Source Type: _____
3. Day/Month/Year: _____/_____/_____
4. Page(s): _____
5. Source Name: _____
(optional) _____

CONTENT INFORMATION

6. Key words/phrases (freq.) _____   7.(_____)
8.   _____   9.(_____)
10.   _____   11.(_____)
12.   _____   13.(_____)
14.   _____   15.(_____)
16.   _____   17.(_____)
18. Overall perception: _____   [] Vulnerable [1]
                                        [] Secure [2]
                                        [] Even/Neither [3]
19. Trigger(s): _____
20. _____
21. _____
22. _____
23. _____

Data on Elite Perceptions of Security/Vulnerability

Source Materials

IRAN

1. Primary Source: Foreign Broadcast Information Service (FBIS) records, 1979–1991.

2. Collections of Speeches and Interviews used to supplement/check primary source:

Khomeini (1979a,b; 1981; 1982)
Motahari (1985)

3. Additional Materials used as retrospective check (memoirs, letters, reflections):

Montazam (1994)
Snare (1997)

CUBA

1. Gopher site used as Primary Source: *gopher://lanic.utexas.edu/11/la/Cuba/Castro*

Below is a description of the site and its contents, taken directly from the site itself:

"Castro Speech" is a database containing the full text of English translations of speeches, interviews, and press conferences by Fidel Castro, based upon the records of the Foreign Broadcast Information Service (FBIS), a U.S. government agency responsible for monitoring broadcast and print media in countries throughout the world. These records are in the public domain.

The Department of Research of the Radio Marti Program, part of the U.S. Information Agency, undertook the task of digitizing FBIS reports from 1959 through the end of the 1980s. FBIS records are now produced online and updates to the Castro Speech database are made electronically.

The files are organized by year and with files named according to the date of the speech, interview, or event (e.g., 13 July 1987 =19870713). If there are two or more events on the same date, files are named sequentially by adding extensions (e.g., 19870713.1, 19870713.2, etc.) The file naming convention has been to name file in accordance with the date of the event; however, file names may vary in that the date of event, date of broadcast, and date of report are often different and inconsistencies will occur.

As suggested in the notes of the database, I compared the text of many FBIS translations with an original source such as the newspaper Granma or other collections of speeches by Fidel Castro (see below).

2. Collections of Speeches and Interviews used to supplement/check primary source:

Brenner, LeoGrande, Rich and Siegel (1989)
Castro (1963; 1964; 1968)
Deutschmann (1987)
Franqui (1976)
Kenner and Petras (1972)

Lockwood (1969)
Matthews (1969; 1975)
Mina (1991)
Sobel (1964)
Taber (1983)

3. Additional Materials used as retrospective check (memoirs, letters, reflections):

Betto (1985)
Castro (1985)
Elliot and Dymally (1986)
Lockwood (1969)
Matthews (1975)
Mina (1991)
Szulc (1986)
Taber (1983)
Urrutia (1964)

NICARAGUA

1. Primary Source: Foreign Broadcast Information Service (FBIS) records, 1979–1991.

2. Collections of Speeches and Interviews used to supplement/check primary source:

Arce (1984)
Dreifus (1983a,b)
Ezcurra (1984)
FSLN (1986 [1979])
Gentile (1989)
Gilbert (1988)
Leiken and Rubin (1987)
Marcus (1982; 1985)
Rosset and Vandermeer (1983)
Stahel (1985)
Wheelock (1984)

3. Additional Materials used as retrospective check (memoirs, letters, reflections):

Hoyt (1997)
Miranda and Ratliff (1993)
Wheelock (1997)

BOLIVIA

1. Primary Sources: Collections of Speeches and Interviews.

Alexander (1994)
Arze Murillo (1962)
Escobari Cusicanqui (1961)
Fellmann Velarde (1955)
Fortún Sanjinés (1963; 1964)
Lechin (1956)
Libermann (1962)
López Muñoz (1958)
Movimiento Nacionalista Revolucionario (1953; 1960a,b,c; 1962a,b; 1963; 1964a,b)
Paz Estenssoro (1953; 1954; 1956; 1959; 1960a,b,c ; 1962; 1964a,b,c; 1965)
Presidencia Dirección De Informaciones (1957)
Siles Zuazo (1952; 1958; 1959; 1960a,b)

2. Journal, Newspaper, or Magazine Articles used to supplement/check primar sources:

Hispanic American Report, 1952–1964.

"Bolivia: Republic Up in the Air," *Time,* December 15, 1952, pp.34–36.

"Bolivia Swings 'Left' - How Far?" *U.S. News and World Report,* June 5, 1953.

"Bolivians Install Paz Estenssoro," *New York Times,* April 17, 1952.

"Civil War Threat Seen," *New York Times,* June 28, 1953.

"High Bolivian Sets Anti-Marxist Aim," *New York Times,* May 4, 1952.

"Paz Estenssoro Returns to Bolivia; Says He Plans to Nationalize Tin," *New York Times,* April 16, 1952.

"President Paz's Independence Day Message," *New York Times,* August 7, 1952.

"President Warns La Paz Newspaper," *New York Times,* April 20, 1952.

3. Additional Materials used as retrospective check (memoirs, letters, reflections):

Alexander (1994)
Andrade(1976)
Paz Estenssoro (1994)

206

Table D.1 Speeches

Year	Iran (t = 1979)	Cuba (t = 1959)	Nicaragua (t = 1979)	Bolivia (t = 1952)
t	17/18	33/39	6/16	3/11
t + 1	17/19	34/41	5/12	2/7
t + 2	7/8	20/25	4/11	1/10
t + 3	5/6	23/31	5/13	0/12
t + 4	10/11	15/20	2/7	1/14
t + 5	6/9	6/7	2/9	0/10
t + 6	13/15	11/13	4/10	1/12
t + 7	6/8	9/12	4/10	1/9
t + 8	8/9	7/10	4/15	1/12
t + 9	15/17	10/11	3/11	1/7
t + 10	16/19	8/10	2/10	2/9
t + 11	6/7	8/12	2/13	1/8
t + 12	7/9	29/35	5/17	2/15

Notes: All ratios above represent number of documents denoting security to number of total documents
Score = Perception of security (high = high degree of security; low = low degree of security)

Table D.2 Interviews

Year	Iran (t = 1979)	Cuba (t = 1959)	Nicaragua (t = 1979)	Bolivia (t = 1952)
t	4/6	4/5	2/5	2/5
t + 1	10/11	4/6	2/5	0/3
t + 2	2/4	3/4	1/3	0/4
t + 3	4/4	4/5	2/7	1/4
t + 4	2/3	6/6	3/9	0/5
t + 5	2/2	2/3	1/3	1/5
t + 6	3/5	3/4	1/4	0/5
t + 7	4/5	3/3	2/8	0/3
t + 8	2/3	2/2	1/6	1/6
t + 9	6/8	2/3	1/4	0/3
t + 10	4/6	4/5	0/3	0/4
t + 11	5/6	4/4	1/5	0/2
t + 12	4/5	5/7	1/4	0/3

Notes: All ratios above represent number of documents denoting security to number of total documents
Score = Perception of security (high = high degree of security; low = low degree of security)

Table D.3 Total

Year	Iran (t = 1979) Total	Iran (t = 1979) Score	Cuba (t = 1959) Total	Cuba (t = 1959) Score	Nicaragua (t = 1979) Total	Nicaragua (t = 1979) Score	Bolivia (t = 1952) Total	Bolivia (t = 1952) Score
t	21/24	0.88	37/44	0.84	8/21	0.38	5/16	0.31
t + 1	27/30	0.90	38/47	0.81	7/17	0.41	2/10	0.20
t + 2	11/12	0.92	23/29	0.79	5/14	0.36	1/14	0.07
t + 3	9/10	0.90	27/36	0.75	7/20	0.35	1/16	0.06
t + 4	12/14	0.86	21/26	0.81	5/16	0.31	1/19	0.05
t + 5	8/11	0.82	8/10	0.80	3/12	0.25	1/15	0.07
t + 6	16/20	0.80	14/17	0.82	5/14	0.36	1/17	0.06
t + 7	10/13	0.77	12/15	0.80	6/18	0.33	1/12	0.08
t + 8	10/12	0.83	9/12	0.75	5/21	0.24	2/18	0.11
t + 9	21/25	0.84	12/14	0.86	4/15	0.27	1/10	0.10
t + 10	20/25	0.80	12/15	0.80	2/13	0.15	2/13	0.15
t + 11	11/13	0.85	12/16	0.75	3/18	0.17	1/10	0.10
t + 12	11/14	0.79	34/42	0.81	6/21	0.29	2/18	0.11

Notes: All ratios above represent number of documents denoting security to number of total documents

Score = Perception of security (high = high degree of security; low = low degree of security)

APPENDIX E.

Opposition Activity—CODEBOOK

Variables	Operationalization	Values
WAR#	Internal war number, as coded by Singer and Small (1994)	811 = Bolivia 829 = Cuba 904 = Iran 907 = Nicaragua
EVENT#	Number designated for each event	Sequential by discovery, not temporal order
YR	Year event began	Bolivia = 1952–1964 Cuba = 1959–1971 Iran = 1979–1991 Nicaragua = 1979–1991
MM	Month event began	1–12
DD	Day event began	1–31
CASE TYPE	Type of opposition activity	0 = NA/don't know 1 = Violent protest 2 = Nonviolent protest 3 = Violent strikes 4 = Nonviolent strikes 5 = Noncooperation 6 = Pro-government rally 7 = Coup plot/attempt 8 = Assassination attempt 11 = Armed attack
TARGET	Target of opposition activity	0 = Non-governmental actor 1 = Governmental actor
SOURCES	Sources in which event was found, described	4 = *New York Times* (NYT) 5 = *Foreign Broadcast Information Service* (FBIS) 6 = *Hispanic American Report* (HAR) 7 = *Times of the Americas* (TOTA) 8 = *Times of Havana* (TOH) 9 = other regional news sources
DESCRIPTION	Description of event, if necessary	Textual description of event

OPPOSITION ACTIVITY: CODING SHEET
"Repression and Accommodation in Post-Revolutionary States"

WAR#	EVENT#	YR	MM	DD	CASE TYPE	TARGET	SOURCE	DESCRIPTION

Notes

Chapter 1

1. See John Vasquez, *The War Puzzle*. Cambridge: Cambridge University Press, 1993: 53; Peter Wallensteen and Margareta Sollenberg, "The End of International War? Armed Conflict, 1989–1995," *Journal of Peace Research,* 33 (1996): 353–370. Systematic studies of recent wars have established the existence of this conflict trend. For a brief review of these studies, see Roy Licklider, ed., *Stopping the Killing: How Civil Wars End.* New York: New York University Press, 1993.
2. See Samuel P. Huntington, "The Clash of Civilizations?" *Foreign Affairs,* 79 (1993): 22–49; Ted Robert Gurr, "Peoples against States: Ethnopolitical Conflict and the Changing World System," *International Studies Quarterly,* 38 (1994): 347–377.
3. Revolutions and civil wars are thus subsets of this larger concept of internal wars. The differences between the two, and between these concepts and the larger umbrella concept *internal wars* will be discussed further in Chapter 3.
4. See Roy Licklider, "The Consequences of Negotiated Settlements In Civil Wars, 1945–1993," *American Political Science Review,* 89 (1995): 688.
5. John Foran and Jeff Goodwin, "Revolutionary Outcomes in Iran and Nicaragua: Coalition Fragmentation, War, and the Limits of Social Transformation," *Theory and Society,* 22 (1993): 234.
6. Eric Selbin, *Modern Latin American Revolutions.* Boulder: Westview Press, 1993: 29.
7. For example, see Susan Eckstein, "Revolutions and the Restructuring of National Economies: The Latin American Experience," *Comparative Politics,* 17 (1985): 73–494. Eckstein finds that position in the world economy, internal resources, and domestic state/class relations affect post-revolutionary economic developments. Others have found that revolutions benefit peasants, but actually do more for those already possessing "human capital," often creating greater inequality in the long run. See for instance, Susan Eckstein, "The Impact of Revolution on Social Welfare in Latin

America," *Theory and Society*, 11 (1982): 43–94; Jonathan Kelley and Herbert S. Klein, *Revolution and the Rebirth of Inequality: A Theory Applied to the National Revolution in Bolivia*. Berkeley: University of California Press, 1981; Jonathan Kelley and Herbert S. Klein. "Revolution and the Rebirth of Inequality: A Theory of Stratification in a Postrevolutionary Society," *American Journal of Sociology*, 83 (1977): 78–99. Alf Edeen finds that, despite its vast expansion and short run increased opportunities for upward mobility, social mobility declined within the post-revolutionary Soviet bureaucracy in the long run. See Alf Edeen, "The Soviet Civil Service: Its Composition and Status," in *The Transformation of Russian Society: Aspects of Social Change Since 1861*, edited by C. Black. Cambridge: Harvard University Press, 1960. For an examination of the various sources of inequalities in post-revolutionary China, see Martin King Whyte, "Inequality and Stratification in China," *The China Quarterly*, 64 (1975): 684–711. For an examination of the effects of post-revolutionary policies on families and/or women, see: Judith Stacey, *Patriarchy and Socialist Revolution in China*. Berkeley: University of California Press, 1983; Margaret Randall, *Women in Cuba: Twenty Years Later*. Brooklyn: Smyrna Press, 1981; Johnnetta B. Cole, "Women in Cuba: The Revolution within the Revolution," in *Comparative Perspectives of Third World Women*, edited by B. Lindsay. New York: Praeger, 1980. For more on effects on communal groups, see Robert Melson, *Revolution and Genocide: On the Origins of the Armenian Genocide and the Holocaust*. Chicago: University of Chicago Press, 1992; Ted Robert Gurr, "Minorities in Revolution," in *Revolutions: Theoretical, Comparative, and Historical Studies*. 2nd ed., edited by J. Goldstone, 308–314. Fort Worth: Harcourt Brace, 1994.

8. Joel S. Migdal, *Strong Societies and Weak States*. Princeton: Princeton University Press, 1989: 225.

9. See S. N. Eisenstadt, *Revolution and the Transformation of Societies: A Comparative Study of Civilizations*. New York: Free Press, 1978; Charles Tilly, *From Mobilization to Revolution*. New York: McGraw-Hill, 1978; Theda Skocpol, *States and Social Revolutions: A Comparative Analysis of France, Russia, and China*. Cambridge: Cambridge University Press, 1979.

10. Licklider, *Stopping the Killing*, 1993; Licklider, "The Consequences of Negotiated Settlements," 1995; T. David Mason and Patrick J. Fett, "How Civil Wars End: A Rational Choice Approach," *Journal of Conflict Resolution*, 40 (1996): 546–568.

11. See Zeev Maoz, "Joining the Club of Nations: Political Development and International Conflicts, 1816–1976," *International Studies Quarterly*, 33 (1989): 199–231; Stephen M. Walt, "Revolution and War," *World Politics*, 44 (1992): 321–368; Harvey Starr, "Revolution and War: Rethinking the Linkage between Internal and External Conflict," *Political Research Quarterly*, 47 (1994): 481–507.

12. Matthew Krain, "State-Sponsored Mass Murder: The Onset and Severity of Genocides and Politicides," *Journal of Conflict Resolution*, 41 (1997): 331–360; R. J. Rummel, "Democracy, Power, Genocide, and Mass Murder," *Journal of Conflict Resolution*, 39 (1995): 3–26.

13. Alexis de Tocqueville, *The Old Regime and the French Revolution*. Garden City, New York: Doubleday, 1955.

14. Max Weber, "Bureaucracy and Revolution," in *From Max Weber: Essays in Sociology*, edited by H. H. Gerth and C. W. Mills. New York: Oxford University Press, 1958.

15. Skocpol, *States and Social Revolutions*, 1979.

16. Ellen Kay Trimberger, *Revolution from Above: Military Bureaucrats and Development in Japan, Turkey, Egypt, and Peru*. New Brunswick: Transaction Books, 1978.

17. See for instance, Richard F. Bensel, *Yankee Leviathan: The Origins of Central State Authority in America, 1859–1877*. Cambridge: Cambridge University Press, 1990.

18. Eisenstadt, *Revolution and the Transformation of Societies*, 1978.

19. These elements of the revolutionary polity model are elaborated upon more thoroughly in Tilly, *From Mobilization to Revolution*, 1978.

20. See Eric Selbin, *Modern Latin American Revolutions*. Boulder: Westview Press, 1993: 19.

21. See Helen Fein, *Accounting for Genocide: National Responses and Jewish Victimization during the Holocaust*. New York: Free Press, 1979; Barbara Harff, "Genocide as State Terrorism," in *Government Violence and Repression: An Agenda for Research*, edited by M. Stohl and G. A. Lopez, 165–188. New York: Greenwood Press, 1986.

22. Tilly, *From Mobilization to Revolution*, 1978: 220–221.

23. Eisenstadt, *Revolution and the Transformation of Societies*, 1978.

24. This, in turn, leads to ever-increasing amounts of either coercion or cooperation (or both) in order to enable further extraction, creating an interaction spiral whose dynamics are similar to that of a security dilemma. If decisionmakers do not exercise caution this "extraction dilemma" spiral can continue unabated. See Samuel E. Finer, "State- and Nation- Building in Europe: The Role of the Military," in *The Formation of National States in Western Europe*, edited by C. Tilly, 84–163. Princeton: Princeton University Press, 1975.

25. Licklider, ed., *Stopping the Killing*, 1993: 19.

26. See Stephen John Stedman, "The End of the American Civil War," in Licklider, ed., *Stopping the Killing*, 1993: 164–188. For an excellent discussion of the use of repression and accommodation by the U.S. federal government in the course of antebellum state building, and in particular, in implementing Southern Reconstruction, see Bensel, *Yankee Leviathan*, 1990.

27. Stedman, "The End of the American Civil War," 1993: 180–183.

28. See Theda Skocpol, *Protecting Soldiers and Mothers: The Political Origins of Social Policy in the United States.* Cambridge: Harvard University Press, 1992. Besides this short-run political outcome, the American Civil War also had a long-lasting effect on American social policy. Skocpol finds that the Civil War was primarily responsible for the emergence of the welfare state in the United States, and that the political, economic, and social forces it created perpetuated and enlarged this social insurance policy.

29. Bensel, *Yankee Leviathan,* 1990.

30. Trimberger, *Revolution from Above,* 1978.

31. Eisenstadt, *Revolution and the Transformation of Societies,* 1978.

32. Skocpol, *States and Social Revolutions,* 1979: 231.

33. Theda Skocpol and Ellen Kay Trimberger, "Revolutions and the World-Historical Development of Capitalism," *Berkeley Journal of Sociology,* 22 (1977): 104.

34. Jonathan R. Adelman, *Revolution, Armies, and War: A Political History.* Boulder: Lynne Rienner Publishers, 1985.

35. Ted Robert Gurr, "War, Revolution, and the Growth of the Coercive State," *Comparative Political Studies,* 21 (1988): 45–65.

36. Maoz, "Joining the Club of Nations," 1989.

37. Walt, "Revolution and War," 1992; Maoz, "Joining the Club of Nations," 1989; Examples of this phenomenon include the Soviet invasion of Afghanistan and U.S. support of the Contras against the Sandinistas in Nicaragua. Another more ambiguous example is the development of the Iran-Iraq War as a consequence of the Iranian Revolution. "The official position of Iraq is that the war started out of an Iraqi fear that the Khomeini regime had been planning to overthrow the Ba'ath party in Iraq" (Maoz, 1989: 206). However, it is also possible that the Iraqi regime saw the revolution as presenting an opportunity rather than a threat. Post-internal war Iran appeared to be in disarray, and the new regime's determination to spread its revolution led to isolation within the international community. For an argument that suggests it is possible that Saddam Hussein saw this moment as a window of political opportunity in which it would be possible to fight a quick, successful war against its neighbor to the east, see Forrest D. Colburn, *The Vogue of Revolution in Poor Countries.* Princeton: Princeton University Press, 1994: 80.

38. Tilly, *From Mobilization to Revolution,* 1978.

39. Licklider, ed., *Stopping the Killing,* 1993.

40. Margaret Levi, "The Predatory Theory of Rule," *Politics and Society,* 10 (1981): 441.

41. Pitrim A. Sorokin, *Social and Cultural Dynamics,* rev. ed. Boston: Porter Sargent, 1957: 596–598; Gil Friedman and Harvey Starr, "The Nexus of Civil and International Conflict Revisited: Opportunity, Willingness, and the Internal-External Linkage," presented at the 29th Annual North American

Meeting of the Peace Science Society (International), Columbus, Ohio, October 13–15, 1995.

42. Rosemary H. T. O'Kane, "The National Causes of State Construction in France, Russia and China," *Political Studies*, 43 (1995): 20.

43. See for instance, Steven C. Poe and C. Neal Tate, "Repression of Human Rights to Personal Integrity in the 1980s: A Global Analysis," *American Political Science Review*, 88 (1994): 853–872; Andrew D. McNitt, "Government Coercion: An Exploratory Analysis," *Social Science Journal*, 32 (1995): 195–205; Conway Henderson, "Military Regimes and Human Rights in Developing Countries: A Comparative Perspective," *Human Rights Quarterly*, 4 (1992): 110–123; Conway Henderson, "Conditions Affecting the Use of Political Repression," *Journal of Conflict Resolution*, 35 (1991): 120–142.

44. Krain, "State-Sponsored Mass Murder," 1997; These findings confirmed a body of previous research that argued that state-sponsored mass murder resulted from large-scale domestic upheaval up to and including internal wars. See for instance, Fein, *Accounting for Genocide*, 1979; Harff, "Genocide as State Terrorism," 1986; Melson, *Revolution and Genocide*, 1992. For more recent discussion of these findings and their implications, see Daniel C. Esty, Jack A. Goldstone, Ted Robert Gurr, Barbara Harff, Marc Levy, Geoffrey D. Dabelko, Pamela T. Surko, and Alan N. Unger, *State Failure Task Force Report: Phase II Findings*. McLean: Science Applications International Corporation, 1998; Matthew Krain, "Democracy, Internal War, and State-Sponsored Mass Murder," *Human Rights Review*, 1,3 (2000): 40–48.

45. Maoz, "Joining the Club of Nations," 1989; Walt, "Revolution and War," 1992.

46. Ted Robert Gurr, ed., *Handbook of Political Conflict: Theory and Research*. New York: Free Press, 1980: 291.

47. See for instance, Otto Hintze, "Military Organization and the Organization of the State," in *The Historical Essays of Otto Hintze*, edited by F. Gilbert, 178–215. New York: Oxford University Press, 1975; Charles Tilly, "War Making and State Making as Organized Crime," in *Bringing the State Back In*, edited by P. Evans, D. Reuschemeyer, and T. Skocpol, 169–191. Cambridge: Cambridge University Press, 1985; Karen A. Rasler and William R. Thompson, *War and State Making: The Shaping of the Global Powers*, Boston: Unwin and Hyman, 1989.

48. For the only study of which I am aware that deals specifically with the importance of elite policy mix choices in understanding post-internal war outcomes, see John Foran and Jeff Goodwin, "Revolutionary Outcomes in Iran and Nicaragua: Coalition Fragmentation, War, and the Limits of Social Transformation," *Theory and Society*, 22 (1993): 209–247. Their comparative case study of post-revolutionary Iran and Nicaragua finds that, despite essentially similar advantages possessed by the these countries' post-internal war elites, the way in which power was consolidated

(via the predominance of repression vs. accommodation) differed significantly. However, despite attributing the overall divergent outcomes to external aggression, the nature of the fragmentation of the revolutionary coalition, and the continuing dependency of the elites on either domestic or international groups, Foran and Goodwin do not discuss specifically what caused these divergent patterns of policy mix choices. Neither do they discuss how these choices affected later political developments in these states.

49. See Migdal, Strong Societies and Weak States, 1989.

Chapter 2

1. J. David Singer and Melvin Small, *Correlates of War Project: International and Civil War Data, 1815–1992,* computer file. Ann Arbor: Inter-university Consortium for Political and Social Research, 1994.

2. Roy Licklider, "The Consequences of Negotiated Settlements in Civil Wars, 1945–1993," *American Political Science Review,* 89 (1995): 681–690; Roy Licklider, ed., *Stopping the Killing: How Civil Wars End.* New York: New York University Press, 1993. Licklider, citing Charles Tilly, defines multiple sovereignty as when the population of an area obeys more than one institution. "They pay taxes [to the opposition], provide men to its armies, feed its functionaries, honor its symbols, give time to its service, or yield other resources despite the prohibitions of a still-existing government they formerly obeyed," Licklider, "The Consequences of Negotiated Settlements," 1995: 682.

3. Licklider, "The Consequences of Negotiated Settlements," 1995.

4. Theda Skocpol, *States and Social Revolutions: A Comparative Analysis of France, Russia, and China.* Cambridge: Cambridge University Press, 1979: 189.

5. Ben Kiernan, ed., *Genocide and Democracy in Cambodia,* monograph #41. New Haven: Yale University Southeast Asia Studies, 1993; Ben Kiernan, "Genocidal Targeting: Two Groups of Victims in Pol Pot's Cambodia," in *State Organized Terror: The Case of Violent Internal Repression,* edited by P. T. Bushnell, V. Shlapentokh, C. K. Vanderpool and J. Sundram, 207–226. Boulder: Westview Press, 1991.

6. Yet another reason why coalition-reduction is necessary immediately following the end of the internal war is the problem of "over-mobilization." Too many groups remain active in the aftermath of the fall of the old regime. This stems from the fact that it "takes a larger mobilized mass to seize power than to maintain it." See Charles Tilly, *From Mobilization to Revolution.* New York: McGraw-Hill, 1978: 218. The result is confusion and competition in the decisionmaking and state-building processes, making the reduction of the coalition necessary to overcome the problem of "too many cooks."

7. John Foran and Jeff Goodwin, "Revolutionary Outcomes in Iran and Nicaragua: Coalition Fragmentation, War, and the Limits of Social Transformation," *Theory and Society,* 22 (1993): 210.

8. Rosemary H. T. O'Kane, "The National Causes of State Construction in France, Russia and China," *Political Studies,* 43 (1995): 15; Rosemary H. T. O'Kane, *The Revolutionary Reign of Terror: The Role of Violence in Political Change.* Hants: Edward Elgar Publishing, 1991.

9. Tilly, *From Mobilization to Revolution,* 1978: 218; Margaret Levi, "The Predatory Theory of Rule," *Politics and Society,* 10 (1981): 441.

10. Skocpol, *States and Social Revolutions,* 1979: 165.

11. O'Kane, "The National Causes," 1995. This is not to say that state building does not occur during the coalition-reduction phase. What is meant, however, is that the primary foci of the elites are the maintenance of their positions within the new government, the accumulation of more power, and the elimination of rivals at the center. Once survival is insured, the elites can wholeheartedly turn their attention to consolidation of power and state building. Until their positions can be secured, survival is the key issue occupying the elites' agenda.

12. Jack A. Goldstone, "An Analytical Framework," in *Revolutions of the Late Twentieth Century,* edited by J. Goldstone, T. R. Gurr, and F. Moshiri, 37–51. Boulder: Westview Press, 1991: 47.

13. O'Kane demonstrates that in the cases of "Great Revolutions" analyzed by Skocpol—France, Russia, and China—early state building was more a function of the coalition-reduction process that immediately followed the internal war than a response to war. She argues that the fundamental basis of permanent state building in these states is "the establishment of central control over the revolutionary forces of internal coercion." See O'Kane, "The National Causes," 1995: 3.

14. Crane Brinton, *The Anatomy of Revolution,* rev. ed. New York: Vintage Books, 1965.

15. S.N. Eisenstadt, *Revolution and the Transformation of Societies: A Comparative Study of Civilizations.* New York: Free Press, 1978.

16. State building is also highly intense (and highly necessary) following complete state collapse in the aftermath of invasion, internal war, or defeat in an international war. Often in such cases a third party, the intervener, acts as state builder. State building from outside the polity is difficult, and rare. Examples include post–World War II Germany and Japan, whose Phoenix-like rise from the ashes was thanks in large part to the state-building efforts of the United States. See A.F.K. Organski and Jacek Kugler, *The War Ledger.* Chicago: University of Chicago Press, 1980; A.F.K. Organski and Jacek Kugler, "The Costs of Major Wars: The Phoenix Factor," *American Political Science Review,* 71 (1977): 1347–1366. Licklider's preliminary study of such situations, comparing United States state-building efforts in Somalia and

Panama under the Bush administration to the post–World War II cases of Germany and Japan, finds that a number of similarities among the cases exists. While historically rare, this type of state building may grow more common with the growing involvement of the UN, NATO, and the United States in peacekeeping operations in the post–Cold War era. See Roy Licklider, "State Building after Invasion: Somalia and Panama," paper presented at the International Studies Association annual convention, San Diego, California, April 1996.

17. The best example of this is the Khmer Rouge's Cambodia/Kampuchea after the 1970–75 internal war. Following their victory, the Khmer Rouge leveled off the old state and society, and initiated the construction of a completely new state, fueled by the fear generated by the severely repressive government.

18. Charles Tilly, "War Making and State Making as Organized Crime," in *Bringing the State Back In,* edited by P. Evans, D. Reuschemeyer, and T. Skocpol, 169–191. Cambridge: Cambridge University Press, 1985: 181.

19. Tilly, "War Making and State Making as Organized Crime," 1985; Karen A. Rasler and William R. Thompson, *War and State Making: The Shaping of the Global Powers.* Boston: Unwin and Hyman, 1989.

20. Samuel E. Finer, "State- and Nation-Building in Europe: The Role of the Military," in *The Formation of National States in Western Europe,* edited by C. Tilly, 84–163. Princeton: Princeton University Press, 1975; Charles Tilly, "Reflections on the History of European State Making," in *The Formation of National States in Western Europe,* edited by C. Tilly, 3–83. Princeton: Princeton University Press, 1975.

21. Youssef Cohen, Brian R. Brown, and A.F.K. Organski, "The Paradoxical Nature of State Making: The Violent Creation of Order," *American Political Science Review,* 75 (1981): 901–910; Ted Robert Gurr, "War, Revolution, and the Growth of the Coercive State," *Comparative Political Studies,* 21 (1988): 45–65.

22. Alan T. Peacock and Jack Wiseman, *The Growth of Public Expenditure in the United Kingdom.* Princeton: Princeton University Press, 1961; Tilly, "War Making and State Making as Organized Crime," 1985: 181; Rasler and Thompson, *War and State Making,* 1989.

23. O'Kane, "The National Causes," 1995.

24. Barbara Harff, "Cambodia: Revolution, Genocide, Intervention," in *Revolutions of the Late Twentieth Century,* edited by J. Goldstone, T. R. Gurr, and F. Moshiri. Boulder: Westview Press, 1991: 227.

25. Harff, "Cambodia: Revolution, Genocide, Intervention," 1991; Ben Kiernan, "Genocidal Targeting: Two Groups of Victims in Pol Pot's Cambodia," in *State Organized Terror: The Case of Violent Internal Repression,* edited by P. T. Bushnell, V. Shlapentokh, C. K. Vanderpool, and J. Sundram, 207–226. Boulder: Westview Press, 1991; Ben Kiernan, ed., *Genocide and Democracy in*

Cambodia, monograph #41. New Haven: Yale University Southeast Asia Studies, 1993.

26. Rasler and Thompson, *War and State Making,* 1989.

27. Historian Paul W. Schroeder argues that alliances between nation-states are often made with the intention of "restraining or controlling the actions of the partners in the alliance themselves." See Paul W. Schroeder, "Alliances, 1815–1945: Weapons of Power and Tools of Management," in *Historical Dimensions of National Security Problems,* edited by K. Knorr. Lawrence: University Press of Kansas, 1976: 230. The same logic is applied here to the temporary domestic alliance made between the accommodators and the accommodated. The elites can and often do accommodate in order to co-opt potential adversaries.

28. Rasler and Thompson, *War and State Making,* 1989: 18.

29. Finer, "State- and Nation-Building in Europe," 1975: 96.

30. Few other options exist. However, while not a normal tactic in a leader's policy mix, nonaccommodating nonviolent direct action is possible, although not very likely. See Matthew Krain, "In Harm's Way: Leaders and Nonviolent Direct Action," paper presented at the 57th Annual Meeting of the Midwest Political Science Association, Chicago, Illinois, April 15–18, 1999.

31. That is not to say that a strategy of "doing nothing" is impossible to employ. For example, Wilson documents the French government's "feather quilt" strategy of absorbing the blows from protesters and not responding with either repression or accommodation. See Frank L. Wilson, "French Interest Group Politics: Pluralist or Neocorporatist?" *American Political Science Review,* 77 (1983): 895–910. Tilly provides three reasons why a state might choose to do nothing rather than repress: "(a) sheer insufficiency of the available means of coercion; (b) inefficiency in applying the means; (c) inhibitions to their application." See Tilly, *From Mobilization to Revolution,* 1978. The same reasoning can be applied to the decision not to use policies of accommodation. However, in the post-internal war state, the pressing need for state building makes action an imperative and inaction a failed strategy. Doing nothing results in an inability to replenish the state treasury, which reduces the elites' future abilities to make war, defend their status, deal effectively with the opposition, protect clients, or further develop policies that expand the state.

32. Gurr, "War, Revolution," 1988: 53.

33. Samuel P. Huntington, *Political Order in Changing Societies.* New Haven: Yale University Press, 1968; Ellen Kay Trimberger, *Revolution from Above: Military Bureaucrats and Development in Japan, Turkey, Egypt, and Peru.* New Brunswick: Transaction Books, 1978; Skocpol, *States and Social Revolutions,* 1979.

34. Theda Skocpol and Ellen Kay Trimberger, "Revolutions and the World-Historical Development of Capitalism," *Berkeley Journal of Sociology,* 22 (1977): 101–113.

35. Cohen, Brown, and Organski, "The Paradoxical Nature of State Making," 1981.

36. Huntington, *Political Order in Changing Societies,* 1968.

37. O'Kane, "The National Causes," 1995.

38. Stephen John Stedman, "The End of the American Civil War," in *Stopping the Killing: How Civil Wars End,* edited by R. Licklider, 164–188. New York: New York University Press, 1993: 181.

39. Sepehr Zabih, *The Left in Contemporary Iran.* Stanford: Hoover Institution Press, 1986.

40. Levi, "The Predatory Theory of Rule," 1981.

41. Michael Mastanduno, David A. Lake, and G. John Ikenberry, "Toward a Realist Theory of State Action," *International Studies Quarterly,* 33 (1989): 457–474.

42. Skocpol and Trimberger, "Revolutions and the World-Historical Development of Capitalism," 1977.

43. R.J. Rummel, "Democracy, Power, Genocide, and Mass Murder," *Journal of Conflict Resolution,* 39 (1995): 3–26; Rummel, R.J. *Death by Government.* New Brunswick: Transaction Books, 1994; O'Kane, *The Revolutionary Reign of Terror,* 1991.

44. See J. Craig Jenkins and Charles Perrow, "Insurgency of the Powerless: Farm Workers Movements," *Annual Review of Sociology,* 42 (1977): 249–268; Tilly, *From Mobilization to Revolution,* 1978. This is not to say that the use of repression will always result in decreased levels of mobilization. In fact, if the necessary resources (micromobilization networks, organizational capital, etc.) are not neutralized by the use of repressive practices, then repression may actually have the opposite effect. In some cases the use of repression can actually initiate new micromobilization processes, increasing the overall level of resistance. See Karl-Dieter Opp and Wolfgang Ruehl, "Repression, Micromobilization and Political Protest," *Social Forces,* 69 (1990): 521–547. Repression can act to curtail resistance in the short run while increasing protest activity in the long run. See Karen A. Rasler, "Concessions, Repression, and Political Protest in the Iranian Revolution," *American Sociological Review,* 61 (1996): 132–152. Severity of repression has also been found to affect resistance levels (Olivier, 1991; Khawaja, 1993). See Johan L. Olivier, "State Repression and Collective Action in South Africa, 1970–1984," *South African Journal of Sociology,* 22 (1991): 109–117; Marwan Khawaja, "Repression and Popular Collective Action: Evidence from the West Bank," *Sociological Forum,* 8 (1993): 47–71.

45. Otto Hintze, "Military Organization and the Organization of the State," in *The Historical Essays of Otto Hintze,* edited by F. Gilbert, 178–215. New York: Oxford University Press, 1975; Tilly, "Reflections on the History of European State Making," 1975; Reinhardt Bendix, *Kings or People.* Berkeley: University of California Press, 1978; Edgar Kiser and Yarom Barzel,

"The Origins of Democracy in England," *Rationality and Society,* 3 (1991): 396–422.

46. James R. Scarritt, "Zimbabwe: Revolutionary Violence Resulting in Reform," in *Revolutions of the Late Twentieth Century,* edited by J. Goldstone, T. R. Gurr, and F. Moshiri, 235–271. Boulder: Westview Press, 1991; Stephen John Stedman, "The End of the Zimbabwean Civil War," in *Stopping the Killing: How Civil Wars End,* edited by R. Licklider, 125–163. New York: New York University Press, 1993.

47. Marc V. Simon and Harvey Starr, "Extraction, Allocation, and the Rise and Decline of States: A Simulation Analysis of Two-Level Security Management," *Journal of Conflict Resolution,* 40 (1996): 272–297.

48. However, Simon and Starr argue that in the long run a consistent strategy of repression can lead to decreased viability of the elites. See Simon and Starr, "Extraction, Allocation," 1996. This is consistent with studies that show that while repression may have short term negative effects on opposition, it can actually exacerbate it in the long run. I shall examine this question more closely in Chapter 5.

49. Ted Robert Gurr, "The Political Origins of State Violence and Terror: A Theoretical Analysis," in *Government Violence and Repression: An Agenda for Research,* edited by M. Stohl and G. A. Lopez. New York: Greenwood Press, 1986; William Stanley, "The Factional Rationality of Mass Murder: A Level of Analysis Problem in the Study of State Violence," unpublished manuscript, 1998.

50. Machiavelli understood the desirability of repression over accommodation as an issue of the security of fear tactics versus the instability of purchased allegiance: "Upon this a question arises: whether it be better to be loved than feared or feared than loved? It may be answered that one should wish to be both, but, because it is difficult to unite them in one person, is much safer to be feared than loved, when, of the two, either must be dispensed with, because friendships that are obtained by payments, and not by greatness or nobility of mind, may indeed be earned, but they are not secured, and in time of need cannot be relied upon; and men have less scruple in offending one who is beloved than one who is feared, for love is preserved by the link of obligation which, owing to the baseness of men, is broken at every opportunity for their advantage; but fear preserves you by a dread of punishment which never fails." Niccolo Machiavelli, *The Prince,* reprint. New York: Norton, 1980.

51. Other examples include: the gradual extension of some freedoms in post-Tiananmen China despite a continued heavy reliance on repression and the improved status of women in Communist states such as the Soviet Union, China, Cuba, and others. See for instance, Amnesty International, *Amnesty International Report: 1994.* New York: Amnesty International USA, 1994; Johnnetta B. Cole, "Women in Cuba: The Revolution Within the

Revolution," in *Comparative Perspectives of Third World Women,* edited by B. Lindsay. New York: Praeger, 1980; Margaret Randall, *Women in Cuba: Twenty Years Later.* Brooklyn: Smyrna Press, 1981.

52. Mark I. Lichbach, "Deterrence or Escalation?: The Puzzle of Aggregate Studies of Repression and Dissent," *Journal of Conflict Resolution,* 32 (1987): 266–297.

53. Some who utilize the individual level of analysis examine personality rather than perceptions of elites. A number of scholars point to the existence of a "revolutionary personality" common to elites who successfully lead violent opposition against the old regime. This personality type usually consists of the following traits: authoritarianism, suspiciousness, stubbornness, narcissism, extreme self-confidence. See M. N. Hagopian, *The Phenomenon of Revolution.* New York: Dodd, Mead and Company, 1974; Mustafa Rejai, *Leaders of Revolution.* Beverly Hills: Sage, 1979. However, Snare demonstrates that even small samples of revolutionaries consist of a number of differing types of personalities rather than one common "revolutionary personality." In fact, he concludes that "successful, revolutionaries do not seem much different than other world leaders in general." See Charles Snare, "Testing the Usefulness of Political Personality Models: How Well Do Political Personality Types Predict Policy Preferences?" unpublished manuscript, 1997. And while revolutionary leaders are extraordinary historical figures, and appear to be prime candidates for the "uniqueness of the great figure in history" approach, assumptions of uniqueness allow us little in the way of generalizable explanatory power. Indeed, both Walt and Calvert find that focusing on the personality of a revolutionary leader furnishes the researcher with severely limited explanations at best. See Stephen M. Walt, "Revolution and War," *World Politics,* 44 (1992): 321–368; Peter Calvert, *Revolution and Counter-Revolution.* Minneapolis: University of Minnesota Press, 1990. I therefore refrain from this line of inquiry.

54. Richard Snyder, H. W. Bruck, and Burton Sapin, eds., *Foreign Policy Decision-Making: An Approach to the Society of International Politics.* New York: Free Press of Glencove, 1962; M. Brewster Smith, Jerome S. Bruner, and Robert W. White, *Opinions and Personality.* New York: Wiley, 1956; Milton Rokeach, *The Open and Closed Mind: Investigations into the Nature of Belief Systems and Personality Systems.* New York: Basic Books, 1960.

55. Ole R. Holsti, "The Belief System and National Images: A Case Study," *Journal of Conflict Resolution,* 6 (1962): 244–252; Harold Sprout and Margaret Sprout, *The Ecological Perspective on Human Affairs.* Princeton: Princeton University Press, 1965.

56. Robert Jervis, *Perception and Misperception in International Relations.* Princeton: Princeton University Press, 1976.

57. William Gamson, *The Strategy of Social Protest.* 2nd ed. Belmont: Wadsworth Publishing, 1990: 82.

58. By intervening so directly and dramatically (on either side), a foreign power can effectively become a challenger or a member of the polity in its own right. As an ally, it may provide a new, previously untapped source of extraction and protection, which can artificially stabilize the regime. By aiding the new regime in the first place, and by remaining on as a source of added protection and funds, the U.S. became an active player in South Vietnamese domestic politics. As such, I consider it to have been a member of the new, restructured polity, one which had formed an alliance with the ruling elite, and was a primary source of protection and extraction.

59. Stanley Karnow, *Vietnam: A History.* New York: Viking, 1983; H. John LeVan, "Vietnam: Revolution of Postcolonial Consolidation," in *Revolutions of the Late Twentieth Century,* edited by J. Goldstone, T. R. Gurr, and F. Moshiri, 52–87. Boulder: Westview Press, 1991.

60. Karnow, *Vietnam: A History,* 1983.

61. LeVan, "Vietnam: Revolution of Postcolonial Consolidation," 1991: 76.

62. The North Vietnamese revolutionary elites saw their revolution as having two fronts—one in the North and one in the South. See J. Woddis, *Ho Chi Minh: Selected Articles and Speeches.* New York: International Publishers, 1970: 149. The Communist revolution in the North had already been consolidated for a few years by the time the North successfully took the South. But it was the taking of the South that completed the revolutionary period, and ushered in the post-internal war period for the new Communist state of Vietnam. Therefore, consolidation of the revolution could not have truly begun until 1975. See LeVan, "Vietnam: Revolution of Postcolonial Consolidation," 1991: 75.

63. Karnow, *Vietnam: A History,* 1983: 29.

64. LeVan, "Vietnam: Revolution of Postcolonial Consolidation," 1991: 76.

65. Jenkins and Perrow, "Insurgency of the Powerless," 1977; Tilly, *From Mobilization to Revolution,* 1978.

66. LeVan, "Vietnam: Revolution of Postcolonial Consolidation," 1991: 76.

67. Carl Leiden and Karl M. Schmitt, *The Politics of Violence: Revolution in the Modern World.* Englewood Cliffs, NJ: Prentice-Hall, 1968: 131; Eric Wolf, *Peasant Wars of the Twentieth Century.* New York: Knopf, 1970: 47.

68. Leiden and Schmitt, *The Politics of Violence,* 1968: 127.

69. For a good discussion of the extensive reforms instituted in post-internal war Mexico, see: Howard F. Cline, *The United States and Mexico.* Cambridge: Harvard University Press, 1963; Leiden and Schmitt, *The Politics of Violence,* 1968.

70. Leiden and Schmitt, *The Politics of Violence,* 1968: 128.

71. Eisenstadt, *Revolution and the Transformation of Societies,* 1978; Tilly, *From Mobilization to Revolution,* 1978; Trimberger, *Revolution from Above,* 1978; Skocpol, *States and Social Revolutions,* 1979.

72. Sidney Tarrow, *Power in Movement: Social Movements, Collective Action and Politics.* Cambridge: Cambridge University Press, 1994; Matthew Krain, "State-Sponsored Mass Murder: The Onset and Severity of Genocides and Politicides," *Journal of Conflict Resolution,* 41 (1997): 331–360. Much of the recent work on political violence has focused on theories of *political opportunity structure.* An assumption of these theories is that political violence is a function of the political opportunities and constraints of the immediate political environment. When openings in the structure of political opportunities change the configurations of power, this in turn affects the strategies used by the elites against their (potential) challengers. As Boudreau notes, "[s]tructural shifts, influence the probable ramifications of collective action, and therefore change how participants behave." See Vincent Boudreau, "Northern Theory, Southern Protest: Opportunity Structure Analysis in Cross-National Perspective," *Mobilization,* 1 (1996): 186. Recent works find that changes in the international political opportunity structure (often caused by war) have important structural effects on the national political opportunity structure. International relations scholars have also begun to incorporate the role of opportunity into a broader understanding of how war and internal conflict are interrelated. See Harvey Starr, "Revolution and War: Rethinking the Linkage between Internal and External Conflict," *Political Research Quarterly,* 47 (1994): 481–507.

73. Tilly, *From Mobilization to Revolution,* 1978; Skocpol, *States and Social Revolutions,* 1979.

74. Arthur A. Stein, *The Nation at War,* Baltimore: Johns Hopkins University Press, 1980.

75. Bruce Bueno de Mesquita, Randolph M. Siverson, and Gary Woller, "War and The Fate of Regimes: A Comparative Analysis," *American Political Science Review,* 86 (1992): 638–646.

76. Robert Higgs, *Crisis and Leviathan : Critical Episodes in the Growth of American Government.* New York: Oxford University Press, 1987: 17.

77. Quoted in Harold D. Lasswell, *National Security and Individual Freedom.* New York: McGraw-Hill, 1950: 23. Even in the most democratic of states, individual rights are abridged and civil liberties are suspended during wartime. For example, President Lincoln suspended the writ of *habeas corpus* during the American Civil War, allowing army officers to arrest civilians and hold them in prison indefinitely without trial or the sanction of civil courts. See James McPhereson, *Battle Cry of Freedom.* New York: Oxford University Press, 1988. In World War II, the governor of Hawaii ceded his authority to the U.S. military after the Japanese bombing of Pearl Harbor. Martial law was immediately proclaimed in Hawaii. The commanding general closed all civil courts on December 8, 1941. See Lasswell, *National Security and Individual Freedom,* 1950. The internment of Japanese-American citizens without statutory authority is yet another example of how

legal barriers are sidestepped in war. For studies focusing on the use of repression in the United States during and in the aftermath of war, see: Michael Stohl, *War and Domestic Political Violence: The American Capacity for Repression and Reaction.* Beverly Hills: Sage, 1976; Michael Stohl, "War and Domestic Violence: The Case of the United States, 1890–1970," *Journal of Conflict Resolution,* 19 (1975): 379–416; Karen A. Rasler, "War, Accommodation, and Violence in the United States, 1890–1970," *American Political Science Review,* 80 (1986): 921–945; Karen A. Rasler and William R. Thompson, *War and State Making: The Shaping of the Global Powers.* Boston: Unwin and Hyman, 1989.

78. Harold D. Lasswell, "The Garrison-State Hypothesis Today," in *Changing Patterns in Military Politics,* edited by S. P. Huntington, 51–70. New York: Free Press, 1962; Gurr, "War, Revolution," 1988.

79. Zeev Maoz, "Joining the Club of Nations: Political Development and International Conflicts, 1816–1976," *International Studies Quarterly,* 33 (1989): 199–231; Gil Friedman, and Harvey Starr, "The Nexus of Civil and International Conflict Revisited: Opportunity, Willingness, and the Internal-External Linkage," paper presented at the 29th Annual North American Meeting of the Peace Science Society (International), Columbus, Ohio, October 13–15, 1995: 10.

80. Michael Stohl, "The Nexus of Civil and International Conflict," in *Handbook of Political Conflict: Theory and Research,* edited by T. R. Gurr, 297–330. New York: Free Press, 1980.

81. Andrew D. McNitt, "Government Coercion: An Exploratory Analysis," *The Social Science Journal,* 32 (1995): 195–205.

82. Steven C. Poe and C. Neal Tate, "Repression of Human Rights to Personal Integrity in the 1980s: A Global Analysis," *American Political Science Review,* 88 (1994): 853–872.

83. Krain, "State-Sponsored Mass Murder," 1997.

84. Politicides are mass killings in which "victim groups are defined primarily in terms of their hierarchical position or political opposition to the regime and dominant groups." See Barbara Harff and Ted Robert Gurr, "Toward an Empirical Theory of Genocides and Politicides: Identification and Measurement of Cases Since 1945," *International Studies Quarterly,* 32 (1988): 360.

85. Charles Tilly, *Coercion, Capital and European States, A.D. 990–1990.* Cambridge: Basil Blackwell, 1990: 20.

86. Occasionally, war also provides leaders with the rationale to justify repressive or accommodative action that they could not justify before the war (Porter, 1994: 10).

87. Peacock and Wiseman, *The Growth of Public Expenditure in the United Kingdom,* 1961.

88. Tilly, From Mobilization to Revolution, 1978; Tilly, Coercion, Capital and European States, 1990: 28.

Chapter 3

1. Later (in Chapters 5 and 6) I will engage in rigorous within-case large-*n* statistical methodology to test some of the hypothetical implications of my model. However, even this large-*n* methodology occurs within the overall framework of a small-*n* structured-focused "most similar case" comparative design.

2. Arend Lijphart, "Comparative Politics and Comparative Method," *American Political Science Review*, 65 (1971): 682–698; Alexander L. George and Timothy J. McKeown, "Case Studies and Theories of Organizational Decision Making," *Advances in Information Processing in Organizations*, 2 (1985): 21–58; Charles C. Ragin, *The Comparative Method: Moving beyond Qualitative and Quantitative Strategies*. Berkeley: University of California Press, 1987: 47–48. For an excellent discussion of the problems inherent in this line of inquiry, see pages 48–51 in Ragin's book. For a discussion of how this method relates to John Stuart Mill's ideas of methods of agreement and method of difference, see pages 36–41 in Ragin's book. See also Gary King, Robert O. Keohane, and Sidney Verba, *Designing Social Inquiry: Scientific Inference in Qualitative Research*. Princeton: Princeton University Press, 1994: 168.

3. However, the researcher must also be wary not to control for a variable that is in part a consequence of the main independent variable(s) of theoretical interest. See King, Keohane, and Verba, *Designing Social Inquiry*, 1994: 173–174.

4. King, Keohane, and Verba, *Designing Social Inquiry*, 1994: 168.

5. While not creating a perfect experimental environment in which to test hypotheses, this method does increase the leverage that researchers using small-*n* comparative methodology have on a given problem. See King, Keohane, and Verba, *Designing Social Inquiry*, 1994: 206.

6. J. David Singer and Melvin Small, *Correlates of War Project: International and Civil War Data, 1815–1992*, computer file. Ann Arbor: Inter-university Consortium for Political and Social Research, 1994.

7. This definition is but one interpretation. Many who study these cases call all such internal conflicts *civil wars*. See for instance: Roy Licklider, "The Consequences of Negotiated Settlements in Civil Wars, 1945–1993," *American Political Science Review*, 89, 3 (1995): 681–690; Singer and Small, "Correlates of War Project," 1994. However, as Licklider later notes, definitions of these phenomena vary considerably. See his article, "Early Returns: Results of the First Wave of Statistical Studies of Civil War Termination," *Civil Wars*, 1,3 (1998): 121–132. I choose the term *internal war* because the term is descriptively accurate, and is not associated with a type of conflict (i.e., the American Civil War).

8. Theda Skocpol, *States and Social Revolutions: A Comparative Analysis of France, Russia, and China*. Cambridge: Cambridge University Press, 1979.

9. Ellen Kay Trimberger, *Revolution from Above: Military Bureaucrats and Development in Japan, Turkey, Egypt, and Peru*. New Brunswick: Transaction Books, 1978.

10. By this admittedly rough definition, civil wars might therefore be thought of as separatist conflicts that escalate to full-blown war. Many separatist conflicts do not reach this level of escalation. Recent examples include the as yet unsuccessful efforts of the Quebeçois and the negotiated settlement between the Inuit and the Canadian government creating the new territory Nunavut.

11. This coding rule is adequate when considering revolutionary success only if the revolution is not a "revolution from above." Although they code the "winner" of the internal war, the Correlates of War (COW) data set codes this variable as either "government" or "opposition." See Singer and Small, *Correlates of War Project*. This is problematic for two reasons. First, government winners are not always the same elites who began the struggle. In such cases, while leadership and social and economic policies change, the political structures and institutions remain intact. Second, the term "opposition" can refer to either type of internal war. Both cases of changes "from above" as Yemen [1948] and "changes from below" such as Bolivia [1952] and Iran [1979] have all been coded as having been won by the "opposition" by COW. Therefore, any further tests of this model using cases other than revolutions from below should consider an alternate decision rule regarding internal war success.

12. See for example, Arthur A. Stein, *The Nation at War*. Baltimore: Johns Hopkins University Press, 1980; Ted Robert Gurr, "War, Revolution, and the Growth of the Coercive State," *Comparative Political Studies*, 21 (1988): 45–65; Gil Friedman and Harvey Starr, "The Nexus of Civil and International Conflict Revisited: Opportunity, Willingness, and the Internal-External Linkage," paper presented at the 29th Annual North American Meeting of the Peace Science Society (International), Columbus, Ohio, October 13–15, 1995; Roy Licklider, "The Consequences of Negotiated Settlements in Civil Wars, 1945–1993," *American Political Science Review*, 89 (1995): 681–690.

13. See Robert Harrison Wagner, "The Causes of Peace," in *Stopping the Killing: How Civil Wars End*, edited by R. Licklider, 235–268. New York: New York University Press, 1993; Licklider, "The Consequences of Negotiated Settlements," 1995.

14. Licklider, "The Consequences of Negotiated Settlements," 1995: 686.

15. T. David Mason and Patrick J. Fett, "How Civil Wars End: A Rational Choice Approach," *Journal of Conflict Resolution*, 40 (1996): 563.

16. For an excellent summary and critique of these arguments, see Mark I. Lichbach, "An Evaluation of 'Does Economic Inequality Breed Political Conflict?' Studies," *World Politics*, 41 (1989): 431–470. For empirical examples of

work exploring this relationship, see T. David Mason and Dale A. Krane, "The Political Economy of Death Squads: Toward a Theory of the Impact of State-Sanctioned Terror," *International Studies Quarterly*, 33 (1989): 175–198; Conway Henderson, "Conditions Affecting the Use of Political Repression," *Journal of Conflict Resolution*, 35 (1991): 120–142; Steven C. Poe and C. Neal Tate, "Repression of Human Rights to Personal Integrity in the 1980s: A Global Analysis," *American Political Science Review*, 88 (1994): 853–872; Mansoor Moaddel, "Political Conflict in the World Economy: A Cross-National Analysis of Modernization and World-System Theories," *American Sociological Review* 59 (1994): 276–303; Christian A. Davenport, "Multi-Dimensional Threat Perception and State Repression: An Inquiry into Why States Apply Negative Sanctions," *American Journal of Political Science*, 39 (1995): 683–713.

17. Michael Freeman, "The Theory and Prevention of Genocide," *Holocaust and Genocide Studies*, 6 (1991): 188.

18. Michael T. Hannan, "The Dynamics of Ethnic Boundaries in Modern States," in *National Development and the World System: Educational, Economic, and Political Change, 1950–1970*, edited by J. W. Meyer and M. T. Hannan, 253–275. Chicago: University of Chicago Press, 1979: 254.

19. Gurr, "War, Revolution, and the Growth of the Coercive State," 1988: 46.

20. Charles Tilly, "Reflections on the History of European State Making," in *The Formation of National States in Western Europe*, edited by C. Tilly, 3–83. Princeton: Princeton University Press, 1975: 79.

21. Leo Kuper, *The Pity of it All: Polarisation of Racial and Ethnic Relations*. Minneapolis: University of Minnesota Press, 1977.

22. Matthew Krain, "State-Sponsored Mass Murder: The Onset and Severity of Genocides and Politicides," *Journal of Conflict Resolution*, 41 (1997): 341–342. This measure is a reworking of Taylor and Hudson's measure of ethnolinguistic fractionalization. See Charles Lewis Taylor and Michael C. Hudson. *The World Handbook of Political and Social Indicators*, 2nd ed., New Haven: Yale University Press, 1972. While their measure is often used in studies of this sort, the Taylor and Hudson data misrepresents the true nature of ethnic cleavages in many societies. Linguistic cleavages do not always correspond with ethnic ones, creating, for example, misleadingly lower scores for Latin America and higher scores for Africa. While linguistic differences are often important, most ethnopolitical conflict centers around the primary cleavage of ethnicity. My index is identical to the Taylor and Hudson measure in many cases (84 percent correlated), but differs significantly in particular in the Latin American cases. Given the three Latin American cases examined here, I have more confidence in the accuracy of my measure in the context of this study.

23. Using my measure, ethnic fractionalization scores for the four cases chosen for this study are: Cuba [1958–59] = 0.43; Nicaragua [1978–79] = 0.47; Iran [1978–79] = 0.53; Bolivia [1952] = 0.59.

24. See the next chapter for a discussion of how I determined elite perceptions of security or vulnerability in these cases. See Tables D.1-D.3 in Appendix D for an annual measure of elite perceptions.

25. See for instance, the studies listed in Table 4.7 in the next chapter.

26. Jonathan Kelley and Herbert S. Klein, *Revolution and the Rebirth of Inequality: A Theory Applied to the National Revolution in Bolivia.* Berkeley: University of California Press, 1981: 93.

27. James M. Malloy, *Bolivia's MNR: A Study of a National Popular Movement in Latin America.* Buffalo: Council on International Studies, State University of New York at Buffalo, 1971: 38–40.

28. James Dunkerley, *Rebellion in the Veins: Political Struggle in Bolivia, 1952–1982.* London: Verso, 1984: 41.

29. James M. Malloy, "Revolutionary Politics," in *Beyond the Revolution: Bolivia since 1952,* edited by J. Malloy and R. Thorn, 111–156. Pittsburgh: University of Pittsburgh Press, 1971: 117.

30. Malloy, "Revolutionary Politics," 1971: 117.

31. Herbert L. Matthews, "Commentary: The Cuban Revolution," *Hispanic American Report,* August 29, 1960: iii.

32. Eric Wolf, *Peasant Wars of the Twentieth Century.* New York: Knopf, 1970.

33. For a more detailed account of the revolutionary conflict, see Herbert L. Matthews, *Revolution in Cuba.* New York: Charles Scribner's Sons, 1975; Juan M. del Aguila, *Cuba: Dilemmas of a Revolution.* Boulder: Westview Press, 1984: 30–40; Marifeli Perez-Stable, *The Cuban Revolution: Origins, Course, and Legacy.* New York: Oxford University Press, 1993: 52–60.

34. Eric Selbin, *Modern Latin American Revolutions.* Boulder: Westview Press, 1993: 44.

35. Moshen Milani, *The Making of Iran's Islamic Revolution.* Boulder: Westview Press, 1994: 41–43.

36. Shaul Bakhash, *The Reign of the Ayatollahs: Iran and the Islamic Revolution.* New York: Basic Books, 1984: 10–11.

37. Bakhash, *The Reign of the Ayatollahs,* 1984: 12.

38. Karen A. Rasler, "Concessions, Repression, and Political Protest in the Iranian Revolution," *American Sociological Review,* 61 (1996): 132–152.

39. Farrokh Moshiri, "Iran: Islamic Revolution Against Westernization," in *Revolutions of the Late Twentieth Century,* edited by J. Goldstone, T. R. Gurr, and F. Moshiri, 116–135. Boulder: Westview Press, 1991: 129.

40. John D. Stempel, *Inside the Iranian Revolution.* Bloomington: Indiana University Press, 1981: 163–164.

41. Thomas W. Walker, *Nicaragua: The Land of Sandino.* Boulder: Westview Press, 1991: 31.

42. Walker, *Nicaragua: The Land of Sandino,* 1991: 40–42; Gary Ruchwarger, *People in Power: Forging a Grassroots Democracy in Nicaragua.* South Hadley: Bergin and Garvey Publishers, 1987.

43. Selbin, *Modern Latin American Revolutions,* 1993: 53.
44. For a more complete account see Walker, *Nicaragua: The Land of Sandino.* 1991: 34–40; Devora Grynspan, "Nicaragua: A New Model for Popular Revolution in Latin America," in *Revolutions of the Late Twentieth Century,* edited by J. Goldstone, T. R. Gurr, and F. Moshiri, 88–115. Boulder: Westview Press, 1991.
45. James DeFronzo, *Revolutions and Revolutionary Movements.* Boulder: Westview Press, 1991: 201.

Chapter 4

1. Despite the dual nature of this variable within the larger context of this project, for the sake of simplicity I refer to these variables throughout the rest of this chapter as the dependent variables, as that is how they will be used in both this chapter and the next.
2. Conway Henderson, "Conditions Affecting the Use of Political Repression," *Journal of Conflict Resolution,* 35 (1991): 120–142; Conway Henderson, "Population Pressures and Political Repression," *Social Science Quarterly,* 74 (1993): 322–333; Steven C. Poe and C. Neal Tate, "Repression of Human Rights to Personal Integrity in the 1980s: A Global Analysis," *American Political Science Review,* 88 (1994): 853–872; David L. Cingranelli and David L. Richards, "Measuring the Level, Pattern, and Sequence of Government Respect for Physical Integrity Rights," *International Studies Quarterly,* 43 (1999): 407–418.
3. See for instance, Neil J. Mitchell and James J. McCormick, "Economic and Political Explanations of Human Rights Violations," *World Politics,* 40 (1988): 476–498.
4. See for instance, Henderson, "Conditions Affecting the Use of Political Repression," 1991; Henderson, "Population Pressures and Political Repression," 1993.
5. Poe and Tate find that both *Amnesty International Reports* and *U.S. State Department Reports* have a zero-order correlation of 0.83. See Poe and Tate, "Repression of Human Rights," 1994: 855. More generally, McBride finds that measures developed using *State Department Reports* exhibited the same patterns as those developed using *Amnesty International Reports.* See Jeffrey Scott McBride, "Political Repression and Regime Transition: Latin America, 1980–1993," paper presented at the Annual Meeting of the American Political Science Association, Washington, DC, August 28–31, 1997: fn.9.
6. Mitchell and McCormick, "Economic and Political Explanations," 1988.
7. Cingranelli and Richards, "Measuring the Level," 1999.
8. Raymond D. Gastil, *Freedom in the World: Political Rights and Civil Liberties, 1980.* New Brunswick: Transaction Books, 1980.
9. Mitchell and McCormick, "Economic and Political Explanations," 1988.

10. Cingranelli and Richards, "Measuring the Level," 1999.

11. Edward E. Azar, *Conflict and Peace Data Bank (COPDAB), 1948–1978.* ICPSR Study #7767. Ann Arbor: Inter-university Consortium for Political and Social Research, 1993.

12. Charles McClelland, *World Events Interaction Survey,* ICPR ed. Los Angeles: University of Southern California, 1972.

13. For a recent attempt to splice together these two data series to form one continuous series from 1948 to the present, see Rafael Reuveny and Hee-joon Kang, "International Conflict and Cooperation: Splicing COPDAB and WEIS Series," *International Studies Quarterly,* 40 (1996): 281–306.

14. Charles Lewis Taylor and Michael C. Hudson, *The World Handbook of Political and Social Indicators,* 2nd ed. New Haven: Yale University Press, 1972; Charles Lewis Taylor and David A. Jodice, *World Handbook of Political and Social Indicators.* New Haven: Yale University Press, 1983.

15. For a more detailed critique of *The World Handbook* data, see Leeds, et al. (1995).

16. Additionally, Goldstein questions the reliability of many *World Handbook* measures. See Robert J. Goldstein, "The Limitations of Using Quantitative Data in Studying Human Rights Abuses," *Human Rights Quarterly,* 8 (1986): 607–627.

17. Will H. Moore and Ronny Lindstrom, "The Violent Intranational Conflict Data Project (VICDP) Codebook." Department of Political Science, University of California- Riverside, 1996.

18. Will H. Moore, "Repression and Dissent: Substitution, Context, and Timing," *American Journal of Political Science,* 42 (1998): 851–873.

19. VICDP examines the following cases: Colombia, Lebanon, Nigeria, Peru, the Philippines, Sri Lanka, and Zimbabwe. See Moore and Lindstrom, "The Violent Intranational Conflict Data Project (VICDP) Codebook," 1996.

20. Brett Ashley Leeds, David R. Davis, and Will H. Moore, with Christopher McHorney, *The Intranational Political Interactions (IPI) Codebook.* Atlanta: Department of Political Science, Emory University, 1995.

21. IPI examines the following cases: Argentina, Belgium, Brazil, Chile, Colombia, Greece, Hungary, India, Indonesia, Iraq, Kenya, Lebanon, Mexico, Nigeria, Pakistan, Peru, the Philippines, South Africa, South Korea, Spain, Sri Lanka, Syria, Taiwan, Venezuela, Zaire, and Zimbabwe.

22. John L. Davies, "The Global Event-Data System Manual," Center for International Development and Conflict Management, University of Maryland, 1993.

23. Deborah J. Gerner, Philip A. Schrodt, Ronald A. Francisco, and Judith L. Weddle, "Machine Coding of Event Data Using Regional and International Sources," *International Studies Quarterly,* 38 (1994): 91–120.

24. Reuveny and Kang, "International Conflict and Cooperation," 1996.

25. This strategy of utilizing the evaluations of expert judges to create weights or value scales has been used successfully in other studies of conflict and conflict resolution. See for example: Joshua S. Goldstein, "A Conflict-Cooperation Scale for WEIS Events Data," *Journal of Conflict Resolution*, 36 (1991): 369–385; Leeds, Davis, and Moore, with McHorney, *The Intranational Political Interactions (IPI) Codebook*, 1995; Will H. Moore, "Reciprocity and the Domestic-International Conflict Nexus During the 'Rhodesia Problem,'" *Journal of Conflict Resolution*, 39 (1995): 129–167; Moore and Lindstrom, "The Violent Intranational Conflict Data Project (VICDP) Codebook," 1996.

26. In order to allow for confidentiality I have subsequently referred to each expert who did respond, by number (1–15) only (see for example Tables 4.3 and 4.4).

27. I distributed the same survey to a class of 23 undergraduate political science students to check "face validity" of the experts' average scores. The correlations between the experts' scores and the undergraduate class' scores were 0.85 on the repression scale and 0.79 on the accommodation scale.

28. I have considered that coverage may have been better for the later cases (Iran, Nicaragua) than for the earlier cases (Bolivia, Cuba) because of the technological advances made in communications and the accompanying "shrinking of the globe" over time. However, Gibney and Caliendo find that media coverage of events across the globe does not increase significantly with the development of these technological advances. See Mark Gibney and Stephen M. Caliendo, "'All the News That's Fit to Print?': *New York Times* Coverage of Human Rights Violations," paper presented at the Annual Meeting of the American Political Science Association, August 28–31, 1997. Washington, DC.

29. The *New York Times Index* has been employed as a key source in many events data collection projects including Intranational Political Interactions [IPI] and International Military Intervention [IMI]. However, I have reservations about employing the *New York Times Index* as a primary source for the collection of data on repression and accommodation. Brockett (1992: 170–171) points out numerous problems, including the bias against events in the periphery, discussed earlier, and the fact that there can even be discrepancies between the *Index* and the *New York Times* news story itself. See Charles Brockett, "Measuring Political Violence and Land Inequality in Central America," *American Political Science Review*, 86 (1992): 169–176. Additionally, Gibney and Caliendo find that the *Times'* coverage of human rights is seriously lacking. Accommodation and the more subtle types of repression are often not reported, while conflict and crisis receive press coverage. See Gibney and Caliendo, "All the News That's Fit to Print?" 1997.

30. Frederic S. Pearson and Robert A. Baumann, *International Military Intervention, 1946–1988 (Codebook)*, ICPSR #6035. Ann Arbor: Inter-university

Consortium for Political and Social Research, 1993. Tillema's data set of international armed conflict (wars and military interventions), similar in many ways to IMI, also employs *Keesing's Contemporary Archives* as a primary source. See Herbert K. Tillema, *International Armed Conflict Since 1945.* Boulder: Westview Press, 1991.

31. Many other data collection projects, including the Correlates of War (COW), have used *Keesing's Contemporary Archives* as a supplemental source.

32. For example, even throughout a two-month newspaper strike during the Iranian Revolution, FBIS remained a reliable source of event data. See Karen A. Rasler, "Concessions, Repression, and Political Protest in the Iranian Revolution," *American Sociological Review,* 61 (1996): 136.

33. Originally known as *The Times of Havana* (TOH) and published out of the capital city of Cuba, its editors were soon forced to flee to the United States. There they continued publication from Miami, under the new name.

34. The name refers to the boat that Castro and his followers used during the Sierra Maestra landing. See John Spencer Nichols, "The Press in Cuba, " in *The Cuba Reader: The Making of a Revolutionary Society,* edited by P. Brenner, W. M. LeoGrande, D. Rich, and D. Siegel, New York: Grove Press, 1989: 221.

35. If TOTA were the only source used one might be worried that both repression and accommodation could be overreported. However, TOTA is one of many sources to be used. Given the coding rule requirement of a confirming source, if an event reported in TOTA was not confirmed by one of the other sources used it was dropped from consideration.

36. The problem of source bias is common in this type of research. Mitchell and McCormick argue that among the most commonly used sources of human rights data—*Amnesty International Reports, Freedom House,* and *U.S. State Department Reports*—only *Amnesty International Reports* can "make a reasonable claim to being politically uncommitted." See Mitchell and Mc-Cormick, "Economic and Political Explanations," 1988. Yet all three continue to be used, sometimes interchangeably, in research on human rights.

37. Gibney and Caliendo, "All the News That's Fit to Print?" 1997: 22.

38. United States Congress—House Committee on Foreign Affairs. *Religious Persecution of the Baha'is in Iran, 1988.* 100th Congress, 2nd Session. Washington, DC: United States Government Printing Office, 1988.

39. Anoushiravan Ehteshami, *After Khomeini: The Iranian Second Republic.* London: Routledge, 1995.

40. Despite the shortcomings of the *New York Times Index* discussed in footnote 7 (above), it may still be useful for confirmation of material gathered using other sources. Gibney and Caliendo find that human rights stories in the *New York Times* were plentiful in states in which U.S. interests were high, while lacking in countries in which U.S. interests were low. See Gibney and Caliendo, "All the News That's Fit to Print?" 1997;

Michael Stohl, "Outside a Small Circle of Friends: States, Genocide, Mass Killing and the Role of Bystanders," *Journal of Peace Research* 24 (1987): 151–166. All four cases used in this study are cases in which the U.S. had high levels of interest, either economically (Bolivia, Iran) or politically (Cuba, Iran, Nicaragua). Additionally, Ovsiovitch demonstrates that human rights coverage is greater in *The New York Times* than in other media sources such as *Time* magazine or the CBS *Evening News*. See Jay S. Ovsiovitch, "A Distant Image? Factors Influencing the U.S. Media's Coverage of Human Rights," in *Human Rights in Developing Countries,* edited by David L. Cingranelli. Greenwich: JAI Press, 1996; Jay S. Ovsiovitch, "News Coverage of Human Rights," *Political Research Quarterly,* 46 (1993): 671–689. Thus, while not the best original source for data on repression and accommodation, it appears that it is the best candidate for a source whose sole purpose is to confirm instances of repression or accommodation in the cases examined in this study. Therefore, I employ the *New York Times Index* in Step 4 as a check on previous citations of events.

41. J. David Singer and Melvin Small, *Correlates of War Project: International and Civil War Data, 1815–1992,* computer file. Ann Arbor: Inter-university Consortium for Political and Social Research, 1994.

42. Ben Kiernan, "Genocidal Targeting: Two Groups of Victims in Pol Pot's Cambodia," in *State Organized Terror: The Case of Violent Internal Repression,* edited by P. T. Bushnell, V. Shlapentokh, C. K. Vanderpool, and J. Sundram, 207–226. Boulder: Westview Press, 1991.

43. Events like the hypothetical one described here were unfortunately all too common in post-internal war Cambodia/Kampuchea. For a good description of the tactics used by the Khmer Rouge against the Eastern Zoners and the Chams, see Kiernan, "Genocidal Targeting," 1991. For a detailed account of the slaughter of the Buddhist Monks, see Chanthou Boua, "Genocide of a Religious Group: Pol Pot and Cambodia's Buddhist Monks," in Bushnell, et al., 1991: 227–242.

44. Interestingly, when severity of repression is accounted for (Figure 4.3), repressive levels of the three Latin American countries all but converge in the final five years of observation (t+8 through t+12). This makes sense, considering that two of the cases (Cuba, Bolivia) have avoided a war, while the third (Nicaragua) spent this period trying to comply with a peace plan that would end their devastating war.

45. Misagh Parsa, *Social Origins of the Iranian Revolution.* New Brunswick: Rutgers University Press, 1989.

46. Shaul Bakhash, *The Reign of the Ayatollahs: Iran and the Islamic Revolution.* New York: Basic Books, 1984: 228.

47. Said Amir Arjomand, *The Turban for the Crown: The Islamic Revolution in Iran.* New York: Oxford University Press, 1988: 154.

48. Moshen Milani, *The Making of Iran's Islamic Revolution*. Boulder: Westview Press, 1994.

49. The remaining Mujahedin rebels fled to Iraq to fight with Saddam Hussein's troops against Iran. See Sepehr Zabih, *The Left in Contemporary Iran*. Stanford: Hoover Institution Press, 1986.

50. Bakhash, *The Reign of the Ayatollahs*, 1984: 223; Zabih, *The Left in Contemporary Iran*. 1986.

51. David Menashri, *Iran: A Decade of War and Revolution*. New York: Holmes and Meier, 1990.

52. Bakhash, *The Reign of the Ayatollahs*, 1984: 223.

53. Lester A. Sobel, ed., *Cuba, the US, and Russia: 1960–63*. New York: Facts on File Interim History, 1964.

54. Manuel Urrutia, *Fidel Castro and Company, Inc.: Communist Tyranny in Cuba*. New York: Praeger, 1964; Eric Selbin, *Modern Latin American Revolutions*. Boulder: Westview Press, 1993.

55. Lowry Nelson, *Cuba: The Measure of a Revolution*. Minneapolis: University of Minnesota Press, 1972: 25.

56. Andres Suarez, *Cuba: Castroism and Communism, 1959–1966*. Cambridge: MIT Press, 1967; Edward Gonzalez, *Cuba under Castro: The Limits of Charisma*. Boston: Houghton Mifflin Company, 1974.

57. The next three years see smaller differences as well, although Nicaragua does repress more than Cuba. This is primarily a function of the role of the war in affecting policy mix choices.

58. Roger Miranda and William Ratliff. *The Civil War in Nicaragua: Inside the Sandinistas*. New Brunswick: Transaction Books, 1993.

59. Americas Watch Committee, *Human Rights in Nicaragua: August 1987–August 1988*. New York: Human Rights Watch, 1988: 95–96; Devora Grynspan, "Nicaragua: A New Model for Popular Revolution in Latin America," in *Revolutions of the Late Twentieth Century*, edited by J. Goldstone, T. R. Gurr, and F. Moshiri, 88–115. Boulder: Westview Press, 1991: 106.

60. Ted Robert Gurr and Barbara Harff, *Ethnic Conflict in World Politics*. Boulder: Westview Press, 1994: 49–51; Bernard Nietschmann, *The Unknown War: The Miskito Nation, Nicaragua, and the United States*. New York: Freedom House, 1989.

61. Grynspan, "Nicaragua," 1991: 109.

62. A majority (almost 58 percent) of the instances of repression in Bolivia in the last three years (1962–1964) consisted of repression of factions within the governmental coalition, including the political wing of the labor unions (COB), led by Juan Lechin, as well as the far right faction, led by Walter Guevara Arce.

63. Christopher Mitchell, *The Legacy of Populism in Bolivia: From the MNR to Military Rule*. New York: Praeger, 1977: 44–45; Herbert S. Klein, *Bolivia:*

The Evolution of a Multi-Ethnic Society, 2nd ed. New York: Oxford University Press, 1992.

64. Jonathan Kelley and Herbert S. Klein, *Revolution and the Rebirth of Inequality: A Theory Applied to the National Revolution in Bolivia.* Berkeley: University of California Press, 1981; Jonathan Kelley and Herbert S. Klein, "Revolution and the Rebirth of Inequality: A Theory of Stratification in a Postrevolutionary Society," *American Journal of Sociology,* 83 (1977): 78–99.

65. James M. Malloy, "Revolutionary Politics," in *Beyond the Revolution: Bolivia since 1952,* edited by J. Malloy and R. Thorn, 111–156. Pittsburgh: University of Pittsburgh Press, 1971; James M. Malloy, *Bolivia: The Uncompleted Revolution.* Pittsburgh: University of Pittsburgh Press, 1970.

66. Bakhash, *The Reign of the Ayatollahs,* 1984; Dilip Hiro, *Iran under the Ayatollahs.* London: Routledge and Kegan Paul, 1985.

67. Arjomand, *The Turban for the Crown,* 1988

68. Milani, *The Making of Iran's Islamic Revolution,* 1994: 214–215.

69. Milani, *The Making of Iran's Islamic Revolution,* 1994: 199.

70. Ehteshami, *After Khomeini,* 1995.

71. Urrutia, *Fidel Castro and Company, Inc.,* 1964.

72. Juan M. del Aguila, *Cuba: Dilemmas of a Revolution.* Boulder: Westview Press, 1984: 46–47; Nelson, *Cuba: The Measure of a Revolution,* 1972: 17–22.

73. Alan Benjamin, *Nicaragua: Dynamics of an Unfinished Revolution.* San Francisco: Walnut Publishing Company, 1989: 19–29.

74. Thomas W. Walker, *Nicaragua: The Land of Sandino.* Boulder: Westview Press, 1991: 44.

75. Grynspan, "Nicaragua," 1991: 105–107.

76. The 1984 Nicaraguan election accounts for the huge spike in Figure 4.3 at year t+5. However, while the sheer number of accommodation events is high, their weights are less impressive. The spike disappears in Figure 4.4, showing that despite sheer numbers, the Sandinistas were not unusually accommodative in that year. In fact, the level attained in 1984 fits the general incremental upward trend demonstrated in Figure 4.4, culminating in the second Nicaraguan election in 1990 (t+11).

77. Americas Watch Committee, *Human Rights in Nicaragua,* 1988: 9–12.

78. Robert J. Alexander, *The Bolivian National Revolution.* New Brunswick: Rutgers University Press, 1958.

79. Mitchell, *The Legacy of Populism in Bolivia,* 1977: 49.

80. Selbin, *Latin American Revolutions,* 1993: 40–41.

81. James M. Malloy, *Bolivia's MNR: A Study of a National Popular Movement in Latin America.* Buffalo: Council on International Studies, State University of New York at Buffalo, 1971: 44.

82. Mitchell, *The Legacy of Populism in Bolivia,* 1977: 92–96; Dunkerley, *Rebellion in the Veins,* 1984: 117–119.

Chapter 5

1. George Bernard Shaw, *The Revolutionist's Handbook*. New York: Limited Editions Club, 1962.

2. Charles R. Morris, ed., *Burke's Speech on Conciliation with America*. New York and London: Harper & Brothers, 1945.

3. Marwan Khawaja, "Repression and Popular Collective Action: Evidence from the West Bank," *Sociological Forum*, 8 (1993): 67.

4. See for instance, Mark I. Lichbach, "Deterrence or Escalation?: The Puzzle of Aggregate Studies of Repression and Dissent," *Journal of Conflict Resolution*, 32 (1987): 266–297; Karl-Dieter Opp and Wolfgang Ruehl, "Repression, Micromobilization and Political Protest," *Social Forces*, 69 (1990): 521–547; Johan L. Olivier, "State Repression and Collective Action in South Africa, 1970–1984," *South African Journal of Sociology*, 22 (1991): 109–117; Mark I. Lichbach, *The Rebel's Dilemma*. Ann Arbor: University of Michigan Press, 1995; Karen A. Rasler, "Concessions, Repression, and Political Protest in the Iranian Revolution," *American Sociological Review*, 61 (1996): 132–152.

5. David Davis and Michael D. Ward, "They Dance Alone: Death and the Disappeared in Contemporary Chile," *Journal of Conflict Resolution* 34 (1990): 449–475

6. Charles Tilly, *From Mobilization to Revolution*. New York: McGraw-Hill, 1978; Lichbach, "Deterrence or Escalation?" 1987; Lichbach, *The Rebel's Dilemma,* 1995.

7. Douglas A. Hibbs, Jr., *Mass Political Violence: A Cross-National Causal Analysis*. New York: Wiley, 1973; Davis and Ward, "They Dance Alone," 1990; Dean Hoover and David Kowalewski, "Dynamic Models of Dissent and Repression," *Journal of Conflict Resolution*, 58 (1992): 637–658.

8. An earlier version of this study was conducted using only total frequency counts of opposition activity rather than disaggregated (violent/nonviolent) measures of opposition. See Matthew Krain, "Factors Affecting the Use of Repression and Accommodation in Post-internal War States," presented at the Annual Meeting of the American Political Science Association, August 28–31, 1997, Washington, DC. That study found that opposition activity was not a significant predictor of repression or accommodation, consistent with the arguments and findings presented by others, including: Christian A. Davenport, "Multi-Dimensional Threat Perception and State Repression: An Inquiry into Why States Apply Negative Sanctions," *American Journal of Political Science*, 39 (1995): 683–713; Jeffrey Scott McBride, "Political Repression and Regime Transition: Latin America, 1980–1993," paper presented at the Annual Meeting of the American Political Science Association, Washington, DC, August 28–31, 1997.

9. Sabine Karstedt-Henke, "Theorien zur Erkldrung terroristischer Bewegungen" (Theories for the Explanation of Terrorist Movements), in *Politik der inneren Sicherheit* (The Politics of Internal Security), edited by E. Blankenberg, 198–234. Frankfurt: Suhrkamp, 1980. Ruud Koopmans confirms Karstedt-Henke's work in his study of new social movements in West Germany. See Ruud Koopmans, *Democracy from Below: New Social Movements and the Political System in West Germany.* Boulder: Westview Press, 1995.

10. Davenport, "Multi-Dimensional Threat Perception and State Repression," 1995: 687.

11. Hibbs, *Mass Political Violence,* 1973; Tilly, *From Mobilization to Revolution,* 1978; Raymond Duvall and Michael Shamir, "Governance by Terror," in *The Politics of Terrorism,* 3rd ed., edited by R. Duvall and M. Stohl. New York: Marcel Dekker, 1983; Steven C. Poe and C. Neal Tate, "Repression of Human Rights to Personal Integrity in the 1980s: A Global Analysis," *American Political Science Review,* 88 (1994): 853–872.

12. Karstedt-Henke, "Theorien zur Erkldrung terroristischer Bewegungen," 1980.

13. Davenport, "Multi-Dimensional Threat Perception and State Repression," 1995: 687.

14. Lichbach, "Deterrence or Escalation?" 1987.

15. Karen A. Rasler, "War, Accommodation, and Violence in the United States, 1890–1970," *American Political Science Review,* 80 (1986): 921–945.

16. Karstedt-Henke, "Theorien zur Erkldrung terroristischer Bewegungen," 1980.

17. Ted Robert Gurr, "The Political Origins of State Violence and Terror: A Theoretical Analysis," in *Government Violence and Repression: An Agenda for Research,* edited by M. Stohl and G. A. Lopez. New York: Greenwood Press, 1986; Poe and Tate, "Repression of Human Rights to Personal Integrity," 1994; Davenport, "Multi-Dimensional Threat Perception and State Repression," 1995.

18. Gurr, "The Political Origins of State Violence and Terror," 1986: 49.

19. Harold D. Lasswell, "The Garrison-State Hypothesis Today," in *Changing Patterns in Military Politics,* edited by S. P. Huntington, 51–70. New York: Free Press, 1962; Ted Robert Gurr, "War, Revolution, and the Growth of the Coercive State," *Comparative Political Studies,* 21 (1988): 45–65.

20. I employed ratios instead of a count of the number of documents to avoid overcounting elites who speak in public (or in interviews) more frequently than others. For example, Fidel Castro was often seen speaking at mass rallies or on Cuban television multiple times per month. In contrast, the Ayatollah Khomeini appeared relatively infrequently in public, but when he did his words carried great weight. By employing ratios instead of frequency counts, the measure would not overcount the speeches by Castro,

or undercount Khomeini's speeches. Similarly, word counts were not used either. Castro's speeches often lasted up to five hours, while Khomeini's were considerably shorter. Using ratios instead of word counts avoids over-counting more loquacious speakers or interviewees.

21. The new, relaxed inclusion criterion (1000 annual average battle deaths sustained per year by *all* participants, as opposed to by each side) is used. For more details, see J. David Singer and Melvin Small, *Correlates of War Project: International and Civil War Data, 1815–1992,* computer file. Ann Arbor: Inter-university Consortium for Political and Social Research, 1994.

22. Singer and Small, *Correlates of War Project,* 1994.

23. Singer and Small, *Correlates of War Project,* 1994.

24. William H. LeoGrande, "The United States in Nicaragua," in *Nicaragua: The First Five Years,* edited by T. W. Walker. New York: Praeger, 1985; Peter Kornbluh, "The Covert War," in *Reagan versus the Sandinistas: The Undeclared War on Nicaragua,* edited by T. W. Walker, 21–38. Boulder: Westview Press, 1987.

25. In fact, the EPS's plans for war, both before and after the U.S. invasion of Grenada in 1983, were based on the assumption of a military confrontation with the United States. The invasion of Grenada changed the strategy of the war from one of direct confrontation to one of making the territory won by the superpower ungovernable. This strategy was developed in conjunction with Cuban advisors, based on lessons learned in Vietnam and Grenada. See Roger Miranda and William Ratliff. *The Civil War in Nicaragua: Inside the Sandinistas.* New Brunswick: Transaction Books, 1993: 221–230.

26. Miranda and Ratliff, *The Civil War in Nicaragua,* 1993: 231. Speeches and interviews by leaders of the Sandinista government support this observation (see for instance: Daniel Ortega [July, 1983], "We Are a Very Small Country Confronting a Truly Colossal Force;" Sergio Ramirez [August, 1983] "U.S. Destabilization in Nicaragua"; Tomas Borge [December 1983], "We Speak to You from a Country at War;" Luis Carrion [November, 1984], "Is It Possible for Nicaragua to Defeat the War of Yankee Imperialism?" (Marcus, 1985). While these views were disseminated widely as propaganda, Miranda and Ratliff maintain that the Sandinista elites actually believed them to be true. As proof beyond the recollections of the first author, they point out that this view is overtly expressed in the EPS's top secret documents such as *Outline History of the Growth of the Counterrevolutionary Organization FDN.*

27. Unlike in the coding procedure for repression and accommodation, no confirmation of opposition activity is deemed necessary. Policies such as repression can be hard to account for as both sides have incentives to either obfuscate or exaggerate (Stohl and Lopez, 1984), and are often more

subtle policies rather than physical confrontations or events. By contrast, opposition activity is more tangible, and thus more difficult to hide.

28. Gary King, "Event Count Models for International Relations: Generalizations and Applications," *International Studies Quarterly,* 33 (1989): 128.

29. King, "Event Count Models for International Relations," 1989: 126.

30. Gary King, "Statistical Models for Political Science Event Counts: Bias in Conventional Procedures and Evidence for the Exponential Poisson Regression Model," *American Journal of Political Science,* 32 (1988): 838–863.

31. Gary King, *Unifying Political Methodology: The Likelihood Theory of Statistical Inference.* Cambridge: Cambridge University Press, 1989: 126.

32. Tim F. Liao, *Interpreting Probability Models: Logit, Probit, and Other Generalized Linear Models,* Sage University Paper Series on Quantitative Applications in the Social Sciences, 7–101. Thousand Oaks: Sage, 1994; J. Scott Long, *The Analysis of Categorical and Limited Dependent Variables.* Sage University Paper Series on Advanced Quantitative Techniques in the Social Sciences. Thousand Oaks: Sage, 1997.

33. William Gardner, Edward P. Mulvey, and Esther C. Shaw. "Regression Analyses of Counts and Rates: Poisson, Overdispersed Poisson, and Negative Binomial Models," *Psychological Bulletin,* 1 (1995): 392–404.

34. Another potential strategy would be to run pooled cross-sectional time series models of event count data. This would allow the researcher to pool all of the data across 13 years for all four countries into one model, but would still allow differentiation by case. However, the methodological technology needed for such a procedure is, at this writing, in its infancy. For a new and promising approach to this method, see Patrick T. Brandt, John T. Williams, and Benjamin Fordham, "Modeling Time Series Count Data: A State-Space Approach to Event Counts," paper presented at the Society for Political Methodology Meeting, University of California at San Diego, July 22–26, 1998.

35. Robert W. White and Terry Falkenberg White, "Repression and the Liberal State: The Case of Northern Ireland, 1969–1972," *Journal of Conflict Resolution,* 39 (1995): 341.

36. Additionally, many of the independent variables are, by their very nature, lagged variables, such as previous histories of repression, accommodation, and opposition.

37. See Jack Levy, "The Diversionary Theory of War: A Critique," in *The Handbook of War Studies,* edited by M. I. Midlarsky, 259–288. Boston: Unwin Hyman, 1989.

38. See for instance, G. Simmel, *Conflict.* translated by K. H. Woldff. Glencoe: Free Press, 1956; John E. Mueller, *War, Presidents, and Public Opinion.* New York: Wiley, 1973; See also Levy, "The Diversionary Theory of War," 1989.

39. See for instance, Michael Stohl, "War and Domestic Violence: The Case of the United States, 1890–1970," *Journal of Conflict Resolution,* 19 (1975):

379–416; Michael Stohl, *War and Domestic Political Violence: The American Capacity for Repression and Reaction.* Beverly Hills: Sage, 1976; Brett Ashley Leeds and David R. Davis, "Domestic Political Vulnerability and International Disputes," *Journal of Conflict Resolution,* 41 (1997): 814–834.

40. Patrick J. Conge, *From Revolution to War: State Relations in a World of Change.* Ann Arbor: University of Michigan Press, 1996: 137.

Chapter 6

1. Margaret Levi, "The Predatory Theory of Rule," *Politics and Society,* 10 (1981): 441.

2. Charles Tilly, *From Mobilization to Revolution.* New York: McGraw-Hill, 1978.

3. Roy Licklider, ed., *Stopping the Killing: How Civil Wars End.* New York: New York University Press, 1993.

4. Theda Skocpol, *States and Social Revolutions: A Comparative Analysis of France, Russia, and China.* Cambridge: Cambridge University Press, 1979: 165; Rosemary H. T. O'Kane, "The National Causes of State Construction in France, Russia and China," *Political Studies,* 43 (1995): 2–21.

5. Jack A. Goldstone, "An Analytical Framework," in *Revolutions of the Late Twentieth Century,* edited by J. Goldstone, T. R. Gurr, and F. Moshiri, Boulder: Westview Press, 1991: 47.

6. Samuel E. Finer, "State- and Nation-Building in Europe: The Role of the Military," in *The Formation of National States in Western Europe,* edited by C. Tilly, Princeton: Princeton University Press, 1975: 96; Tilly, *From Mobilization to Revolution,* 1978: 211.

7. Doug McAdam, *Political Process and the Development of Black Insurgency, 1930–1970.* Chicago: University of Chicago Press, 1982: 42.

8. Tilly, *From Mobilization to Revolution,* 1978: 218.

9. Michael Schwartz, *Radical Protest and Social Structure.* New York: Academic Press, 1976; Stephen John Stedman, "The End of the American Civil War," in *Stopping the Killing: How Civil Wars End,* edited by R. Licklider, 164–188. New York: New York University Press, 1993.

10. O'Kane, "The National Causes," 1995: 95–101.

11. Fred Halliday and Maxine Molyneux, *The Ethiopian Revolution.* London: Verso, 1981: 119–127; Rosemary H. T. O'Kane, *The Revolutionary Reign of Terror: The Role of Violence in Political Change.* Hants: Edward Elgar Publishing, 1991; Anwar–ul–Haq Ahady, "Afghanistan: State Breakdown," in *Revolutions of the Late Twentieth Century,* edited by J. Goldstone, T. R. Gurr, and F. Moshiri. Boulder: Westview Press, 1991: 191; I. William Zartman, "The Unfinished Agenda: Negotiating Internal Conflicts," in *Stopping the Killing: How Civil Wars End,* edited by R. Licklider. New York: New York University Press, 1993: 24.

12. Tilly, *From Mobilization to Revolution*, 1978: 218; Levi, "The Predatory Theory of Rule," 1981: 441.

13. John Foran and Jeff Goodwin, "Revolutionary Outcomes in Iran and Nicaragua: Coalition Fragmentation, War, and the Limits of Social Transformation," *Theory and Society.* 22 (1993): 210.

14. Crane Brinton, *The Anatomy of Revolution*. rev. ed. New York: Vintage Books, 1965.

15. Sabine Karstedt-Henke, "Theorien zur Erkldrung terroristischer Bewegungen" (Theories for the Explanation of Terrorist Movements), in *Politik der inneren Sicherheit* (The Politics of Internal Security), edited by E. Blankenberg, 198–234. Frankfurt: Suhrkamp, 1980.

16. Moshen Milani, *The Making of Iran's Islamic Revolution*. Boulder: Westview Press, 1994: Chapter 11; Anoushiravan Ehteshami, *After Khomeini: The Iranian Second Republic*. London: Routledge, 1995. Interestingly, note that in the year of Khomeini's death, 1989, the opposition engaged in a moratorium on nonviolent opposition.

17. Richard Stahler-Sholk, "The Dog That Didn't Bark: Labor Autonomy and Economic Adjustment in Nicaragua under the Sandinista and UNO Governments," *Comparative Politics,* 28 (1995): 77–102.

18. These factors have all been shown to be key elements in my model, as well as key determinants of opposition activity (see text below). I acknowledge that some variables that have been found to be key explanatory variables in the study of dissent such as inequality and economic development are not examined here. However, I have carefully controlled for these variables during case selection, meaning that there will be little if any variation between cases (see Chapter 2). Additionally, within each case, variables such as inequality vary little because of their slow pace of change over time. Therefore I do not examine the impact of these variables on dissent. For a recent treatment of this subject, see Mansoor Moaddel, "Political Conflict in the World Economy: A Cross-National Analysis of Modernization and World-System Theories," *American Sociological Review,* 59 (1994): 276–303.

19. David Snyder and Charles Tilly, "Hardship and Collective Violence in France: 1830–1960," *American Sociological Review,* 37 (1972): 520–532; Charles Tilly, Louise Tilly, and Richard Tilly, *The Rebellious Century: 1830–1930*. Cambridge: Harvard University Press, 1975; Tilly, *From Mobilization to Revolution*, 1978; McAdam, *Political Process*, 1982.

20. Edward N. Muller and Erich Weede, "Cross-National Variation in Political Violence: A Rational Action Approach," *Journal of Conflict Resolution,* 34 (1990): 635.

21. William Gamson, *The Strategy of Social Protest,* 2nd ed. Belmont: Wadsworth Publishing, 1990: 156.

22. Peter K. Eisinger, "The Conditions of Protest Behavior in American Cities," *American Political Science Review,* 67 (1973): 27–28.

23. Moaddel suggests three possible reasons as to why this relationship is not strongly significant. First, he suggests that the measures used are inadequate to capture the full scope and force of regime repressiveness. Second, he notes that in the wake of controls for economic (peripheralization, economic vulnerability, economic growth, income inequality) and social (presence of separatism) variables, repression may not be as effective as once thought at controlling dissent. Finally, Moaddel suggests that international pressure plays a role in opening up the political opportunity structure for protest without significantly altering the regime's repressive structure, making repression's effect weaker. See Moaddel, "Political Conflict in the World Economy," 1994: 296.

24. David Davis and Michael D. Ward, "They Dance Alone: Death and the Disappeared in Contemporary Chile," *Journal of Conflict Resolution,* 34 (1990): 451.

25. By far the largest number of empirical studies report a positive linear effect of repression on protest activity. Hoover and Kowalewski surveyed over one hundred studies published between 1965 and 1990. They found that 70 percent of these studies confirmed the hypothesis that repression increased opposition activity. See Dean Hoover and David Kowalewski, "Dynamic Models of Dissent and Repression," *Journal of Conflict Resolution,* 58 (1992): 637–658.

26. Ted Robert Gurr, *Why Men Rebel.* Princeton: Princeton University Press, 1970.

27. Douglas A. Hibbs, Jr., *Mass Political Violence: A Cross-National Causal Analysis.* New York: Wiley, 1973.

28. Ted Robert Gurr and Raymond Duvall, "Civil Conflict in the 1960s: A Reciprocal Theoretical System with Parameter Estimates," *Comparative Political Studies,* 6 (1973): 160.

29. Marwan Khawaja, "Repression and Popular Collective Action: Evidence from the West Bank," *Sociological Forum,* 8 (1993): 47–71.

30. Ruud Koopmans, *Democracy from Below: New Social Movements and the Political System in West Germany.* Boulder: Westview Press, 1995.

31. See Johan L. Olivier, "State Repression and Collective Action in South Africa, 1970–1984," *South African Journal of Sociology,* 22 (1991): 109–117. Also, Ruud Koopmans found that different types of repression (institutional and situational) had different impacts on the two types of opposition activity (violent and nonviolent). See Ruud Koopmans, "Dynamics of Repression and Mobilization: The German Extreme Right in the 1990s," *Mobilization,* 2 (1997): 149–164. And Lichbach theorizes that when the state responds with repression to one type of strategy, the opposition substitutes the other (i.e., if the state represses following a violent protest, the opposition response with nonviolent tactics). See Mark I. Lichbach, "Deterrence or Escalation?: The Puzzle of Aggregate Studies of Repression and Dissent,"

Journal of Conflict Resolution, 32 (1987): 266–297. Using historical sequencing analysis, Moore finds some empirical support for this hypothesis. See Will H. Moore, "Repression and Dissent: Substitution, Context, and Timing," *American Journal of Political Science,* 42 (1998): 851–873. Each of these hypotheses are important in understanding the interrelationship between elite policy mix choices and opposition activity choices. However, limited space does not allow for me to retest these hypotheses using the data collected for this project. In some of my future work I plan to examine this and other questions regarding less aggregate notions of repression, accommodation, and opposition in the context of post-internal war states.

32. Davis and Ward, "They Dance Alone," 1990: 451.

33. See for instance, Edward N. Muller, "Income Inequality, Regime Repressiveness, and Political Violence," *American Sociological Review,* 50 (1985): 47–61; Muller and Weede. "Cross-National Variation in Political Violence," 1990.

34. Ronald A. Francisco, "The Relationship between Coercion and Protest: An Empirical Evaluation in Three Coercive States," *Journal of Conflict Resolution,* 39 (1995): 265.

35. Karen A. Rasler, "Concessions, Repression, and Political Protest in the Iranian Revolution," *American Sociological Review,* 61 (1996): 133.

36. Lichbach, "Deterrence or Escalation?" 1987.

37. Koopmans goes further, pointing out *three* major flaws of the literature. First, the quality of the data used in many of these studies is suspect, and may not actually measure repression directly. Second, despite theorizing that the repression–dissent links are dynamic, most studies employ either static analyses or cross-sectional data. Finally, the level of theorizing has been too general. Koopmans suggests that instead of theorizing about these processes across all regimes, it might be wiser to stick to specific regime types at first. See Ruud Koopmans, "Dynamics of Repression and Mobilization: The German Extreme Right in the 1990s," *Mobilization,* 2 (1997): 151–152.

   Heeding Koopmans' warnings, I hope to overcome these obstacles in this study. The data employed here, for repression, accommodation, and opposition, are reliable data, and measure the phenomena in question directly (see Chapter 3). The data set is both cross-sectional and longitudinal, and the analyses have incorporated time in two ways: by accounting for phases in the post-internal war state, and by considering the possibility that policy mix choices have both short- and long-term effects. Finally, I restrict the application of my theoretrical model to post-internal war regimes. Even more narrowly, I test my historical process model using only post-revolutionary states in the current study. Future studies will attempt to expand the range of the theory by testing it on other types of regimes.

38. Lichbach, "Deterrence or Escalation?" 1987.

39. Karl-Dieter Opp and Wolfgang Ruehl, "Repression, Micromobilization and Political Protest," *Social Forces*, 69 (1990): 521–547; Rasler, "Concessions, Repression, and Political Protest," 1996.

40. Opp and Ruehl, "Repression, Micromobilization and Political Protest," 1990.

41. Rasler, "Concessions, Repression, and Political Protest," 1996: 133.

42. As we have seen earlier, accommodation and repression are often born of the same processes. Yet in the study of policy mix choices, accommodation has more often than not been neglected in favor of repression. Lichbach warns that repression cannot be assessed independently from accommodation. See Lichbach, "Deterrence or Escalation?" 1987: 286. This holds true in examining their effects as well as their determinants.

43. Mark I. Lichbach, "An Evaluation of 'Does Economic Inequality Breed Political Conflict?' Studies," *World Politics*, 41 (1989): 431–470.

44. Edward N. Muller and Karl-Dieter Opp, "Rational Choice and Rebellious Collective Behavior," *American Political Science Review*, 80 (1986): 871–887.

45. Dennis Chong, *Collective Action and the Civil Rights Movement*. Chicago: University of Chicago Press, 1991: 116–125.

46. Anthony Oberschall, "Rational Choice in Collective Protests," *Rationality and Society*, 6 (1994): 79–100.

47. Karen A. Rasler, "War, Accommodation, and Violence in the United States, 1890–1970," *American Political Science Review*, 80 (1986): 941.

48. Rasler, "Concessions, Repression, and Political Protest," 1996: 148–149.

49. Rasler, "War, Accommodation, and Violence," 1986: 941.

50. Paul W. Schroeder, "Alliances, 1815–1945: Weapons of Power and Tools of Management," in *Historical Dimensions of National Security Problems*, edited by K. Knorr. Lawrence: University Press of Kansas, 1976: 230.

51. Gamson, *The Strategy of Social Protest*, 1990: 116.

52. For example, this was certainly the thinking behind the decision of the ruling clerics in Iran to ally with their natural enemies, Tudeh (the Iranian Communist Party), in the first years following the revolution. By accommodating Tudeh in the short run, the regime was able to keep the Communist Party in check long enough to dispose of its other rivals. Once this was done, the ruling elites turned their attentions toward eliminating Tudeh, a task all but completed by 1983. See Sepehr Zabih, *The Left in Contemporary Iran*. Stanford: Hoover Institution Press, 1986; Robin Wright, *In the Name of God: The Khomeini Decade*. New York: Simon and Schuster, 1989: 124–125.

53. See Mark Granovetter, "Threshold Models of Collective Behavior," *American Sociological Review*, 39 (1978): 335–373. Typically, individuals calculate that their chances for successful opposition are greatest when acting in a group. Therefore, individuals require assurances regarding the willingness of others such as themselves to engage in opposition activity. Social networks

(formal and informal associations) allow for the transmission of information regarding the intentions and degree of commitment of others. See Chong, *Collective Action and the Civil Rights Movement,* 1991: 116–125; Doug McAdam and Ronnelle Paulsen, "Specifying the Relationship between Social Ties and Activism," *American Journal of Sociology,* 99 (1993): 641–645. This information enables them to commit to opposition activity with the knowledge that they will be relatively anonymous within a large group of protesters. That is because the probability of apprehension decreases as the number of participants increases.

54. See Timur Kuran, "Now Out of Never: The Element of Surprise in the East European Revolution of 1989," *World Politics,* 44 (1991): 7–48; Timur Kuran, "Sparks and Prairie Fires: A Theory of Unanticipated Political Revolution," *Public Choice,* 61 (1989): 41–74. Similarly, J. White developed a bandwagon model to explain why people participated in riots in early modern Japan. White concluded that people participated because the likelihood of success increased with each new participant, making each individual's participant meaningful. Additionally, the probable costs of punishment were negligible because of the anonymity that increasing numbers provide. Following Granovetter's work, White points out that those with the lowest threshold necessary for participation, leaders, play a key role in making further participation possible. He points to leaders' roles in focusing the potential power of the crowd. He also notes that the potential costs and benefits for leaders are greater than for the population as a whole. This may explain why regimes target leaders in an attempt to preempt opposition. See J. White, "Rational Rioters: Leaders, Followers and Popular Protest in Early Modern Japan," *Politics and Society,* 16 (1988): 35–70.

55. Davis and Ward, "They Dance Alone," 1990.

56. Davis and Ward, "They Dance Alone," 1990.

57. Sidney Tarrow, *Power in Movement: Social Movements, Collective Action and Politics.* Cambridge: Cambridge University Press, 1994: 68.

58. Tilly, *From Mobilization to Revolution,* 1978: 211.

59. Tilly, *From Mobilization to Revolution,* 1978; Charles Tilly, "War Making and State Making as Organized Crime," in *Bringing the State Back In,* edited by P. Evans, D. Reuschemeyer, and T. Skocpol, 169–191. Cambridge: Cambridge University Press, 1985; Karen A. Rasler and William R. Thompson, *War and State Making: The Shaping of the Global Powers.* Boston: Unwin and Hyman, 1989.

60. Finer, "State- and Nation-Building in Europe," 1975: 96; Tilly, *From Mobilization to Revolution,* 1978: 211.

61. Gamson, *The Strategy of Social Protest,* 1990: 116.

62. McAdam, *Political Process,* 1982; See Chapter 2, footnote 17 for a more detailed discussion of political opportunity structure.

63. Skocpol, *States and Social Revolutions,* 1979.

64. Tarrow, *Power in Movement,* 1994.

65. McAdam, *Political Process,* 1982.

66. Rasler, "War, Accommodation, and Violence," 1986: 925; Ted Robert Gurr, *Minorities at Risk: A Global View of Ethnopolitical Conflict.* Washington, DC: United States Institute for Peace Press, 1993: 133.

67. Gurr and Duvall, "Civil Conflict in the 1960s," 1973.

68. Tarrow, *Power in Movement,* 1994: 68.

69. Lewis A. Coser, *The Function of Social Conflict.* New York: Free Press, 1956; G. Simmel, *Conflict,* translated by K. H. Woldff. Glencoe: Free Press, 1956.

70. John E. Mueller, *War, Presidents, and Public Opinion.* New York: Wiley:, 1973.

71. Quincy Wright, *A Study of War.* Chicago: University of Chicago Press, 1964: 1516; See also Jack Levy, "The Diversionary Theory of War: A Critique," in *The Handbook of War Studies,* edited by M. I. Midlarsky, 259–288. Boston: Unwin Hyman, 1989.

72. Brett Ashley Leeds and David R. Davis, "Domestic Political Vulnerability and International Disputes," *Journal of Conflict Resolution,* 41 (1997): 814–834.

73. Levy, "The Diversionary Theory of War: A Critique," 1989: 282.

74. Arthur A. Stein, *The Nation at War.* Baltimore: Johns Hopkins University Press, 1980.

75. Gamson, *The Strategy of Social Protest,* 1990: 116.

76. Consider the case of the Iranian Communist Party, Tudeh, discussed earlier from the point of view of the regime. Tudeh leaders consciously allowed themselves to be co-opted in the first years of the post-internal war period and the beginning of the Iran-Iraq War. Despite serious ideological and practical differences with the ruling clerics, Tudeh saw short-term advantage in supporting the regime, even while their sister party on the left, the Mujahedin-e Khalq resisted assiduously during the first years of the war. Regardless, in the long run the regime went a long way toward eliminating both Tudeh and the Mujahedin. See Wright, *In the Name of God,* 1989; Zabih, *The Left in Contemporary Iran,* 1986.

77. Oberschall, "Rational Choice in Collective Protests," 1994: 88.

78. Some would argue that opposition in the form of the Contras actually increased. However, for the purposes of this study I was unable to count Contra activity as domestic opposition activity. To do so would be to double-count the effect of the war. Opposition was counted if it came from non-combatants, even those sympathetic to or aiding the Contras.

79. Opp and Ruehl, "Repression, Micromobilization and Political Protest," 1990; Rasler, "Concessions, Repression, and Political Protest," 1996.

80. Thomas W. Walker, *Nicaragua: The Land of Sandino.* Boulder: Westview Press, 1991: 46–47.

81. Eric Selbin, *Modern Latin American Revolutions.* Boulder: Westview Press, 1993: 58.

82. Walker, *Nicaragua: The Land of Sandino,* 1991: 48.

83. Toward the end of the post-internal war period, at the height of opposition activity, much of the opposition actually came from the Sandinistas. By mid-1990 the Sandinistas were out of power, and were spearheading opposition activity against the UNO government of Violetta Chamorro. See Richard Stahler-Sholk, "The Dog That Didn't Bark: Labor Autonomy and Economic Adjustment in Nicaragua under the Sandinista and UNO Governments," *Comparative Politics,* 28 (1995): 77–102.

Chapter 7

1. Daniel Defoe, "The Kentish Petition," (addenda), in *Later Stuart Tracts,* edited by George A. Aitken. New York: Cooper Square Publishers, 1964.

2. H. L. Menken, ed. *A Mencken Chrestomathy.* New York: A. A. Knopf, 1949: 152.

3. Terry Lynn Karl, "Dilemmas of Democratization in Latin America," *Comparative Politics,* 23 (1990): 8.

4. Karl, "Dilemmas of Democratization," 1990; Samuel P. Huntington, *The Third Wave: Democratization in the Late Twentieth Century.* Norman: University of Oklahoma Press, 1991: Chapter 3.

5. Jack A. Goldstone, "Revolutions," in *Encyclopedia of Government and Politics*—Volume I," edited by M. Hawkesworth and M. Kogan, 1049–1060. New York: Routledge, 1992: 1057.

6. See, for instance, Karl, "Dilemmas of Democratization," 1990: 15; Perhaps the most influential work examining historical patterns in the development of political form is Barrington Moore's *Social Origins of Dictatorship and Democracy* (1966). Moore examines three historical paths to political modernity—the paths to early democracy (in England, France, and the United States), fascist dictatorship (in Germany and Japan), and Communist dictatorship (in Russia and China). However, the generalizability of Moore's arguments to any study of post–World War II political system development is not necessarily apparent. The rhythm of change is much faster and more compressed in the contemporary world environment than that which existed previously. Moore himself suggests as much, arguing that these three route are not alternatives currently open to any and all states, but are rather tied to particular historical processes and preconditions. In particular, the path examined by Moore that was most favorable to early democracies "was itself a part of history that almost certainly will not be repeated" (Moore, 1966: 5). For an excellent critique of Moore's argument, see Theda Skocpol, "A Critical Review of Barrington Moore's *Social Origins of Dictatorship and Democracy,*" in *Social Revolutions in the Modern World,* by Theda Skocpol, 25–54. New York: Cambridge University Press, 1994.

7. For more on the PRI and their control of Mexican politics since the revolution, see: Howard F. Cline, *The United States and Mexico*. Cambridge: Harvard University Press, 1963; Eric Wolf, *Peasant Wars of the Twentieth Century*. New York: Knopf, 1970; Daniel C. Levy, "Mexico: Sustained Civilian Rule without Democracy," in *Politics in Developing Countries: Comparing Experiences with Democracy*, edited by L. Diamond, J. Linz, and S. M. Lipset, 135–174. Boulder: Lynne Rienner, 1990. For more on the origins of the ZANU-PF coalition and their subsequent rule in Zimbabwe, see Anthony Verrier, *The Road to Zimbabwe: 1890–1980*. London: Jonathan Cape, 1986; Masipula Sithole, "Zimbabwe: In Search of a Stable Democracy," in *Politics in Developing Countries: Comparing Experiences with Democracy*, edited by L. Diamond, J. Linz, and S. M. Lipset, 449–490. Boulder: Lynne Rienner, 1990; Geroges Nzongola-Ntalaja. *Nation-Building and State Building in Africa*. Harare: SAPES Books, 1993.

8. Dietrich Rueschemeyer, Evelyne Huber Stephens, and John D. Stephens, *Capitalist Development and Democracy*. Chicago: University of Chicago Press, 1991: 305.

9. Davis S. Mason, *Revolution and Transition in East-Central Europe*, 2nd ed. Boulder: Westview Press, 1996: 106; David Close, "Central American Elections 1989–90: Costa Rica, El Salvador, Honduras, Nicaragua, Panama," *Electoral Studies*, 10 (1991): 60–76; John A. Booth and Patricia Bayer Richard, "The Nicaraguan Elections of October 1996," *Electoral Studies*, 16 (1997): 386–393.

10. Ted Robert Gurr, "War, Revolution, and the Growth of the Coercive State," *Comparative Political Studies*, 21 (1988): 53.

11. Kevin J. Middlebrook, "Organized Labor and Democratization in Postrevolutionary Regimes: Transition Politics in Nicaragua, Russia, and Mexico," paper presented at the Annual Meeting of the American Political Science Association, Washington, DC, August 28–31, 1997: 7–9.

12. Interestingly, Rueschemeyer, Stephens, and Stephens find that political parties are important in determining elite reaction to democratization. In particular, when elites are represented by strong political parties, they are less likely to feel threatened by the mobilization of the working and middle classes, and they are less likely to develop into an anti-democratic force. See Rueschemeyer, Stephens, and Stephens, *Capitalist Development and Democracy*, 1991.

13. Michelle Benson and Jacek Kugler, "Power Parity, Democracy, and the Severity of Internal Violence," *Journal of Conflict Resolution*, 42 (1998): 196–209.

14. See, for instance, Douglas A. Hibbs, Jr., *Mass Political Violence: A Cross-National Causal Analysis*. New York: Wiley, 1973; Neil J. Mitchell and James J. McCormick, "Economic and Political Explanations of Human Rights Violations," *World Politics*, 40 (1988): 476–498; Steven C. Poe and C. Neal

Tate, "Repression of Human Rights to Personal Integrity in the 1980s: A Global Analysis," *American Political Science Review,* 88 (1994): 853–872. This may also be true at the highest levels of repression. Rummel argues that regime type is strongly associated with state-sponsored mass murder. His argument is based on the observation that "power kills; absolute power kills absolutely." See R.J. Rummel, *Death by Government.* New Brunswick: Transaction Books, 1994: 1. Democracies offer fewer institutional opportunities to employ power, and are therefore less likely to kill their own people. But elsewhere I find that variables such as war and internal war explain the occurrence of genocides and politicides better than does regime type. These more dynamic "big opportunities" are potentially more salient than institutional, static opportunities, in explaining the onset and severity of state-sponsored mass murder. See Matthew Krain, "State-Sponsored Mass Murder: The Onset and Severity of Genocides and Politicides," *Journal of Conflict Resolution,* 41 (1997): 331–360.

15. Frances Fox Piven and Richard A. Cloward, *Why Americans Don't Vote.* New York: Pantheon Books, 1988: xiv; Christian A. Davenport, "Censorship, Political Restrictions and the Democratic Proposition," paper presented at the Annual Meeting of the Midwest Political Science Association, Chicago, Illinois, April 10–12, 1997. Additionally, democracies are relatively successful at diffusing conflict via means other than coercion. See Gurr, "War, Revolution," 1988: 54. One reason for this success is that the very nature of a democratic system implies to participating groups that even if they "lose" this time, they will get another chance to "win" next time. However, when democracies do employ repression, they incite protest.

16. G. Bingham Powell, *Contemporary Democracies: Participation, Stability, and Violence.* Cambridge: Harvard University Press, 1982; Matthew Krain, "Contemporary Democracies Revisited: Democracy, Political Violence, and Event Count Models," *Comparative Political Studies,* 31 (1998): 139–164.

17. Arend Lijphart, "Democracies: Forms, Performance, and Constitutional Engineering," *European Journal of Political Research,* 25 (1994): 1–17; Arend Lijphart. *Democracy in Plural Societies: A Comparative Exploration.* New Haven: Yale University Press, 1977; Krain, "Contemporary Democracies Revisited," 1998.

18. Christian A. Davenport, "From Ballots to Bullets: An Empirical Assessment of How National Elections Influence State Uses of Political Repression," *Electoral Studies,* 16 (1997): 517–540; Christian A. Davenport, "Censorship, Political Restrictions and the Democratic Proposition," paper presented at the Annual Meeting of the Midwest Political Science Association, Chicago, Illinois, April 10–12, 1997. Curiously, Davenport finds that elections significantly decrease levels of repression in non-democracies, but have no such effect in transitional states and in democracies. He suggests three possible explanations: first, elections happen infrequently (especially relative to

repression) in transitional states; second, elections happen frequently and in a ritualized, habitual manner in established democracies, making them a routine part of the political landscape often taken for granted by policymakers and opposition groups alike; finally, elections are only one of many participatory opportunities in democracies.

19. Christian A. Davenport, "From Ballots to Bullets," 1997. However, a recent preliminary study calls these findings into question. David Richards finds that the presence of national elections, even including its interaction with suffrage, is not a good predictor of a regime's respect for human rights. See David L. Richards, "Settling the Score: Elections and Physical Integrity," paper presented at the Annual Meeting of the New York State Political Science Association, Ithaca College, 1996.

20. See Michael Stohl, *War and Domestic Political Violence: The American Capacity for Repression and Reaction*. Beverly Hills: Sage, 1976; Michael Stohl, "War and Domestic Violence: The Case of the United States, 1890–1970," *Journal of Conflict Resolution,* 19 (1975): 379–416; Karen A. Rasler, "War, Accommodation, and Violence in the United States, 1890–1970," *American Political Science Review,* 80 (1986): 921–945; Robert W. White and Terry Falkenberg White, "Repression and the Liberal State: The Case of Northern Ireland, 1969–72," *Journal of Conflict Resolution,* 39 (1995): 330–352; Ronald A. Francisco, "Coercion and Protest: An Empirical Test in Two Democratic States," *American Journal of Political Science,* 40 (1996): 1179–1204.

21. Powell, *Contemporary Democracies,* 1982; Lijphart, "Democracies," 1994; Krain, "Contemporary Democracies Revisited," 1998.

22. Conway Henderson, "Conditions Affecting the Use of Political Repression," *Journal of Conflict Resolution.* 35 (1991): 120–142; Poe and Tate, "Repression of Human Rights," 1994.

23. Sidney Tarrow, *Power in Movement: Social Movements, Collective Action and Politics.* Cambridge: Cambridge University Press, 1994.

24. Ted Robert Gurr, *Why Men Rebel.* Princeton: Princeton University Press, 1970.

25. Benson and Kugler, "Power Parity, Democracy," 1998: 199.

26. Matthew Krain and Marissa Edson Myers, "Democracy and Civil War: A Note on the Democratic Peace Proposition," *International Interactions,* 23 (1997): 87–94; Jeff Goodwin, "Is the Age of Revolutions Over?" paper presented at the 39th Annual Meeting of the International Studies Association, Minneapolis, Minnesota, March 18–21, 1998.

27. Currently a controversy rages in the international relations literature on the application of the democratic peace proposition to "new democracies." This proposition argues that democracies generally do not fight each other, although it is generally understood that they do engage in international conflict as frequently as other states. See Stuart A. Bremer, "Dangerous Dyads: Conditions Affecting the Likelihood of Interstate War,

1816–1965," *Journal of Conflict Resolution,* 36 (1992): 231–249; Zeev Maoz and Bruce Russett, "Normative and Structural Causes of Democratic Peace, 1946–1986," *American Political Science Review,* 87 (1993): 624–638. Mansfield and Snyder find that new democracies are not subject to this democratic peace principle, and are in fact more war-prone than states that do not undergo a regime change. See Edward D. Mansfield and Jack Snyder, "Democratization and the Danger of War," *International Security,* 20 (1995): 5–38. But others present empirical evidence refuting these claims. See Andrew J. Enterline, "Driving While Democratizing (DWD)," *International Security,* 20 (1996): 183–196; William R. Thompson and Richard Tucker, "A Tale of Two Democratic Peace Critiques," *Journal of Conflict Resolution,* 41 (1997): 428–451. Current research points out that while successful democratization leads to a more peaceful international environment, democratic reversals increase the likelihood of warfare. See Michael D. Ward and Kristian S. Gleditsch, "Democratizing for Peace," *American Political Science Review,* 92 (1998): 51–61.

28. Andrew J. Enterline, "Fledgling Regimes: Is the Case of Inter-War Germany Generalizable?" *International Interactions,* 22 (1997): 245–277; However, Enterline earlier found that new autocracies are subject to more severe domestic conflict for a longer duration than that experienced by new democracies. See Enterline, "Driving While Democratizing," 1996.

29. While R. J. Rummel's work shows that democratic states do not kill their own people, work by Harff, Gurr, and others demonstrates that transitions to democracy yields these lethal policies. See R.J. Rummel, "Democracy, Power, Genocide, and Mass Murder," *Journal of Conflict Resolution,* 39 (1995): 3–26; Ted Robert Gurr, "Peoples Against States: Ethnopolitical Conflict and the Changing World System," *International Studies Quarterly,* 38 (1994): 347–377; Barbara Harff, "Genocide as State Terrorism," in *Government Violence and Repression: An Agenda for Research,* edited by M. Stohl and G. A. Lopez, 165–188. New York: Greenwood Press, 1986. Why the discrepancy? Perhaps it is because these transitions yield openings in the political opportunity structure. Elites in these countries can justify such repressive policies by claiming the necessity of maintaining order during the transition process. In addition, the norms and institutions of democracy, which negatively affect the use of repression, are not solidified (consolidated) in transitional regimes. If experience with these mechanisms and ideas leads to a less repressive society, perhaps inexperience with the tools of democracy allow for their misuse. See Krain, "State-Sponsored Mass Murder," 1997; For an alternative explanation, see William Stanley, "The Factional Rationality of Mass Murder: A Level of Analysis Problem in the Study of State Violence," unpublished manuscript, 1998.

30. Frank S. Cohen, "Ethnic Conflict Governance and the Conflict between Nation and State," paper presented at the 39th Annual Meeting of the International Studies Association, March 18–21, 1998, Minneapolis, Minnesota.

31. Guillermo O'Donnell and Philippe C. Schmitter, *Transitions from Authoritarian Rule: Tentative Conclusions about Uncertain Democracies*. Baltimore: Johns Hopkins University Press, 1986; Philippe C. Schmitter and Javier Santiso, "Three Temporal Dimensions to the Consolidation of Democracy," *International Political Science Review,* 19 (1998): 79.

32. Charles Tilly, *From Mobilization to Revolution*. New York: McGraw-Hill, 1978.

33. Benson and Kugler, "Power Parity, Democracy," 1998: 206.

34. This potential problem with the democratic peace argument has been pointed out before in regard to the effects of regime type on war propensity. William R. Thompson develops an explanation of the democratic peace that emphasizes the role of international conflict (or the lack thereof) in the development of different regime types. He argues that zones of peace facilitate democratization, and that the absence of a peaceful environment impeded moves toward democracy. Thompson's analysis shows that democratic peace researchers may have misattributed the direction of causality. See William R. Thompson, "Democracy and Peace: Putting the Cart Before the Horse?" *International Organization,* 50 (1996): 141–174.

35. See Valerie Bunce and M. Csanadi, "Uncertainty in the Transition: Post-Communism in Hungary," *East European Politics and Societies,* 7 (1993): 240–275. The study of democratization has undergone a transition in the last ten years, during which many factors previously thought to be preconditions of democracy have been found to be effects of democratization. Before the wave of democratization in the 1980s, the majority of the literature focused on preconditions necessary for the development of democracy. That literature emphasizes that high levels of five interrelated macro-quantitative structural variables are necessary for democratization: economic development, education, literacy, urbanization, and communication. See for instance, Seymour Martin Lipset, Kyoung-Ryung Seong, and John Charles Torres, "A Comparative Analysis of the Social Requisites of Democracy," *International Social Science Journal,* 136 (1993): 155–175. Various critiques have been written about this approach, including Guillermo O'Donnell, *Modernization and Bureaucratic Authoritarianism: Studies in South American Politics*. Berkeley: Institute of International Studies, University of California at Berkeley, 1973; Guiseppe DiPalma, *To Craft Democracies*. Berkeley: University of California Press, 1990. Indeed, recent work has shown that what had in the past been seen as preconditions of democracy may actually number among its outcomes. See Karl, "Dilemmas of Democratization," 1990: 5.

36. DiPalma, *To Craft Democracies.* 1990; Huntington, *The Third Wave,* 1991; Bermeo, "Democracy and the Lessons of Dictatorship," *Comparative Politics,* 24 (1992): 273–291.

37. Level of opposition activity is a key component in my explanation of how policy mix choices affect political system development. Is it possible that the type of opposition activity also impacts regime type? Recent research suggests otherwise. Despite expectations of such a relationship, Vogele's cross-national longitudinal analysis uncovers no significant relationship between a country's experience with nonviolent struggle and an increase in levels of democracy. See William B. Vogele, "Struggle and Democracy: Nonviolent Action and Democratization," paper presented at the Annual Meeting of the International Studies Association, Chicago, Illinois, February 21–25, 1995. Indeed, transitions to democracy have been the product of both violent (i.e., Romania) and nonviolent (i.e., Poland, Czechoslovakia, Hungary) opposition. See Larry Diamond, Juan J. Linz, and Seymour Martin Lipset, eds., *Politics in Developing Countries: Comparing Experiences with Democracy.* Boulder: Lynne Rienner, 1990; Terry Lynn Karl, "Dilemmas of Democratization in Latin America," *Comparative Politics,* 23 (1990): 1–21. Terry Lynn Karl and Philippe Schmitter, "Modes of Transition in Latin America, Southern and Eastern Europe," *International Social Science Journal,* 128 (1991): 269–284.

38. Robert A. Dahl, *Polyarchy: Participation and Opposition.* New Haven: Yale University Press, 1971; Tatu Vanhanen, *The Process of Democratization: A Comparative Study of 147 States, 1980–88.* New York: Crane Russak, 1990; Mancur Olson, "Dictatorship, Democracy, and Development," *American Political Science Review,* 87 (1993): 567–576; Tatu Vanhanen and Richard Kimber, "Predicting and Explaining Democratization in Eastern Europe," in *Democratization in Eastern Europe,* edited by G. Pridham and T. Vanhanen. New York: Routledge, 1994.

39. O'Donnell and Schmitter, *Transitions from Authoritarian Rule,* 1986.

40. Adam Przeworski, "The Games of Transition," in *Issues in Democratic Consolidation,* edited by S. Mainwaring, G. O'Donnell, and J. S. Valenzuela. Notre Dame: University of Notre Dame Press, 1992: 119; William Stanley, "The Factional Rationality of Mass Murder: A Level of Analysis Problem in the Study of State Violence," unpublished manuscript, 1998.

41. O'Donnell and Schmitter, *Transitions From Authoritarian Rule.* 1986.

42. See Otto Hintze, "Military Organization and the Organization of the State," in *The Historical Essays of Otto Hintze,* edited by F. Gilbert, 178–215. New York: Oxford University Press, 1975; Charles Tilly, "Reflections on the History of European State Making," in *The Formation of National States in Western Europe,* edited by C. Tilly, 3–83. Princeton: Princeton University Press, 1975; Edgar Kiser and Yarom Barzel. "The Origins of Democracy in England," *Rationality and Society,* 3 (1991): 396–422.

43. Eric Selbin, *Modern Latin American Revolutions.* Boulder: Westview Press, 1993.

44. Michael Bratton and Nicholas van de Walle, "Popular Protest and Political Reform in Africa," *Comparative Politics,* 24 (1992): 419–442.

45. Przeworski, "The Games of Transition," 109.

46. Philippe C. Schmitter and Javier Santiso, "Three Temporal Dimensions to the Consolidation of Democracy," *International Political Science Review,* 19 (1998): 74.

47. DiPalma, *To Craft Democracies,* 1990.

48. Lawson argues that the presence of constitutional opposition is necessary in order to consider a state a democracy. She adds that constitutional opposition "does not seek to oppose the regime itself, only the government." See Stephanie Lawson, "Conceptual Issues in the Comparative Study of Regime Change and Democratization," *Comparative Politics,* 25 (1993): 200.

49. Gurr, "War, Revolution," 1988: 55.

50. This is not to imply that elites in such states do not benefit from accommodating. Rulers who provide rights and insure the rule of law can best maximize the efficiency of their extraction, as well as generate economic growth and thereby increase the pool of societal resources from which they can extract in the future. This turns out to be mutually beneficial to elites and masses, regardless of whether this is intentional or not. Elites accommodate in return for harvesting societal resources. Masses gain rights and privileges, and society becomes more democratic. This yields greater overall wealth, and a greater yield for the extracting elites. The more wealth the masses provide, the greater the rights and privileges they are granted. See Kiser and Barzel, "The Origins of Democracy in England," 1991; Olson, "Dictatorship, Democracy, and Development," 1993.

51. Karl, "Dilemmas of Democratization in Latin America," 1990: 16.

52. DiPalma, *To Craft Democracies,* 1990; Huntington, *The Third Wave,* 1991: 114. Pacts also allow the elites to better position themselves for the time when they no longer hold power. By negotiating with this eventuality in mind, the elites can insure that their interests are represented, even if they do not hold the reigns of government. Alternatively, elites can create a "new" system that reflects the economic and social relations of the old system. The end result is political change without "revolutionary" alterations of society. For example, Staniszkis argues that the old *nomenklatura* bureaucrats in Communist Poland became the new capitalists in post-transition Poland. See Jadwiga Staniszkis, *The Dynamics of the Breakthrough in Eastern Europe.* Berkeley: University of California Press, 1991: 176.

53. Karl, "Dilemmas of Democratization in Latin America," 1990: 12.

54. Benson and Kugler, "Power Parity, Democracy," 1998: 204.

55. Scott Mainwaring, "Transitions to Democracy and Democratic Consolidation: Theoretical and Conceptual Issues," in *Issues in Democratic Consolidation,*

edited by S. Mainwaring, G. O'Donnell, and J. S. Valenzuela, 294–342. Notre Dame: University of Notre Dame Press, 1992. For more on the debate as to whether democracy and/or democratic transitions decrease or increase uncertainty, see: O'Donnell and Schmitter, *Transitions from Authoritarian Rule,* 1986; Przeworski, *Democracy and the Market,* 1991.

56. John Higley, Judith Kullberg, and Jan Pakulski, "The Persistence of Post-communist Elites," *Journal of Democracy,* 7 (1996): 146.

57. Dahl, *Polyarchy,* 1971: 38–39.

58. Percy C. Hintzen, *The Costs of Regime Survival: Racial Mobilization, Elite Domination, and Control of the State in Guyana and Trinidad.* Cambridge: Cambridge University Press, 1989: 2.

59. Juan M. del Aguila, *Cuba: Dilemmas of a Revolution.* Boulder: Westview Press, 1984.

60. Gurr, "War, Revolution," 1988: 50.

61. Remmer, Karen. *Military Rule in Latin America.* Boston: Unwin Hyman, 1989.

62. Rueschemeyer, Stephens, and Stephens, *Capitalist Development and Democracy.* 1991.

63. Rueschemeyer, Stephens, and Stephens, *Capitalist Development and Democracy,* 1991: 279.

64. S.N. Eisenstadt, *Revolution and the Transformation of Societies: A Comparative Study of Civilizations.* New York: Free Press, 1978.

65. Conversely, they find that in the absence of war the rule of law and "proto-democracy" evolved as an unintended consequence of the interactions between rulers and their subjects. See Kiser and Barzel, "The Origins of Democracy in England," 1991.

66. Thompson, "Democracy and Peace," 1996: 142.

67. Lasswell, Harold D. "The Garrison-State Hypothesis Today," in *Changing Patterns in Military Politics,* edited by S. P. Huntington, 51–70. New York: Free Press, 1962; Gurr, "War, Revolution," 1988.

68. Rueschemeyer, Stephens and Stephens, *Capitalist Development and Democracy,* 1991: 279.

69. David Collier and Steven Levitsky, "Democracy with Adjectives: Conceptual Innovation in Comparative Research," *World Politics,* 49 (1997): 430–451.

70. Karl, "Dilemmas of Democratization in Latin America," 1990: 2.

71. Dahl, *Polyarchy,* 1971.

72. Barrington Moore, *The Social Origins of Dictatorship and Democracy.* Boston: Beacon, 1966; Dahl, *Polyarchy,* 1971; Karl, "Dilemmas of Democratization in Latin America," 1990; Vanhanen, *The Process of Democratization,* 1990; Przeworski, *Democracy and the Market,* 1991.

73. Constitutional political opposition in a democracy opposes the government, but not the regime itself. See Lawson, "Conceptual Issues," 1993: 200.

74. Lawson, "Conceptual Issues," 1993: 194. For a discussion of what makes elections free and fair, see Jorgen Elklit and Palle Svensson, "What Makes Elections Free and Fair?" *Journal of Democracy,* 8 (1997): 32–46. For a discussion of the role of domestic and international observers in determining whether elections are free and fair, see Thomas Carothers, "The Observers Observed," *Journal of Democracy,* 8 (1997): 17–31; Neil Nevitte and Santiago A. Canton, "The Role of Domestic Observers," *Journal of Democracy,* 8 (1997): 47–61.

75. Scott Mainwaring, Guillermo O'Donnell, and J. Samuel Valenzuela, eds., *New Issues in Democratic Consolidation.* Notre Dame: University of Notre Dame Press, 1992. Schmitter and Santiso suggest that, as a rule of thumb, consolidation should take at minimum, 12 years, given that consolidation is often considered achieved when two consecutive peaceful turnovers of government have occurred. This minimum time required for "the second transition" assumes that consolidation begins with the seating of the first freely elected legislature, is followed by a turnover in government without regime change in elections four years later, followed by another turnover in government four years hence. See Schmitter and Santiso, "Three Temporal Dimensions," 1997: 83–84.

76. Morris M. Mottale, *Iran: The Political Sociology of the Islamic Revolution.* New York: University Press of America, 1995: 30–35.

77. Dilip Hiro, *Iran under the Ayatollahs.* London: Routledge and Kegan Paul, 1985: 217; Sepehr Zabih, *The Left in Contemporary Iran.* Stanford: Hoover Institution Press, 1986: 106.

78. Theda Skocpol, "Rentier State and Shi'a Islam in the Iranian Revolution," *Theory and Society,* 11 (1982): 276; Richard Cottam, "Inside Revolutionary Iran," in *Iran's Revolution: The Search for Consensus,* edited by R. K. Ramazani, 3–26. Bloomington: Indiana University Press, 1990: 4.

79. David Menashri, *Iran: A Decade of War and Revolution.* New York: Holmes and Meier, 1990: Zabih, *The Left in Contemporary Iran,* 1986.

80. John Foran and Jeff Goodwin, "Revolutionary Outcomes in Iran and Nicaragua: Coalition Fragmentation, War, and the Limits of Social Transformation," *Theory and Society,* 22 (1993): 216.

81. For more on presidential-parliamentary hybrid political systems, see Matthew Soberg Shugart and John M. Carey, *Presidents and Assemblies: Constitutional Design and Electoral Dynamics.* Cambridge: Cambridge University Press, 1992.

82. Skocpol, "Rentier State," 1982: 276.

83. Shaul Bakhash, *The Reign of the Ayatollahs: Iran and the Islamic Revolution.* New York: Basic Books, 1984: 259.

84. Bakhash, *The Reign of the Ayatollahs,* 1984: 52–70; H. E. Chehabi, "The Provisional Government and the Transition from Monarchy to Islamic Republic in Iran," in *Between States: Interim Governments and Democratic*

Transitions, edited by Y. Shain and J. Linz, 127–143. Cambridge: Cambridge University Press, 1995.

85. Farrokh Moshiri, "Iran: Islamic Revolution against Westernization," in *Revolutions of the Late Twentieth Century,* edited by J. Goldstone, T. R. Gurr, and F. Moshiri, 116–135. Boulder: Westview Press, 1991: 130.

86. Cottam, "Inside Revolutionary Iran," 1990: 8; Foran and Goodwin, "Revolutionary Outcomes," 1993: 238.

87. Human Rights Watch/Middle East, "Power Versus Choice: Human Rights and Parliamentary Elections in the Islamic Republic of Iran," *Human Rights Watch/Middle East Report,* 8 (1996): 3.

88. Foran and Goodwin, "Revolutionary Outcomes," 1993: 217.

89. Skocpol, "Rentier State," 1982: 278.

90. Bahman Baktiari, *Parliamentary Politics in Revolutionary Iran: The Institutionalization of Factional Politics.* Gainesville: University Press of Florida, 1996: 69.

91. Human Rights Watch/Middle East, "Power versus Choice," 1996: 1.

92. Skocpol, "Rentier State," 1982.

93. Foran and Goodwin. "Revolutionary Outcomes," 1993: 217; Human Rights Watch/Middle East, "Power Versus Choice" 1996: 3.

94. See Reza Afshari, "An Essay on Scholarship, Human Rights, and State Legitimacy: The Case of the Islamic Republic of Iran," *Human Rights Quarterly,* 18 (1996): 544–593; John Kifner, "Khomeini Discounts Report on Strife," The *New York Times,* November 10, 1986, A14; Roberto Suro, "Iran's Unpredictable Behavior Reflects Rivalries in Regime," The *New York Times,* February 4, 1987: A1. While contestation, participation, and accountability were minimized in post-revolutionary Iran, a different (perhaps non-Western) type of democratization occurred—democratization "understood not as an extension of political liberalism or the realization of democratic socialism, but as an enhancement of popular involvement in national political life." See Theda Skocpol, "Social Revolutions and Mass Military Mobilization," *World Politics,* 40 (1988): 148–149. Additionally, there was significant, lively debate at the top levels of government, particularly in the *majlis.* See Baktiari, *Parliamentary Politics in Revolutionary Iran,* 1996. Finally, the regime can legitimately claim the support of the masses. The ability of the regime to avoid Western-style democratic liberalization, and to instead develop this alternate model involving mass mobilization and a degree of democratic centralism, hints at similarities with the Cuban case (below).

95. Menashri, *Iran: A Decade of War and Revolution,* 1990: 389.

96. Baktiari, *Parliamentary Politics in Revolutionary Iran,* 1996: 236–237; Hiro, *Iran Under the Ayatollahs,* 1985: 179–184.

97. Moshiri, "Iran: Islamic Revolution Against Westernization," 1991: 132.

98. Menashri, *Iran: A Decade of War and Revolution*, 1990; Barbara Harff, "Minorities, Rebellion, and Repression in North Africa and the Middle East," in *Minorities at Risk: A Global View of Ethnopolitical Conflict*, by T. R. Gurr, 217–251. Washington, DC: United States Institute for Peace Press, 1993. By 1986 these benefits had been all but exhausted. The fact that the regime had been able to oust the majority of their domestic opposition early on may explain why, despite the increasingly negative effects of the war from 1986 to 1988, levels of opposition did not increase dramatically (see Figure 6.1). Nevertheless, some increase is evident. The regime responded by increasing its use of repressive tactics (see Figures 4.2 and 4.3).

99. Benard and Khalilzad take this one step further, arguing that a review of the steps taken by the clerics to consolidate their regime shows a striking similarity to those taken by totalitarian dictatorships. See Cheryl Benard and Zalmay Khalilzad, *The Government of God: Iran's Islamic Republic*. New York: Columbia University Press, 1984.

100. Marifeli Perez-Stable, *The Cuban Revolution: Origins, Course, and Legacy*. New York: Oxford University Press, 1993: 62–63.

101. Eisenstadt, *Revolution and the Transformation of Societies*, 1978: 297.

102. Lowry Nelson, *Cuba: The Measure of a Revolution*. Minneapolis: University of Minnesota Press, 1972: 19.

103. Tad Szulc, *Fidel: A Critical Portrait*. New York: William Morrow, 1986.

104. Manuel Urrutia, *Fidel Castro and Company, Inc.: Communist Tyranny in Cuba*. New York: Praeger, 1964; Perez-Stable, *The Cuban Revolution*, 1993: 78–79.

105. Nelson, *Cuba: The Measure of a Revolution*, 1972: 21.

106. Selbin, *Modern Latin American Revolutions*, 1993: 43.

107. Juan M. del Aguila, *Cuba: Dilemmas of a Revolution*, 1984: 159; Selbin, *Modern Latin American Revolutions*, 1993: 47.

108. Marta Harnecker, ed., *Cuba: Dictatorship or Democracy*. Westport: Lawrence Hill, 1978: xxix.

109. Juan M. del Aguila, *Cuba: Dilemmas of a Revolution*, 1984: 141,168. For a contrary view, see Peter Roman, "Representative Government in Socialist Cuba," *Latin American Perspectives*, 20 (1993): 7–27. For a good discussion of these reforms, see: Rhonda Pearl Rabkin, "Cuban Political Structure: Vanguard Party and the Masses," in *Cuba: Twenty-Five Years of Revolution, 1959–1984*, edited by S. Halebsky and J. Kirk, 251–269. New York: Praeger, 1985; Archibald R. M. Ritter, "The Organs of People's Power and the Communist Party: The Nature of Cuban Democracy," in Halebsky and Kirk, eds., *Cuba: Twenty-Five Years of Revolution*, 1985: 270–290.

110. Herbert L. Matthews, "Commentary: The Cuban Revolution," *Hispanic American Report*, August 29, 1960: iii.

111. Nelson, *Cuba: The Measure of a Revolution*, 1972: 198.

112. Selbin, *Modern Latin American Revolutions*, 1993: 44.

113. Juan M. del Aguila, *Cuba: Dilemmas of a Revolution,* 1984: 49; Human Rights Watch/Americas, "Cuba: Improvements without Reform," *Human Rights Watch/Americas Report,* 7 (1995): 8.

114. Matthews, "Commentary: The Cuban Revolution," 1960: iii-vii.

115. Selbin, *Modern Latin American Revolutions,* 1993: 47–49.

116. Donald W. Bray and Timothy F. Harding, "Cuba," in *Latin America: The Struggle with Dependency and Beyond,* edited by R. Chilcote and J. Edelstein, 583–730. New York: Wiley, 1974: 622–623.

117. Juan M. del Aguila, *Cuba: Dilemmas of a Revolution,* 1984: 63.

118. Juan M. del Aguila, *Cuba: Dilemmas of a Revolution,* 1984: 98.

119. John Griffiths and Peter Griffiths, *Cuba: The Second Decade.* London: Writers and Readers Publishing Cooperative, 1979: 11.

120. Devora Grynspan, "Nicaragua: A New Model for Popular Revolution in Latin America," in *Revolutions of the Late Twentieth Century,* edited by J. Goldstone, T. R. Gurr, and F. Moshiri, 88–115. Boulder: Westview Press, 1991: 100–102.

121. In a meeting in Havana soon after the Sandinistas took power, Humberto Ortega was heard to remark to Fidel Castro, "we are sharing the cake because that is the only way to control the whole thing." See Roger Miranda and William Ratliff, *The Civil War in Nicaragua: Inside the Sandinistas.* New Brunswick: Transaction Books, 1993: 20; Forrest D. Colburn, *The Vogue of Revolution in Poor Countries.* Princeton: Princeton University Press, 1994: 53.

122. Michael E. Conroy and Manuel Pastor, Jr. "The Nicaraguan Experiment: Characteristics of a New Economic Model," in *Crisis in Central America: Regional Dynamics and U.S. Policy in the 1980s,* edited by N. Hamilton, J. Frieden, L. Fuller, and M. Pastor, Jr., 207–226. Boulder: Westview Press, 1988: 221.

123. Colburn, *The Vogue of Revolution in Poor Countries,* 1994. What the directorate did envision was the type of "democracy" that Fidel Castro claimed was the result of the Cuban revolution—mass mobilization and "direct democracy." See Harry E. Vanden, "Democracy Derailed: The 1990 Elections and After," in *The Undermining of the Sandinista Revolution,* edited by G. Prevost and H. Vanden, 45–73. New York: St. Martin's Press, 1997: 48.

124. Miranda and Ratliff, *The Civil War in Nicaragua,* 1993: 23.

125. L. Serra, "The Sandinista Mass Organizations," in *Nicaragua in Revolution,* edited by T. W. Walker, New York: Praeger, 1982: 96.

126. Przeworski, "The Games of Transition," 1992: 115.

127. Gary Prevost, "The Role of the Sandinista Revolution in the Process of Democratization in Nicaragua," *Democratization,* 2 (1995): 98–99.

128. Gary Ruchwarger. *People in Power: Forging a Grassroots Democracy in Nicaragua.* South Hadley: Bergin and Garvey Publishers, 1987.

129. Gary Prevost, "The Status of the Sandinista Revolutionary Project," in *The Undermining of the Sandinista Revolution,* edited by G. Prevost and H. Vanden, 9–44. New York: St. Martin's Press, 1997: 14.

130. Andrew J. Stein, "Public Perceptions and Evaluations of Corruption in Nicaragua: Consequences for Democracy," paper presented at the Annual Meeting of the Midwest Political Science Association, Chicago, Illinois, April 23–25, 1998.

131. Foran and Goodwin, "Revolutionary Outcomes in Iran and Nicaragua," 1993: 229.

132. David Close, "The Nicaraguan Elections of 1984," *Electoral Studies,* 4 (1985): 152–158.

133. Close, "The Nicaraguan Elections of 1984," 1985; LASA Forum, *Report of the Latin American Studies Association Delegation to Observe the Nicaraguan General Election of November 4, 1984.* Pittsburgh: Latin American Studies Association, 1985; Rueschemeyer, Stephens, and Stephens, *Capitalist Development and Democracy,* 1991: 246.

134. Selbin, *Latin American Revolutions,* 1993: 56.

135. Grynspan, "Nicaragua," 1991: 106–107.

136. Dennis Gilbert, "Nicaragua," in *Confronting Revolution: Security through Diplomacy in Central America,* edited by M. J. Blachman, W. M. LeoGrande, and K. E. Sharpe, 88–125. New York: Pantheon Books, 1986: 105.

137. These measures were lifted as part of the liberalization effort surrounding the 1984 elections, but were reinstated soon thereafter. See Richard Stahler-Sholk, "The Dog That Didn't Bark: Labor Autonomy and Economic Adjustment in Nicaragua under the Sandinista and UNO Governments," *Comparative Politics,* 28 (1995): 84; Middlebrook, "Organized Labor and Democratization in Postrevolutionary Regimes," 1997: 15.

138. Rueschemeyer, Stephens, and Stephens, *Capitalist Development and Democracy.* 1991: 246; Stahler-Sholk, "The Dog That Didn't Bark," 1995: 84; Kevin J. Middlebrook, "Organized Labor and Democratization in Postrevolutionary Regimes," 1997: 15.

139. Bernard Nietschmann, *The Unknown War: The Miskito Nation, Nicaragua, and the United States.* New York: Freedom House, 1989; Ted Robert Gurr and Barbara Harff, *Ethnic Conflict in World Politics.* Boulder: Westview Press, 1994: 49–50.

140. Selbin, *Latin American Revolutions,* 1993: 118.

141. David Close, "Central American Elections 1989–90: Costa Rica, El Salvador, Honduras, Nicaragua, Panama," *Electoral Studies,* 10 (1991): 70.

142. Jaime Wheelock Roman, "Revolution and Democratic Transition in Nicaragua," in *Democratic Transitions in Central America,* edited by J. Dominguez and M. Lindenberg, 67–85. Gainesville: University Press of Florida, 1997: 82–83; William A. Barnes, with Kenneth M. Coleman,

"Incomplete Democracy and Voter Turnout in Nicaragua and El Salvador," presented at the Annual Meeting of the Midwest Political Science Association. Chicago, Illinois, April 10–12, 1997: 33.

143. Prevost, "The Role of the Sandinista Revolution," 1995: 104. For an excellent account of the processes of institutionalization and consolidation of the revolution and their culmination in the end of the Contra War and the election of 1990, see Selbin, *Latin American Revolutions,* 1993.

144. Foran and Goodwin, "Revolutionary Outcomes in Iran and Nicaragua," 1993: 233.

145. Rueschemeyer, Stephens, and Stephens, *Capitalist Development and Democracy,* 1991: 246.

146. Samuel J. Valenzuela, "Democratic Consolidation in Post-Transitional Settings: Notion, Process, and Facilitating Conditions, " in *Issues in Democratic Consolidation,* edited by S. Mainwaring, G. O'Donnell, and J. S. Valenzuela, 157–104. Notre Dame: University of Notre Dame Press, 1992: 78.

147. Prevost, "The Status of the Sandinista Revolutionary Project," 1997.

148. Steven Kent Smith, "Renovation and Orthodoxy: Debate and Transition within the Sandinista National Liberation Front," *Latin American Perspectives,* 24 (1997): 102–116.

149. However, the fact that free and fair elections occurred does not mean that corruption was absent in the highest levels of power in Nicaragua. For more about corrupt practices by the Sandinistas, the UNO and Aleman, along with an examination of public perceptions of corruption in the Nicaraguan government, see Stein (1998).

150. Outside observers included former United States President Jimmy Carter, former Secretary of State James Baker, former Costa Rican President Oscar Arias, and former President of Ecuador Osvaldo Hurtado. Additionally, a group of Nicaraguan citizens and non-governmental organizations called Ethics and Transparency (ET) monitored the 1996 elections and certified their fairness. See Nevitte and Canton, "The Role of Domestic Observers," 1997: 56; Carter Center, "Democracy Prevails in Nicaragua's 1996 Presidential Election," *The Carter Center News,* winter, 1997: 1; Booth and Richard, "The Nicaraguan Elections of October 1996," 1997.

151. Barnes, with Kenneth M. Coleman, "Incomplete Democracy and Voter Turnout," 1997. The significance of his election was not lost on the victor. In his initial statement confirming his (and his party's) electoral victory, Aleman proudly announced "we have consolidated democracy in Nicaragua." See Larry Rohter, "Rightist is Victor over Sandinistas in Nicaraguan Vote," The *New York Times,* October 22, 1996: A1.

152. Robert J. Alexander, *Bolivia: Past, Present, and Future of its Politics.* Stanford: Praeger, 1982: 81.

153. James M. Malloy, "Revolutionary Politics," in *Beyond the Revolution: Bolivia since 1952*, edited by J. Malloy and R. Thorn, 111–156. Pittsburgh: University of Pittsburgh Press, 1971: 118–119.

154. James M. Malloy, *Bolivia: The Uncompleted Revolution*. Pittsburgh: University of Pittsburgh Press, 1970; Malloy, "Revolutionary Politics," 1971; J. Calderon, *The Bolivian Coup of 1964: A Sociological Analysis*. Buffalo: Council on International Studies, State University of New York at Buffalo, 1972.

155. Susan Eckstein, *The Impact of Revolution: A Comparative Analysis of Mexico and Bolivia*. London: Sage Publications, 1976; Herbert S. Klein, *Bolivia: The Evolution of a Multi-Ethnic Society*, 2nd ed. New York: Oxford University Press, 1992.

156. Laurence Whitehead, "Bolivia's Failed Democratization, 1977–1980," in *Transitions from Authoritarian Rule: Latin America*, edited by G. O'Donnell, P. Schmitter, and L. Whitehead. Baltimore: Johns Hopkins University Press, 1986: 54.

157. Susan Eckstein, "Revolutions and the Restructuring of National Economies: The Latin American Experience," *Comparative Politics*, 17 (1985): 73–494; James M. Malloy and Eduardo A. Gamarra, "The Transition to Democracy in Bolivia," in *Authoritarians and Democrats: Regime Transition in Latin America*, edited by J. Malloy and M. Seligson, 94. Pittsburgh: University of Pittsburgh Press, 1987.

158. Waltraud Queiser Morales, *Bolivia: Land of Struggle*. Boulder: Westview Press, 1992: 81.

159. James Dunkerley, *Rebellion in the Veins: Political Struggle in Bolivia, 1952–1982*. London: Verso, 1984: 46.

160. Klein, *Bolivia*, 1992: 233–234.

161. Malloy, *Bolivia*, 1970: 30; Jonathan Kelley and Herbert S. Klein, *Revolution and the Rebirth of Inequality: A Theory Applied to the National Revolution in Bolivia*. Berkeley: University of California Press, 1981: 102.

162. Rueschemeyer, Stephens, and Stephens, *Capitalist Development and Democracy*, 1991: 194.

163. Queiser Morales, *Bolivia: Land of Struggle*, 1992: 78; Klein, *Bolivia*. 1992: 232.

164. Kelley and Klein, *Revolution and the Rebirth of Inequality*, 1981: 96–99.

165. Kelley and Klein, *Revolution and the Rebirth of Inequality*, 1981: 95. The COB fanned the flames further, encouraging the radicalization of the peasants. See Selbin, *Latin American Revolutions*, 1993: 41.

166. Selbin, *Latin American Revolutions*, 1993: 41.

167. Malloy, *Bolivia*, 1970: 30; Klein, *Bolivia*, 1992: 234.

168. Malloy, "Revolutionary Politics," 1971: 128.

169. Dunkerley, *Rebellion in the Veins*, 1984: 64.

170. See Alexander, *Bolivia*, 1982: 85; Queiser Morales, *Bolivia: Land of Struggle*, 1992: 78. Indeed the regime did try other options. Soon after the 1953 coup attempt, Paz Estenssoro called for the creation of a "Popular and Revolutionary army" (Dunkerley, 1984: 81). For more on the resurrection of the army in post-1953 Bolivia, see Corbett (1972).

171. Selbin, *Latin American Revolutions*, 1993: 41.

172. Malloy, *Bolivia*, 1970: 187–222.

173. Malloy, "Revolutionary Politics," 1971: 131; Klein, *Bolivia*. 1992: 237.

174. Malloy, *Bolivia*, 1970.

175. Rueschemeyer, Stephens, and Stephens. *Capitalist Development and Democracy*. 1991: 305.

176. Christopher Mitchell, *The Legacy of Populism in Bolivia: From the MNR to Military Rule*. New York: Praeger, 1977: 45–49.

177. Alexander, *Bolivia,* 1982: 97.

178. Rueschemeyer, Stephens, and Stephens, *Capitalist Development and Democracy*. 1991: 305.

179. Queiser Morales, *Bolivia: Land of Struggle*, 1992: 81; Malloy and Gamarra, "The Transition to Democracy in Bolivia," 1987: 94.

180. Malloy, "Revolutionary Politics," 1971: 138.

181. Rueschemeyer, Stephens, and Stephens, *Capitalist Development and Democracy*, 1991: 305.

182. It is easier for a less repressive regime to undergo the transition toward a more democratic regime. As O'Donnell and Schmitter point out, the more repressive the regime, the more they will block any such transition. See O'Donnell and Schmitter, *Transitions from Authoritarian Rule*, 1986.

183. Valerie Bunce, *Do New Leaders Make a Difference?* Princeton: Princeton University Press, 1981.

Chapter 8

1. Days before Nicaraguan election on February 25th, 1990, Daniel Ortega authorized an election slogan to remind illiterate voters that the Sandinistas were the fifth slot on the ballot: "(mark your ballot in) the fifth on the 25th." In an interview in 1995, William A. Barnes was told by Augustin Jarquin, a top UNO campaign leader, that on election morning, Catholic clergy all around Nicaragua read this passage (5: 25) from the book of Daniel to their parishioners. See William A. Barnes, with Kenneth M. Coleman. "Incomplete Democracy and Voter Turnout in Nicaragua and El Salvador," paper presented at the Annual Meeting of the Midwest Political Science Association, Chicago, Illinois, April 10–12, 1997: 24.

2. This assumption is common throughout the political science literature. For examples of its use in the study of American politics, see David R. Mayhew, *Congress: The Electoral Connection*. New Haven: Yale University Press,

1974; Richard F. Fenno, *Home Style: House Members in Their Districts.* Boston: Little Brown, 1978. For examples of its use in the study of comparative politics, see Ted Robert Gurr, "War, Revolution, and the Growth of the Coercive State," *Comparative Political Studies,* 21 (1988): 45–65; Michael Bratton and Nicholas van de Walle, "Popular Protest and Political Reform in Africa," *Comparative Politics,* 24 (1992): 419–442. For examples of its use in international relations, see Jack Levy, "The Diversionary Theory of War: A Critique," in *The Handbook of War Studies,* edited by M. I. Midlarsky, 259–288. Boston: Unwin Hyman, 1989; Bruce Bueno de Mesquita and Randolph Siverson, "War and the Survival of Political Leaders: A Comparative Study of Regime Types and Political Accountability," *American Political Science Review,* 89 (1995): 841–855.

3. See Barry Ames, *Political Survival: Politicians and Public Policy in Latin America.* Berkeley: University of California Press, 1987: 211, 242; Bueno de Mesquita and Siverson, "War and the Survival of Political Leaders," 1995: 842. At this point I wish to differentiate between political system survival and elite political survival. For example, Samuel P. Huntington argues that political institutionalization is necessary for political durability. See his book *Political Order in Changing Societies,* New Haven: Yale University Press, 1968. Yet Joel Migdal points out that political survival may involve a degree of deinstitutionalization, and is even more dependent on the effective and timely use of repression by elites. See Migdal's book *Strong Societies and Weak States.* Princeton: Princeton University Press, 1989. The apparent contradiction is clarified when one realizes that, while Huntington is describing the political stability of the *state,* Migdal is describing the political survival of the *elites.* Indeed, I make no argument in this chapter regarding political system survivability. In fact, I would expect that in many cases, particularly in democracies, when elites lose power the system survives. This is precisely the definition of a consolidated democracy often used in the process theory literature—(multiple) turnover of elites while the rules of the game remain constant. See for instance: Scott Mainwaring, Guillermo O'Donnell, and J. Samuel Valenzuela, eds., *New Issues in Democratic Consolidation.* Notre Dame: University of Notre Dame Press, 1992; Stephanie Lawson, "Conceptual Issues in the Comparative Study of Regime Change and Democratization," *Comparative Politics,* 25 (1993): 183–205. Instead, I focus on *elite* political survival in his study.

4. Migdal, *Strong Societies, Weak States,* 1989: 226.

5. See Valerie Bunce, *Do New Leaders Make a Difference?* Princeton: Princeton University Press, 1981; Valerie Bunce, "The Succession Connection: Policy Cycles and Political Change in the Soviet Union and Eastern Europe," *American Political Science Review,* 74 (1980): 966–977; Valerie Bunce, "Elite Succession, Petrification, and Policy Innovation in Communist Systems: An Empirical Assessment," *Comparative Political Studies,* 9 (1976): 3–41.

Philip Roeder critiques, retests, and revises Bunce's original argument. While he finds a different "succession connection" than the one posited by Bunce, Roeder confirms the more general finding that new leaders mean new policies. See Philip G. Roeder, "Do New Soviet Leaders Really Make a Difference? Rethinking the 'Succession Connection,'" *American Political Science Review,* 79 (1985): 958–976.

6. Ironically, the possibility of ouster is demonstrated by the very elites whose concern it now is to retain power.

7. For example, when asked what he had done during the French Revolution, Sieyes replied "I survived." See Ezra N. Suleiman, *Elites in French Society: The Politics of Survival.* Princeton: Princeton University Press, 1978: 6. As this reply demonstrates, post-internal war elites often see survival as an end of its own, and one that is difficult to come by in and of itself.

8. Henry Bienen and Nicholas Van de Walle, *Of Time and Power: Leadership Duration in the Modern World.* Stanford: Stanford University Press, 1991.

9. Charles S. Maier, *Recasting Bourgeois Europe: Stabilization in France, Germany and Italy in the Decade After World War I.* Princeton: Princeton University Press, 1975: 3.

10. For more on the 1964 Bolivian coup, see J. Calderon, *The Bolivian Coup of 1964: A Sociological Analysis.* Buffalo: Council on International Studies, State University of New York at Buffalo, 1972. For a brief discussion of the 1983 coup in Grenada see Eric Selbin, *Modern Latin American Revolutions.* Boulder: Westview Press, 1993: 69.

11. For more on the electoral defeat of the Sandinistas, see Gary Prevost, "The Role of the Sandinista Revolution in the Process of Democratization in Nicaragua," *Democratization,* 2 (1995): 85–108. For more on the defeat of Solidarity see John Higley, Judith Kullberg, and Jan Pakulski, "The Persistence of Postcommunist Elites," *Journal of Democracy,* 7 (1996): 133–147.

12. Andrew J. Enterline and Kristian S. Gleditsch, "Threats, Force, and Survival: A Study of Latin American Leaders," paper presented at the annual meeting of the Peace Science Society (International), Indianapolis, Indiana, November 21–23, 1997: 1.

13. Bueno de Mesquita and Siverson, "War and the Survival of Political Leaders," 1995: 842–843.

14. See for instance, Migdal, *Strong Societies, Weak States,* 1989; Enterline and Gleditsch, "Threats, Force, and Survival," 1997.

15. Enterline and Gleditsch, "Threats, Force, and Survival," 1997: 1; See also Tatu Vanhanen, *The Process of Democratization: A Comparative Study of 147 States,* 1980–88. New York: Crane Russak, 1990; Mancur Olson, "Dictatorship, Democracy, and Development," *American Political Science Review,* 87 (1993): 567–576.

16. Frances Hagopian, "After Regime Change: Authoritarian Legacies, Political Representation, and the Democratic Future of South America," *World Politics,* 45 (1993): 490.

17. However, recent research has determined that, while democracies do oc-casionally experience internal wars, non-democracies experience such up-heavals significantly more frequently. See for instance, Matthew Krain and Marissa Edson Myers, "Democracy and Civil War: A Note on the Demo-cratic Peace Proposition," *International Interactions*, 23 (1997): 87–94. Jeff Goodwin also notes that no democracy has *ever* been overthrown by a rev-olution. See his paper "Is the Age of Revolutions Over?" presented at the 39th Annual Meeting of the International Studies Association, Minneapo-lis, MN, March 18–21, 1998. In other words, while democracies provide institutional opportunities to oust leaders, they impede many forms of extra-constitutional ouster. Yet democracy does not necessarily inhibit the frequency of other types of rollback. For more on rollback of democracies, see Juan J. Linz, *The Breakdown of Democratic Regimes: Crisis, Breakdown and Reequilibration*. Baltimore: Johns Hopkins University Press, 1978; Samuel P. Huntington, *The Third Wave: Democratization in the Late Twentieth Century.* Norman: University of Oklahoma Press, 1991.

18. Juan J. Linz, "Democracy's Time Constraints," *International Political Science Review*, 19 (1998): 19.

19. Despite this, leaders in authoritarian political systems also experience sub-stantial limits to their political autonomy. As such, constraints on political leaders are not solely characteristics of democratic systems. See Enterline and Gleditsch, "Threats, Force, and Survival," 1997: 1.

20. However, Bienen and Van de Walle find that initially the risk of ouster is higher for authoritarian leaders than for democratic leaders. See their book *Of Time and Power,* 1991.

21. Keith Jaggers, "War and the Three Faces of Power: War Making and State Making in Europe and the Americas," *Comparative Political Studies,* 25 (1992): 39.

22. Percy C. Hintzen, *The Costs of Regime Survival: Racial Mobilization, Elite Domination, and Control of the State in Guyana and Trinidad.* Cambridge: Cambridge University Press, 1989.

23. This tactic has been shown to work in states that have not experienced an internal war as well. For instance, Percy C. Hintzen demonstrates that the perpetual campaigns of repressive, reactive crisis management by the elites in Guyana and Trinidad prevented mass dissafection from growing into a serious threat to the regimes, thereby insuring the elites' survival in power. See Hintzen's *The Costs of Regime Survival,* 1989.

24. When repressive elites are replaced, it is for reasons other than their policy mix choices. See Mancur Olson, "Dictatorship, Democracy, and Develop-ment," 1993: 573.

25. Niccolo Machiavelli, *The Prince,* reprint. New York: Norton, 1980: 55.

26. Some argue that regimes that employ repression in an effort to assure sur-vival will be unable to adequately provide for the collective needs and/or desires of society. See for instance, Migdal, *Strong Societies, Weak States,* 1989:

225. This, in turn, might lead to greater unrest and further repression, and perhaps regime collapse or overthrow. However, Hintzen shows that collective needs can be sacrificed without jeopardizing elite survival. He argues that the state is able to do so by playing different roles for different sectors of society. This allows the elites to effectively bypass a majority of the masses and still maintain power and a resource base. For example:

> Regime survival in Trinidad came to be rooted in an ability to satisfy the accumulative claims of the country's middle and upper classes and continued ability to deny full and equal political participation to the country's rural East Indian population. Black lower-class dissent, the result of outbidding, was contained through coercion and control and lower-class political movements were demobilized.

Hintzen concludes that "survival can, and usually does, come at the cost of the satisfaction of the collective needs of society." See Hintzen, *The Costs of Regime Survival,* 1989. For more on the elites' use of alliances with different sectors of society to establish or maintain regimes, see Charles Tilly, *From Mobilization to Revolution.* New York: McGraw-Hill, 1978; Guillermo O'Donnell and Philippe C. Schmitter, *Transitions from Authoritarian Rule: Tentative Conclusions about Uncertain Democracies.* Baltimore: Johns Hopkins University Press, 1986; Gregory M. Luebbert, *Liberalism, Fascism, or Social Democracy: Social Classes and the Political Origins of Regimes in Interwar Europe.* New York: Oxford University Press, 1991; Dietrich Rueschemeyer, Evelyne Huber Stephens, and John D. Stephens, *Capitalist Development and Democracy.* Chicago: University of Chicago Press, 1991.

27. O'Donnell and Schmitter, *Transitions from Authoritarian Rule,* 1986.

28. Hintzen, *The Costs of Regime Survival,* 1989: 2.

29. See O'Donnell and Schmitter, Transitions From Authoritarian Rule, 1986; Guiseppe DiPalma, *To Craft Democracies.* Berkeley: University of California Press, 1990.

30. This is sometimes due to the very nature of democratic or semi-democratic regimes. As noted earlier, democracy is, by its very nature, government *pro tempore* (Linz, 1998: 119). "[T]he power of the government in a democratic regime is always conditional and always temporary. It is conditional because it is subject to the limitations on its power imposed by the doctrine of constitutionalism, and it is temporary because it is subject to the periodic judgment of the people, who may choose to replace it with an alternative government, the opposition" (Lawson, 1993).

31. Higley, Kullberg, and Pakulski, "The Persistence of Postcommunist Elites," 1996; David S. Mason, *Revolution and Transition in East-Central Europe,* 2nd ed. Boulder: Westview Press, 1996.

32. Jonathan Kelley and Herbert S. Klein, *Revolution and the Rebirth of Inequality: A Theory Applied to the National Revolution in Bolivia*. Berkeley: University of California Press, 1981; Herbert S. Klein, Bolivia: *The Evolution of a Multi-Ethnic Society*, 2nd ed. New York: Oxford University Press, 1992.

33. Bueno de Mesquita and Siverson, "War and the Survival of Political Leaders," 1995: 853.

34. Bruce Bueno de Mesquita, Randolph M. Siverson, and Gary Woller. "War and the Fate of Regimes: A Comparative Analysis," *American Political Science Review*, 86 (1992): 638–646. This result is confirmed by Bueno de Mesquita and Siverson, who show that leaders who lead their nations into war subject themselves to a domestic political hazard that threatens their political survival. See Bueno de Mesquita and Siverson, "War and the Survival of Political Leaders," 1995.

35. Enterline and Gleditsch, "Threats, Force, and Survival," 1997.

36. Hypothesis 8.3 is not significantly different from Hypothesis 8.1. Both argue that perceptions and the timing of policy mix choices matter most. But Hypothesis 8.3 focuses on the more direct comparison between Type I and Type III cases in order to determine the nature of war's direct effect on elite survivability.

37. Boolean algebra is a method of qualitative comparison that allows for a more "holistic approach" toward cases, with a bias toward complexity of causation. There are benefits that this approach brings to comparative analysis. The method of data presentation—truth tables—enables one to present the data in a more intuitive fashion to those not quantitatively inclined, thus reaching a wider audience. Truth tables are "used in the comparative analysis of configurations of similar ties and differences to summarize the different patterns that exist in a set of cases. It summarizes [*sic*] a data matrix by sorting cases according to their combinations of values on dichotomous causal variables." See Charles C. Ragin, *Constructing Social Research*. Thousand Oaks: Pine Forge Press, 1994: 193. Additionally, this type of analysis allows for comparative examination of conjunctural configurations of causes rather than simply the presence or absence of causal conditions. This leads to the third benefit of Boolean algebra. This method enables one to account for the possibility that multiple patterns of causal variables may result in the same outcome. Also, Boolean algebra allows one to account for "complex and seemingly contradictory patterns of causation" such as when the presence of one variable in one configuration and the absence of the same variable in another configuration both lead to the same result, but in opposite ways. See Ragin, *Constructing Social Research*, 1994: 118.

38. Moshen Milani, *The Making of Iran's Islamic Revolution*. Boulder: Westview Press, 1994: 246.

39. Theda Skocpol, "Rentier State and Shi'a Islam in the Iranian Revolution," *Theory and Society,* 11 (1982): 276.

40. Farrokh Moshiri, "Iran: Islamic Revolution Against Westernization," in *Revolutions of the Late Twentieth Century,* edited by J. Goldstone, T. R. Gurr, and F. Moshiri, 116–135. Boulder: Westview Press, 1991: 132.

41. Ahmad Ghoreishi and Dariush Zahedi, "Prospects for Regime Change in Iran," *Middle East Policy,* 5 (1997): 99.

42. Bahman Baktiari, *Parliamentary Politics in Revolutionary Iran: The Institutionalization of Factional Politics.* Gainesville: University Press of Florida, 1996: 236.

43. James DeFronzo, *Revolutions and Revolutionary Movements.* Boulder: Westview Press, 1991: 268.

44. Moshiri, "Iran: Islamic Revolution against Westernization," 1991: 133; John Foran and Jeff Goodwin, "Revolutionary Outcomes in Iran and Nicaragua: Coalition Fragmentation, War, and the Limits of Social Transformation," *Theory and Society.* 22 (1993): 238.

45. Mehran Kamrava, "Non-democratic States and Political Liberalisation in the Middle East: A Structural Analysis," *Third World Quarterly,* 19 (1998): 71.

46. Ghoreishi and Zahedi, "Prospects for Regime Change in Iran," 1997: 98.

47. Dilip Hiro, *Iran under the Ayatollahs.* London: Routledge and Kegan Paul, 1985: 217; David Menashri, *Iran: A Decade of War and Revolution.* New York: Holmes and Meier, 1990: 184–187.

48. Milani, *The Making of Iran's Islamic Revolution.* 1994: 219–221.

49. H. E. Chehabi, "The Provisional Government and the Transition from Monarchy to Islamic Republic in Iran," in *Between States: Interim Governments and Democratic Transitions,* edited by Y. Shain and J. Linz, 127–143. Cambridge: Cambridge University Press, 1995: 143.

50. Baktiari, *Parliamentary Politics in Revolutionary Iran,* 1996.

51. Reza Afshari, "An Essay on Scholarship, Human Rights, and State Legitimacy: The Case of the Islamic Republic of Iran," *Human Rights Quarterly,* 18 (1996): 544–593.

52. See John Foran, "The Future of Revolutions at the *fin-de-siecle,*" *Third World Quarterly,* 18 (1997): 791–820; Ghoreishi and Zahedi, "Prospects for Regime Change in Iran," 1997: 98; Mark N. Katz, "The Khatemi Factor: How Much Does it Matter?" *The National Interest,* spring, 1998: 85–90.

53. See Selbin, *Modern Latin American Revolutions,* 1993: 50; Antoni Kapcia, "Politics in Cuba: Beyond the Stereotypes," *Bulletin of Latin American Research,* 15 (1996): 247–253.

54. The leader of the exile community, Jorge Mas Canosa, recently died, leaving the hierarchy of the opposition-in-exile in disarray. See "The Fading of Fidel," *The Economist,* January 15, 1998.

55. Kapcia, "Politics in Cuba," 1996: 249.

56. Lowry Nelson, *Cuba: The Measure of a Revolution.* Minneapolis: University of Minnesota Press, 1972: 19.

57. Tad Szulc, *Fidel: A Critical Portrait*. New York: William Morrow, 1986; Rosemary H. T. O'Kane, *The Revolutionary Reign of Terror: The Role of Violence in Political Change*. Hants: Edward Elgar Publishing, 1991: 59–60.

58. Juan M. del Aguila, *Cuba: Dilemmas of a Revolution*. Boulder: Westview Press, 1984: 63.

59. See Donald W. Bray and Timothy F. Harding, "Cuba," *Latin America: The Struggle with Dependency and Beyond,* edited by R. Chilcote and J. Edelstein, 583–730. New York: Wiley, 1974: 669–670; Selbin, *Modern Latin American Revolutions,* 1993: 44. The one issue that has not been addressed sufficiently by the Cuban elites is succession. Fidel has designated his brother, Raul, as his successor, but no mechanism is in place to guarantee a smooth transition, or to explain how future successions might work. As Eric Selbin argues, "the true test of the revolution will be when Fidel Castro has left the scene." See Marifeli Perez-Stable, *The Cuban Revolution: Origins, Course, and Legacy.* New York: Oxford University Press, 1993: 178; Selbin, *Modern Latin American Revolutions,* 1993: 51.

60. Foran and Goodwin, "Revolutionary Outcomes in Iran and Nicaragua," 1993: 238.

61. Michael E. Conroy and Manuel Pastor, Jr., "The Nicaraguan Experiment: Characteristics of a New Economic Model, in *Crisis in Central America: Regional Dynamics and U.S. Policy in the 1980s,* edited by N. Hamilton, et.al., 207–226. Boulder: Westview Press, 1988.

62. This is not to say that repression was not employed (Wheelock, 1997: 82–83). Indeed, repression appears to have been an effective tactic in reducing opposition activity amongst non-Contra opposition (Table 6.3 in Chapter 6). Unfortunately, it also drove many opposition groups to leave the domestic arena and become a direct part of the war effort against the Sandinistas. Because all wartime fighting is excluded from the events examined in the data analysis run in previous chapters, it is impossible to determine the precise effect of repression on the defection of opposition groups to the anti-Sandinista war effort. Examples of such defections resulting from regime repression include the activity of large portions of the Miskito population during the Contra War (Nietschmann, 1989; Gurr and Harff, 1994: 49–50).

63. Prevost, "The Role of the Sandinista Revolution," 1995; Gary Prevost, "The Status of the Sandinista Revolutionary Project," in *The Undermining of the Sandinista Revolution,* edited by G. Prevost and H. Vanden, 9–44. New York: St. Martin's Press, 1997.

64. Katherine Hoyt, *The Many Faces of Sandinista Democracy,* monographs in International Studies, Latin American Series, number 27. Athens: Ohio University Press, 1997: 31.

65. Foran and Goodwin, "Revolutionary Outcomes in Iran and Nicaragua," 1993: 238.

66. Kevin J. Middlebrook, "Organized Labor and Democratization in Postrevolutionary Regimes: Transition Politics in Nicaragua, Russia, and Mexico," paper presented at the Annual Meeting of the American Political Science Association, Washington, DC, August 28–31, 1997: 16.

67. Roger Miranda and William Ratliff, *The Civil War in Nicaragua: Inside the Sandinistas.* New Brunswick: Transaction Books, 1993: 272.

68. See Jaime Wheelock Roman, "Revolution and Democratic Transition in Nicaragua," in *Democratic Transitions in Central America,* edited by J. Dominguez and M. Lindenberg, 67–85. Gainesville: University Press of Florida, 1997: 82. However, similar actions did not yield similar results in 1984. The Sandinistas had also moved up the first set of elections from 1985 to November of 1984 in order to undercut U.S. influence in both the electoral campaign and the Contra War. Yet they were victorious, capturing 67 percent of the vote. Recent analysis of these results have led the FSLN leadership to believe that had those parties that boycotted the 1984 election participated, the Sandinista margin of victory would have been significantly smaller (Hoyt, 1997: 31). This may explain the discrepancy in the effect of war-driven electoral maneuvering on outcomes in Nicaragua.

69. Thomas W. Walker, *Nicaragua: The Land of Sandino.* Boulder: Westview Press, 1991: 143.

70. Hoyt, *The Many Faces of Sandinista* Democracy. 1997: 31.

71. Wheelock Roman, "Revolution and Democratic Transition in Nicaragua," 1997: 82–83.

72. See Devora Grynspan, "Nicaragua: A New Model for Popular Revolution in Latin America," in *Revolutions of the Late Twentieth Century,* edited by J. Goldstone, T. R. Gurr, and F. Moshiri, 88–115. Boulder: Westview Press, 1991: 110; David Close, "Central American Elections 1989–90: Costa Rica, El Salvador, Honduras, Nicaragua, Panama," *Electoral Studies,* 10 (1991): 72. See also Harry E. Vanden, "Democracy Derailed: The 1990 Elections and After," in *The Undermining of the Sandinista Revolution,* edited by G. Prevost and H. Vanden, 45–73. New York: St. Martin's Press, 1997: 59.

73. Wheelock Roman, "Revolution and Democratic Transition in Nicaragua," 1997: 82–83.

74. Calderon, *The Bolivian Coup of 1964,* 1972: 109.

75. Klein, *Bolivia: The Evolution of a Multi-Ethnic Society,* 1992: 236.

76. Laurence Whitehead, "Bolivia's Failed Democratization, 1977–1980," in *Transitions from Authoritarian Rule: Latin America,* edited by G. O'Donnell, P. Schmitter, and L. Whitehead, 49–71. Baltimore: Johns Hopkins University Press, 1986: 54.

77. Leslie Bethell, ed., *The Cambridge History of Latin America,* volume 6, part 2. Cambridge: Cambridge University Press, 1984: 427.

78. William H. Brill, *Military Intervention in Bolivia: The Overthrow of Paz Estenssoro and the MNR.* Washington, DC: Institute for the Comparative Study of Political Systems, 1967.

79. Bethell, *The Cambridge History of Latin America*. 1984: 427.

80. James M. Malloy, "Revolutionary Politics," in *Beyond the Revolution: Bolivia since 1952*, edited by J. Malloy and R. Thorn, 111–156. Pittsburgh: University of Pittsburgh Press, 1971: 136.

81. Brill, *Military Intervention in Bolivia*, 1967.

82. Susan Eckstein, *The Impact of Revolution: A Comparative Analysis of Mexico and Bolivia*. London: Sage Publications, 1976.

83. Calderon, *The Bolivian Coup of 1964*, 1972: 109.

84. Robert J. Alexander, *Bolivia: Past, Present, and Future of its Politics*. Stanford: Praeger, 1982: 81.

85. James M. Malloy, *Bolivia's MNR: A Study of a National Popular Movement in Latin America*. Buffalo: Council on International Studies, State University of New York at Buffalo, 1971: 39; Robert J. Alexander, *Bolivia: Past, Present, and Future of its Politics*, 1982: 94.

86. James M. Malloy and Eduardo A. Gamarra, "The Transition to Democracy in Bolivia," in *Authoritarians and Democrats: Regime Transition in Latin America*, edited by J. Malloy and M. Seligson, 93–120. Pittsburgh: University of Pittsburgh Press, 1987: 95.

87. Robert J. Alexander, *Bolivia: Past, Present, and Future of its Politics*, 1982: 93.

88. Charles D. Corbett, "Military Institutional Development and Sociopolitical Change: The Bolivian Case," *Journal of Inter-American Affairs*. 14 (1972): 405.

89. Christopher Mitchell, *The Legacy of Populism in Bolivia: From the MNR to Military Rule*. New York: Praeger, 1977: 90.

90. Eckstein, *The Impact of Revolution*, 1976: 35.

91. Corbett, "Military Institutional Development," 1972: 409.

92. Bueno de Mesquita and Siverson, "War and the Survival of Political Leaders," 1995.

93. Bienen and Van de Walle, *Of Time and Power*, 1991: 99.

94. Guy D. Whitten, and Henry S. Bienen, "Political Violence and Time in Power," *Armed Forces and Society*, 23 (1996): 227.

95. Bienen and Van de Walle, *Of Time and Power*, 1991.

96. Bienen and Van de Walle, *Of Time and Power*, 1991: 106.

97. Other social scientists have made similar predictions regarding the survivability of these elites, including Foran, "The Future of Revolutions," 1997; Ghoreishi and Zahedi. "Prospects for Regime Change in Iran," 1997; Katz, "The Khatemi Factor," 1998

Chapter 9

1. Philip Gourevitch, "Letter from the Congo: Continental Shift," The *New Yorker*, August 4, 1997: 42–55; Dan Connell and Frank Smyth, "Africa's New Bloc," *Foreign Affairs*, 77 (1998): 80–94.

2. John F. Burns, "Kabul's Rulers Face Rivals and Unpopular Unrest," The *New York Times*, October 22, 1996: A6.

3. Ted Robert Gurr, *Minorities at Risk: A Global View of Ethnopolitical Conflict*. Washington, DC: United States Institute for Peace Press, 1993; Ted Robert Gurr, "Peoples against States: Ethnopolitical Conflict and the Changing World System," *International Studies Quarterly*, 38 (1994): 347–377.

4. Stephen Van Evera, "Hypotheses on Nationalism and War," *International Security*, 18 (1994): 5–39.

5. R. J. Rummel, *Death by Government*. New Brunswick: Transaction Books, 1994; R. J. Rummel, "Democracy, Power, Genocide, and Mass Murder," *Journal of Conflict Resolution*, 39 (1995): 3–26.

6. Jack A. Goldstone, "An Analytical Framework," in *Revolutions of the Late Twentieth Century*, edited by J. Goldstone, T. R. Gurr, and F. Moshiri, 37–51. Boulder: Westview Press, 1991.

7. Roy Licklider, ed., *Stopping the Killing: How Civil Wars End*. New York: New York University Press, 1993.

8. For some notable exceptions who explicitly examine the outcomes of internal wars, see: S. N. Eisenstadt, *Revolution and the Transformation of Societies: A Comparative Study of Civilizations*. New York: Free Press, 1978; Ted Robert Gurr, "War, Revolution, and the Growth of the Coercive State," *Comparative Political Studies*, 21 (1988): 45–65; John Foran and Jeff Goodwin, "Revolutionary Outcomes in Iran and Nicaragua: Coalition Fragmentation, War, and the Limits of Social Transformation," *Theory and Society*, 22 (1993): 209–247; Roy Licklider, "The Consequences of Negotiated Settlements in Civil Wars, 1945–1993," *American Political Science Review*, 89 (1995): 681–690.

9. Paul Diehl, Daniel Druckman, and James Wall, "International Peacekeeping and Conflict Resolution: A Taxonomic Analysis with Implications," *Journal of Conflict Resolution*, 42 (1998): 33.

10. Anthony Lake, ed. *After the Wars: Reconstruction in Afghanistan, Indochina, Central America, Southern Africa, and the Horn of Africa*. New Brunswick: Transaction Books, 1990; Diehl, Druckman, and Wall, "International Peacekeeping and Conflict Resolution," 1998.

11. Roy Licklider, "State Building After Invasion: Somalia and Panama," paper presented at the International Studies Association annual convention, San Diego, California, April 1996.

12. Lenard J. Cohen, "Whose Bosnia?: The Politics of Nation Building," *Current History*, 97 (March, 1998): 103–114.

13. Among those who categorize the conflict in which Kabila and his allies ousted the Mobutu government as revolutionary are: John Foran, "The Future of Revolutions at the *fin-de-siecle*," *Third World Quarterly*, 18 (1997): 791–820; Daniel C. Esty, Jack A. Goldstone, Ted Robert Gurr, Barbara Harff, Marc Levy, Geoffrey D. Dabelko, Pamela T. Surko, and Alan N. Unger, *State Failure Task Force Report: Phase II Findings*. McLean: Science Applications International Corporation, 1998.

14. See Paul Williams, "Kabila Blocks UN Investigation into Massacres," *Human Rights Tribune,* 4 (1997): 18–23; Gourevitch, "Letter from the Congo," 1997; Connell and Smyth, "Africa's New Bloc," 1998.

15. Michael G. Schatzberg, "Beyond Mobutu: Kabila and the Congo," *The Journal of Democracy,* 8 (1997): 70–84.

16. Peter Rosenblum, "Kabila's Congo," *Current History,* 97 (May 1998): 196.

17. Rosenblum, "Kabila's Congo," 1998: 199.

18. Barbara Harff, "Genocide as State Terrorism," in *Government Violence and Repression: An Agenda for Research,* edited by M. Stohl and G. A. Lopez, 165–188. New York: Greenwood Press, 1986; Steven C. Poe and C. Neal Tate, "Repression of Human Rights to Personal Integrity in the 1980s: A Global Analysis," *American Political Science Review,* 88 (1994): 853–872; Licklider, "The Consequences of Negotiated Settlements," 1995; Matthew Krain, "State-Sponsored Mass Murder: The Onset and Severity of Genocides and Politicides," *Journal of Conflict Resolution,* 41 (1997): 331–360; Esty et al., *State Failure Task Force Report.* 1998.

19. Rummel, *Death by Government,* 1994; Rummel, "Democracy, Power, Genocide, and Mass Murder," 1995.

20. Samuel P. Huntington, *The Third Wave: Democratization in the Late Twentieth Century.* Norman: University of Oklahoma Press, 1991.

21. Richard Joseph, "Africa, 1990–1997: From *Abertura* to Closure," *The Journal of Democracy,* 9 (1998): 7.

22. Gurr, "Peoples Against States," 1994; Esty, et al., *State Failure Task Force Report: Phase II Findings,* 1998.

23 Guillermo O'Donnell and Philippe C. Schmitter, *Transitions from Authoritarian Rule: Tentative Conclusions about Uncertain Democracies.* Baltimore: Johns Hopkins University Press, 1986; Guiseppe DiPalma, *To Craft Democracies.* Berkeley: University of California Press, 1990; Terry Lynn Karl and Philippe Schmitter, "Modes of Transition in Latin America, Southern and Eastern Europe," *International Social Science Journal,* 128 (1991): 269–284.

24. Scott Mainwaring, Guillermo O'Donnell, and J. Samuel Valenzuela, eds., *New Issues in Democratic Consolidation.* Notre Dame: University of Notre Dame Press, 1992; Philippe C. Schmitter and Javier Santiso, "Three Temporal Dimensions to the Consolidation of Democracy," *International Political Science Review,* 19 (1998): 69–92.

25. Yossi Shain and Juan J. Linz, eds., *Between States: Interim Governments and Democratic Transitions.* Cambridge: Cambridge University Press, 1995.

26. Edward D. Mansfield and Jack Snyder, "Democratization and the Danger of War," *International Security,* 20 (1995): 5–38; William R. Thompson and Richard Tucker, "A Tale of Two Democratic Peace Critiques," *Journal of Conflict Resolution,* 41 (1997): 428–451; Michael D. Ward and Kristian S. Gleditsch, "Democratizing for Peace," *American Political Science Review,* 92 (1998): 51–61.

27. Licklider, "The Consequences of Negotiated Settlements," 1995: 686.

28. Michelle Benson and Jacek Kugler, "Power Parity, Democracy, and the Severity of Internal Violence," *Journal of Conflict Resolution,* 42 (1998): 196–209

29. Bruce Bueno de Mesquita and Randolph Siverson, "War and the Survival of Political Leaders: A Comparative Study of Regime Types and Political Accountability," *American Political Science Review,* 89 (1995): 841–855.

30. Gurr, "War, Revolution, and the Growth of the Coercive State," 1988: 50–53.

31. Human Rights Watch/Middle East, "Power versus Choice: Human Rights and Parliamentary Elections in the Islamic Republic of Iran," *Human Rights Watch/Middle East Report,* 8 (1996): 1–19.

32. Diehl, Druckman, and Wall, "International Peacekeeping and Conflict Resolution," 1998.

33. Zeev Maoz, "Joining the Club of Nations: Political Development and International Conflicts, 1816–1976," *International Studies Quarterly,* 33 (1989): 199–231.

34. Gil Friedman and Harvey Starr, "The Nexus of Civil and International Conflict Revisited: Opportunity, Willingness, and the Internal-External Linkage," paper presented at the 29th Annual North American Meeting of the Peace Science Society (International), Columbus, Ohio, October 13–15, 1995.

35. Ekkart Zimmermann, "On the Outcomes of Revolutions: Some Preliminary Considerations," *Sociological Theory* (1988): 37.

36. Mark I. Lichbach, "Deterrence or Escalation?: The Puzzle of Aggregate Studies of Repression and Dissent," *Journal of Conflict Resolution,* 32 (1987): 266–297.

37. See, for instance, Conway Henderson, "Conditions Affecting the Use of Political Repression," *Journal of Conflict Resolution,* 35 (1991): 120–142; Seymour Martin Lipset, Kyoung-Ryung Seong, and John Charles Torres, "A Comparative Analysis of the Social Requisites of Democracy," *International Social Science Journal,* 136 (1993): 155–175.

38. Charles Tilly, *European Revolutions, 1492–1992.* Oxford: Basil Blackwell, 1993; Harvey Starr, "Revolution and War: Rethinking the Linkage between Internal and External Conflict," *Political Research Quarterly,* 47 (1994): 481–507; Doug McAdam, Sidney Tarrow, and Charles Tilly, "To Map Contentious Politics," *Mobilization,* 1 (1996): 17–34.

39. Licklider, *Stopping the Killing,* 1993: 19.

40. Michael Schwartz, *Radical Protest and Social Structure.* New York: Academic Press, 1976; Richard F. Bensel, *Yankee Leviathan: The Origins of Central State Authority in America, 1859–1877.* Cambridge: Cambridge University Press, 1990; Stephen John Stedman, "The End of the American Civil War," in *Stopping the Killing: How Civil Wars End,* edited by R. Licklider, 164–188. New York: New York University Press, 1993.

41. Robert Fisk, *Pity the Nation: The Abduction of Lebanon*. New York: Simon and Schuster, 1990.

42. Licklider, *Stopping the Killing*, 1993: 320.

43. Some scholars of social movements have begun to explicitly incorporate multiple groups into their models of elite-mass interaction dynamics. See for instance, David S. Meyer and Suzanne Staggenborg, "Movements, Countermovements, and the Structure of Political Opportunity," *American Journal of Sociology*, 101 (1996): 1628–1660.

44. Charles Tilly, *From Mobilization to Revolution*. New York: McGraw-Hill, 1978: 104; Marwan Khawaja, "Repression and Popular Collective Action: Evidence from the West Bank," *Sociological Forum*, 8 (1993): 67.

45. Ruud Koopmans, "Dynamics of Repression and Mobilization: The German Extreme Right in the 1990s," *Mobilization*, 2 (1997): 149–164.

46. Ted Robert Gurr and Barbara Harff, *Ethnic Conflict in World Politics*. Boulder: Westview Press, 1994.

47. Will H. Moore, "Repression and Dissent: Substitution, Context, and Timing," *American Journal of Political Science*, 42 (1998): 851–873.

48. Debra C. Minkoff, "The Sequencing of Social Movements," *American Sociological Review*, 62 (1997): 779–799; Moore, "Repression and Dissent," 1998.

49. On the effect of perceptions on foreign policy behavior, see: Robert Jervis, *Perception and Misperception in International Relations*. Princeton: Princeton University Press, 1976; Brett Ashley Leeds and David R. Davis, "Domestic Political Vulnerability and International Disputes," *Journal of Conflict Resolution*, 41 (1997): 814–834. On the effect of policy mix choices on international interactions, see: Michael Stohl, "The Nexus of Civil and International Conflict," in *Handbook of Political Conflict: Theory and Research*, edited by T. R. Gurr, 297–330. New York: Free Press, 1980. On the effect of dissent on international behavior, see: John E. Mueller, *War, Presidents, and Public Opinion*. New York: Wiley, 1973; Jack Levy, "The Diversionary Theory of War: A Critique," in *The Handbook of War Studies*, edited by M. I. Midlarsky, 259–288. Boston: Unwin Hyman, 1989; Andrew J. Enterline and Kristian S. Gleditsch, "Threats, Force, and Survival: A Study of Latin American Leaders," paper presented at the annual meeting of the Peace Science Society (International), Indianapolis, Indiana, November 21–23, 1997. On the effects of regime type on international conflict propensity, see: Stuart Bremer, "Dangerous Dyads: Conditions Affecting the Likelihood of Interstate War, 1816–1965," *Journal of Conflict Resolution* 36 (1992): 231–249; Zeev Maoz and Bruce Russett, "Normative and Structural Causes of Democratic Peace, 1946–1986," *American Political Science Review*, 87 (1993): 624–638.

50. See Foran, "The Future of Revolutions at the *fin-de-siecle*," 1997; Mark N. Katz, *Revolutions and Revolutionary Waves*. New York: St. Martin's Press,

1997; Eric Selbin, "Same As It Ever Was: The Future of Revolution at the End of the Century," paper presented at the 39th Annual Meeting of the International Studies Association, Minneapolis, Minnesota, March 18–21, 1998.

51. Licklider, *Stopping the Killing,* 1993: 5–6; Peter Wallensteen and Margareta Sollenberg, "The End of International War? Armed Conflict, 1989–1995," *Journal of Peace Research,* 33 (1996): 353–370.

52. Diehl, Druckman, and Wall, "International Peacekeeping and Conflict Resolution," 1998.

Bibliography

Adelman, Jonathan R. *Revolution, Armies, and War: A Political History.* Boulder: Lynne Rienner Publishers, 1985.

Afshari, Reza. "An Essay on Scholarship, Human Rights, and State Legitimacy: The Case of the Islamic Republic of Iran," *Human Rights Quarterly,* 18 (1996): 544–593.

del Aguila, Juan M. *Cuba: Dilemmas of a Revolution.* Boulder: Westview Press, 1984.

Ahady, Anwar-ul-Haq. "Afghanistan: State Breakdown," in *Revolutions of the Late Twentieth Century,* edited by J. Goldstone, T. R. Gurr, and F. Moshiri, 162–193. Boulder: Westview Press, 1991.

Alexander, Robert J. *The Bolivian National Revolution.* New Brunswick: Rutgers University Press, 1958.

Alexander, Robert J. *Bolivia: Past, Present, and Future of Its Politics.* Stanford: Praeger, 1982.

Americas Watch Committee. *Human Rights in Nicaragua: August 1987–August 1988.* New York: Human Rights Watch, 1988.

Ames, Barry. *Political Survival: Politicians and Public Policy in Latin America.* Berkeley: University of California Press, 1987.

Amnesty International. *Amnesty International Report: 1994.* New York: Amnesty International USA, 1994.

Andrade, Victor. *My Missions for Revolutionary Bolivia, 1944–1962.* Pittsburgh: University of Pittsburgh Press, 1976.

Arjomand, Said Amir. *The Turban for the Crown: The Islamic Revolution in Iran.* New York: Oxford University Press, 1988.

Arze Murillo, Jos J Antonio. *Los Comunistas Disfrazados No Tienen Sitio En El MNR.* La Paz: Direcci\n Nacional de Informaciones, 1962.

Azar, Edward E. *Conflict and Peace Data Bank (COPDAB), 1948–1978.* ICPSR Study #7767. Ann Arbor: Inter-university Consortium for Political and Social Research, 1993.

Bakhash, Shaul. *The Reign of the Ayatollahs: Iran and the Islamic Revolution.* New York: Basic Books, 1984.

Baktiari, Bahman. *Parliamentary Politics in Revolutionary Iran: The Institutionalization of Factional Politics.* Gainesville: University Press of Florida, 1996.

Barnes, William A., with Kenneth M. Coleman. "Incomplete Democracy and Voter Turnout in Nicaragua and El Salvador," paper presented at the Annual Meeting of the Midwest Political Science Association, Chicago, Illinois, April 10–12, 1997.

Belli, Humberto. *Breaking Faith: The Sandinista Revolution and the Impact on Freedom and Christian Faith in Nicaragua.* Westchester: Crossway Books, 1985.

Benard, Cheryl and Zalmay Khalilzad. *The Government of God: Iran's Islamic Republic.* New York: Columbia University Press, 1984

Bendix, Reinhardt. *Nation-Building and Citizenship.* New York: Wiley, 1964.

Bendix, Reinhardt. *Kings or People.* Berkeley: University of California Press, 1978.

Benjamin, Alan. *Nicaragua: Dynamics of an Unfinished Revolution.* San Francisco: Walnut Publishing, 1989.

Bensel, Richard F. *Yankee Leviathan: The Origins of Central State Authority in America, 1859–1877.* Cambridge, UK: Cambridge University Press, 1990

Benson, Michelle, and Jacek Kugler. "Power Parity, Democracy, and the Severity of Internal Violence," *Journal of Conflict Resolution,* 42 (1998): 196–209

Bermeo, Nancy. "Democracy and the Lessons of Dictatorship," *Comparative Politics,* 24 (1992): 273–291.

Bernard, Jean-Pierre. "Bolivia," in *Guide to the Political Parties of South America,* edited by J. Bernard, S. Cerqueira, P. Gilhodes, H. Graillot, L. Manigat, and H. Neira, 107–149. Translated by Michael Perl. Baltimore: Penguin Books, 1973.

Bethell, Leslie, ed. *The Cambridge History of Latin America.* Volume 6, Part 2. Cambridge: Cambridge University Press, 1984.

Betto, Frei. *Fidel and Religion.* New York: Simon and Schuster, 1987.

Bienen, Henry and Nicholas Van de Walle. *Of Time and Power: Leadership Duration in the Modern World.* Stanford: Stanford University Press, 1991.

Booth, John A. and Patricia Bayer Richard. "The Nicaraguan Elections of October 1996," *Electoral Studies,* 16 (1997): 386–393.

Boua, Chanthou. "Genocide of a Religious Group: Pol Pot and Cambodia's Buddhist Monks," *State Organized Terror: The Case of Violent Internal Repression,* edited by P. T.

Bushnell, V. Shlapentokh, C. K. Vanderpool, and J. Sundram, 227–242. Boulder: Westview Press, 1991.

Boudreau, Vincent. "Northern Theory, Southern Protest: Opportunity Structure Analysis in Cross-National Perspective," *Mobilization,* 1 (1996): 175–189.

Brandt, Patrick T., John T. Williams, and Benjamin Fordham, "Modeling Time Series Count Data: A State-Space Approach to Event Counts," paper presented at the Society for Political Methodology Meeting, University of California at San Diego, July 22–26, 1998.

Bratton, Michael and Nicholas van de Walle. "Popular Protest and Political Reform in Africa," *Comparative Politics,* 24 (1992): 419–442.

Bray, Donald W. and Timothy F. Harding. "Cuba," in *Latin America: The Struggle with Dependency and Beyond,* edited by R. Chilcote and J. Edelstein, 583–730. New York: Wiley, 1974.

Bremer, Stuart. "Dangerous Dyads: Conditions Affecting the Likelihood of Interstate War, 1816 - 1965," *Journal of Conflict Resolution,* 36 (1992): 231–249.

Brenner, Philip, William M. LeoGrande, Donna Rich, and Daniel Siegel, eds. *The Cuba Reader: The Making of a Revolutionary Society.* New York: Grove Press, 1989.

Brill, William H. *Military Intervention in Bolivia: The Overthrow of Paz Estenssoro and the MNR.* Washington, DC: Institute for the Comparative Study of Political Systems, 1967.

Brinton, Crane. *The Anatomy of Revolution.* Rev. ed. New York: Vintage Books, 1965.

Brockett, Charles. "Measuring Political Violence and Land Inequality in Central America," *American Political Science Review,* 86 (1992): 169–176.

Brown, Gillian. "Miskito Revindication: Between Revolution and Resistance," in *Nicaragua: A Revolution under Siege,* edited by R. Harris and C. M. Vilas, 175–201. London: Zed Books, 1985.

Brownmiller, Susan. *Against Our Will: Men, Women and Rape.* New York: Simon and Schuster, 1975.

Bueno de Mesquita, Bruce and Randolph Siverson. "War and the Survival of Political Leaders: A Comparative Study of Regime Types and Political Accountability," *American Political Science Review,* 89 (1995): 841–855.

Bueno de Mesquita, Bruce, Randolph M. Siverson, and Gary Woller. "War and the Fate of Regimes: A Comparative Analysis," *American Political Science Review,* 86 (1992): 638-646.

Bunce, Valerie. "Elite Succession, Petrification, and Policy Innovation in Communist Systems: An Empirical Assessment," *Comparative Political Studies,* 9 (1976): 3–41.

Bunce, Valerie. "The Succession Connection: Policy Cycles and Political Change in the Soviet Union and Eastern Europe," *American Political Science Review,* 74 (1980): 966–977.

Bunce, Valerie. *Do New Leaders Make a Difference?* Princeton: Princeton University Press, 1981.

Bunce, Valerie and M. Csanadi. "Uncertainty in the Transition: Post-Communism in Hungary," *East European Politics and Societies,* 7 (1993): 240–275.

Bunce, Valerie and Philip Roeder. "The Effects of Leadership Succession in the Soviet Union," *American Political Science Review,* 80 (1986): 215–244.

Burns, John F. "Kabul's Rulers Face Rivals and Unpopular Unrest," The *New York Times,* October 22, 1996: A6.

Burton, Michael, Richard Gunther, and John Higley. "Elites and Democratic Consolidation in Latin America and Southern Europe: An Overview," in *Elites and Democratic Consolidation in Latin America and Southern Europe,* edited by J. Higley and R. Gunther, 323–348. Cambridge: Cambridge University Press, 1992.

Burton, Michael, Richard Gunther, and John Higley. "Introduction: Elite Transformations and Democratic Regimes," in *Elites and Democratic Consolidation in*

Latin America and Southern Europe, edited by J. Higley and R. Gunther, 1–37. Cambridge: Cambridge University Press, 1992.

Calderon, J. *The Bolivian Coup of 1964: A Sociological Analysis.* Buffalo: Council on International Studies, State University of New York at Buffalo, 1972.

Calvert, Peter. *Revolution and Counter-Revolution.* Minneapolis: University of Minnesota Press, 1990.

Carey, Peter. "Foreward," in J. G. Taylor, *The Indonesian Occupation of East Timor, 1974–1989: A Chronology.* London: Catholic Institute for International Relations, 1993.

Carothers, Thomas. "The Observers Observed," *Journal of Democracy,* 8 (1997): 17–31.

Carter Center. "Democracy Prevails in Nicaragua's 1996 Presidential Election," *The Carter Center News,* winter, 1997: 1.

Chehabi, H.E. "The Provisional Government and the Transition from Monarchy to Islamic Republic in Iran," in *Between States: Interim Governments and Democratic Transitions,* edited by Y. Shain and J. Linz, 127–143. Cambridge: Cambridge University Press, 1995.

Chilcote, Ronald H. and Joel C. Edelstein, eds. *Latin America: The Struggle with Dependency and Beyond.* New York: Wiley, 1974.

Chong, Dennis. *Collective Action and the Civil Rights Movement.* Chicago: University of Chicago Press, 1991.

Cingranelli, David L. and David L. Richards. "Measuring the Level, Pattern, and Sequence of Government Respect for Physical Integrity Rights." *International Studies Quarterly,* 43 (1999): 407–418.

Cline, Howard F. *The United States and Mexico.* Cambridge: Harvard University Press, 1963

Close, David. "The Nicaraguan Elections of 1984," *Electoral Studies,* 4 (1985): 152–158.

Close, David. *Nicaragua: Politics, Economics and Society.* London: Pinter Publishers, 1988.

Close, David. "Central American Elections 1989–90: Costa Rica, El Salvador, Honduras, Nicaragua, Panama," *Electoral Studies,* 10 (1991): 60–76.

Cohen, Frank S. "Ethnic Conflict Governance and the Conflict between Nation and State," paper presented at the 39th Annual Meeting of the International Studies Association, March 18- 21, 1998, Minneapolis, Minnesota.

Cohen, Lenard J. "Whose Bosnia?: The Politics of Nation Building," *Current History,* 97 (March, 1998): 103–114.

Cohen, Youssef, Brian R. Brown, and A.F.K. Organski. "The Paradoxical Nature of State Making: The Violent Creation of Order." *American Political Science Review,* 75 (1981): 901–910.

Colburn, Forrest D. *The Vogue of Revolution in Poor Countries.* Princeton: Princeton University Press, 1994.

Cole, Johnnetta B. "Women in Cuba: The Revolution within the Revolution," in *Comparative Perspectives of Third World Women,* edited by B. Lindsay. New York: Praeger, 1980.

Collier, David and Ruth Berins Collier. *Shaping the Political Arena: Critical Junctures, the Labor Movement, and Regime Dynamics in Latin America.* Princeton: Princeton University Press, 1991.

Collier, David and Steven Levitsky. "Democracy with Adjectives: Conceptual Innovation in Comparative Research," *World Politics,* 49 (1997): 430–451.

Conge, Patrick J. *From Revolution to War: State Relations in a World of Change.* Ann Arbor: University of Michigan Press, 1996.

Connell, Dan and Frank Smyth, "Africa's New Bloc," *Foreign Affairs,* 77 (1998): 80–94.

Conroy, Michael E. and Manuel Pastor, Jr. "The Nicaraguan Experiment: Characteristics of a New Economic Model," in *Crisis in Central America: Regional Dynamics and U.S. Policy in the 1980s.* edited by N. Hamilton, J. Frieden, L. Fuller, and M. Pastor, Jr. Boulder: Westview Press, 1988.

Corbett, Charles D. "Military Institutional Development and Sociopolitical Change: The Bolivian Case," *Journal of Inter-American Affairs,* 14 (1972): 399–436.

Coser, Lewis A. *The Function of Social Conflict.* New York: Free Press, 1956.

Cottam, Richard. "Inside Revolutionary Iran," in *Iran's Revolution: The Search for Consensus,* edited by R. K. Ramazani, 3–26. Bloomington: Indiana University Press, 1990.

Dahl, Robert A. *Polyarchy: Participation and Opposition.* New Haven: Yale University Press, 1971.

Davenport, Christian A. "Multi-Dimensional Threat Perception and State Repression: An Inquiry into Why States Apply Negative Sanctions," *American Journal of Political Science,* 39 (1995): 683–713.

Davenport, Christian A. "Constitutional Promises and Repressive Reality: A Cross-National Time-Series Investigation of Why Political and Civil Liberties are Suppressed," *Journal of Politics,* 58 (1996): 627–654.

Davenport, Christian A. "Censorship, Political Restrictions and the Democratic Proposition," paper presented at the Annual Meeting of the Midwest Political Science Association, Chicago, Illinois, April 10–12, 1997.

Davenport, Christian A. "From Ballots to Bullets: An Empirical Assessment of How National Elections Influence State Uses of Political Repression," *Electoral Studies,* 16 (1997): 517–540.

David, Shelton H. and Julie Hodson. *Witnesses to Political Violence in Guatemala: The Suppression of a Rural Development Movement.* Boston: Oxfam America, 1982.

Davies, John L. "The Global Event-Data System Manual." Center for International Development and Conflict Management, University of Maryland, 1993.

Davis, David and Michael D. Ward. "They Dance Alone: Death and the Disappeared in Contemporary Chile," *Journal of Conflict Resolution,* 34 (1990): 449–475.

DeFronzo, James. *Revolutions and Revolutionary Movements.* Boulder: Westview Press, 1991.

Diamond, Larry, Juan J. Linz, and Seymour Martin Lipset, eds. *Politics in Developing Countries: Comparing Experiences with Democracy.* Boulder: Lynne Rienner, 1990.

Diehl, Paul, Daniel Druckman, and James Wall. "International Peacekeeping and Conflict Resolution: A Taxonomic Analysis with Implications," *Journal of Conflict Resolution,* 42 (1998): 33–55

DiPalma, Guiseppe. *To Craft Democracies.* Berkeley: University of California Press, 1990.

Dixon, William. "Democracy and the Management of International Conflict," *Journal of Conflict Resolution,* 37 (1993): 42–68.

Dunkerley, James. *Rebellion in the Veins: Political Struggle in Bolivia, 1952–1982.* London: Verso, 1984.

Dunkerley, James. *Power in the Isthmus: A Political History of Modern Central America.* London: Verso, 1988.

Durban, E. F. M. *The Politics of Democratic Socialism.* reproduced in *Communism, Fascism, and Democracy,* edited by C. Cohen. New York: Random House, 1962 [1940].

Duvall, Raymond and Michael Shamir. "Governance by Terror," in *The Politics of Terrorism,* 3rd ed., edited by R. Duvall and M. Stohl. New York: Marcel Dekker, 1983.

Eckstein, Susan. *The Impact of Revolution: A Comparative Analysis of Mexico and Bolivia.* London: Sage Publications, 1976.

Eckstein, Susan. "The Impact of Revolution on Social Welfare in Latin America," *Theory and Society,* 11 (1982): 43–94.

Eckstein, Susan. "Revolutions and the Restructuring of National Economies: The Latin American Experience," *Comparative Politics,* 17 (1985): 73–494.

The Economist. "The Fading of Fidel," *The Economist,* January 15, 1998.

Edeen, Alf. "The Soviet Civil Service: Its Composition and Status," in *The Transformation of Russian Society: Aspects of Social Change since 1861,* edited by C. Black. Cambridge: Harvard University Press, 1960.

Ehteshami, Anoushiravan. *After Khomeini: The Iranian Second Republic.* London: Routledge, 1995.

Eisenstadt, S.N. *Revolution and the Transformation of Societies: A Comparative Study of Civilizations.* New York: Free Press, 1978.

Eisinger, Peter K. "The Conditions of Protest Behavior in American Cities," *American Political Science Review,* 67 (1973).

Elklit, Jorgen and Palle Svensson. "What Makes Elections Free and Fair?" *Journal of Democracy,* 8 (1997): 32–46.

Enterline, Andrew J. "Driving While Democratizing (DWD)," *International Security,* 20 (1996): 183–196.

Enterline, Andrew J. "Fledgling Regimes: Is the Case of Inter-War Germany Generalizable?" *International Interactions,* 22 (1997): 245–277.

Enterline, Andrew J. and Kristian S. Gleditsch. "Threats, Force, and Survival: A Study of Latin American Leaders," paper presented at the annual meeting of the Peace Science Society (International), Indianapolis, Indiana, November 21–23, 1997.

Esty, Daniel C., Jack A. Goldstone, Ted Robert Gurr, Barbara Harff, Marc Levy, Geoffrey D. Dabelko, Pamela T. Surko, and Alan N. Unger. *State Failure Task Force Report: Phase II Findings.* McLean: Science Applications International Corporation, 1998.

Evans, Peter, Dietrich Reuschemeyer, and Theda Skocpol, eds. *Bringing the State Back In.* Cambridge: Cambridge University Press, 1985.

Fein, Helen. *Accounting for Genocide: National Responses and Jewish Victimization during the Holocaust.* New York: Free Press, 1979.

Fenno, Richard F. *Home Style: House Members in Their Districts.* Boston: Little Brown, 1978.

Finer, Samuel E. "State- and Nation-Building in Europe: The Role of the Military," in *The Formation of National States in Western Europe,* edited by C. Tilly, 84–163. Princeton: Princeton University Press, 1975.

Fisk, Robert. *Pity the Nation: The Abduction of Lebanon.* New York: Simon and Schuster, 1990.

Foran, John. "The Future of Revolutions at the *fin-de-siecle*," *Third World Quarterly,* 18 (1997): 791–820.

Foran, John and Jeff Goodwin. "Revolutionary Outcomes in Iran and Nicaragua: Coalition Fragmentation, War, and the Limits of Social Transformation," *Theory and Society,* 22 (1993): 209–247.

Francisco, Ronald A. "The Relationship between Coercion and Protest: An Empirical Evaluation in Three Coercive States," *Journal of Conflict Resolution,* 39 (1995): 263–282.

Francisco, Ronald A. "Coercion and Protest: An Empirical Test in Two Democratic States," *American Journal of Political Science,* 40 (1996): 1179–1204.

Freeman, Michael. "The Theory and Prevention of Genocide," *Holocaust and Genocide Studies,* 6 (1991): 185–199.

Friedman, Gil and Harvey Starr. "The Nexus of Civil and International Conflict Revisited: Opportunity, Willingness, and the Internal-External Linkage," paper presented at the 29th Annual North American Meeting of the Peace Science Society (International), Columbus, Ohio, October 13–15, 1995.

Gamson, William. *The Strategy of Social Protest.* Homewood: Dorsey Press, 1975.

Gamson, William. *The Strategy of Social Protest.* 2nd ed. Belmont: Wadsworth Publishing, 1990.

Gardner, William, Edward P. Mulvey, and Esther C. Shaw. "Regression Analyses of Counts and Rates: Poisson, Overdispersed Poisson, and Negative Binomial Models." *Psychological Bulletin,* 1 (1995): 392–404.

Gartner, Scott S. and Patrick M. Regan. "Threat and Repression: The Non-Linear Relationship between Government and Opposition Violence," *Journal of Peace Research,* 33 (1996): 273–287.

Gastil, Raymond D. *Freedom in the World: Political Rights and Civil Liberties, 1980.* New Brunswick: Transaction Books, 1980.

Geddes, Barbara. "A Game Theoretic Model of Reform in Latin American Democracies," *American Political Science Review,* 85 (1991): 371–393.

George, Alexander L. and Timothy J. McKeown. "Case Studies and Theories of Organizational Decision Making," *Advances in Information Processing in Organizations,* 2 (1985): 21- 58.

Gerner, Deborah J, Philip A. Schrodt, Ronald A. Francisco, and Judith L. Weddle. "Machine Coding of Event Data Using Regional and International Sources," *International Studies Quarterly,* 38 (1994): 91–120.

Ghoreishi, Ahmad and Dariush Zahedi. "Prospects for Regime Change in Iran," *Middle East Policy,* 5 (1997): 85–101.

Gibney, Mark and Stephen M. Caliendo. "'All the News That's Fit to Print?': *New York Times* Coverage of Human Rights Violations," paper presented at the Annual Meeting of the American Political Science Association, Washington, DC, August 28–31, 1997.

Gilbert, Dennis. "Nicaragua," in *Confronting Revolution: Security through Diplomacy in Central America,* edited by M. J. Blachman, W. M. LeoGrande, and K. E. Sharpe, 88- 125. New York: Pantheon Books, 1986.

Goldstein, Joshua S. "A Conflict-Cooperation Scale for WEIS Events Data," *Journal of Conflict Resolution,* 36 (1991): 369–385.

Goldstein, Robert J. "The Limitations of Using Quantitative Data in Studying Human Rights Abuses," *Human Rights Quarterly,* 8 (1986): 607–627.

Goldstone, Jack A. "An Analytical Framework," in *Revolutions of the Late Twentieth Century,* edited by J. Goldstone, T. R. Gurr, and F. Moshiri, 37–51. Boulder: Westview Press, 1991.

Goldstone, Jack A. "Revolutions," in *Encyclopedia of Government and Politics–Volume I,"* edited by M. Hawkesworth and M. Kogan, 1049–1060. New York: Routledge, 1992.

Gonzalez, Edward. *Cuba under Castro: The Limits of Charisma.* Boston: Houghton Mifflin, 1974.

Goodwin, Jeff. "Is the Age of Revolutions Over?" paper presented at the 39th Annual Meeting of the International Studies Association, Minneapolis, Minnesota, March 18–21, 1998.

Gourevitch, Philip. "Letter from the Congo: Continental Shift," The *New Yorker,* August 4, 1997: 42–55.

Granovetter, Mark. "Threshold Models of Collective Behavior," *American Sociological Review,* 39 (1978): 335–373.

Griffiths, John and Peter Griffiths. *Cuba: The Second Decade.* London: Writers and Readers Publishing Cooperative, 1979.

Grynspan, Devora. "Nicaragua: A New Model for Popular Revolution in Latin America," in *Revolutions of the Late Twentieth Century,* edited by J. Goldstone, T. R. Gurr, and F. Moshiri, 88–115. Boulder: Westview Press, 1991.

Gurr, Ted Robert. *Why Men Rebel.* Princeton: Princeton University Press, 1970.

Gurr, Ted Robert, ed. *Handbook of Political Conflict: Theory and Research*. New York: Free Press, 1980.

Gurr, Ted Robert. "The Political Origins of State Violence and Terror: A Theoretical Analysis," in *Government Violence and Repression: An Agenda for Research*, edited by M. Stohl and G. A. Lopez. New York: Greenwood Press, 1986.

Gurr, Ted Robert. "War, Revolution, and the Growth of the Coercive State," *Comparative Political Studies*, 21 (1988): 45–65.

Gurr, Ted Robert. "Polity II: Political Structures and Regime Change, 1800–1986," Ann Arbor: Inter-university Consortium for Political and Social Research, 1990.

Gurr, Ted Robert. *Minorities at Risk: A Global View of Ethnopolitical Conflict*. Washington, DC: United States Institute for Peace Press, 1993.

Gurr, Ted Robert. "The Internationalization of Protracted Communal Conflicts since 1945: Which Groups, Where and How?" in *The Internationalization of Communal Strife*, edited by M. I. Midlarsky. London: Routledge, 1992.

Gurr, Ted Robert. "Minorities in Revolution," in *Revolutions: Theoretical, Comparative, and Historical Studies*. 2nd ed., edited by J. Goldstone, 308–314. Fort Worth: Harcourt Brace, 1994.

Gurr, Ted Robert. "Peoples against States: Ethnopolitical Conflict and the Changing World System," *International Studies Quarterly*, 38 (1994): 347–377.

Gurr, Ted Robert and Raymond Duvall. "Civil Conflict in the 1960s: A Reciprocal Theoretical System with Parameter Estimates," *Comparative Political Studies*, 6 (1973): 135–169.

Gurr, Ted Robert and Barbara Harff. *Ethnic Conflict in World Politics*. Boulder: Westview Press, 1994.

Gurr, Ted Robert, Keith Jaggers, and Will Moore. *Polity II Codebook*. Boulder: University of Colorado, 1989.

Gurr, Ted Robert, Keith Jaggers, and Will Moore. "The Transformation of the Western State: The Growth of Democracy, Autocracy, and State Power since 1800," in *On Measuring Democracy: Its Consequences and Concomitants*, edited by A. Inkeles, 69–104. New Brunswick: Transaction Books, 1991.

Hagopian, Frances. "After Regime Change: Authoritarian Legacies, Political Representation, and the Democratic Future of South America," *World Politics*, 45 (1993): 464–500.

Hagopian, M. N. *The Phenomenon of Revolution*. New York: Dodd, Mead, 1974.

Halebsky, Sandor and John M. Kirk. *Cuba: Twenty-Five Years of Revolution, 1959–1984*. New York: Praeger, 1985.

Halliday, Fred and Maxine Molyneux. *The Ethiopian Revolution*. London: Verso, 1981.

Halperin, Morton H. and Kristen Lomasney. "Guaranteeing Democracy: A Review of the Record," *The Journal of Democracy*, 9 (1998): 134–147.

Hannan, Michael T. "The Dynamics of Ethnic Boundaries in Modern States," in *National Development and the World System: Educational, Economic, and Political*

Change, 1950–1970, edited by J. W. Meyer and M. T. Hannan, 253–275. Chicago: University of Chicago Press, 1979.

Harff, Barbara. "Genocide as State Terrorism," in *Government Violence and Repression: An Agenda for Research,* edited by M. Stohl and G. A. Lopez, 165–188. New York: Greenwood Press, 1986.

Harff, Barbara. "Cambodia: Revolution, Genocide, Intervention," in *Revolutions of the Late Twentieth Century,* edited by J. Goldstone, T. R. Gurr, and F. Moshiri, 218–234. Boulder: Westview Press, 1991.

Harff, Barbara. "Minorities, Rebellion, and Repression in North Africa and the Middle East," in *Minorities at Risk: A Global View of Ethnopolitical Conflict,* by T. R. Gurr, 217–251. Washington, DC: United States Institute for Peace Press, 1993.

Harff, Barbara and Ted Robert Gurr. "Toward an Empirical Theory of Genocides and Politicides: Identification and Measurement of Cases since 1945," *International Studies Quarterly,* 32 (1988): 357–71.

Harnecker, Marta, ed. *Cuba: Dictatorship or Democracy.* Westport: Lawrence Hill.

Harris, Richard and Carlos M. Vilas, eds. *Nicaragua: A Revolution under Siege.* London: Zed Books, 1985.

Henderson, Conway. "Conditions Affecting the Use of Political Repression," *Journal of Conflict Resolution,* 35 (1991): 120–142.

Henderson, Conway. "Military Regimes and Human Rights in Developing Countries: A Comparative Perspective," *Human Rights Quarterly,* 4 (1992): 110–123.

Henderson, Conway. "Population Pressures and Political Repression," *Social Science Quarterly,* 74 (1993): 322–333.

Hibbs, Douglas A, Jr. *Mass Political Violence: A Cross-National Causal Analysis.* New York: Wiley, 1973.

Higgs, Robert. *Crisis and Leviathan : Critical Episodes in the Growth of American Government.* New York: Oxford University Press, 1987.

Higley, John, Judith Kullberg, and Jan Pakulski. "The Persistence of Postcommunist Elites," *Journal of Democracy,* 7 (1996): 133–147.

Hintze, Otto. "Military Organization and the Organization of the State," in *The Historical Essays of Otto Hintze,* edited by F. Gilbert, 178–215. New York: Oxford University Press, 1975.

Hintzen, Percy C. *The Costs of Regime Survival: Racial Mobilization, Elite Domination, and Control of the State in Guyana and Trinidad.* Cambridge: Cambridge University Press, 1989.

Hiro, Dilip. *Iran under the Ayatollahs.* London: Routledge and Kegan Paul, 1985.

Holsti, Ole R. "The Belief System and National Images: A Case Study," *Journal of Conflict Resolution,* 6 (1962): 244–252.

Hoover, Dean and David Kowalewski. "Dynamic Models of Dissent and Repression," *Journal of Conflict Resolution,* 58 (1992): 637–658.

Hoyt, Katherine. *The Many Faces of Sandinista Democracy.* Monographs in International Studies. Latin American Series, Number 27. Athens: Ohio University Press, 1997.

Human Rights Watch/Americas. "Cuba: Improvements without Reform," *Human Rights Watch/Americas Report,* 7 (1995): 1–34.

Human Rights Watch/Middle East. "Power versus Choice: Human Rights and Parliamentary Elections in the Islamic Republic of Iran," *Human Rights Watch/Middle East Report,* 8 (1996): 1–19.

Huntington, Samuel P. *Political Order in Changing Societies.* New Haven: Yale University Press, 1968.

Huntington, Samuel P. *The Third Wave: Democratization in the Late Twentieth Century.* Norman: University of Oklahoma Press, 1991.

Huntington, Samuel P. "The Clash of Civilizations?" *Foreign Affairs,* 79 (1993): 22–49.

Jaggers, Keith. "War and the Three Faces of Power: War Making and State Making in Europe and the Americas," *Comparative Political Studies,* 25 (1992): 26–62.

Jenkins, J. Craig and Charles Perrow. "Insurgency of the Powerless: Farm Workers Movements," *Annual Review of Sociology,* 42 (1977): 249–268.

Jervis, Robert. *Perception and Misperception in International Relations.* Princeton: Princeton University Press, 1976.

Joseph, Richard. "Africa, 1990 - 1997: From *Abertura* to Closure," *Journal of Democracy,* 9 (1998): 3–17.

Kamrava, Mehran. "Non-democratic States and Political Liberalisation in the Middle East: A Structural Analysis," *Third World Quarterly,* 19 (1998): 63–85.

Kapcia, Antoni. "Politics in Cuba: Beyond the Stereotypes," *Bulletin of Latin American Research,* 15 (1996): 247–253.

Kaplan, Morton A. "Intervention in Internal War: Some Systemic Sources," in *International Aspects of Civil Strife,* edited by J. Rosenau, 92–121. Princeton: Princeton University Press, 1964.

Karl, Terry Lynn. "Dilemmas of Democratization in Latin America," *Comparative Politics,* 23 (1990): 1–21.

Karl, Terry Lynn and Philippe Schmitter. "Modes of Transition in Latin America, Southern and Eastern Europe," *International Social Science Journal,* 128 (1991): 269–284.

Karstedt-Henke, Sabine. "Theorien zur Erkldrung terroristischer Bewegungen" (Theories for the Explanation of Terrorist Movements), in *Politik der inneren Sicherheit* (The Politics of Internal Security), edited by E. Blankenberg, 198–234. Frankfurt: Suhrkamp, 1980.

Katz, Mark N. *Revolutions and Revolutionary Waves.* New York: St. Martin's Press, 1997.

Katz, Mark N. "The Khatemi Factor: How Much Does it Matter?" *The National Interest,* spring, 1998: 85–90.

Keddie, Nikki R. and Eric Hooglund, eds. *The Iranian Revolution and the Islamic Republic.* Syracuse: Syracuse University Press, 1985.

Kelley, Jonathan and Herbert S. Klein. "Revolution and the Rebirth of Inequality: A Theory of Stratification in a Postrevolutionary Society," *American Journal of Sociology,* 83 (1977): 78–99.

Kelley, Jonathan and Herbert S. Klein. *Revolution and the Rebirth of Inequality: A Theory Applied to the National Revolution in Bolivia.* Berkeley: University of California Press, 1981.

Khawaja, Marwan. "Repression and Popular Collective Action: Evidence from the West Bank," *Sociological Forum,* 8 (1993): 47–71.

Kiernan, Ben. "Genocidal Targeting: Two Groups of Victims in Pol Pot's Cambodia," in *State Organized Terror: The Case of Violent Internal Repression,* edited by P. T. Bushnell, V. Shlapentokh, C. K. Vanderpool, and J. Sundram, 207–226. Boulder: Westview Press, 1991.

Kiernan, Ben, ed. *Genocide and Democracy in Cambodia.* Monograph #41. New Haven: Yale University Southeast Asia Studies, 1993.

Kifner, John. "Khomeini Discounts Report on Strife," The *New York Times,* November 10, 1986, A14.

Kimmel, Michael S. *Revolution: A Sociological Interpretation.* Cambridge: Polity Press, 1990.

King, Gary. "Statistical Models for Political Science Event Counts: Bias in Conventional Procedures and Evidence for the Exponential Poisson Regression Model," *American Journal of Political Science,* 32 (1988): 838–863.

King, Gary. "Event Count Models for International Relations: Generalizations and Applications," *International Studies Quarterly,* 33 (1989): 123–147.

King, Gary. *Unifying Political Methodology: The Likelihood Theory of Statistical Inference.* Cambridge: Cambridge University Press, 1989.

King, Gary, Robert O. Keohane, and Sidney Verba. *Designing Social Inquiry: Scientific Inference in Qualitative Research.* Princeton: Princeton University Press, 1994.

Kiser, Edgar and Yarom Barzel. "The Origins of Democracy in England," *Rationality and Society,* 3 (1991): 396–422.

Klein, Herbert S. *Bolivia: The Evolution of a Multi-Ethnic Society.* 2nd ed. New York: Oxford University Press, 1992.

Koopmans, Ruud. "The Dynamics of Protest Waves: West Germany, 1965 to 1989," *American Sociological Review,* 58 (1993): 637–658.

Koopmans, Ruud. *Democracy from Below: New Social Movements and the Political System in West Germany.* Boulder: Westview Press, 1995.

Koopmans, Ruud. "Dynamics of Repression and Mobilization: The German Extreme Right in the 1990s," *Mobilization,* 2 (1997): 149–164.

Kornbluh, Peter. "The Covert War," in *Reagan Versus the Sandinistas: The Undeclared War on Nicaragua,* edited by T. W. Walker, 21–38. Boulder: Westview Press, 1987.

Krain, Matthew. "Factors Affecting the Use of Repression and Accommodation in Post-Internal War States," paper presented at the Annual Meeting of the American Political Science Association, August 28–31, 1997, Washington, DC.

Krain, Matthew. "State-Sponsored Mass Murder: The Onset and Severity of Genocides and Politicides," *Journal of Conflict Resolution,* 41 (1997): 331–360.

Krain, Matthew. "Contemporary Democracies Revisited: Democracy, Political Violence, and Event Count Models," *Comparative Political Studies,* 31 (1998): 139–164.

Krain, Matthew. "In Harm's Way: Leaders and Nonviolent Direct Action," paper presented at the 57th Annual Meeting of the Midwest Political Science Association, Chicago, Illinois. April 15–18, 1999.

Krain, Matthew. "Democracy, Internal War, and State-Sponsored Mass Murder," *Human Rights Review,* 1,3 (2000): 40–48.

Krain, Matthew and Marissa Edson Myers. "Democracy and Civil War: A Note on the Democratic Peace Proposition," *International Interactions,* 23 (1997): 87–94.

Krasner, Stephen D. "Approaches to the State: Alternative Conceptions and Historical Dynamics," *Comparative Politics,* (1984): 223–246.

Kriesi, Hanspeter. "The Political Opportunity Structure of New Social Movements: Its Impact on Their Mobilization," in *The Politics of Social Protest: Comparative Perspectives on States and Social Movements,* edited by J. C. Jenkins and B. Klandermans, 167–198. Minneapolis: University of Minnesota Press, 1995.

Kuper, Leo. *The Pity of It All: Polarisation of Racial and Ethnic Relations.* Minneapolis: University of Minnesota Press, 1977.

Kuper, Leo. *Genocide: Its Political Use in the Twentieth Century.* New Haven: Yale University Press, 1981.

Kuran, Timur. "Sparks and Prairie Fires: A Theory of Unanticipated Political Revolution," *Public Choice,* 61 (1989): 41–74.

Kuran, Timur. "Now Out of Never: The Element of Surprise in the East European Revolution of 1989," *World Politics,* 44 (1991): 7–48.

Ladman, Jerry R., ed. *Modern-Day Bolivia: Legacy of the Revolution and Prospects for the Future.* Tempe: Center for Latin American Studies, Arizona State University, 1983.

Lake, Anthony, ed. *After the Wars: Reconstruction in Afghanistan, Indochina, Central America, Southern Africa, and the Horn of Africa.* New Brunswick: Transaction Books, 1990.

Lane, Frederic C. "The Economic Meaning of War and Protection," in *Venice and History: The Collected Papers of Frederic C. Lane.* Baltimore: Johns Hopkins University Press, 1966.

LASA Forum. *Report of the Latin American Studies Association Delegation to Observe the Nicaraguan General Election of November 4, 1984.* Pittsburgh: Latin American Studies Association, 1985.

Lasswell, Harold D. *National Security and Individual Freedom.* New York: McGraw-Hill, 1950.

Lasswell, Harold D. "The Garrison-State Hypothesis Today," in *Changing Patterns in Military Politics,* edited by S. P. Huntington, 51–70. New York: Free Press, 1962.

Lawson, Stephanie. "Conceptual Issues in the Comparative Study of Regime Change and Democratization," *Comparative Politics,* 25 (1993): 183–205.

Leeds, Brett Ashley and David R. Davis. "Domestic Political Vulnerability and International Disputes," *Journal of Conflict Resolution*, 41 (1997): 814–834.

Leeds, Brett Ashley, David R. Davis, and Will H. Moore, with Christopher McHorney. *The Intranational Political Interactions (IPI) Codebook*. Atlanta: Department of Political Science, Emory University, 1995.

Leiden, Carl and Karl M. Schmitt. *The Politics of Violence: Revolution in the Modern World*. Englewood Cliffs, NJ: Prentice-Hall, 1968.

LeoGrande, William H. "The United States in Nicaragua," in *Nicaragua: The First Five Years,* edited by T. W. Walker. New York: Praeger, 1985.

LeoGrande, William H. "Political Parties and Postrevolutionary Politics in Nicaragua," in *Political Parties and Democracy in Central America*, edited by L. W. Goodman, W. M. LeoGrande, and J. M. Forman, 187–202. Boulder: Westview Press, 1990.

LeVan, H. John. "Vietnam: Revolution of Postcolonial Consolidation," in *Revolutions of the Late Twentieth Century,* edited by J. Goldstone, T. R. Gurr, and F. Moshiri, 52–87. Boulder: Westview Press, 1991.

Levi, Margaret. "The Predatory Theory of Rule," *Politics and Society,* 10 (1981): 431–465.

Levy, Daniel C. "Mexico: Sustained Civilian Rule without Democracy," in *Politics in Developing Countries: Comparing Experiences with Democracy,* edited by L. Diamond, J. Linz, and S. M. Lipset, 135–174. Boulder: Lynne Rienner, 1990.

Levy, Jack. "The Diversionary Theory of War: A Critique," in *The Handbook of War Studies,* edited by M. I. Midlarsky, 259–288. Boston: Unwin Hyman, 1989.

Levy, Jack and L. I. Vakili. "Diversionary Action by Authoritarian Regimes: Argentina and the Falklands/Malvinas Case," in *The Internationalization of Communal Strife,* edited by M. I. Midlarsky, 118–148. London: Routledge, 1992.

Liao, Tim F. *Interpreting Probability Models: Logit, Probit, and Other Generalized Linear Models*. Sage University Paper Series on Quantitative Applications in the Social Sciences, 7–101. Thousand Oaks: Sage, 1994.

Lichbach, Mark I. "Deterrence or Escalation?: The Puzzle of Aggregate Studies of Repression and Dissent," *Journal of Conflict Resolution,* 32 (1987): 266–297.

Lichbach, Mark I. "An Evaluation of 'Does Economic Inequality Breed Political Conflict?' Studies," *World Politics,* 41 (1989): 431–470.

Lichbach, Mark I. *The Rebel's Dilemma*. Ann Arbor: University of Michigan Press, 1995.

Licklider, Roy, ed. *Stopping the Killing: How Civil Wars End*. New York: New York University Press, 1993.

Licklider, Roy. "The Consequences of Negotiated Settlements in Civil Wars, 1945–1993," *American Political Science Review,* 89 (1995): 681–690.

Licklider, Roy. "State Building after Invasion: Somalia and Panama," paper presented at the International Studies Association annual convention, San Diego, California, April 1996.

Lieberson, Stanley. *Making It Count: The Improvement of Social Research and Theory.* Berkeley: University of California Press, 1985.

Lijphart, Arend. "Comparative Politics and Comparative Method," *American Political Science Review,* 65 (1971): 682–698.

Lijphart, Arend. *Democracy in Plural Societies: A Comparative Exploration.* New Haven: Yale University Press, 1977.

Lijphart, Arend. "Democracies: Forms, Performance, and Constitutional Engineering," *European Journal of Political Research,* 25 (1994): 1–17.

Linz, Juan J. *The Breakdown of Democratic Regimes: Crisis, Breakdown and Reequilibration.* Baltimore: Johns Hopkins University Press, 1978.

Linz, Juan J. "Democracy's Time Constraints," *International Political Science Review,* 19 (1998): 19–38.

Lipset, Seymour Martin, Kyoung-Ryung Seong, and John Charles Torres. "A Comparative Analysis of the Social Requisites of Democracy," *International Social Science Journal,* 136 (1993): 155–175.

Long, J. Scott. *The Analysis of Categorical and Limited Dependent Variables.* Sage University Paper Series on Advanced Quantitative Techniques in the Social Sciences, Thousand Oaks: Sage, 1997.

Luce, Henry R., ed. *Time Capsule: 1959.* New York: Time-Life Books, 1968.

Luebbert, Gregory M. *Liberalism, Fascism, or Social Democracy: Social Classes and the Political Origins of Regimes in Interwar Europe.* New York: Oxford University Press, 1991.

Lustick, Ian. *State-Building Failure in British Ireland and French Algeria.* Berkeley: Institute of International Studies, 1985.

Lustick, Ian. *Unsettled States, Disputed Lands: Britain and Ireland, France and Algeria, Israel and the West Bank-Gaza.* Ithaca: Cornell University Press, 1993.

Machiavelli, Niccolo. *The Prince.* Reprint. New York: Norton, 1980.

Maier, Charles S. *Recasting Bourgeois Europe: Stabilization in France, Germany and Italy in the Decade after World War I.* Princeton: Princeton University Press, 1975.

Mainwaring, Scott. "Transitions to Democracy and Democratic Consolidation: Theoretical and Conceptual Issues," in *Issues in Democratic Consolidation,* edited by S. Mainwaring, G. O'Donnell, and J. S. Valenzuela, 294–342. Notre Dame: University of Notre Dame Press, 1992.

Mainwaring, Scott, Guillermo O'Donnell, and J. Samuel Valenzuela, eds. *New Issues in Democratic Consolidation.* Notre Dame: University of Notre Dame Press, 1992.

Malhuret, Claude. *Mass Deportations in Ethiopia.* Confidential Report, Medecins Sans Frontieres, 1985.

Malloy, James M. *Bolivia: The Uncompleted Revolution.* Pittsburgh: University of Pittsburgh Press, 1970.

Malloy, James M. *Bolivia's MNR: A Study of a National Popular Movement in Latin America.* Buffalo: Council on International Studies, State University of New York at Buffalo, 1971.

Malloy, James M. "Revolutionary Politics," in *Beyond the Revolution: Bolivia since 1952,* edited by J. Malloy and R. Thorn, 111–156. Pittsburgh: University of Pittsburgh Press, 1971.

Malloy, James M. and Eduardo A. Gamarra. "The Transition to Democracy in Bolivia," in *Authoritarians and Democrats: Regime Transition in Latin America,* edited by J. Malloy and M. Seligson, 93–120. Pittsburgh: University of Pittsburgh Press, 1987.

Malloy, James M. and Richard S. Thorn, eds. *Beyond the Revolution: Bolivia since 1952.* Pittsburgh: University of Pittsburgh Press, 1971.

Mansfield, Edward D. and Jack Snyder. "Democratization and the Danger of War," *International Security,* 20 (1995): 5–38.

Maoz, Zeev. "Joining the Club of Nations: Political Development and International Conflicts, 1816–1976," *International Studies Quarterly,* 33 (1989): 199–231.

Maoz, Zeev and Bruce Russett. "Alliance, Contiguity, Wealth, and Political Stability: Is the Lack of Conflict among Democracies a Statistical Artifact?" *International Interactions,* 17 (1992): 245–267.

Maoz, Zeev and Bruce Russett. "Normative and Structural Causes of Democratic Peace, 1946–1986," *American Political Science Review,* 87 (1993): 624–638.

Marcus, Bruce, ed. *Nicaragua: The Sandinista People's Revolution—Speeches by Sandinista Leaders.* New York: Pathfinder Press, 1985.

Mason, Davis S. *Revolution and Transition in East-Central Europe.* 2nd ed. Boulder: Westview Press, 1996.

Mason, T. David and Dale A. Krane. "The Political Economy of Death Squads: Toward a Theory of the Impact of State-Sanctioned Terror," *International Studies Quarterly,* 33 (1989): 175–198.

Mason, T. David and Patrick J. Fett. "How Civil Wars End: A Rational Choice Approach," *Journal of Conflict Resolution,* 40 (1996): 546–568.

Mastanduno, Michael, David A. Lake, and G. John Ikenberry. "Toward a Realist Theory of State Action," *International Studies Quarterly,* 33 (1989): 457–474.

Matthews, Herbert L. "Commentary: The Cuban Revolution," *Hispanic American Report,* August 29, 1960: i–viii.

Matthews, Herbert L. *Revolution in Cuba.* New York: Charles Scribner's Sons, 1975.

Mayhew, David R. *Congress: The Electoral Connection.* New Haven: Yale University Press, 1974.

McAdam, Doug. *Political Process and the Development of Black Insurgency, 1930–1970.* Chicago: University of Chicago Press, 1982.

McAdam, Doug and Ronnelle Paulsen. "Specifying the Relationship between Social Ties and Activism," *American Journal of Sociology,* 99 (1993): 640–667.

McAdam, Doug, Sidney Tarrow, and Charles Tilly. "To Map Contentious Politics," *Mobilization,* 1 (1996): 17–34.

McBride, Jeffrey Scott. "Political Repression and Regime Transition: Latin America, 1980–1993," paper presented at the Annual Meeting of the American Political Science Association, Washington, DC, August 28–31, 1997.

McClelland, Charles. *World Events Interaction Survey,* ICPSR ed. Los Angeles: University of Southern California, 1972.

McLaughlin, Sara, Scott Gates, Havard Hegre, Ranveig Gissinger, and Nils Petter Gleditsch. "Timing the Changes in Political Structures: A New Polity Database," *Journal of Conflict Resolution,* 42 (1998): 231–242.

McNitt, Andrew D. "Government Coercion: An Exploratory Analysis," *The Social Science Journal,* 32 (1995): 195–205.

McPhereson, James. *Battle Cry of Freedom.* New York: Oxford University Press, 1988.

Melson, Robert. *Revolution and Genocide: On the Origins of the Armenian Genocide and the Holocaust.* Chicago: University of Chicago Press, 1992.

Menashri, David. *Iran: A Decade of War and Revolution.* New York: Holmes and Meier, 1990.

Merritt, Richard L. and Dina A. Zinnes. "Data Development for International Research—Phase I: International Conflict and National Characteristics," *International Interactions,* 20 (1994): 227–247.

Meyer, David S. and Suzanne Staggenborg. "Movements, Countermovements, and the Structure of Political Opportunity," *American Journal of Sociology,* 101 (1996): 1628–1660.

Middlebrook, Kevin J. "Organized Labor and Democratization in Postrevolutionary Regimes: Transition Politics in Nicaragua, Russia, and Mexico," paper presented at the Annual Meeting of the American Political Science Association, Washington, DC, August 28–31, 1997.

Migdal, Joel S. *Strong Societies and Weak States.* Princeton: Princeton University Press, 1989.

Milani, Moshen. *The Making of Iran's Islamic Revolution.* Boulder: Westview Press, 1994.

Minkoff, Debra C. "The Sequencing of Social Movements," *American Sociological Review,* 62 (1997): 779–799.

Miranda, Roger and William Ratliff. *The Civil War in Nicaragua: Inside the Sandinistas.* New Brunswick: Transaction Books, 1993.

Mitchell, Christopher. *The Legacy of Populism in Bolivia: From the MNR to Military Rule.* New York: Praeger, 1977.

Mitchell, Neil J. and James J. McCormick. "Economic and Political Explanations of Human Rights Violations," *World Politics,* 40 (1988): 476–498.

Moaddel, Mansoor. "Political Conflict in the World Economy: A Cross-National Analysis of Modernization and World-System Theories." *American Sociological Review,* 59 (1994): 276–303.

Modelski, George. "International Settlement of Internal War," in *International Aspects of Civil Strife,* edited by J. Rosenau, 122–153. Princeton: Princeton University Press, 1964.

Moghadam, Val. "Islamic Populism, Class, and Gender in Postrevolutionary Iran," in *A Century of Revolution: Social Movements in Iran,* edited by J. Foran, 189–222. Minneapolis: University of Minnesota Press, 1994.

Montazam, Mir Ali Asghar. *The Life and Times of Ayatollah Khomeini.* London: Anglo-European Publishing Limited, 1994.

Moore, Barrington. *The Social Origins of Dictatorship and Democracy.* Boston: Beacon, 1966.

Moore, Will H. "Reciprocity and the Domestic-International Conflict Nexus during the 'Rhodesia Problem,'" *Journal of Conflict Resolution,* 39 (1995): 129–167.

Moore, Will H. "Repression and Dissent: Substitution, Context, and Timing," *American Journal of Political Science,* 42 (1998): 851–873.

Moore, Will H. and Ronny Lindstrom. "The Violent Intranational Conflict Data Project (VICDP) Codebook." Department of Political Science, University of California—Riverside, 1996.

Moshiri, Farrokh. "Iran: Islamic Revolution against Westernization," in *Revolutions of the Late Twentieth Century,* edited by J. Goldstone, T. R. Gurr, and F. Moshiri, 116–135. Boulder: Westview Press, 1991.

Mottale, Morris M. *Iran: The Political Sociology of the Islamic Revolution.* New York: University Press of America, 1995.

Mueller, John E. *War, Presidents, and Public Opinion.* New York: Wiley, 1973.

Muller, Edward N. "Income Inequality, Regime Repressiveness, and Political Violence." *American Sociological Review,* 50 (1985): 47–61.

Muller, Edward N. and Karl-Dieter Opp. "Rational Choice and Rebellious Collective Behavior," *American Political Science Review,* 80 (1986): 871–887.

Muller, Edward N. and Erich Weede. "Cross-National Variation in Political Violence: A Rational Action Approach," *Journal of Conflict Resolution,* 34 (1990): 624–651.

Nagorski, Andrew. "The Return of the Reds," *Newsweek,* December 4, 1995: 47–48.

Nelson, Lowry. *Cuba: The Measure of a Revolution.* Minneapolis: University of Minnesota Press, 1972.

Nevitte, Neil and Santiago A. Canton. "The Role of Domestic Observers," *Journal of Democracy,* 8 (1997): 47–61.

Nichols, John Spencer. "The Press in Cuba," in *The Cuba Reader: The Making of a Revolutionary Society,* edited by P. Brenner, W. M. LeoGrande, D. Rich, and D. Siegel, 219–227. New York: Grove Press, 1989.

Nietschmann, Bernard. *The Unknown War: The Miskito Nation, Nicaragua, and the United States.* New York: Freedom House, 1989.

Nzongola-Ntalaja, Geroges. *Nation-Building and State-Building in Africa.* Harare: SAPES Books, 1993.

O'Donnell, Guillermo. *Modernization and Bureaucratic Authoritarianism: Studies in South American Politics.* Berkeley: Institute of International Studies, University of California at Berkeley, 1973.

O'Donnell, Guillermo and Philippe C. Schmitter. *Transitions from Authoritarian Rule: Tentative Conclusions about Uncertain Democracies.* Baltimore: Johns Hopkins University Press, 1986.

O'Kane, Rosemary H. T. *The Revolutionary Reign of Terror: The Role of Violence in Political Change*. Hants: Edward Elgar Publishing, 1991.

O'Kane, Rosemary H. T. "The National Causes of State Construction in France, Russia and China," *Political Studies*, 43 (1995): 2–21.

Oberschall, Anthony. "Rational Choice in Collective Protests," *Rationality and Society*, 6 (1994): 79–100.

Odom, William E. *On Internal War: American and Soviet Approaches to Third World Clients and Insurgents*. Durham: Duke University Press, 1992.

Olivier, Johan L. "State Repression and Collective Action in South Africa, 1970–1984," *South African Journal of Sociology*, 22 (1991): 109–117.

Olson, Mancur. *The Logic of Collective Action*. Cambridge: Harvard University Press, 1965.

Olson, Mancur. "Dictatorship, Democracy, and Development," *American Political Science Review*, 87 (1993): 567–576.

Opp, Karl-Dieter and Wolfgang Ruehl. "Repression, Micromobilization and Political Protest," *Social Forces*, 69 (1990): 521–547.

Organski, A.F.K and Jacek Kugler. "The Costs of Major Wars: The Phoenix Factor," *American Political Science Review*, 71 (1977): 1347–1366.

Organski, A.F.K and Jacek Kugler. *The War Ledger*. Chicago: University of Chicago Press, 1980.

Ostria Gutierrez, Alberto. *The Tragedy of Bolivia: A People Crucified*. New York: Devin-Adair, 1958.

Ovsiovitch, Jay S. "News Coverage of Human Rights," *Political Research Quarterly*, 46 (1993): 671–689.

Ovsiovitch, Jay S. "A Distant Image? Factors Influencing the U.S. Media's Coverage of Human Rights," in *Human Rights in Developing Countries*, edited by David L. Cingranelli. Greenwich: JAI Press, 1996.

Parsa, Misagh. *Social Origins of the Iranian Revolution*. New Brunswick: Rutgers University Press, 1989.

Peacock, Alan T. and Jack Wiseman. *The Growth of Public Expenditure in the United Kingdom*. Princeton: Princeton University Press, 1961.

Pearson, Frederic S. "Foreign Military Intervention and Domestic Disputes," *International Studies Quarterly*, 18 (1974): 259–290.

Pearson, Frederic S. and Robert A. Baumann. *International Military Intervention, 1946–1988 (Codebook)*. ICPSR #6035. Ann Arbor: Inter-university Consortium for Political and Social Research, 1993.

Perez-Stable, Marifeli. *The Cuban Revolution: Origins, Course, and Legacy*. New York: Oxford University Press, 1993.

Pion-Berlin, David. "The Political Economy of State Repression in Argentina," in *The State as Terrorist: The Dynamics of Governmental Violence and Repression*, edited by M. Stohl and G. A. Lopez, 99–122. Westport: Greenwood Press, 1984.

Piven, Frances Fox and Richard A. Cloward. *Why Americans Don't Vote*. New York: Pantheon Books, 1988.

Poe, Steven C. and C. Neal Tate. "Repression of Human Rights to Personal Integrity in the 1980s: A Global Analysis," *American Political Science Review,* 88 (1994): 853–872.

Porter, Bruce. *War and the Rise of the State: The Military Foundations of Modern Politics.* New York: Free Press, 1994.

Powell, G. Bingham. *Contemporary Democracies: Participation, Stability, and Violence.* Cambridge: Harvard University Press, 1982.

Prevost, Gary. "The Role of the Sandinista Revolution in the Process of Democratization in Nicaragua," *Democratization,* 2 (1995): 85–108.

Prevost, Gary. "The Status of the Sandinista Revolutionary Project," in *The Undermining of the Sandinista Revolution,* edited by G. Prevost and H. Vanden, 9–44. New York: St. Martin's Press, 1997.

Przeworski, Adam. *Democracy and the Market.* London: Cambridge University Press, 1991.

Przeworski, Adam. "The Games of Transition," in *Issues in Democratic Consolidation,* edited by S. Mainwaring, G. O'Donnell, and J. S. Valenzuela, 105–152. Notre Dame: University of Notre Dame Press, 1992.

Putnam, Robert. "Diplomacy and Domestic Politics: The Logic of Two-Level Games," *American Political Science Review,* 85 (1988): 1303–1320.

Queiser Morales, Waltraud. *Bolivia: Land of Struggle.* Boulder: Westview Press, 1992.

Rabkin, Rhonda Pearl. "Cuban Political Structure: Vanguard Party and the Masses," in *Cuba: Twenty-Five Years of Revolution, 1959 - 1984,* edited by S. Halebsky and J. Kirk, 251–269. New York: Praeger, 1985.

Ragin, Charles C. *The Comparative Method: Moving beyond Qualitiative and Quantitative Strategies.* Berkeley: University of California Press, 1987.

Ragin, Charles C. *Constructing Social Research.* Thousand Oaks: Pine Forge Press, 1994.

Ramazani, R.K., ed. *Iran's Revolution: The Search for Consensus.* Bloomington: Indiana University Press, 1990.

Randall, Margaret. *Women in Cuba: Twenty Years Later.* Brooklyn: Smyrna Press, 1981.

Rasler, Karen A. "War, Accommodation, and Violence in the United States, 1890–1970," *American Political Science Review,* 80 (1986): 921–945.

Rasler, Karen A. "Concessions, Repression, and Political Protest in the Iranian Revolution," *American Sociological Review,* 61 (1996): 132–152.

Rasler, Karen A. and William R. Thompson. *War and State Making: The Shaping of the Global Powers.* Boston: Unwin and Hyman, 1989.

Rasler, Karen A. and William R. Thompson. *The Great Powers and Global Struggle, 1490–1990.* Lexington: University of Kentucky Press, 1994.

Rejai, Mustafa. *Leaders of Revolution.* Beverly Hills: Sage, 1979.

Remmer, Karen. *Military Rule in Latin America.* Boston: Unwin Hyman, 1989.

Reuveny, Rafael and Heejoon Kang. "International Conflict and Cooperation: Splicing COPDAB and WEIS Series," *International Studies Quarterly*, 40 (1996): 281–306.

Richards, David L. "Settling the Score: Elections and Physical Integrity," paper presented at the Annual Meeting of the New York State Political Science Association, Ithaca College, 1996.

Ritter, Archibald R. M. "The Organs of People's Power and the Communist Party: The Nature of Cuban Democracy," in *Cuba: Twenty-Five Years of Revolution, 1959–1984*, edited by S. Halebsky and J. Kirk, 270–290. New York: Praeger, 1985.

Roeder, Philip G. "Do New Soviet Leaders Really Make a Difference? Rethinking the 'Succession Connection,'" *American Political Science Review*, 79 (1985): 958–976.

Rohter, Larry. "Rightist is Victor over Sandinistas in Nicaraguan Vote," The *New York Times*, October 22, 1996: A1.

Rokeach, Milton. *The Open and Closed Mind: Investigations into the Nature of Belief Systems and Personality Systems*. New York: Basic Books, 1960.

Roman, Peter. "Representative Government in Socialist Cuba," *Latin American Perspectives*, 20 (1993): 7–27.

Rosenblum, Peter. "Kabila's Congo," *Current History*, 97 (May, 1998): 193–199.

Ruchwarger, Gary. *People in Power: Forging a Grassroots Democracy in Nicaragua*. South Hadley: Bergin and Garvey Publishers, 1987.

Rueschemeyer, Dietrich, Evelyne Huber Stephens, and John D. Stephens. *Capitalist Development and Democracy*. Chicago: University of Chicago Press, 1991.

Rummel, R.J. *Death by Government*. New Brunswick: Transaction Books, 1994.

Rummel, R.J. "Democracy, Power, Genocide, and Mass Murder," *Journal of Conflict Resolution*, 39 (1995): 3–26.

Scarritt, James R. "Zimbabwe: Revolutionary Violence Resulting in Reform," in *Revolutions of the Late Twentieth Century*, edited by J. Goldstone, T. R. Gurr, and F. Moshiri, 235–271. Boulder: Westview Press, 1991.

Schatzberg, Michael G. "Beyond Mobutu: Kabila and the Congo," *The Journal of Democracy*, 8 (1997): 70–84.

Schedler, Andreas. "What is Democratic Consolidation?" *The Journal of Democracy*, 9 (1998): 91–107.

Schmitter, Philippe C. "Still The Century of Corporatism?" in *Trends toward Corporatist Intermediation*, edited by P. Schmitter and G. Lehmbruch. Beverly Hills: Sage, 1974.

Schmitter, Philippe C. and Javier Santiso. "Three Temporal Dimensions to the Consolidation of Democracy," *International Political Science Review*, 19 (1998): 69–92.

Schroeder, Paul W. "Alliances, 1815 - 1945: Weapons of Power and Tools of Management," in *Historical Dimensions of National Security Problems*, edited by K. Knorr, 227–262. Lawrence: University Press of Kansas, 1976.

Schwartz, Michael. *Radical Protest and Social Structure*. New York: Academic Press, 1976.

Selbin, Eric. *Modern Latin American Revolutions*. Boulder: Westview Press, 1993.

Selbin, Eric. "Same As It Ever Was: The Future of Revolution at the End of the Century," paper presented at the 39th Annual Meeting of the International Studies Association, Minneapolis, Minnesota, March 18–21, 1998.

Serra, L. "The Sandinista Mass Organizations," in *Nicaragua in Revolution*, edited by T. W. Walker, New York: Praeger, 1982.

Shain, Yossi and Juan J. Linz, eds. *Between States: Interim Governments and Democratic Transitions*. Cambridge: Cambridge University Press, 1995.

Shugart, Matthew Soberg and John M. Carey. *Presidents and Assemblies: Constitutional Design and Electoral Dynamics*. Cambridge: Cambridge University Press, 1992.

Sick, Gary. "Trial by Error: Reflections on the Iran-Iraq War," in *Iran's Revolution: The Search for Consensus*, edited by R. K. Ramazani, 104–142. Bloomington: Indiana University Press, 1990.

Simmel, G. *Conflict*. Translated by K. H. Woldff. Glencoe: Free Press, 1956.

Simon, Marc V. and Harvey Starr. "Extraction, Allocation, and the Rise and Decline of States: A Simulation Analysis of Two-Level Security Management," *Journal of Conflict Resolution*, 40 (1996): 272–297.

Singer, J. David and Melvin Small. *Correlates of War Project: International and Civil War Data, 1815–1992*. Computer file. Ann Arbor: Inter-university Consortium for Political and Social Research, 1994.

Sithole, Masipula. "Zimbabwe: In Search of a Stable Democracy," in *Politics in Developing Countries: Comparing Experiences with Democracy*, edited by L. Diamond, J. Linz, and S. M. Lipset, 449–490. Boulder: Lynne Rienner, 1990.

Siverson, Randolph M. "War and Change in the International System," in *Change in the International System*, edited by O. R. Holsti, R. M. Siverson, and A. George. Boulder: Westview Press, 1980.

Skocpol, Theda. *States and Social Revolutions: A Comparative Analysis of France, Russia, and China*. Cambridge: Cambridge University Press, 1979.

Skocpol, Theda. "Rentier State and Shi'a Islam in the Iranian Revolution," *Theory and Society*, 11 (1982): 265–283.

Skocpol, Theda. "Social Revolutions and Mass Military Mobilization," *World Politics*, 40 (1988).

Skocpol, Theda. *Protecting Soldiers and Mothers: The Political Origins of Social Policy in the United States*. Cambridge: Harvard University Press, 1992.

Skocpol, Theda. "A Critical Review of Barrington Moore's *Social Origins of Dictatorship and Democracy*," in *Social Revolutions in the Modern World*, by Theda Skocpol, 25–54. New York: Cambridge University Press, 1994.

Skocpol, Theda and Ellen Kay Trimberger. "Revolutions and the World-Historical Development of Capitalism," *Berkeley Journal of Sociology*, 22 (1977): 101–113.

Smith, M. Brewster, Jerome S. Bruner, and Robert W. White. *Opinions and Personality.* New York: Wiley, 1956.

Smith, Steven Kent. "Renovation and Orthodoxy: Debate and Transition within the Sandinista National Liberation Front," *Latin American Perspectives,* 24 (1997): 102–116.

Smolar, Aleksander. "Poland's Emerging Party System," *The Journal of Democracy,* 9 (1998): 122–133.

Snare, Charles. "Testing the Usefulness of Political Personality Models: How Well Do Political Personality Types Predict Policy Preferences?" Unpublished manuscript, 1997.

Snyder, David, and Charles Tilly. "Hardship and Collective Violence in France: 1830–1960," *American Sociological Review,* 37 (1972): 520–532.

Snyder, Richard, H. W. Bruck, and Burton Sapin, eds. *Foreign Policy Decision-Making: An Approach to the Society of International Politics.* New York: Free Press of Glencove, 1962.

Sobel, Lester A., ed. *Cuba, the US, and Russia: 1960–63.* New York: Facts on File Interim History,1964.

Sorokin, Pitrim A. *Social and Cultural Dynamics.* Rev. ed. Boston: Porter Sargent, 1957.

Sprout, Harold and Margaret Sprout. *The Ecological Perspective on Human Affairs.* Princeton: Princeton University Press, 1965.

Stacey, Judith. *Patriarchy and Socialist Revolution in China.* Berkeley: University of California Press, 1983.

Stahler-Sholk, Richard. "The Dog That Didn't Bark: Labor Autonomy and Economic Adjustment in Nicaragua under the Sandinista and UNO Governments," *Comparative Politics,* 28 (1995): 77–102.

Staniszkis, Jadwiga. *The Dynamics of the Breakthrough in Eastern Europe.* Berkeley: University of California Press, 1991.

Stanley, William. "The Factional Rationality of Mass Murder: A Level of Analysis Problem in the Study of State Violence," Unpublished Manuscript, 1998.

Starr, Harvey. "Revolution and War: Rethinking the Linkage between Internal and External Conflict," *Political Research Quarterly,* 47 (1994): 481–507.

Staub, Ervin. *The Roots of Evil: The Origins of Genocide and Other Group Violence.* Cambridge: Cambridge University Press, 1989.

Stedman, Stephen John. "The End of the American Civil War," in *Stopping the Killing: How Civil Wars End,* edited by R. Licklider, 164–188. New York: New York University Press, 1993.

Stedman, Stephen John. "The End of the Zimbabwean Civil War," in *Stopping the Killing: How Civil Wars End,* edited by R. Licklider, 125–163. New York: New York University Press, 1993.

Stein, Andrew J. "Public Perceptions and Evaluations of Corruption in Nicaragua: Consequences for Democracy," paper presented at the Annual

Meeting of the Midwest Political Science Association, Chicago, Illinois, April 23–25, 1998.

Stein, Arthur A. *The Nation at War.* Baltimore: Johns Hopkins University Press, 1980.

Stempel, John D. *Inside the Iranian Revolution.* Bloomington: Indiana University Press, 1981.

Stohl, Michael. "War and Domestic Violence: The Case of the United States, 1890–1970," *Journal of Conflict Resolution,* 19 (1975): 379–416.

Stohl, Michael. *War and Domestic Political Violence: The American Capacity for Repression and Reaction.* Beverly Hills: Sage, 1976.

Stohl, Michael. "The Nexus of Civil and International Conflict," in *Handbook of Political Conflict: Theory and Research,* edited by T. R. Gurr, 297–330. New York: Free Press, 1980.

Stohl, Michael. "Outside a Small Circle of Friends: States, Genocide, Mass Killing and the Role of Bystanders." *Journal of Peace Research,* 24 (1987): 151–166.

Stohl, Michael and George A. Lopez, eds. *The State as Terrorist: The Dynamics of Governmental Violence and Repression.* Westport: Greenwood Press, 1984.

Stohl, Michael and George A. Lopez, eds. *Government Violence and Repression: An Agenda for Research.* New York: Greenwood Press, 1986.

Stone, Bailey. *The Genesis of the French Revolution: A Global-Historical Interpretation.* Cambridge: Cambridge University Press, 1994.

Strobel, Warren P. *Late-Breaking Foreign Policy: The News Media's Influence on Peace Operations.* Washington, DC: United States Institute of Peace Press, 1997.

Suarez, Andres. *Cuba: Castroism and Communism, 1959–1966.* Cambridge: MIT Press, 1967.

Suleiman, Ezra N. *Elites in French Society: The Politics of Survival.* Princeton: Princeton University Press, 1978.

Suro, Roberto. "Iran's Unpredictable Behavior Reflects Rivalries in Regime," The *New York Times,* February 4, 1987: A1.

Szulc, Tad. *Fidel: A Critical Portrait.* New York: William Morrow, 1986.

Tarrow, Sidney. *Power in Movement: Social Movements, Collective Action and Politics.* Cambridge: Cambridge University Press, 1994.

Taylor, Charles Lewis and Michael C. Hudson. *The World Handbook of Political and Social Indicators,* 2nd ed. New Haven: Yale University Press, 1972.

Taylor, Charles Lewis and David A. Jodice. *World Handbook of Political and Social Indicators.* New Haven: Yale University Press, 1983.

Tétrault, Nancy. "Accountability or Justice? Rape as a War Crime," paper presented at the Annual Meeting of the International Studies Association, Chicago, Illinois, February 21- 25, 1995.

Thompson, William R. "The Consequences of War." *International Interactions,* 19 (1993): 125–147.

Thompson, William R. "Democracy and Peace: Putting the Cart before the Horse?" *International Organization,* 50 (1996): 141–174.

Thompson, William R. and Richard Tucker. "A Tale of Two Democratic Peace Critiques," *Journal of Conflict Resolution,* 41 (1997): 428–451.

Tillema, Herbert K. *International Armed Conflict since 1945.* Boulder: Westview Press, 1991.

Tilly, Charles. "Reflections on the History of European State Making," in *The Formation of National States in Western Europe,* edited by C. Tilly, 3–83. Princeton: Princeton University Press, 1975.

Tilly, Charles. *From Mobilization to Revolution.* New York: McGraw-Hill, 1978.

Tilly, Charles. "War Making and State Making as Organized Crime," in *Bringing the State Back In,* edited by P. Evans, D. Reuschemeyer, and T. Skocpol, 169–191. Cambridge: Cambridge University Press, 1985.

Tilly, Charles. *Coercion, Capital and European States, A.D. 990 – 1990.* Cambridge: Basil Blackwell, 1990.

Tilly, Charles. *European Revolutions, 1492–1992.* Oxford: Basil Blackwell, 1993.

Tilly, Charles, Louise Tilly, and Richard Tilly. *The Rebellious Century: 1830–1930.* Cambridge: Harvard University Press, 1975.

Tocqueville, Alexis de. *The Old Regime and the French Revolution.* Garden City, New York: Doubleday, 1955.

Trimberger, Ellen Kay. *Revolution from Above: Military Bureaucrats and Development in Japan, Turkey, Egypt, and Peru.* New Brunswick: Transaction Books, 1978.

United States Congress. House Committee on Foreign Affairs. *Religious Persecution of the Baha'is in Iran, 1988.* 100th Congress, 2nd Session. Washington, DC: United States Government Printing Office, 1988.

Urrutia, Manuel. *Fidel Castro and Company, Inc.: Communist Tyranny in Cuba.* New York: Praeger, 1964.

Valenta, Jiri and Esperanza Duran. *Conflict in Nicaragua: A Multidimensional Perspective.* Boston: Allen & Unwin, 1987.

Valenzuela, J. Samuel. "Democratic Consolidation in Post-Transitional Settings: Notion, Process, and Facilitating Conditions," in *Issues in Democratic Consolidation,* edited by S. Mainwaring, G. O'Donnell, and J. S. Valenzuela, 157–104. Notre Dame: University of Notre Dame Press, 1992.

Van Evera, Stephen. "Hypotheses on Nationalism and War," *International Security,* 18 (1994): 5–39.

Vanden, Harry E. "Democracy Derailed: The 1990 Elections and After," in *The Undermining of the Sandinista Revolution,* edited by G. Prevost and H. Vanden, 45–73. New York: St. Martin's Press, 1997.

Vanhanen, Tatu. *The Emergence of Democracy: A Comparative Study of 119 States, 1850–1979.* Helsinki: Societas Scientiarum Fennica, 1984.

Vanhanen, Tatu. *The Process of Democratization: A Comparative Study of 147 States, 1980–88.* New York: Crane Russak, 1990.

Vanhanen, Tatu and Richard Kimber. "Predicting and Explaining Democratization in Eastern Europe," in *Democratization in Eastern Europe,* edited by G. Pridham and T. Vanhanen. New York: Routledge, 1994.

Vasquez, John. *The War Puzzle*. Cambridge: Cambridge University Press, 1993.

Verrier, Anthony. *The Road to Zimbabwe: 1890–1980*. London: Jonathan Cape, 1986.

Vogele, William B. "Struggle and Democracy: Nonviolent Action and Democratization," paper presented at the Annual Meeting of the International Studies Association, Chicago, Illinois, February 21–25, 1995.

Wagner, Robert Harrison. "The Causes of Peace," in *Stopping the Killing: How Civil Wars End,* edited by R. Licklider, 235–268. New York: New York University Press, 1993.

Walker, Thomas W., ed. *Nicaragua in Revolution*. New York: Praeger, 1982.

Walker, Thomas W. *Nicaragua: The Land of Sandino*. Boulder: Westview Press, 1991.

Wallensteen, Peter and Margareta Sollenberg. "The End of International War? Armed Conflict, 1989–1995," *Journal of Peace Research,* 33 (1996): 353–370.

Walt, Stephen M. "Revolution and War," *World Politics,* 44 (1992): 321–368.

Ward, Michael D. and Kristian S. Gleditsch. "Democratizing for Peace," *American Political Science Review,* 92 (1998): 51–61.

Ward, Michael D. and Ulrich Widmaier. "The Domestic-International Conflict Nexus: New Evidence and Old Hypotheses," *International Interactions,* 9 (1982): 75–101.

Waterman, Harvey. "Political Order and the 'Settlement' of Civil Wars," in *Stopping the Killing: How Civil Wars End,* edited by R. Licklider, 292–302. New York: New York University Press, 1993.

Weber, Max. "Bureaucracy and Revolution," in *From Max Weber: Essays in Sociology,* edited by H. H. Gerth and C. W. Mills. New York: Oxford University Press, 1958.

Wheelock Roman, Jaime. "Revolution and Democratic Transition in Nicaragua," in *Democratic Transitions in Central America,* edited by J. Dominguez and M. Lindenberg, 67–85. Gainesville: University Press of Florida, 1997.

White, J. "Rational Rioters: Leaders, Followers and Popular Protest in Early Modern Japan," *Politics and Society,* 16 (1988): 35–70.

White, Robert W. and Terry Falkenberg White. "Repression and the Liberal State: The Case of Northern Ireland, 1969–1972," *Journal of Conflict Resolution,* 39 (1995): 330–352.

Whitehead, Laurence. "Bolivia's Failed Democratization, 1977–1980," in *Transitions from Authoritarian Rule: Latin America,* edited by G. O'Donnell, P. Schmitter, and L. Whitehead, 49–71. Baltimore: Johns Hopkins University Press, 1986.

Whitten, Guy D. and Henry S. Bienen. "Political Violence and Time in Power," *Armed Forces and Society,* 23 (1996): 209–234.

Whyte, Martin King. "Inequality and Stratification in China," *The China Quarterly,* 64 (1975): 684–711.

Williams, Paul. "Kabila Blocks UN Investigation into Massacres," *Human Rights Tribune,* 4 (1997): 18–23.

Wilson, Frank L. "French Interest Group Politics: Pluralist or Neocorporatist?" *American Political Science Review,* 77 (1983): 895–910.

Woddis, J. *Ho Chi Minh: Selected Articles and Speeches.* New York: International Publishers, 1970.

Wolf, Eric. *Peasant Wars of the Twentieth Century.* New York: Knopf, 1970.

Wright, Quincy. *A Study of War.* Chicago: University of Chicago Press, 1964.

Wright, Robin. *In the Name of God: The Khomeini Decade.* New York: Simon and Schuster, 1989.

Zabih, Sepehr. *The Left in Contemporary Iran.* Stanford: Hoover Institution Press, 1986.

Zartman, I. William. "The Unfinished Agenda: Negotiating Internal Conflicts," in *Stopping the Killing: How Civil Wars End,* edited by R. Licklider, 20–36. New York: New York University Press, 1993.

Zimmermann, Ekkart. *Political Violence, Crises, and Revolutions: Theories and Research.* Boston: G. K. Hall, 1983.

Zimmermann, Ekkart. "On the Outcomes of Revolutions: Some Preliminary Considerations," *Sociological Theory,* (1988): 33–47.

Index